**Dr Sam Willis** is one of the world's leading authorities on the sailing navy. He is an Honorary Fellow at the University of Exeter's Centre for Maritime Historical Studies and a Fellow of the Royal Historical Society. He has consulted widely on maritime affairs for clients including the BBC, Channel 4 and Christie's. He is the author of several books on naval and maritime history including the *Hearts of Oak* trilogy and the highly successful *Fighting Ships* series.

'Those who would attempt to explain a great battle at sea in the age of sail need salt water in the veins and a skilled pen. In this marvellous book Dr Sam Willis proves that he has both'

*BBC History Magazine*

'One of the things that makes Willis such a joy to read is the blazing clarity of his explanations. By the time you've finished his book you'll appreciate every nuance of naval tactics'

*Mail on Sunday*

'With a great gift for making complex events exceptionally clear, and an authentically salty understanding of the workings of wind, sea, sail and rig, Willis describes how in the four days running up to the climax of the battle the two fleets had been grappling, and then drifting apart, losing each other in the fog or the darkness of the short nights, like a pair of lumbering, half-blind wrestlers, looking for a fight, not sure where to find it'

Adam Nicolson, *Sunday Times*

# THE GLORIOUS FIRST OF JUNE

*Fleet Battle in the Reign of Terror*

Sam Willis

Quercus

First published in Great Britain in 2011 by Quercus
This paperback edition published in 2012 by
Quercus
55 Baker Street
7th Floor, South Block
W1U 8EW



A CIP catalogue record for this book is available from the British Library

TPB ISBN 978 1 84916 039 1
EBOOK ISBN 978 0 85738 758 5

10 9 8 7 6 5 4 3 2 1

Text and plates designed and typeset by Helen Ewing

Printed and bound in Great Britain by Clays Ltd. St Ives plc

# THE HEARTS OF OAK TRILOGY

This is the third book of the *Hearts of Oak* trilogy, which explores three of the most iconic and yet largely unexplored stories of the Great Age of Sail. *The Fighting Temeraire*, *The Admiral Benbow* and *The Glorious First of June* are the biographies of a ship, a man and a battle that will splice together to form a narrative of an era that stretches from the English Civil War of the 1640s to the coming of steam two centuries later. This Great Age of Sail was once written about in heroic terms but many of those legends have since been overlooked. The details of the stories themselves have become confused and the reasons behind the formation of those legends ignored. With more than a century of professional naval history to draw from, together with new access to previously restricted archives, now is the time to look afresh at those stories of heroism from the perspective of the modern historian; now is the time to understand how and why *The Fighting Temeraire*, *The Admiral Benbow* and *The Glorious First of June* became legends.

> Heart of oak are our ships, jolly tars are our men,
> We always are ready; Steady, boys, steady!
> We'll fight and we'll conquer again and again.
>
> D. GARRICK, *Heart of Oak* (1759)

# Acknowledgements

Many people have made this book better than it otherwise would have been. Fenton Burgin kindly let me look at a previously unstudied account of the battle; Sim Comfort knows as much about naval swords and badges as anyone alive; Mark Barker's ability to visualise battle plans is priceless; both Lucy Morris and Gareth Cole gave their time, knowledge and skill; and Christine Reynolds knows her way around Westminster Abbey in both present and past. Mike Duffy, Nicholas Blake and Andrew Bond read all, or part of this book through in draft. It is a better book because of them.

But in particular I must thank the staff on the Yarty Ward of the Royal Devon and Exeter Hospital and the inventors of chemotherapy who made sure that my family is as big as it was when I started writing this book. Our families have also provided unceasing support during these Dark Ages, which has meant that this book was not put aside on a dusty shelf even when my mind was full of anything but naval history. There are, in fact, entire sections of this book that I can't remember writing. When I eventually came back to the manuscript, it was like reading something new but very obviously mine: a very strange experience. I particularly enjoyed the bit about the Revolutionaries banning kings, queens and jacks in playing cards and their new rule of allowing an ace to beat any other card – the lowest thus rising to the top. They also reinvented time. How mad is that! But what I think is irrelevant of course – what's *your* favourite bit? Let me know at www.sam-willis.com or on Twitter @navalhistoryguy. I'll see you there. Bring your friends.

Sam

Heading home to glorious Devon on a train, October 2010

For Tors

'. . . totally beyond my powers of description… of magnificence and importance, not of common occurrence, and not often equalled.'*

*From the private diaries of Admiral Sir William Dillon, then a fourteen-year-old midshipman of the 74-gun *Defence*, describing the fleets on the morning of 1 June 1794.

Howe's daring signal floats on high;
I see through roaring cannon's smoke –
Their awful line subdued and broke
They strike, they sink, they fly.

Earl of Mulgrave, 1794

The Main Mast to be half the breadth
in a midships

# Contents


List of Illustrations xvii

Maps xxi

Prologue: The First Regicide xxvii

Introduction xxxiii

1. The First Terror 1
2. The First Surrender 19
3. The First and Greatest Sea Officer 41
4. The First War Artist 69
5. The First Convoy 91
6. The First Contact 127
7. The First Blood 151
8. The First of June 183
9. The First Reaction: Honour and Glory 227
10. The Second Reaction: Acrimony and Disgrace 257
11. The Second Terror 285

Epilogue 317

APPENDIX I: The Chronology 329

APPENDIX II: The Fleets 333

APPENDIX III: The Pocock Sketches 352

APPENDIX IV: The Biographies 367

Glossary 383
Notes 394
Bibliography 416
Index 425

# List of Illustrations

FRONTISPIECE

*La Montagne* by Philip James de Loutherbourg, c.1794. (Victoria & Albert Museum, London, UK/The Bridgeman Art Library)

CHAPTER OPENER DETAIL

Commemorative gold anchor badge. (Sim Comfort Collection)

PLATES

1. Memorial to James Montagu, Westminster Abbey by John Flaxman, 1798. (© Dean and Chapter of Westminster)
2. Marble Sculpture at the Panthéon in Paris dedicated to the *Vengeur* by Ernest Dubois, 1908. (Caroline Rose © CMN/Paris)
3. Execution of Louis XVI, 21st January 1793. (Private Collection/Archives Charmet/The Bridgeman Art Library)
4. Admiral Earl Howe by John Singleton Copley, 1794. (National Maritime Museum)
5. Vice Admiral Louis-Thomas-Villaret de Joyeuse. (Malmaison, Châteaux de Malmaison et Bois-Préau/©RMN/Gérard Blot)
6. Portrait of Maximilien de Robespierre. (Musee de la Ville de Paris/Musee Carnavalet, Paris, France/The Bridgeman Art Library)
7. Portrait of Jeanbon Saint-André by Jacques Louis David, 1795. (Helen Regenstein Collection, 1973.153/The Art Institute of Chicago)
8. Danton Led to His Execution by Pierre Alexandre Wille, 1794. (Musee de la Ville de Paris/Musee Carnavalet, Paris, France/ Giraudon/The Bridgeman Art Library)
9. The Battle of Scheveningen, 31 July 1653 by Willem van de Velde, the Elder, 1655. (National Maritime Museum)

10. View of the Port at Brest by Jean-Francois Hue. (Musee de la Marine, Paris, France/Giraudon/The Bridgeman Art Library)
11. *Queen Charlotte*'s Union flag. (National Maritime Museum)
12. Schematic view of Barker's Panorama. (The National Archives)
13. Section of the Rotunda, Leicester Square, in which is exhibited the Panorama by Robert Mitchell, 1801. (Private collection/The Bridgeman Art Library)
14. Nicholas Pocock's logbook of the *Betsey* 1766-7. (National Maritime Museum)
15. French Boarding flag from *L'America*. (National Maritime Museum)
16. The Battle of the First of June, 1794 by Loutherbourg. (National Maritime Museum)
17. The *Brunswick* and *Vengeur* at the Glorious First of June, by Nicholas Pocock. (National Maritime Museum)
18. *Le Vengeur du Peuple* sinking at the Battle of Ouessant, 1st June 1794 by Louis Lafitte. (Bibliotheque Nationale, Paris, France/Giraudon/The Bridgeman Art Library)
19. Admiral Earl Howe on the deck of the *Queen Charlotte* during the Glorious First of June by Mather Brown. (National Maritime Museum)
20. Portsmouth Harbour, Lord Howe's victory, the French prizes brought into the harbour by Thomas Rowlandson, 1780. (Victoria & Albert Museum, London, UK)
21. Caricature of Admiral Earl Howe, Anonymous. (National Maritime Museum)
22. *Le Juste* and *L'America* both captured and added 1 June 1794 aquatint engraved by J Wells after an original by R Livesay (National Maritime Museum)
23. French ship *Sans Pareil* 3rd Rate 80 guns captured at First of June. Watercolour attributed to Dominic Serres, c. 1800. (National Maritime Museum)
24. The sterns of three French prizes by Loutherbourg, 1794. (British Museum)
25. Commemorative uniform badge. (National Maritime Museum)

IN TEXT IMAGES

i. Breaking the Line by Jamie Whyte

ii. Battle plan depicting morning of 28 May by Matthew Flinders (National Maritime Museum)

iii. Battle plan depicting evening of 28 May by Matthew Flinders (National Maritime Museum)

iv. Battle plan depicting 29 May by Matthew Flinders (National Maritime Museum)

v. Battle plan depicting 29 May (2) by Matthew Flinders (National Maritime Museum)

vi. Battle plan depicting evening of 31 May by Matthew Flinders (National Maritime Museum)

vii. Battle plan depicting morning of 1 June by Matthew Flinders (National Maritime Museum)

viii. A new method of securing guns to a ship's side, 1794 (The National Archives)

APPENDIX III

All by Nicholas Pocock (National Maritime Museum)

26. Battle View 1: The Engagement of 28 May.

27. Battle View 2: The Engagement of 29 May.

28. Battle View 3: The Battle of 1 June.

29. Battle View 4: The End of the Battle.

30. Battle Plan 1 June.

31. HMS *Invincible* raking *La Juste.*

32. HMS *Brunswick* and *Le Vengeur du Peuple.*

33. Frigate towing HMS *Defence.*

34. HMS *Queen* and HMS *Queen Charlotte.*

35. *The French Admiral ... No.1.*

36. *French Ships to Windward ... No.2.*

37. Stern views of the captured French ships *L'America* and *La Juste.*

38. Lord Howe to windward of the French Line on the same tack

# Maps

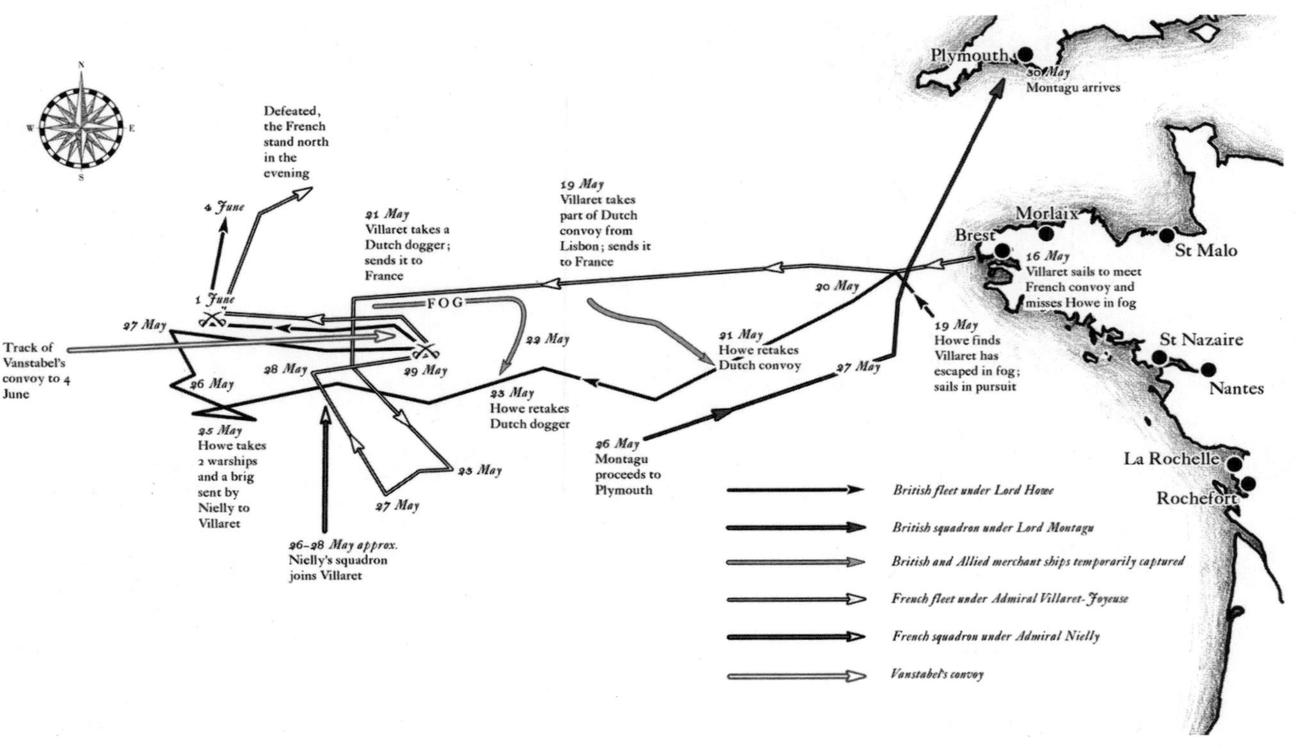

Plymouth
30 May Montagu arrives
Defeated, the French stand north in the evening
4 June
21 May Villaret takes a Dutch dogger; sends it to France
19 May Villaret takes part of Dutch convoy from Lisbon; sends it to France
Morlaix
Brest
St Malo
16 May Villaret sails to meet French convoy and misses Howe in fog
20 May
1 June
FOG
27 May
22 May
21 May Howe retakes Dutch convoy
19 May Howe finds Villaret has escaped in fog; sails in pursuit
St Nazaire
Track of Vanstabel's convoy to 4 June
28 May
29 May
27 May
Nantes
26 May
23 May Howe retakes Dutch dogger
25 May Howe takes 2 warships and a brig sent by Nielly to Villaret
26 May Montagu proceeds to Plymouth
23 May
27 May
La Rochelle
Rochefort
26–28 May approx. Nielly's squadron joins Villaret
N
E
S
W
British fleet under Lord Howe
British squadron under Lord Montagu
British and Allied merchant ships temporarily captured
French fleet under Admiral Villaret-Joyeuse
French squadron under Admiral Nielly
Vanstabel's convoy

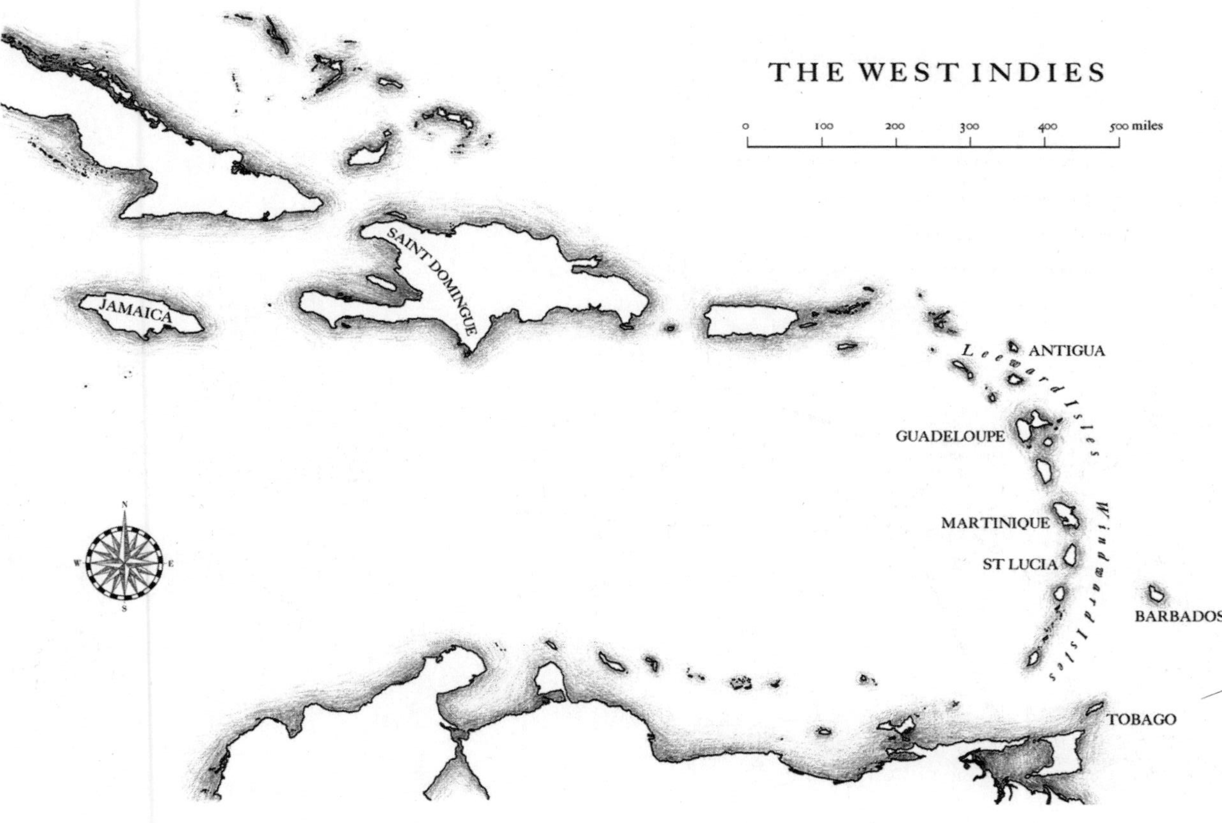
THE WEST INDIES
0 100 200 300 400 500 miles
ANTIGUA
Leeward Isles
Windward Isles
GUADELOUPE
MARTINIQUE
ST LUCIA
BARBADOS
TOBAGO
SAINT DOMINGUE
JAMAICA
N
E
S
W

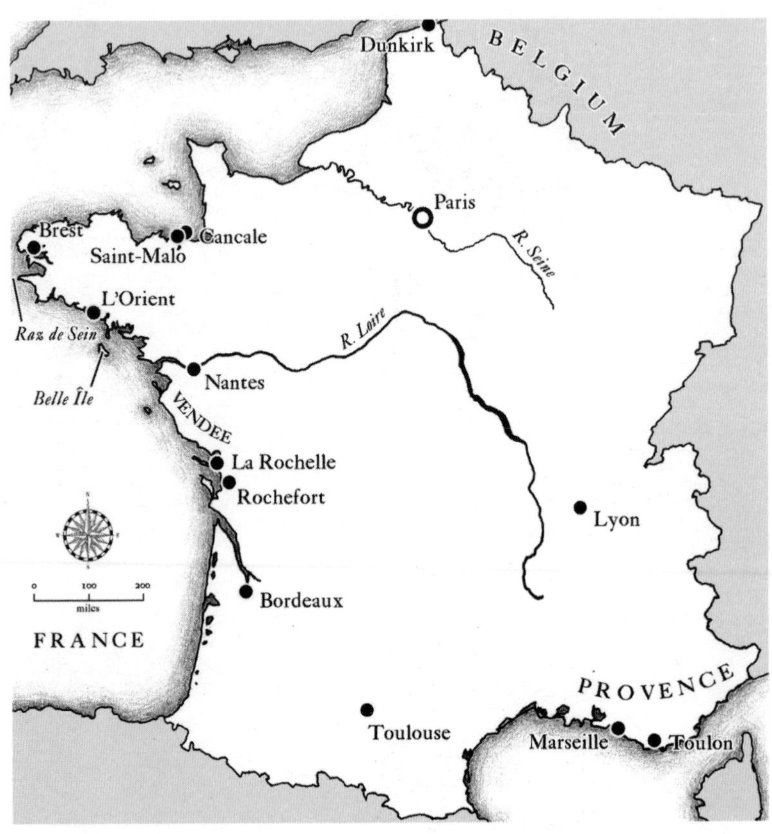
Dunkirk
BELGIUM
Paris
R. Seine
Brest
Cancale
Saint-Malo
L'Orient
Raz de Sein
Belle Île
R. Loire
Nantes
VENDEE
La Rochelle
Rochefort
Lyon
0
100
200
miles
Bordeaux
FRANCE
PROVENCE
Toulouse
Marseille
Toulon

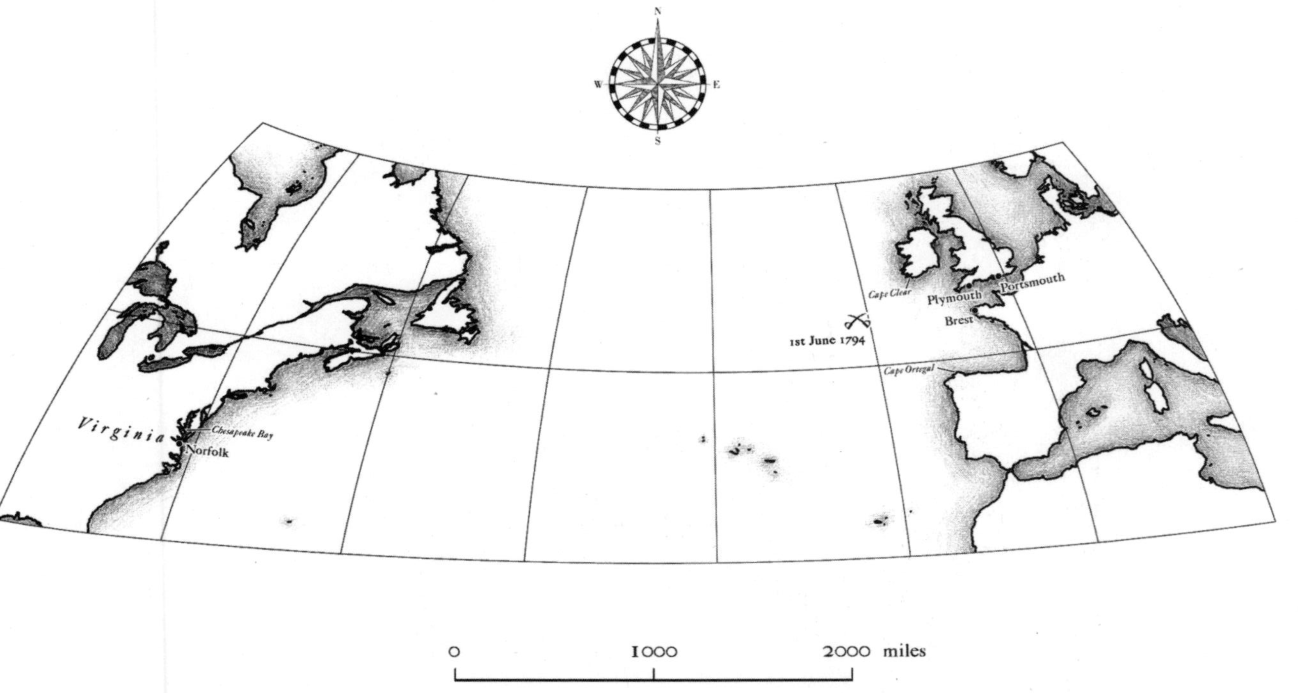
N
W
E
S
Virginia
Chesapeake Bay
Norfolk
Cape Clear
Plymouth
Portsmouth
Brest
1st June 1794
Cape Ortegal
0
1000
2000 miles

# Prologue

# The First Regicide

> No quarter! Whenever we can lay our hands on emperors, kings, queens, empresses, let us rid them from the face of the earth. Better to kill the devil than that the devil should kill us. Never will we do as much harm to these monsters as they have done to us, and would do to us, damn it.
>
> From the radical newspaper *Le Père Duchesne*.[1]

It was a time of mad kings and dead kings. In 1789, the year that a Revolutionary mob stormed the great Bastille prison in Paris, George III of England had to be kept in a straitjacket, occasionally a restraining chair, as he ranted incessantly and often indecently. Three years later Louis XVI of France was put to death on a cold winter's morning in the centre of Paris.

How many members of the National Convention, the governing French body, actually voted for the King's execution is uncertain because each member was allowed to make a speech as he voted and some speeches were highly ambiguous. But all scholars agree that the ballot return was very close. Some claim that a proposal for immediate execution was carried by only one vote. Greater skill and diplomacy could undoubtedly have saved Louis's life. Even a final vote on a stay of execution was carried by 380 to 310, the decision to execute him swung by barely 10 per cent of the whole assembly. While some sections of the public and the gutter press rejoiced, renaming him 'Louis the Last' long before his execution, France was deeply divided over the direction that the Revolution was taking.[2]

One hundred horsemen escorted Louis from the oppressive and long-vanished temple fortress in the east of the city where he had been confined with his family and some 1,200 foot soldiers surrounded the coach. The streets were so thickly lined with onlookers that it took the coach two hours to cover the short distance to the scaffold. The King sat with his confessor, an Irish priest named Henry Edgeworth, and together they murmured the penitential psalms and the traditional prayers for the dying. A feeble attempt to rescue the King was savagely cut down. When he arrived at the square, he left the coach with purpose and climbed the stairs to the scaffold with steady legs and a strong back.

And then it was over, shockingly, deliberately and, disappointingly for some, quickly. The guillotine had been designed to immobilise the head, to severe it far more cleanly and reliably than death by sword (restricted to nobility) or hanging (for everyone else). It had been designed with a revolutionary principle at its heart: this was execution for everyone, with no distinction between rich and poor, enacted anonymously by a machine designed to end life and not to cause pain. The end came so quickly that many believed the victim retained some measure of consciousness as the head fell to the floor. We now know that the catastrophic blood loss would cause unconsciousness in a matter of seconds, if not instantaneously, but the eyes and lips of every severed head twitched and the executioners played to the crowd. On one occasion, the executioner of Charlotte Corday – brazen assassin of the Revolutionary leader Jean Marat – slapped her cheek as he brandished the severed head, and she blushed.

So it was that, atop the scaffold, Louis, manhandled onto the horizontal plank and his neck secured in the brace, looked into the basket and died. A very young guard, perhaps no more than eighteen years old, held the King's head aloft for the crowd.

Louis's execution was a quite extraordinary event whose impact has to be understood if the complex history which followed, and in which the great naval Battle of the Glorious First of June played its part, is to be put in any kind of perspective.

Louis died as a citizen of France rather than its monarch: he died as plain old *citoyen* (citizen) Louis Capet, and not as Louis XVI. Everything about the execution was designed to obliterate the rights and rituals of centuries of French monarchy. The monarchy had been abolished four months earlier and none of his final requests, made in the hope if not the expectation of preferential treatment, were granted. He asked to delay the execution for three days to better prepare himself and to spend more time with his family. This was denied. He asked to keep his hair long for the execution. This, too, was denied and his skull was roughly shaved by the executioner, Charles Sanson. He asked to keep his hands free for the execution. Again, this was denied. He tried to make a brief speech on the scaffold, but it was drowned out as the sixty drums surrounding the scaffold rolled in response to a harsh call from General Santerre. Once severed, the body of the former king, with its head laid between its legs, was taken in a wicker basket to the nearby cemetery of La Madeleine – and not to the ancient burial ground of French monarchy near St Denis – where it was transferred into a plain wooden coffin, covered in two layers of quicklime and then lowered into a communal grave pit.

To comprehend the full significance of Louis's death one must see him not just as a king but as a king of France. Unlike many of its north-European counterparts, the French monarchy had been secure for centuries. Elsewhere, spates of regicide had become the defining characteristic of some monarchies, such as medieval Scandinavia, late medieval England and Stuart Scotland. If we consider the case of medieval England, regicide was surprisingly common. Since 1066, of the forty English monarchs who reigned, six were killed by their subjects, and five of those six murders – the exception of course being the execution of Charles I – occurred in the 158 years between 1327 and 1485. For these dynasties a central feature of kingship was that they were so prone to being killed.[3] Now consider France. The Capetian monarchy was founded in 987 AD. Between then and 1789 – that is 802 years – thirty French kings reigned but none of them was deposed and only two were murdered. The two who were murdered were killed by lone assassins and they were replaced immediately on the throne by the next male heir.

The French monarchy was a shining example of dynastic security, whereas in England, Sweden and Russia, most successions from the eleventh to the early sixteenth centuries violated the rules of succession.[4] New dynasties were forced to secure their rocky claim to the throne through murder and even more murder. In England, for example, both Henry VII and Henry VIII had powerful nobles killed to protect the Tudor crown from Yorkist attack, and in Romanoff Russia a crown prince was killed by his father and a Czar by his wife.

In all of these examples of European regicide, however, the monarch was always replaced. The physical bodies of the monarchs may have been threatened, but at no stage was the divine body of kingship questioned. Monarchs were regarded as central to the prosperity, security and wellbeing of a nation's body and spirit. The king, after all, was divinely anointed and the murder of a monarch was an act not only against humanity, but also an act against God. Modern scholars believe that the majority of regicides performed their dastardly acts in the full expectation of spending the rest of eternity in hell.

Tyranny of course was both loathed and feared, but not so much as anarchy, and nothing suggested anarchy more than the execution and non-replacement of a monarch. Even raving-mad monarchs were endured for considerable periods, sometimes for as long as a decade, purely to secure stability. Charles VI of France thought he was made of glass; Henry VI of England spent several years without moving or speaking; Joanna the Mad of Spain believed the corpse of her husband wasn't actually a corpse; and the ravings of George III of England are infamous. A mad king and a dead king therefore represent the polar opposites of attitudes toward monarchy in the 1790s: George was tolerated even though he was mad while Louis was killed *because* he was a king.

Louis's death had two immediate repercussions that are central to this story. First, by baptising itself in his blood, the new Republic split French society as surely as if it, too, had been struck by the blade of the guillotine. As the blade fell, the head rolled and the royal blood ran, some of those who witnessed the execution shouted '*Vive la République*', but others cut their own throats, drowned themselves in the Seine or dipped their handkerchiefs in the pools of Louis's blood that collected around their feet. The King's death opened up a power vacuum in which tyranny was not just tolerated but flourished. Within a year, the ships of the French navy were painted red ochre for the blood of the enemies of the Revolution that stained the soles and souls of a nation. The death of Louis was not the herald of liberty but the birth of the Terror. Second, the European powers swiftly rose together in defence of sovereign rule: William Pitt the British Prime Minister, though not particularly surprised it had come to pass, declared Louis's execution '...the foulest and most atrocious deed which the history of the world has yet had occasion to attest';[5] the Russian Queen, Catherine the Great, declared nine weeks of mourning for her entire court; Spain recalled its ambassador.

As the French began to expand their territory, so the threatened European powers united against her. France, already lame from the unprecedented internal butchery that had followed the death of Louis, was now threatened by a powerful foreign coalition that dwarfed previous half-hearted international attempts to restrain the Revolutionaries. With Pitt's backing Britain was an integral part of that coalition and so the struggle of the French Revolution burst out of France and its surrounding territories and onto the open sea.

# Introduction

> As our late cruise is rather interesting I shall endeavour to give you some account of it.
>
> Anonymous British sailor writing home in June 1794.[1]

You are standing outside Westminster Abbey, waiting, with all of the other London tourists, to go in through the north door. The route is carefully laid out with barriers and patrolled by security officers who funnel every visitor along a relentless path into the Abbey. Turn around, elbow a few people out of the way and march across the grass toward the larger and much more impressive west door because this – which is now the exit – is the door that the architect of Westminster Abbey's mid-eighteenth-century alterations, Nicholas Hawksmoor, envisaged as the building's grand entrance; this was his bold statement of architectural vision. The fact that visitors must now enter through the north door is upsetting because they are unable to experience one of our finest architectural treasures in the way Hawksmoor intended, but more specifically it is upsetting because, if you are not careful, you miss one of the most magnificent naval monuments ever constructed.

This memorial is in the north tower, immediately to the left of the splendid west door. It is quite the last thing that any tired tourist leaving the Abbey would notice, but it is quite impossible to miss if one enters through the west door. The geography of the Abbey's modern tourist trail has relegated this memorial to the bottom rung, despite its being in one of the most prestigious locations, if not *the* most prestigious location, for a memorial in the entire country. In St Paul's Cathedral, by contrast, even the elaborate tombs of some of Britain's finest are in the quiet sanctuary of the crypt, through the nave and down the stairs: one has to know where they are to find them. But this naval memorial at Westminster Abbey, this is something else entirely. It is quite deliberately provocative and it demands attention from all who enter through the west door. Entirely unexpected, within seconds of entering the Abbey, every visitor is confronted with an image of the Royal Navy. You expect to be awed by British reverence for God but within seconds you are awed by British reverence for seapower. It is a profoundly disorienting experience.

Now, look more closely and it becomes even more interesting, because this is not a memorial to a flag officer decorated many times over a lifetime of naval war, but that to a lowly captain by the name of James Montagu. Nevertheless, there he stands at the entrance to Westminster Abbey, hand on hip in breezy confidence, his waist tilted away from the magnificent sword that balances his pose. Raised on a column carved in relief with a detailed battle scene and with two rather surly lions at his feet, he peers with interest, down a long nose, into the nave while beautiful winged Victory reaches high into the heavens to lower a crown upon his head. Flags carved in marble provide a backdrop alive with movement, like the sea itself. Some flag officers' tombs are more grand, perhaps, but no other naval captain is commemorated with such pomp and in such a nationally significant location as James Montagu. Twenty-two British monarchs lie in Westminster Abbey along with giants of British scientific, political and military history such as Isaac Newton, Charles Darwin, Bonar Law, Neville Chamberlain, Winston Churchill, Francis Drake, James Wolfe, William Shakespeare, Edward Elgar. The list goes on and on, but James Montagu is the one next to the front door (see fig. 1). He is a very lucky man.

A little farther down the north aisle and mounted high on the wall is another monument, this time dedicated to two men who were, again, both lowly naval captains: John Hutt and John Harvey. Compared to the Montagu memorial it is in fact but a tiny proportion and all that remains of what was, once, a monument to rival it in both size and artistic scope. No images of the original survive but we know that it was centred on a large vase decorated with portraits of both men. Set on a pedestal, the vase was flanked by a colossal figure of Britannia who, complete with shield, trident and lion, was placing a laurel on the vessel. Opposite Britannia, and of a similar size, was Fame complete with garland and trumpet and pointing to the officers' names engraved at the base. On the front of the pedestal was a detailed battle relief, overflown by an angel grasping in one hand a palm branch and the other a set of scales, symbols of victory and justice. Behind the pedestal were carved trophies and the officers' weaponry. The whole composition stood some eighteen feet high and was designed specifically 'to tell, to distant ages, the "gallant bearing" of Britons'.[2] Originally, the memorial to Hutt and Harvey was sited very close to that of Montagu. Impressive as it is today, therefore, the Montagu memorial provides only half of the impact that was once intended.

It was following an unscheduled visit to Westminster Abbey one fine spring day in 2009 that I stumbled, quite accidentally, upon these monuments. I was left reeling by the questions they posed. Not least, why did these three captains deserve such magnificent memorials and on such a nationally significant and prominent site? The simple answer is that they died in, or shortly after, the battle in 1794 that became known as the Glorious First of June. But this fact raised yet more questions. I knew that there were numerous fleet battles during the eighteenth century and at least fifty between 1688 and 1815. There was also a near-constant stream of other naval operations and engagements, ranging from clashes between single ships to amphibious warfare and coastal bombardment. The Royal Navy was generally successful, though the tide of British death was as steady as the tide of British victory. So, why was *this* battle so important to the British? What on earth happened in 1794? It was a conundrum in itself, but then I went to Paris and things became even more interesting.

You are now in Paris with your back to the Seine, looking south towards the Latin quarter. If you can find even the slightest vantage point you will be able to see a vast dome dominating the skyline, a dome that is designed to be seen and to attract, a monument that encourages you to visit and to discover. This is the dome of the Panthéon, the great neo-classical mausoleum that shelters the bones of many great and famous Frenchmen. Here, you will find the tombs of eminent writers and philosophers such as Voltaire, Rousseau, Victor Hugo and Alexandre Dumas and it was here that Léon Foucault demonstrated the rotation of the earth.

As Westminster Abbey is in Britain, the Panthéon is one of the most significant monuments in France and, as at Westminster Abbey, you are not allowed to walk in through the front door. You are, however, allowed through a small door just to one side and you are immediately funnelled towards the nave. One's modern impression of the Panthéon, therefore, is very much as was always intended. And what is one of the first things that one sees? The tomb of a king, queen or emperor, a politician or a scientist? No. Just to the right of the nave and fiercely grabbing your attention with its larger-than-life white marble figures that gesture defiantly amongst a mountain of broken rigging, is a sculpture dedicated to the crew of a warship that sank in an engagement known as *La Bataille Prairial* (see fig. 2). The adjective *prairial*, loosely translated as 'pastoral', appears to sit uneasily in the title of a naval battle but it refers, here, to a date, rather than a place. In 1793 when the energy of the young French Revolution was in full spate, one of the many institutions and traditions of France that were reinvented was the calendar.[3] The year began at the autumnal equinox and was divided into twelve months, each consisting of thirty days, and the months were all renamed for natural events corresponding to the season. Mid-February to March became *Ventôse*, from the Latin *ventosus* meaning windy; mid-April to May became *Floréal*, from the Latin *flos* meaning flower, and late May and early June became *Prairial*. *La Bataille Prairial*, therefore, is the very same battle that is known in Britain as the Glorious First of June.

Next, you must head north, back toward the Seine which you cross at the Île de la Cité and strike out across the third arrondissement until you reach that theatre of French Revolutionary heritage, the Place de la République. This was once the location of the great Temple prison where both Louis XVI and Marie Antoinette, along with thousands of other French men and women, were held before their execution during the Terror of 1793–4. The Place de la République was a centrepiece of the rebuilding of Paris in the 1850s and 60s then, in 1879, the monument at its centre was constructed to celebrate the newly proclaimed Third Republic. Around its base at eye-level, bronze reliefs depict significant events in French history, one of them dedicated to the same crew of the same warship commemorated in the Panthéon. Thus, in the historic Place de la République, we find yet another memorial to *La Bataille Prairial* – the Glorious First of June.

Collectively, the memorials in Westminster Abbey, the Panthéon and the Place de la République say something very important about British and French history. The memorials' grandeur and artistry coupled with their high-profile locations leave no doubt that the Glorious First of June once stood high in the national consciousness of both Britain and France. Moreover, the nature and location of all three memorials serve as a powerful reminder that naval history of the Age of Sail has become so dominated by Nelson and his great victories at Trafalgar (1805) and, to a lesser extent, the Nile (1798) that other great and significant battles have been overlooked. The first two volumes of my *Hearts of Oak* trilogy, *The Fighting Temeraire* and *The Admiral Benbow*, were about naval legends that have endured. This third volume rediscovers a naval legend that has been forgotten.

The Battle of the Glorious First of June was fought between Britain and France in the mid-Atlantic between 28 May and 1 June 1794. Beyond that, there are several facts that distinguish it and all are important in their own way. It was the first naval battle of the French Revolutionary War; it was the only fleet battle during the Reign of Terror; it was the first fleet battle in British or French history that was fought for political ideology rather than for territory, religion or trade or at the whim of monarchs;[4] it was the longest fleet battle for 128 years;[5] it was celebrated as a victory by the French and the British navy as well as by the Americans; it was the largest British naval victory for 102 years;[6] it was the first naval battle witnessed and then depicted by a professional artist for 128 years;[7] it was the first battle in the eighteenth century in which an Admiral deliberately tried to break the enemy line; it was the first battle made famous by a 'panorama', an artistic technique which became standard for celebrating naval battles; it was the first battle for which British officers received a medal; it was the first battle to be celebrated by an immediate Royal review of the fleet. But of all of these claims to distinction, the most important and the most interesting is this: The Glorious First of June was, without question, the hardest-fought battle of the Age of Sail.

In every battle fought in that period the men's blood stained the spume amid flotsam, wreckage and bloated corpses. When news of those lost reached home, mothers, sons, daughters and sweethearts mourned their missing and their dead. Gifts wrapped for a happy return were put away; dreams of seaside walks with loved ones were now cherished as memories and not nursed as expectations. So much was the same; this side of warfare never changed. What distinguished The Glorious First of June from other naval battles was the very particular point in time at which it was fought: when the opposing fleets met in June 1794, the French Revolution was at its height. The Bastille had been stormed, Louis XVI had been executed and had lain in his grave for sixteen months and, now, the new French Republic tottered on uncertain legs, blinking at its first sun. With humanitarian ideals unlike any the world had ever seen cradled close to its heart, the Republic faced the enemies it had created at its birth. This was one of the most significant moments in the evolution of the modern world, a great rift in the plains of history. Could the young Republic survive?

Nothing was certain. The young Republic had enemies everywhere. The most significant European powers, the Holy Roman Empire, Prussia, Spain, Portugal and Britain, united in a coalition against the new Republic and the French populace had been shattered into a thousand disparate shards. Politics, religion, class, family and countless other factors had bred a dangerous mix of attraction and repulsion which erupted into one of the most vicious civil wars that has ever been fought. Into this chaos strutted the Jacobins, their tricolour sashes and cockades aggressively displaying their beliefs. A ruthless and radical political faction, the Jacobins chose to save the humanitarian ideals of the Republic through a dedicated programme of institutionalised fear, sustained violence and an absence of justice. This was the Reign of Terror.[8]

The Terror lasted only a short time, perhaps sixteen months from the spring of 1793. Although its start date is uncertain, its end date is quite specific: the Terror met its demise on 27 July 1794 with the death of Maximilien Robespierre, the caring lawyer who became the tyrant largely responsible for its design and implementation. Owing to reprisals against the hated Jacobins, civil unrest and violence did not stop immediately, but the intense politicisation of society gradually fizzled out and with it the denunciations, the propaganda, the fear and the butchery, all of which had blossomed under the Terror. A mere seven weeks before Robespierre's fall from grace, the Jacobins' reign was at its most intense. Everything appeared concentrated, magnified and distorted. In Paris, for example, the guillotine, which had been working at a steady rate for a year or so, was slicing off heads as quickly as the executioners could unstrap the severed bodies and secure the next fresh victim who was forced to lie in the seeping wetness of others' blood. At one stage the guillotine had to be moved from its original position in the Place de la Révolution to the site of the demolished Bastille and then, again, even farther into the suburbs because the blood being shed threatened to pollute the city's water supply.[9] In the beautiful Vendée region of western France, just south of the Loire, women and child 'rebels' were clubbed to death and buried in mass graves while men were taken prisoner, loaded on to boats and executed by mass drownings in the Loire as their land was burned.

It was against this chaotic backdrop that two vast fleets, one British and one French, met in the middle of the north Atlantic, at a point so far from land that, uniquely, the resulting battle is known for its date rather than its location. There was no shadowy bluff, no sheer cliff, no menacing reef, no sandy shoal and no port to name it by. Nothing but the horizon encircled the ships on that misty summer morning while a towering, lumpy, mid-ocean swell rolled under their hulls.

What happened at that spot, where the seabed must still be littered with the debris of war and the shattered hull of the French 74-gunner, the *Vengeur du Peuple*, was unlike any other naval battle before or since.

The French Revolution had tilted the world on its axis. England's traditional enemy was governed, not by a new ruler but by a new system of beliefs. The battle was a clash of philosophies as much as one of oak and iron, flesh and bone with the British fearing that the hideousness of the Terror might be exported across the English Channel. Cuthbert Collingwood, a future star of the Royal Navy but then a lowly captain, wrote to a friend:

> This war is certainly unlike any former, both in its object and execution. The object is a great and serious one, to resist the machinations of a mad people who, under the mask of freedom, wou'd stamp their tyranny in every country in Europe, and support and defend the happiest constitution that ever wisdom formed for the preserving order in civil society...[10]

The French were fighting for the survival of their Republic, for which they had already sacrificed so much. The French navy had been whipped into a frenzy by Jeanbon Saint-André, a Jacobin representative sent directly from Paris to Brest to galvanise naval affairs. He achieved his objective through judicious use of the guillotine and promising a string of punishments and death to those who failed to fight for the Republic in the unforgiving way expected of them. The French navy was fighting out of fear, but it was also fighting for its reputation. Less than a year before, the entire French Mediterranean squadron had surrendered to a British squadron under Samuel Hood without a shot being fired. This, the most disgraceful act in French naval history, was swiftly followed by a mutiny at Brest. Since the outbreak of war in 1792 French and British armies had met and tested each other's strength time and again but thus far, naval contact between the two countries had been inconclusive. The French armies had begun to demonstrate their skill and resolve and now, with the British fleet spoiling for a fight, it was the turn of the navy to prove its loyalty and its value to the new Republic. Both fleets were straining at the leash for a significant battle.

The name of the battle is a little misleading. The Glorious First of June was not a single action but the final act in a week-long struggle between the fleets. There were large-scale battles on both 28 and 29 May followed by two days of excruciating tension with intermittent contact as the damaged ships circled their elusive opponent in thick fog. When they met again on 1 June, the preceding four days and nights had left both fleets very badly damaged and the men exhausted. The British fleet, led by the veteran naval commander Earl Howe, bore down on the French and broke their line in four, or possibly five, places. The French fleet was led by Louis Thomas Villaret de Joyeuse, a nobleman who had survived the Republicans' violent hatred of the aristocracy. Transparently loyal to the Republican cause, Villaret countered the British attack with ferocious resolve.

Both sides hailed a victory. The British claim stemmed from the fact that they had sunk one and captured six French ships and that, while their own fleet suffered severe damage, no ships were lost to the French. The French for their part deemed themselves victors because they had fulfilled their mission. They had been ordered to sea to protect a convoy carrying grain from America. In the chaos of revolution the French economy had imploded, the people were starving and hunger was fuelling the country's instability. The American grain was as vital for the politicians as it was for the starving peasants. Nothing, they ordered, must stop it reaching France. And despite the efforts of the British, the convoy did, indeed, reach Brest unmolested.

Thus the battle was celebrated in Britain and France and also in America. Having recently won independence through revolution in the War of American Independence (1775–83), the United States was openly supporting the French Republicans. In both Britain and France the facts of the battle and the politically induced spin combined to create a legend powerful enough to endure for generations. Incidents such as the single-ship action fought between the British *Brunswick* and the French *Vengeur du Peuple* captured everyone's imagination. Vivid images of French sailors crying '*Vive la République*' as their ship sank beneath them cemented the battle's fame in French history. Entrepreneurs hovered around the Battle like bees around a honey pot, darting in to take out whatever they valued. It became famous in art, theatre, poetry and song. In Paris it impacted on the constantly shifting political situation and became an important factor in the events leading to the fall of Robespierre. Just seven weeks afterwards, the tyrant's jawless head and headless corpse lay in a commoners' mass grave in a Parisian cemetery alongside many others who, by increasing the powers of the state and stripping the powers of the individual had made the Terror a reality. The battle must also be linked to subsequent events in Paris: the confusion and weak leadership that followed the Jacobins and then, from the ashes of their destruction, the meteoric rise of Napoleon Bonaparte, a friend of Robespierre's and witness to his personal ambition and the capability of an infrastructure designed for tyranny.

For this story to make sense, all of these themes must be brought together. It is not just a tale of fleet battle but of revolution, tyranny, mutiny, personal ambition, human endurance, fear and love, gain and loss. Much of the outline is well known to scholars of Robespierre and the Revolution but the naval side is not recognised to the extent a battle of such scale and importance deserves. Inevitably, as a precursor of Nelson, the Glorious First of June has suffered: it must always live in the shadow of his great victories at the Nile and Trafalgar. To understand its full impact at the time, however, we must put aside our knowledge of what followed and place ourselves in the spring of 1794 when the Royal Navy was still plagued by self-doubt. The British had unmistakeably and irrevocably lost the preceding war, the War of American Independence (1775–83). During that conflict, the French navy had fought skilfully in some magnificent ships and had achieved notable strategic and tactical successes at the battles of Ushant (1778) and the Chesapeake (1781). By the end of the war the British had begun to fight well and much of their reputation was restored by Admiral George Rodney in the Battle of the Saints (1782), but significant and lasting damage had been done to their confidence and uncertainty remained. Bitterness surrounded even the Battle of the Saints, caused by a distinct feeling that Rodney could have done more. By 1794 there had not been a fleet action for twelve years. A generation had passed. Some remembered the whistle of the cannonballs and the terrible shrieking of the rigging as it splintered and cracked under a hail of grapeshot, but many did not. Most British sailors were new to naval warfare; many of the newest recruits were so young that they were even new to ships and the sea.

To understand why the fleets met where they did, and how they fought in the way that they did, we must travel widely in our narrative and not only visit Paris and London, Plymouth and Brest, but also Toulon, Italy, Austria, Saint Domingue, Martinique, St Lucia, Tobago, Philadelphia, Virginia and New York. We must go back a full year to the summer of 1793 and then look on, past the battle, to the weeks, months and years that followed. With the traditional geographical and temporal barriers thus removed we can see links where previously none were visible, reach a more profound understanding of the battle itself and hence achieve a new perception of the French Revolution, one of the most important events in the history of the modern world. This is how naval history can give old stories a new voice.

The sources available to the historian wishing to place himself in the spring of 1794 are quite exceptional; indeed, a greater number of fascinating sources for this battle survive than for almost any other in the Age of Sail. Of particular importance, while very few accurate images of sailing warfare are known to exist, at the Glorious First of June, and for the first time since the seventeenth century, the battle was witnessed by an artist, Nicholas Pocock, one of the finest of his day and one who had spent his formative years at sea. Pocock understood the sea, ships and rigging and he worked in an era that sought artistic realism. As a result the paintings that survive of the Glorious First of June are believed to be the most accurate images of sailing warfare ever produced. There are numerous other detailed sketches and plans from eye-witnesses, including battle plans from the master of the *Bellerophon*[11] and the third lieutenant of the *Queen*,[12] a rapidly executed ink sketch by Captain John Duckworth of the *Orion*[13] and, most valuable of all, a series of plans kept by the meticulous hand of none other than Matthew Flinders who fought at the Glorious First of June as a midshipman on board the *Bellerophon* and went on to circumnavigate Australia.[14] A host of other artists, though not present at the scene, also became involved in preserving the memory of the battle and went to great lengths to ensure their images were as accurate as possible by sketching the damaged ships and interviewing sailors and officers. Taken together, all these various depictions form a canon of work unrivalled in naval history.

The relics that survive from the battle are also deeply impressive, not least the magnificent white silk banner flown on French ships proclaiming '*Marins. La République ou la Mort.*', which translates as, 'Sailors. The Republic or Death.' (see fig. 15). Even the ensign flown by Admiral Howe from the mainmast of his flagship, the *Queen Charlotte*, survives (see fig. 11). Very few such flags remain and this is the oldest Admiral's command flag known to exist. Saved by a light-fingered midshipman named William Burgh who slipped it into his kit bag, the flag is vast, measuring four metres by five and a half metres, and is riddled with shot holes, bleached by sea and sun and tattered by the wind. It is shown quite clearly in a very large and very famous painting of the action by the English artist Philippe de Loutherbourg (see fig. 16). It was bought by the National Maritime Museum in London at a snip, only £40,000 for a unique piece of naval heritage, though only after a public appeal to save it from export into the hands of an American collector. To see it in person is a powerful experience, a worthy equal to viewing the foretopsail of HMS *Victory* from the Battle of Trafalgar that survives at the Royal Naval Museum in Portsmouth. A massive body of contemporary written evidence relating to the battle survives, including professional correspondence, love letters, ships' logs and reports from dockyards, naval administrators, diplomats and spies.

This evidence can help explain how and why the battle on 1 June 1794 once enjoyed an exalted status in British and French culture. A fresh analysis can also verify whether basic facts are accurate. It has long been argued, for example, that it was won by superior British seamanship and experience, but this was the British navy's first battle for nearly eleven years. Is such a comparison and judgement fair after such a passage of time? Skill, after all, is much easier to lose than it is to gain and lessons are much easier to forget than to learn. Traditionally, the French crews have also been described as an unskilled mob driven to extremes of courage under the whip-hand of the Jacobins. But if one stops to consider, this picture is not so clear. Certainly a large portion of the experienced French officer corps had left the navy for fear of their lives and been replaced by merchantmen and fishermen. On the other hand, anyone who has tried to enter a port on the north-western coast of France knows that it requires a high degree of seamanship, even in a modern yacht, to survive the tidal races, hidden rocks and constant patchy fog. In fact, the fishermen and merchant captains of north-western France, particularly those from around St Malo, were among the finest seamen afloat. We must ask ourselves anew, therefore, how the change in the social and professional dynamic of French crews actually impacted French naval competence. We also need to think beyond the immediate focus of the battle, beyond the immediate pain and human tragedy of fleet warfare and beyond the seamanship and tactics of victory to explain how the British and French operational capabilities and war strategy were affected by the battle, and how the battle interacted with other events that led to the downfall of Robespierre and eventually to the rise of Napoleon.

Most importantly of all we must ask ourselves if the battle deserves its continuing association with glory, for it is clear that deep in its heart, this battle is a profound paradox. If one could ask the people who fought at the First of June to describe the battle in a single word very few would use the word 'glorious'. Painful and exhilarating, dark and light, wet and dry, hungry and thirsty, frightening and energising, hot and cold? Yes: all of these. But glorious? No. In 1794 the word glorious was used by politicians and historians, not sailors; by observers, not combatants. It fails entirely to capture the pain of trying to eat with teeth shattered by splinters, of the smell of blood like the taste of a copper coin, or the reality of trying to maintain one's balance on a heaving, slippery deck with a sword cut to the hip, a piece of grapeshot in the knee or toes crushed beyond repair. Glorious is a word used with hindsight to embellish and deceive; it is the gold leaf that transforms an iron candlestick into a priceless treasure; the forged label that turns vinegar into claret. Yet that process of transformation is itself part of the history of the battle: it cannot be discarded once identified, but should be celebrated as its own layer of history. The battle may not have been glorious for many who fought it, but the politicians on both sides grasped the opportunity it raised to stoke the fires of propaganda that powered the war.

Simply because of its name, therefore, no other naval battle can demonstrate such important themes so clearly. Equally, no other battle shows so emphatically that naval history is best understood by focusing first on the societies which created and surrounded the navies involved. Naval history is not about ships, powder and geometric lines representing fleets, but about the people who sailed in those ships and, over and above even that, the people who sent them to war. What happened hundreds, or even thousands of miles away from the battle was very often more important than what took place on board the ships themselves. The natural shape of the story of the Glorious First of June shadows so perfectly the rise and fall of Maximilien Robespierre that it is there it must start. It begins not with sweating sailors peering nervously through gunports, ears straining for the order to fire and hearts racing in anticipation, but in the cool of a committee room in the heart of Paris. There stands the vain and dainty Robespierre, in whose mind were conceived some of the purest ideals of human civilisation, in whose hands lay the future of the French republic, and at whose feet lay thousands upon thousands of French corpses.

# The First Terror

## APRIL – AUGUST 1793

My purpose is to burn everything, to leave nothing … all brigands caught bearing arms, or convicted of having taken up arms to revolt against their country, will be bayoneted. The same will apply to girls, women and children in the same circumstances. Those who are merely under suspicion will not be spared either…

General Louis Turreau declares his intentions for the rebellious Vendée region of France, 19 January 1794.[1]

There are many extraordinary characters in the French Revolution, but no one encapsulates better the change in the nature of the Revolution in the aftermath of Louis XVI's death than Maximilien Robespierre. A small, immaculately presented man, fond of his sky-blue frock coat, embroidered waistcoat and silk stockings, he always wore small, circular, green-tinted spectacles through which he peered to read his endless, meandering speeches. A man of slight stature, his words nevertheless carried weight and influence; he could recruit, convince, enthuse, persuade and harangue as no other. His intellect could twist the most clear-cut logic in an age when twisted logic was a currency that could purchase life or death. He was zealous, motivated and ambitious but, above all, he was eloquent, articulate and tenacious, and as with all politicians who are both ambitious and tenacious, Robespierre was prepared to change his mind. Once a moderate lawyer, he had argued passionately against war and specifically against the death penalty with no exception, but by 1792 he was arguing for it, and with no exception. It was chiefly under his impassioned guidance that the Revolution, once a movement steeped in virtue and morality, descended into unprecedented butchery in the first two years of the new Republic.

Only three years previously, the Revolution's humanitarian ideals had been celebrated throughout the western world. The Revolutionaries had argued for popular sovereignty, for civil liberty and for equality before the law; for the legality of divorce and for full status to be granted to illegitimate children; for the abolition of primogeniture, slavery and discrimination against Protestants and Jews. In 1789, the British

Ambassador in Paris wrote: 'The greatest revolution that we know anything of has been effected with, comparatively speaking, if the magnitude of the event is considered, the loss of very few lives: from this moment we may consider France a free country.' In the same year the House of Commons proposed to the Lords a 'day of thanksgiving for the French Revolution' [2] and a popular poem even celebrated the newfound freedom of the old enemy.

> There is not an English heart that would not leap
> That ye were fallen at last, to know
> That even our enemies, so oft employed
> In forging chains for us, themselves were free.[3]

But by the spring of 1794, when Robespierre had achieved tyrannical control, perhaps half a million men and women had been imprisoned for political crimes, almost 16,000 had been officially guillotined with the deaths carefully logged and perhaps a further 40,000 had been executed without any record being kept. Countless corpses, 200,000 at least in the Vendée region alone and, some scholars claim, more than double that figure for all of France, filled rivers, ditches and mass graves.[4]

The night before his election to the Committee of Public Safety (CPS), the body of twelve men instigated in April 1793 and granted exceptionally wide-ranging executive powers to govern France at this time of crisis, Robespierre took up his pen and in his highly distinctive and very exact cursive handwriting, set down his self-styled manifesto for progress. It ended with the following paragraph that reveals how unstable France had become, and the extent to which the Jacobins were prepared to go to secure their dream:

> How can we end the civil war?
> By punishing traitors and conspirators, especially those deputies and administrators who are to blame; by sending patriot troops under patriot leaders to reduce the aristocrats of Lyon, Marseille, Toulon, the Vendée, the Jura, and all other districts where the banner of Royalism and rebellion has been raised; and by making

> a terrible example of all the criminals who have outraged liberty and spilt the blood of patriots.[5]

Just as the initial ideals of the Revolution seem impossible to reconcile with the genocide of 1793–4, so it is with the image of Robespierre as both tolerant and tyrannical and as the incarnation of both moderation and extremism. The origins of this change in both the Revolution and Robespierre are uncertain and debatable but it is clear that, by the time the headless Louis lay in a mass grave in 1792, some of the seeds of extremism had already germinated: the Jacobin regime had embraced and used shocking violence; the Revolutionaries were intrinsically afraid of conspiracy and anyone with alternative views to those of the Jacobins had been branded as enemies.

There was also considerable and rapidly growing antipathy directed toward the ruling politicians. In reality, little had changed for the poorest classes who had placed so much hope in the Revolution. The king was dead but the poor were still poor, the hungry were still hungry and many were now poorer and hungrier than they ever had been. The means by which any change could be brought about were also uncertain; there was a lack of leadership, a gulf of power. The Republic had been declared but the new constitution had not been written, thus there was no legal infrastructure to guarantee its safety and to wield its power.

Enemies of the Revolution chose this moment, the earliest days of the new Republic, to rise up. Sixty of the eighty departments broke into open revolt in June 1793 over the Jacobin expulsion of their opponents, the Girondins, from the National Convention – the legislative assembly. In the Vendée, that beautiful region just south of the Loire, thousands had already formed an army to fight for their freedom: Republicanism not only threatened their Catholic faith, but also imposed the indignity of forced conscription and required them to pay a tax for a war they did not support. The bourgeois middle class of some of France's principal provincial cities, Marseille, Lyon and Toulon, rose under the banner of federalism, a political system favoured by the Girondins. Elsewhere, though in fewer numbers, supporters of the monarchy fought for its restoration.

Hunger remained a problem for everyone in the very hot summer of 1793 because, although the harvest was good, there was little water to run the mills. Flour could not be milled and so bread and biscuits could not be baked. Prices shot up and shops and warehouses were raided of goods. In mid-summer the Convention, in a vain attempt to ease hyperinflation, was forced to fix the price of bread and other necessities and hoarding became punishable by death. This was a time of price control and requisitioning of labour, goods and property to a degree that was unprecedented and remained unmatched until the Second World War.[6]

In the same year France's borders were coming under foreign threat on all sides and her armed forces were incompetent. The Austrians, Prussians and some German states attacked from the north and east. In January, an attempt by the French navy to take Sardinia failed spectacularly and in March French forces were routed by the Austrians at Neerwinden and forced out of the Low Countries. In their wake the Austrians advanced into northern France. Also in March, France tried to send a fleet to the West Indies but it got no farther than Biscay and the Royal Navy occupied the Flanders ports of Nieuport and Ostend. And, again in March, the Austrians took Aix-la-Chapelle and Liège. In April France's General Dumouriez, who had overseen the disaster at Neerwinden, defected to the Austrians. French troops panicked along the Rhine frontier at both Alsace and at Montcheutin.[7] In April, in the West Indies, the British captured the French island of Tobago and in early summer began to move against Martinique. The strategically significant towns of Jérémie, St Nicholas Mole and Léogane on the French colony of Saint Domingue all fell to the British. St Pierre and Miquelon, fishing bases off Newfoundland, also fell to the British. In June 1793 the first frigate to be captured in the first year of war was French: the *Cléopâtre* was boarded by the crew of the British frigate *Nymphe*, commanded by Captain Sir Edward Pellew. In July, Mainz, on the Rhine, fell to the Prussians, bringing to an end its Revolutionary aspirations and excesses. The Piedmontese forced their way over the Alps and the Spaniards over the Pyrenees, as far as the river Têt. In the East Indies hostilities did not break out until June but as soon as they did French possessions, with the exception of Mauritius, fell like dominoes. In total that year almost 19,000 French troops surrendered.

With so much uncertainty surrounding the new Republic and no effective government in place since ridding the country of its monarch, immediate action was needed if France and its colonies were not to fall to the British, Dutch, Austrians or French counter-Revolutionaries, leaving the revolution as nothing more than a broken dream. The one thing that the Jacobins needed more than any other was time to absorb the decisions and actions they had made in the preceding few months. They had abolished the monarchy but all they had to replace it was ideas. There was no sound, responsible government infrastructure ready in the wings and something was desperately needed to fill the vacuum, if only as a temporary measure to save the republic. The answer the Jacobins came up with was the Committee of Public Safety, its job to flex the muscle of the National Convention in Republican interests and secure the military and economic stability the Republic needed to carry out its benevolent work. It was granted extraordinary executive powers to do this, and to do it quickly.

By midsummer 1793, every man, woman, child and inanimate object had been conscripted, by means of the *grande levée*, for the war effort. This was conscription according to Republican ideals, applied equally to everything and to everyone. The decree was sent out:

> The young men shall fight; the married men shall forge weapons and transport supplies; the women will make tents and clothes and will serve in the hospitals; the children will make up old linen into lint; the old men will have themselves carried into the public squares to rouse the courage of fighting men, to preach the unity of the Republic and the hatred of Kings. The public buildings shall be turned into barracks, the public squares into munitions factories, the earthen floors shall be treated with lye to extract saltpetre. All firearms of suitable calibre shall be turned over to the troops: the interior shall be policed with shotguns and with cold steel. All saddle horses shall be seized for the cavalry; all draft horses not employed in cultivation will draw the artillery and supply-wagons.[8]

Scholars no longer believe the Revolutionary propaganda describing hordes of bright-eyed young men willingly rushing to the front or to the dockyards to lay down their lives for the Republic. In fact, conscription was the solution to one problem, the external threat to France, and the cause of the other, the internal threat to the Republican cause. The departments raged against the tally of 300,000 new soldiers they were required to provide in the first levée of February 1793 and the second, of August of that year, which expected to raise 500,000 more. Neither levée raised the expected amount but together they swelled the ranks of the French army to a staggering 750,000.

To bring the country to order, the CPS was also given the power of summary justice. The will of the Republic needed to be wielded powerfully and immediately. Time was now more important than justice. There was no open trial, no fair hearing and no appeal. After the Law of Suspects was introduced on 17 September 1793, even circumstantial evidence became admissible and attempts at self-defence could be twisted easily by paranoid judges. By the end of the summer citizens could find themselves condemned to death for nothing more than 'associations, comments, or writings have[ing] shown themselves partisans of tyranny or federalism and enemies of liberty'. A gunsmith arrested at Versailles called for a fair hearing, citing in his defence the Rights of Man, that document so central to the original Revolution. The judge on the tribunal, however, proclaimed: 'He talks continuously of liberty and the rights of man, which shows clearly enough that he is bent on sedition.'[9] There was little defence against such logic. The debate of the early years had simply vanished: by 1793, to think differently made you an enemy of the Revolution; moderation and counter-Revolution became one and the same. In some areas of the country there were more acquittals than others but they were, still, a rarity. Indictment, prosecution and conviction was the norm.

In the summer of 1793 that power of summary justice, moreover, was not jealously guarded and centrally held by the CPS but was delegated to deputies who travelled throughout France in an attempt to bring the country to order through terror: as the CPS's powers grew, so did it leak through their hands. Frenzied rhetoric and zeal erupted in the freedom of a monarch-less state. The *sans-culottes*, the group of working-class radicals and army volunteers who enacted most of the Revolutionary policy, were at their most powerful in this period characterised by extraordinary executive powers and a total lack of central control. In contrast, the second period of the Terror, in the spring and summer of 1794, while no less bloody was subtly different – by then the CPS had secured a handle on its powers. Its actions, if still shocking, were nevertheless deliberate, methodical and well controlled.

Areas of rebellion suffered most. Armies were sent to the reactionary heartlands of Lyon, Bordeaux, Marseille, Toulon, the Vendée, Brittany and Normandy. The ferocity of the Republic's response to the Vendée uprising was extraordinary by any standard: soldiers burned villages and crops and killed some 117,000 people. Mass executions with grape shot and group drownings were inventive means of genocide. In one instance, thirty children and two women were buried alive in a large pit.[10] Cemeteries grew in number and size and prison populations swelled. By early December 1793 almost 7,000 suspects were incarcerated throughout France.

As the Republic's sword cut down any opposition, so its words began to wage a parallel ideological war and the most radical of policies were now imposed to appease the extremist *sans-culottes*. Most radical of all was the attempted abolition from French society of Christian religion in favour of atheism and, while the policy was opposed by many of the moderates at the very top of the political hierarchy, radical Republicans had power enough to overrule them. Churches were shut and the clergy were encouraged to leave their posts and to marry. The magnificent Catholic cathedral of Notre-Dame in Paris became a temple for the Cult of Reason. Also targeted were the creative arts and other aspects of cultural life with policies ranging from raging iconoclasm – the ritual beheading of royalist statues was a favourite – to the careful deposition of kings and queens in packs of playing cards by figures of brotherhood and liberty, all of which could now be trumped by an Ace, the lowest thus rising to the top. Kings and queens in chess sets suffered a similar fate.

Even the queen bee was dethroned and became *abeille pondeuse* or 'laying bee'.

Plays were all censored. A play about William Tell was taken off stage until it had been rewritten and retitled *Les Sans-Culottes Suisses*.[11] There was a simultaneous explosion in political songs celebrating Republican virtues or caricaturing Royalists. Republicanism bled through society. When naming babies, saints' names were abandoned in favour of names derived from the new Republican calendar such as Rose, Laurier, Floréal, or the slightly more obvious Liberté or Victoire, and birth records reveal that one lucky child was named Faisceau Pique Terreur.[12] The foreign minister Pierre-Henri Lebrun named his daughter Civilisation-Jémappes[13]-République. Even adults renamed themselves: Louis was a moniker that now had to be dropped, for obvious reasons, and the French reached back in time for mythical names relating to strength and endurance. Spartacus, the Roman slave who rose to lead a rebellion, was a particular favourite.

The Jacobins also proposed sweeping programmes of social and economic welfare and education. They made education compulsory for six- to thirteen-year-olds, extended the rights of children and made abandoned children the concern of the State. They instigated changes in weight, distance and volume to provide a uniform, decimal system to ease economic reform. Prostitution, in theory at least, was banned. If they destroyed scores of magnificent buildings and statues, new ones were planned in their stead as a most vivid demonstration of the new order. Designs were proposed for parks, bathhouses, hospitals, schools, libraries, theatres and museums.[14] Civic authorities organised public festivals and fêtes to explain and explore Revolutionary themes such as nation, unity, fraternity and liberty, which focused in particular on the glory of youth.[15]

Nothing was free from Revolutionary idealism: even time. For the Revolutionaries, time began when the French monarchy ended on 22 September 1792. This became the first day, of the first month, of the first year. The months were renamed, weeks were given ten days, each with a new name, and each month consisted of three weeks. The five days left over became public holidays and they were given appropriate names to celebrate virtue, genius, labour, honours and convictions. The reign of the Jacobins, therefore, was far more than a bloodbath, and they certainly viewed the Terror as nothing more than an enabling measure to realise their dreams of social equality, support and fairness. To appreciate the overt politicisation of all of French society during this period is important for our understanding of the naval battle that followed because the navy was in no way isolated from such politics.

The navy posed a unique challenge to Revolutionary thought and the Jacobin response to the navy exemplifies the type of mental cul-de-sac in which Revolutionaries found themselves after the execution of Louis. As an armed force, the navy was both the future protection of the Revolution, providing the means to ensure its survival, and also an obvious threat. The latter proved a far stronger motivation than the former: Revolutionaries at both local and national level were unsettled by the navy more than they were comforted by it.

The specific problem was that the navy was so easily associated with the type of power and authority that had already been so mercilessly cut out of French society. The French officer corps traditionally had been picked from the *crème* of the aristocracy. In 1780 it had even become law that prospective officers had to demonstrate a full four-quarters of nobility to apply. Attempts had been made by Revolutionaries to change this after 1789, but progress had been slow and the association of the naval officer corps with the aristocracy remained strong. The navy had always drawn its authority explicitly from the crown, and it had always been accustomed to furthering the interests of the French monarchy rather than the interests of the French people. It was, in short, all too easy for Republicans to mistrust the navy.

Service in the navy, moreover, was by no means an attractive proposal, and for many Frenchmen it wasn't even a choice. Living conditions in the French navy were deplorable and there was an infamously high mortality rate. As we already know, the French navy had been relatively successful in the War of American Independence but, still, thousands of sailors had died by the guns, swords and fists of the

British, from the bite of the mosquito or after the invisible fetid breath of typhus triggered the rash and fever that signalled certain death. In times of war, imprisonment at the hands of the British was no distant threat, and any promise of pay came with no guarantee.

The navy's system of punishment was particularly severe, even for minor offences, and among the host of barbaric punishments that could be meted out was one known as the 'cale'.[16] The prisoner would be bound and hauled aloft, clear of the ship's sides, before being dropped, repeatedly, head first into the sea as the ship sailed along. The cale shares all of the main characteristics with that now well-known scourge of modern warfare, waterboarding: restriction of movement, disorientation, and near drowning under water. The cale was punishment by torture. If all of this was bad enough, it was made far worse by the fact that, for many, their service was imposed. The navy was manned by a system of *classes* that required all men from the coastal provinces of France to serve one year in every three, four or five years, depending on the size of the province and the needs of the fleet. For many French sailors, therefore, their service was deeply resented as a form of enforced servitude.

Some improvements had been made since 1789: the navy was one of the first targets for the enlightened ideals of the early Revolution. The path to high rank had been cleared of all obstacles associated with social status; the system of punishment had been changed; sailors were given access to reliable medical advice and assistance and there was a far greater focus on washing, airing, and fumigating the ships in an attempt to improve living and working conditions.[17] But the hated *classes* manning system remained and many of the problems were so institutionally deep-set that, even if the reality of life in the navy did improve, any significant alteration in the navy's reputation, as perceived by outsiders, was some way behind. Unfortunately for the navy it was that reputation as an institution that deprived honest citizens of their liberty, health and life in the King's name that mattered most in 1793. The navy remained an obvious target for those Revolutionaries who had been inspired by the spilled blood of their king.

Before the execution of Louis and the rise of the Jacobins, trouble between Revolutionaries and the navy manifested itself in political confrontation between local authorities around the dockyards and the naval hierarchy that ran them. It was a relationship that matters more than one might suspect because of France's geography.

The dockyards were isolated both nationally and locally. It was at least 350 miles from Paris to Brest and almost another hundred miles more to Toulon. Much of the journey was on terrible roads and could take, at very best, eight or nine days in a shaking, juddering carriage. This geographical and social isolation made the French dockyards fertile breeding grounds for radicalism: there was far less of the moderate cosmopolitan thinking that characterised the coastal merchant cities.

Soon after the Jacobins seized control in Paris, and power was placed in the hands of the CPS, Jacobinism, in its most extreme form, began to rear its head in the provinces. This gave local politicians the power and excuse they needed to exert their authority at the expense of the navy, initially over issues of jurisdiction and authority. The navy resented any such local interference but there was no central power to whom they could turn for support and assistance. Precedent had been set in Toulon as early as 1789 when local authorities imprisoned the Commandant of Toulon, Albert de Rioms. The government – then the National Consitutent Assembly – did nothing. A year later, *Le Léopard* was taken into Brest by a crew that had mutinied off Saint Domingue in the West Indies and abandoned the ship's captain and most of her officers ashore there. When they arrived at Brest, the crew reported directly to the civic authorities in Brest who, to the horror of many naval officers, welcomed them ashore as heroes.[18] Only three months earlier, the Brest Jacobin club had been founded, providing a solid foundation for the spread of Jacobinism into the surrounding area and the fleet itself. It was not long before political unrest had spread throughout the fleet, in some but not all cases even aggravated by Jacobin authorities ashore. For those afloat, therefore, there was both reason and inspiration to mutiny.

The traditional order and authority of the navy completely collapsed and this, combined with the Republican threat to noblemen in positions of power, resulted in many experienced officers leaving the service. In the first two years of the Republic the French navy lost a large proportion of its officers: men who knew how to work a warship in a fleet; men who knew how to bring an enemy to battle and how to organise a crew to repair battle damage; men who understood the strategy and tactics of war at sea. In 1791 alone only forty-four of 237 officers granted leave returned to Brest when their leave ran out.[19] By March 1792 there were two vice-admirals left in the entire French navy from a total of nine, and three rear-admirals left from a total of eighteen. Those who remained were openly and aggressively loyal to the Revolution or sufficiently ambitious that they were prepared to accept the new terms of the Revolution to exploit this unique situation.

The huge gap in the navy's officer corps was filled as retired officers loyal to the new regime came back into the service, others were promoted with indecent haste from within and some were drafted in from French merchant ships. A number of the merchant sailors who accepted command were inexperienced in combat, and several could neither read nor write, an omission that was never permitted in the army.[20]

A further and very significant problem with the composition of the French crews was at the level of gunner. In 1787 the French navy had established a corps of specialist seamen gunners and trained future generations to nurture those skills. They swiftly became something of an elite corps that recognised their own value to each ship's crew and thus their influential position within the navy as a whole. This in turn attracted political agitators into the corps as the Revolution gained momentum in the late 1780s. As soon as the corps of seamen gunners became perceived as a significant internal threat to order it was abolished. By the New Year of 1794, the number of trained gunners had shrunk leaving just the odd individual who knew his business among thousands of sailors who did not. On 4 March 1794 Rear-Admiral Villaret reckoned there were not ten men in his entire fleet who were experienced gunners.[21]

Yet another problem lay deeper still. It rather depends on whose interpretation one accepts, but it is quite clear that the Revolution brought to the navy at least as many new problems in relation to social tension, factional strife and ideological struggle as had existed under the *ancien régime*, when the serving officers thought the administration socially inferior and the administration thought the serving officers incompetent. With the introduction of commoners into the officer corps after 1789 a new conflict emerged based on both professional ability and social status, this time between the noble officers, known as the *grand corps*, and *les bleus*, the new breed of officers. And all officers, regardless of background, struggled to control the men: by 1793 no real solution had been found for the inherent tension in the relationship between the Revolutionary ideal of power in which authority came from the people, and the way that the French navy traditionally worked, with the officer's authority coming direct from the King. No navy could work with the power residing in the hands of the crew and yet that is what they had been taught to believe by the new Revolutionary ideals. Yet again the navy had created another reason for it to be mistrusted: its established modes of authority and command simply didn't fit into Revolutionary philosophy.

Serious as they were, these social and manning problems were in some respects irrelevant because the fleet had enjoyed none of the practice it needed to hone an effective fighting force. Regardless of who was in charge or how many ships had been built, navies in this period were particularly sensitive to inactivity. The complexity of the rigs, the difficulty of teamwork and the vagaries of weather and winds ensured that even limited periods of inactivity crippled any navy's efficiency.

The French discovered exactly how much of a problem this had become in March 1793 when the Convention insisted on a naval patrol of the Channel. Led by Morard de Galles, three ships of the line and four frigates made it into the Channel after a lengthy delay caused by a lack of men. Almost immediately they were battered by a spring storm and de Galles's crew stayed below instead of braving the weather to make their ship safe. She soon blew out her headsails. There was similar professional apathy on board *Le Tourville*, whose captain was struck on the head by a swinging block and instantly killed when, his orders ignored, he attempted to secure a flailing sail by himself. 'The spirit of the sailors is lost entirely,' wrote de Galles to the Convention. 'Nothing can make them attend to their duties.'[22] This was dramatically different from the early stages of the War of American Independence, when French fleets had exercised regularly, finely drilling their fleet and crews so that, when the first naval clash occurred at the Battle of Ushant in 1778, their skill and seamanship was exemplary. Then, when the signal for a frigate was raised:

> ...they were in an instant under a cloud of canvas; when they returned to their admiral, or were called to him, they ran close up to his stern with all sail set, when in a moment all disappeared but the topsails. If a ship was but at a small distance, if called to the admiral, she immediately spread all her sail, even to stunsails if they would draw. This appears to be not only seamanship, but the brilliancy of it.[23]

Thus spoke Richard Kempenfelt, one of the most exacting flag officers of his day, and his respect for French seamanship in the early stages of the American War was widely shared. In the limited fleet exercises of 1793, however, there was constant incompetence, cowardice, even sabotage.[24]

It is also important to realise that the French sailors were failing at what we can distinguish as ship and fleet seamanship: the means by which officers judged by eye the distance between ships in line; the means by which they subtly altered their speed to maintain position; the means by which they manoeuvred fleets twenty or thirty strong in a single body; weighing anchor; furling and reefing sails; hoisting and striking topmasts, studdingsails and royals. The seamanship of *fighting*, was another matter entirely that combined the challenges of fleet seamanship with skills specific to battle.

The firing ship moved in several dimensions, all at once, and so did the target ship. The gunner had to account for pitch, roll, heel and speed, none of which was predictable in open water with any swell running. None of this could ever be achieved without practice and it was such an ephemeral skill that even the most experienced of naval gunners could lose their 'eye' after even short periods of inactivity. Furthermore, gunnery was useless if the ship could not be sailed with gunnery in mind. The finest fighting ships used manoeuvrability as a weapon, the sailors and the gunners working together to maximise the effectiveness of their battery.

Before any battle commenced a captain had to bring his ship into range with his adversary, which was far from straightforward unless both captains wanted to fight. Chasing another vessel required the adoption of intercepting courses and taking immediate advantage of any opportunity that arose, however transient – a sudden calm or squall, an unexpected tidal race or sandbank or at night the appearance, or disappearance, of the moon. Once within range, there were still advantages to be won according to factors such as wind direction and strength, the direction and height of the swell and the state and strength of the tide. And then, once engaged in battle, the captain had to keep his ship alongside his enemy's, or at least within range, by adjusting the sail plan, altering course and reacting to the inevitable rig damage. Fighting at sea was a highly skilled occupation. Consider, for example, how a professional boxer trains to fight. He ducks and weaves, dancing in and out, feinting right and left, up and down, learning to attack or defend from positions of advantage: he uses his skill to limit damage as much as to inflict it. Natural ability is not enough to win, he needs the skill learned through experience and constant practice. This, in crude terms, was the problem that the French navy faced. It was not an irretrievable situation, in theory at least, because the gun crews could be drilled by targeting rafts, barrels, old hulks or even old buildings on land. But by August 1793 there was no time left for any training. The French crews were unfit and unskilled, mutinous and morose. And all the while, like sharks, the British fleet circled just out of sight.

One reason that the main French battle fleet had not been to sea very often in the early years of war was money. The financial crisis that had formed the economic background of the Revolution was felt particularly keenly in the naval dockyards. By 1789 the French navy was already 400,000,000 livres in debt and yet, after 1789, the navy continued to build more ships, and at an even faster rate than before.[25] When war was declared, the French navy boasted some seventy-two ships of the line on paper. This included eight that were soon ordered to be reduced to frigates, yet the politicians harbouring grandiose dreams of a fleet of 100 line of battle ships supported by 127 frigates demanded still more be built.[26] Timber, sailcloth, iron and copper all had to be imported, but now there were few friends to supply those resources, nor were there enough shipwrights to build the ships.[27]

In spite of the theoretically effective *classes* manning system, there was never a large enough pool of skilled men for the navy to draw upon. Most estimates put France's population at more than double England, Ireland and Scotland's combined, but she only had 50,000 seamen available. So, while in 1794 the French could raise one of the largest land armies the world had ever seen, there simply weren't enough sailors, let alone sailors experienced in crewing warships and fighting battles.[28] Those who did serve were never paid because of the navy's debt, thus further ruining the reputation of the navy as an employer. Due to its need to defend itself, the problems faced by the Republic were compounded. In the past, France had been able to call on her maritime allies in times of strife, but now the Republic stood alone.

Dark days, then, at the French naval dockyards with the fleet in turmoil, out of practice and poorly equipped. Dark days, too, for the ruling Jacobins, forced to bring in mass conscription, the epitome of tyranny, to defend their beloved new Republic, and forced to wage brutal war against their own people to restore order. Benevolent Republican ideals, such as fairness, liberty, the eradication of poverty and hunger and the protection of children, were all lost or, at best, temporarily misplaced, by the demands of war. Bodies burned, heads rolled and children died. Tyrants ruled, justice evaporated and accountability dissolved. The borders of France were breached and the Revolution hung by a spider's silk thread. And then, in late August 1793, it got worse.

# 2.

# The First Surrender

## FRANCE: AUGUST 1793 – JANUARY 1794

Fathers are here without families, families without fathers. In short, all is horror we hear… Each teller makes the scene more horrible.

Captain Horatio Nelson.[1]

One lesson modern research has taught us about the Revolution is that it did not affect all parts of France in the same way or to the same extent. Outbreaks of political tension, sectarian violence and mass murder were sporadic; vile buboes erupting on the skin of France. If one considers official executions, for example, in six of the departments of France there were none at all, in thirty-one there were fewer than ten and in thirty-two fewer than one hundred. In eighteen departments, however, there were more than 1,000.[2] The department of the Var in the far south-east of the country, with one foot in the lowest hills of the Alps and the other in the Mediterranean, was one of the worst hit and Toulon, its administrative centre and home of the French Mediterranean fleet, suffered particularly badly.

Jacobin extremism was particularly severe in Toulon, where the presence of the navy had both created and exposed social tensions that were then exploited and magnified by *sans-culottes* agitators through powerful political clubs. In the summer of 1792, Jacobins mobilised and marshalled through their newly established *Club Saint-Jean* had seized control of Toulon's civic authority in a particularly violent coup. Several naval officers had been lynched and a mob had beaten up four members of the administration and then hanged them from lampposts. The Toulon Jacobins were then ousted in the summer of 1793 by a rebel group who, while disparate in their political beliefs and social backgrounds, were united by their desire for moderation in the face of Jacobin violence:

> 'We want a Republic one and indivisible,' they cried. '...We want a constitution, fruit of wisdom and reflection, and they [the

> Jacobins] propose to us only a phantom of government which must propagate factions and anarchy, and leave the ship of state tossed ceaselessly by the stormy waves of popular insurrections'.[3]

These moderate but furious men then stormed the *Club Saint-Jean*, 'deep into the dark lair, where they had hatched their wicked plots... This vampire's cave … was then sealed off and the emblems which decorated the walls … were consumed by fire'.[4]

Thirty of the prominent Jacobins responsible for the executions of 1792 were guillotined and in the late summer of 1793 the municipality of Toulon was controlled by a rebel group, dedicated to Republican ideals but dissatisfied with the direction that the Revolution had taken. The naval dockyard, however, remained firmly in the grip of radical Jacobins. This state of affairs was not an insurmountable problem for the Republic in its own right; it was just one of the many cocktails of local politics being mixed in departments throughout France at this time. But there were two problems that would transform the Toulon revolt into the most serious disaster suffered by France in the entire Revolutionary Wars. The first problem was that the Jacobin leaders in Paris, anxious to nip the revolt in the bud, had sent a large army south to deal with the rebels. With the army speeding toward Toulon, the gaze of the Toulonnais turned toward the sea: to survive any forthcoming siege they would need naval support to ship in supplies and troops and to ship out civilians. The second problem was the unwillingness, or inability, of central government to trust in the loyalty of the navy's commanders and specifically that of Admiral Trogoff de Kerlessy. He, indeed, was in charge only because his superior, Admiral Truguet, had been summoned to Paris to explain in person the recent disastrous assault on Sardinia. The mistrustful Jacobins sensed treachery from their commanding officers when in practice all that existed was confusion, poor planning and uncertainty.

Not far offshore, meanwhile, was a powerful British squadron led by Vice-Admiral Samuel, Lord Hood. Almost seventy years old but with a youthful vigour, Hood had been entrusted with the Mediterranean command and instructed to protect trade, blockade or attack the French fleet and secure the interests of Britain's allies.[5] Hood had no instructions to attack Toulon but, intent on nothing more than a little espionage, he sent one of his junior officers into the town, ostensibly to negotiate the release of some prisoners, but actually to gauge the strength of the French fleet. While Hood was within reach of the French coast, a deputation from the nearby city and port of Marseille – like Toulon, rebel-held and also facing the wrath of the Revolutionary armies – approached Hood for help, and encouraged the Toulonnais to do the same.

It was too late to help Marseille, which fell to the Revolutionary army on 25 August, but there was still time for Toulon and Hood brokered a deal. He offered British help on several conditions. First, the Toulonnais had to come out in support of Louis XVII, the young and bewildered son of Louis XVI (executed) and Marie Antoinette (imprisoned), who was now incarcerated in a deep, damp vault beneath the Temple prison in Paris where he was dying of neglect. Second, the Toulonnais had to disarm their warships and place the city's defences under Hood's jurisdiction. Only then would Toulon receive the protection of the British fleet, a guarantee to respect life and private property and, once peace had been agreed and the French monarchy restored, a promise that everything now placed under British control would be returned to France.

The Toulonnais found the proposal difficult to stomach for a number of reasons. The rebel municipal leaders were not anti-Revolutionary but simply anti-Jacobin; they loathed the *ancien régime* and French monarchy. Moreover, Britain was France's traditional and avowed enemy with whom she had been at war for almost half of the preceding century. To consider an alliance of the Royal Navy with a German naval base in 1916 or 1942, or the United States Navy with a Japanese naval base in 1944 gives some sense of the profound discomfort and shock that such a proposal generated, but neither example carries the weight of more than a century of mutual loathing as it did in 1793. Nevertheless, there followed such widespread and horrifying violence after the fall of Marseille that the civic authorities of Toulon accepted Hood's offer.

In between Hood and the rebel municipal leaders, however, stood the French navy, which had taken no part in these discussions and whose dislike of the British was very much stronger than their loyalty to either of the land-locked political factions squabbling over control of Toulon. When the fleet in Toulon was told of the proposal there was widespread outrage, at first vociferous and undirected but then led by Rear-Admiral Saint-Julien de Chambon. Saint-Julien led the protest in the absence of the fleet's commanding officer, Rear-Admiral Trogoff, who had been negotiating with Toulon's civic leaders ashore and who was perceived, unfairly, to have sided with them. A plaque was nailed to the mainmast of the fleet flagship the *Commerce de Marseille* which read, '*La Constitution ou la mort!*' Representatives of the local authorities fled ashore for fear of their lives and halters were raised to yardarms ready to hang any captain suspected of supporting Toulon's treason. For many French sailors the choice was not so simple, however. An alliance with the British was unthinkable but loyalty to the Jacobins meant turning their guns on their homes and families in Toulon to bombard the rebels into subservience. There was, however, a third way, and this was encouraged by the Toulon authorities who made it clear that those sailors who wanted no part in handing over the fleet to the British would be allowed to leave their ships even with the promise of pay. On the night of 27 August hundreds of French sailors fled.

The next morning the fleet remained divided: Saint-Julien urged his men to fire on the British and bombard the town; Admiral Trogoff, by now returned to the fleet, ordered his ships to the inner roadstead as a hermit crab might withdraw into its shell. Trogoff was no traitor to the Revolution, just a man caught up in turmoil. In the end, Trogoff's authority over Saint-Julien was recognised by enough of the few remaining men for the fleet to seek shelter in Toulon's inner roadstead. This allowed Hood to take control of a naval base that had been one of the bastions of French naval power for more than three centuries, the equivalent of the French occupying Plymouth, Portsmouth or Chatham, and he did so without a shot being fired.[6]

It was a perfect coup for the Royal Navy and the British Government who, together, had long fantasised about drawing the sting of French naval power in the Mediterranean. Nevertheless, politicians in Westminster, who were yet to commit to any regime on the other side of the Channel, were uncomfortable about Hood's alignment of the British with Louis XVII. They were equally uncomfortable with the Toulonnais' desire to restore the constitution of 1792 which had greatly reduced the power of the monarch.[7] For the paranoid Jacobins, the Mediterranean fleet's surrender to the British at Toulon appeared to confirm everything they had feared: the navy was treasonous and a threat to the Republic. This, in fact, was not true because, by 1793, most of the officers who had harboured such thoughts had left. The problem facing the French navy was not one of loyalty but of external, political support. The National Convention was, at best, indifferent toward naval affairs and the Republican local authorities were actively hostile.

The calamity at Toulon encapsulates much of what characterised the war in the summer of the Republic's first year with numerous factions involved at all levels: extreme Jacobins, moderate Jacobins, Republicans who despised Jacobinism, Royalists who supported the *ancien régime* and Royalists who wanted a progressive, modern monarchy. Power vacuums at every level of government led to ferocious opportunism by all sides and throughout society. The French navy was inevitably affected by the plight of the Republic and had never been at a lower ebb. News of the navy's betrayal at Toulon burned north to Paris where the National Convention declared its 'indignation', and promised to defeat '*les royalistes, les despots et les traîtres*'.[8] At the same time, the same news had reached Brest: now, not only did the CPS still have to crush the Toulon rebellion, but they also had to stop the rot from spreading.

For once, the majority of the Atlantic fleet was not in its home port at Brest, but a little to the south at the entrance to Quiberon Bay. This part of the coastline edged the rebellious Vendée region, and the fleet had orders to prevent supplies from reaching the rebel armies and to prevent British landings.[9] The men on board were in terrible condition. Weak and sick, they were riddled with scurvy, their gums bled and they suffered open wounds that would not heal. Tension between the officers and men led to outbreaks of open dissent, and the situation escalated amid rumours of a strong British fleet sailing for the Vendée, news of the Mediterranean fleet's surrender at Toulon and whispers of mutiny on board ships of their own fleet lying in Brest.[10]

It would be all too easy for the surrender at Toulon to condemn the French navy as a whole in the eyes of the public and their political leaders. The crews of the Brest fleet knew that the spotlight was shining on them. For those in the Brest fleet with a Republican sympathy and a mistrustful nature, this was the time to anticipate any treachery by seizing the navy in the name of loyalty to the ruling Jacobins. Mutinous sailors demanded that, for their own safety, the ships return to Brest, though this contravened the explicit wishes of the CPS.

By September 1793, therefore, the Republic's naval power had been reduced to practically nothing. The Mediterranean fleet was in the hands of Hood and the Atlantic fleet in the hands of mutineers. The CPS, however, soon began to tidy up the mutinous mess in Brittany by wielding the power of summary justice while in Provence the French army closed on Toulon. Among its number was an ambitious, determined young artillery officer named Napoleon Bonaparte. The Republic was set to regain control.

In London there were high hopes of a swift victory at Toulon. Francis Drake, the British Minister at Genoa, wrote to Lord Grenville the Foreign Secretary exclaiming: 'No event of the war has so much tended to bring about a safe and honourable peace'.[11] On the ground, however, peace was far from certain. Toulon was well fortified but her defences had been built with a seaward enemy in mind, or one coming from the east, from Italy. But now it was facing a powerful army approaching from the north and west, between the mountains and the sea. The guns on board Hood's fleet would be of some use, of course, but his ships were all grouped closely together, and motionless at anchor, like so much firewood just waiting for a spark. The geography made the defenders' situation worse. High peaks dominated the land immediately beyond Toulon, providing the attackers with a fine aerial view of their target. If a perimeter a good distance from the coast could not be held to keep the attackers at bay, the Republicans would turn the sky red with heated shot and burn the ships where they lay.

Troops were sent from Britain, more were donated by Spain and Naples and sailors fought as soldiers but they were too few to be an effective foe, and certainly not enough to stop Napoleon. He took command of the artillery around 16 September and from that moment on the attackers' fire from the heights of La Grasse drove the allied ships from their anchorages. While British shot thudded into rock and dune, Napoleon's guns hulled and burned Hood's ships. The fate of the city shifted from one side to the other throughout September and early October but the Republicans were firmly entrenched on the heights. Simultaneously, more troops were gradually becoming available to the Republicans just as fewer were to Hood who, despite already limited manpower, had been forced to send troops away from Toulon on other missions.

Under Bonaparte's guidance and sparkling heroism, key forts protecting the heights of Toulon and its harbour entrance were taken by Jacobin forces and Hood's position collapsed. There was a scramble to sea to escape the inevitable Jacobin vengeance. 'The poor inhabitants are flocking on board the ships, begging to be received,' wrote the captain of the *Princess Royal* in his log. A flotilla of skiffs, rowing boats, fishing boats and anything else that would float carried at least 8,000 refugees out to the British, Spanish and Neapolitan fleets. British naval officers who had moved ashore abandoned their possessions in the race to escape. There was little room for anything other than muskets. Even soldiers' knapsacks were abandoned onshore. But they were right to leave in a hurry.

As soon as the city fell the Jacobins swiftly tried and executed almost 300 suspected traitors, though this was after a week or more of unofficial reprisal. In one instance, all of the individuals remaining in Toulon were marched across the Champs de Mars outside the city walls. A 'patriotic jury' then selected, and shot in batches, those who had borne arms against the government soldiers, those who might bear arms in the future, those who represented a political threat and those who were personal enemies. One representative sent by the Convention wrote back to his masters with nothing short of glee that 'we are killing everything that moves', and recommended the entire city be razed to the ground. We now suspect that some 200 people were killed every day for the first few days, and perhaps 2,000 in total from a population of around only 28,000. Nelson met some of the lucky few who made it out and he wrote to his wife with some discomfort: 'Fathers are here without families, families without fathers. In short, all is horror we hear… Each teller makes the scene more horrible.'[12]

Before they abandoned Toulon, British and Spanish troops set about burning the French ships and dockyard stores. This, however, was only partially achieved because large parts of Toulon's population and the French crews had never been happy with Hood's occupation and now they did what they could to protect the French ships and stores. The Spaniards had been asked to destroy a number of French ships but baulked at the task, well aware that this would shift the balance of European sea power irrevocably in favour of the Royal Navy, a situation they could not possibly condone: the Spanish alliance with the British at Toulon had been both uneasy and consciously temporary. The final count against the navy was nine French ships of the line and three frigates burned, a section of the dockyard destroyed and twelve more vessels of various sizes seized by the British and Spanish. Decent quantities of naval stores, however, plus a good number of dockyard buildings, thirteen ships of the line and five frigates survived.

For the French, the siege of Toulon was a naval disaster to rival any battle at sea in the preceding century and it carried far deeper consequences because they had lost shipbuilding supplies, accumulated over years, which would be difficult to replace. However, everyone knew that it could have been worse. With a more carefully executed assault on the port, French naval power in the Mediterranean could have been destroyed rather than broken. As it was, within ten months vigorous effort at Toulon had recreated the Mediterranean force as a powerful player in the war strategy.

To understand the wider impact of the Toulon siege, however, we need to look beyond the Mediterranean fleet and consider its outcome in a much broader sense than numbers alone. From the French perspective, it energised the Jacobins, crushed the spirit of moderation that led to the revolts in Marseille and Toulon and it united France against a common, foreign enemy. Representatives from the National Convention were explicit: 'The British came there as traitors, they established themselves as cowards, and they left like scoundrels.' And this was a view shared even by a French Royalist, and hence a supposed British ally, who wrote: 'Toulon has been occupied in order to burn it.'[13] By September 1793 certain parts of the country had already been hooked on the barbs of the Terror for several months, but it is significant that news of the fall of Toulon directly preceded formal government inauguration of the Terror. That news arrived in Paris on 2 September and the city instantly dissolved into anarchy which lasted for several days. On 5 September, in one of the most sinister announcements made by any government in history, the National Convention, faced with a mob at its door, proclaimed that Terror was 'the order of the day'. The Revolutionary Tribunal was expanded and fortified so that it could process more 'trials' more swiftly.

In Brest, meanwhile, a member of the CPS, Jeanbon Saint-André, had begun to take control of the situation by working night and day to unify the French fleet. 'Severity' claimed Jeanbon 'is the only means to make the conspirators tremble and to frighten the intriguers.' He later wrote of his time at Brest: 'Because all here was gangrenous ... all needed the scalpel of patriotism.'[14] And so Jeanbon began to cut.

To understand the impact of Jeanbon's arrival in Brest we must first understand the system of representatives used by the Committee of Public Safety to impose rule, order and republicanism, as perceived and defined by the Montagnard faction of the Jacobins that dominated government from June 1793. France is a vast country, a little over four times the size of England, divided into regions, each with its own, often passionately held, beliefs and traditions. For example, in Alsace in the east it was considered an insult to be called a Frenchman and the insularity of the Provençals of the south-east was matched in its depth only by the

Bretons of the north-west. In the navy, the rivalry between Provençal and Breton was particularly keen, and after the surrender of the Toulon fleet rumour spread of a Breton conspiracy, a rumour that was thereafter propagated by generations of French historians. The Breton sailors, it was claimed by the Provençals, were far stauncher in their resistance to surrender, as they had no qualms in attacking the Provençal citizens of Toulon to bring them to heel.[15]

In the face of long-entrenched regional separatism in France, the CPS would be hard pressed to find a way of uniting the country's various districts and cultures under a single banner. Their solution was to send out agents to recruit men and requisition supplies, to politicise the civilian population and to purge the local authorities of Republican dissidents. Everyone who was too slow to show convincing loyalty to the new regime would be punished. Fifty-eight members of the National Convention were sent throughout France, each imbued with unlimited power.

Each of the fifty-eight members was allotted a huge area of France so they in turn delegated their responsibilities and powers to agents, who then took the message into the villages and farms. The farther away they were from Paris, the focal point of Revolutionary power, the more extreme these agents' behaviour became.[16] The agents maintained superiority by persecuting civilians for any lack of Revolutionary zeal and by their actions and rhetoric proved their own loyalty to the new regime. And so the wheel turned. Set on its way it gathered speed under self-generating momentum and produced outbursts such as:

> Tomorrow at noon at the latest we will be in your area. We will deposit most of our vermin at the louse-ridden château of Chantilly and, in the presence of the guillotine birds who live inside it we will pierce the air with the cries of Liberty that make them shudder with fear and horror. Most likely we will also pierce a cask of wine there.[17]

The hierarchy of government remained strong, however and occasionally a member of the Committee of Public Safety itself would go to a crucial troublespot, and his presence would dominate over any other government representative and set a precedent for expected behaviour. For Louis Antoine de Saint-Just, a leading CPS member and close colleague of Robespierre's, his role was not only about politics but also about lifestyle, self-governance and self-respect. He was concerned with obedience and also with morality, and he came down especially hard on those crimes linked with moral laxity, such as drunkenness and debauchery or licentiousness and greed. And he was not a tolerant man. Saint-Just had recently travelled to Alsace to restore order in a crucial war zone plagued by lack of discipline. One rather unfortunate officer who stopped him in the street to ask directions to the theatre was immediately arrested.[18] Like Saint-Just, Jeanbon was also a veteran CPS member. He was from Toulouse, nearly 1,000 kilometres south of Brest and Brittany but, with some experience of the merchant navy, was the only member of the CPS with any maritime experience and therefore the natural choice to be sent to Brest. The Committee's greatest fear was that the fleet at Brest would act as the fleet had at Toulon and Jeanbon was there in person to stop it. What complicated matters, however, was that the CPS had completely misunderstood the cause of the surrender at Toulon.

The Toulon surrender was the result of tumbling circumstance triggered by a coalition of moderates rebelling against Jacobin extremism, but the Committee believed it a black and white case of premeditated treachery by an officer-led Royalist conspiracy. The Committee's solution for Brest, therefore, was not the moderation of Jacobin extremism but a dramatic purge of the officer corps in which all officers of noble extraction or suspect loyalty had to be removed. It was a heavy-handed approach to a sensitive beast and within a few weeks Jeanbon found himself both unable and unwilling to execute such a purge. Of the noble-blooded officers who had remained in the navy some were extremely talented and many were also popular. Jeanbon also understood from his own seafaring experience that discipline on a ship was not achieved through rules and regulations alone but through constant negotiation between the captain and his men via his officers. The result was that the dramatic purge envisioned by the CPS was not entirely achieved by Jeanbon. Nothing illustrates this more than Jeanbon's selection of a new commander-in-chief for the Brest fleet who, in the words of some fellow sailors:

> … is truly imbued with sincere love for the Republic. We are tormented from all sides and our most cruel enemies surround us. Hasten, citizen Representatives, to name him … the firmness and the talents of citizen Joyeuse render him worthy of your choice: we will never fear a firm man, this is necessary to command a fleet. We are true sans-culottes and republicans who want a Republic one and indivisible.[19]

'Citizen Joyeuse' was none other than Louis-Thomas, the Comte Villaret de Joyeuse. Not only a thoroughbred nobleman, he had also been a member of the Royal Guard. Villaret was, however, respected by his sailors, and known to keep tight discipline on his ships – he was one of the few captains who had retained control during the recent mutiny. He was not the only nobleman promoted by Jeanbon, and Villaret's rise from lieutenant to rear-admiral in less than a year shows in the clearest terms that Jeanbon was happy to promote talent as well as ideology.[20] Hitherto, Villaret had enjoyed a relatively undistinguished career. He had run away to sea after killing his opponent in a duel. Command of a fireship followed when he was in his early twenties but he had then become stuck at the rank of *lieutenant de vaisseau.* The Revolution had provided him with an extraordinary opportunity and he shone immediately by returning a measure of order to the rebellious French colony of Saint Domingue in 1790. Villaret was swiftly promoted to command the 74-gun *Le Trajan* and thereafter gained a fine reputation as an officer and won respect from his sailors. On 16 November 1793 he was made commander of the Brest fleet and he raised his flag in the mighty 120-gun *La Montagne.*[21]

The day Jeanbon arrived from Paris, after six uncomfortable days on the road, he inspected the fleet, first the troublesome ships and then the few on which discipline had held. On the decks of the latter, the brotherhood of republicanism was brought out in its full glory. Political speeches were made and songs were sung, ending with the bellicose Marseillaise. The men reverently fell to one knee as Jeanbon stood above them, his red satin sash denoting officialdom. Today, only the first verse and chorus of the Marseillaise are sung, but allowing for regional and chronological variation the middle section, in 1794, went something like this:

Tremble, tyrants and traitors
The shame of all good men
Tremble! Your parricidal schemes
Will receive their just reward
Against you we are all soldiers
If they fall, our young heroes
France will bear new ones
Ready to join the fight against you

Frenchmen, as magnanimous warriors
Bear or hold back your blows
Spare these sad victims
That they regret taking up arms against us
But not these bloody despots
These accomplices of Bouillé
All these tigers who pitilessly
Ripped out their mothers' wombs

We shall enter into the pit
When our elders will no longer be there
There we shall find their ashes
And the mark of their virtues
We are much less jealous of surviving them
Than of sharing their coffins
We shall have the sublime pride
Of avenging or joining them

Each verse was followed by the resounding chorus, well known to most ears but which, translated, reads:

To arms, citizens,
Form your battalions
Let's march, let's march!
May an impure blood
Water our furrows!

This was strong stuff and Jeanbon stood by every word. Those who were loyal and disciplined were thanked and welcomed into Jeanbon's comforting embrace; those who were not were shunned, their freedom and their very lives in the balance. Thus, Jeanbon instilled immediately a clear vision of right and wrong, of expected behaviour, reward and punishment. The Brest fleet had been spinning in turmoil, confused by a loss of leadership and direction, and Jeanbon provided the solution. He had authority, backed up by the power of tyranny, and he breathed Revolutionary principle. Jeanbon knew that there had to be some kind of reconciliation between the concept of popular sovereignty and the reality of military effectiveness and he set about his task in a fury, urging naval officers to set and then maintain their own expected standards. He also spoke to the crews, urging them to accept and follow their officers. Exhorting personal sacrifice for the good of the *patrie* he also reinvigorated the tradesmen and craftsmen of the slips and docks into frenzied activity.

Jeanbon's purge of the disloyal, meanwhile, was unremitting. The man Villaret had replaced at the top was Morard de Galles. Suspected, unfairly, of involvement in the Atlantic fleet's mutinies, Jeanbon had de Galles sent home where he was subsequently arrested and imprisoned. Two rear-admirals were also dismissed and one resigned, several captains were punished and mutineers were guillotined. This was a very significant step for the navy. Mutiny had been rife for months. The argument ran that mutiny was, in a loose sense, 'revolutionary' but this held no water for Jeanbon; he understood that naval mutiny was the biggest threat of all to the success of the Revolution. To emphasise the extent to which mutiny would not be tolerated he imprisoned or executed many of the 4,000 sailors sent from Toulon to Rochefort by Hood, who believed them to be pro-revolutionary agitators. Those men whom Jeanbon could have seen as supporters of the revolution were punished merely for being associated with the 'treason' at Toulon.[22]

Jeanbon introduced to the navy a new, strict code of discipline that left no room for confusion. Petitions to commanders, the traditional method of airing grievances, were now forbidden and anyone guilty of inciting mutiny would be immediately put to death. To make it clear that this was no idle threat the executions were performed in front of the entire fleet. Officers could not question their captains, and captains their fleet commanders.[23] Any officer, including the captains of the fleet, who failed to carry out an order from his superior officer, or even repeat his signals, would be executed. When fighting, any person of any rank who hauled down the national colours would be declared a traitor and executed, unless the ship was in danger of sinking. Particularly harsh was the decree that the captain or officers of any frigate, corvette or smaller vessel who surrendered to a force *double* their own in size would be executed. To make matters slightly easier, because immediate execution would not always be practicable, Jeanbon introduced a signal to indicate the instant dismissal and replacement of a ship's captain who would then be tried ashore.[24]

In addition to Jeanbon's rejuvenating measures, the National Convention had given the Brest fleet a powerful new focus. They were no longer simply to patrol the western coasts shepherding their own convoys, but were to prepare for a mass invasion of England tapping into the growing tide of xenophobia fuelled by the British occupation of Toulon. The Convention had prohibited from France all goods made by the British Empire and had also passed their own version of the notorious 1651 English Navigation Act: no foreign vessel could trade between French ports. The definition of 'French' was particularly severe as even French-registered vessels, if owned by a foreigner, were to be considered 'foreign'. This hard-line maritime approach was mirrored on land. In January 1794 a decree was passed forbidding the taking of British and Hanoverian prisoners, meaning they were to be killed instead of captured, and when Saint-Just was in Alsace, fortifying the eastern front by his very presence, the Austrians made a diplomatic approach for a parley: 'The French republic takes from and sends to its enemies nothing but lead,' replied Saint-Just.[25]

At Brest, 100,000 men were ordered to be made ready, new warships and landing craft were built, old warships were repaired, recommissioned, and hulks converted. Mooring bollards were replaced along with all of the old iron ballast. Local ropewalks, sail lofts, mines and a cooperage were all requisitioned. A lair of apathy became a hive of industry in a matter of weeks. The energy in the dockyard was, according to Jacobin propaganda, unquestioned. One witness declared:

> Brest was a cross between a workshop and a taproom. At the morning gun the port bore a close resemblance to an anthill. Here a ship was being masted; there provisions were being stowed … the evening offered an entirely different spectacle. At the sound of the bell some twelve to fifteen thousand men dashed through the gates like schoolboys. They wished to profit by their existence while they were sure of it and before they found themselves at sea, on an unstable deck, faced by the guns of an English three-decker. This unpleasant prospect did not depress them; on the contrary I have never seen a more cheerful crowd. In a flash the town became one enormous pot-house, the cafés were crammed, and drinkers lined the streets; outside the gates the distractions were less innocent, dances were held, and the dancers were fixed in propose and indecent in appearance.[26]

The dockyard, which had suffered from four years of absolute neglect, lived once more. 'The sounds of our axes, of our hammers, of our mallets, have reached London,' Jeanbon wrote to the Convention.[27] Extraordinary efforts were made to replace weak masts and the stocks of rotting rope and canvas while the country was scoured for old cannon which had been put to use as civic statues and milestones. Jeanbon raised men for the navy from all walks of life, emphasising that the responsibility to serve fell on all citizens, equally, and he also siphoned men from coastal departments already claimed by the *grande levée*. The inexperienced were trained in seamanship and the young were schooled in reading, writing and arithmetic. Ships were cleaned and captains became directly responsible for keeping them so. Jeanbon insisted that all the men were issued a standard kitbag containing clothes fit for Atlantic waters, and that they be properly fed in relation to the heavy work and long hours expected of them with salt beef, cod or cheese, in rotation.[28] Nothing is more indicative of the great gulf in such standards between the British and French navies than these changes. Ordered for the first time in France in the autumn of 1793, this had long been standard practice in the Royal Navy.

French sailors' leisure time was now taken up with relentless politicisation as they were encouraged to live out Revolutionary beliefs and ideals, all monitored by the classic tools of the Terror, a surveillance committee and a Revolutionary tribunal. Everything was centred upon unity, sacrifice and brotherhood, which was not just to be acknowledged, but shared and celebrated enthusiastically. Jeanbon, as did Robespierre, reserved his greatest scorn for Catholicism, which he believed dangerous as a source of superstition. The churches of Brest were desecrated.[29] Those who did not display sufficient revolutionary enthusiasm could find themselves under the guillotine blade. Seventy men, dockyard workers, sailors, and administrators, died this way in Brest.[30]

Jeanbon sought to generate hope, energy and positive thinking alongside an ideal future when fairness would be the rule, not the exception, and the French would stand proud over the bodies of their enemies.[31] To encourage this brand of confidence and celebrate Revolutionary ideals, the ships were renamed, condemning to obscurity anything associated with the *ancien régime*: the flagship was renamed the *Montagne* for the Montagnard politicians, while others included *Patriote* (Patriot), *Vengeur du Peuple* (People's Avenger), *Tyrannicide* (Tyrannicide), *Révolutionnaire* (Revolutionary), *Juste* (Fair), *Convention* (named for the National Convention) and the eponymous *Jacobin*.[32] The *Royal Louis* became the *Républicaine*, the *Lys*, that ancient fleur-de-lys symbol of French monarchy, became the *Tricolore* and in a nice sleight of hand the *Souverain* (Sovereign) was simply renamed the *Peuple Souverain* (Sovereign People).

The problem of lack of naval matériel was eased greatly by the novel economic philosophy which had been introduced alongside the Terror: absolute state control over the nation's resources. From 1793 *everything* could now be claimed by the state and bought at a fixed price or at the legal maximum rate, usually a gross undervaluation.[33] Wood from private forests deep in the Pyrenees was requisitioned for timber yards[34] Closer to home, a Breton source of coal was surveyed and exploited and a new source of lead was mined in the east of the region. Churches were stripped of their bells for the bronze to cast guns. A new law stating that only one church bell was allowed for each parish had been superseded within ten days by another which made every bell legally forfeit: in the winter of 1793, war was the Revolution's new God.[35] There was a rumour in England, with a strong whiff of anti-French propaganda, that the French cannon were fired with cartridges made 'of the fine painted church music used in the cathedrals, and of the *preuves* [proofs] *de noblesse* of the principal families, many hundred years old, illuminated with the genealogical tree'.[36] With much greater certainty, because one survives in the collection of the National Maritime Museum in London, we can say that white silk flags embroidered in gold thread with the words 'the Republic or death' were distributed to the squadron (see fig. 15)[37] and the ships were painted red ochre – blood-red.[38] The lack of skilled gunners since the dissolution of the corps of seamen gunners was finally addressed when on 2 March the CPS ordered the Minister of the Marine to re-employ most of those disbanded. Only one group was shunned for its suspect loyalties.[39]

Jeanbon's influence was felt far beyond Brest and he paid close attention to Lorient and Rochefort, France's two other major naval shipbuilding ports. But he was proudest of his work at Brest and wrote to the Convention: 'I departed Brest, leaving the work in full swing. If the other ports of the Republic had seconded our zeal or followed our example, the fleet would be at this moment on a respectable footing.'[40] As Jeanbon predicted, Villaret's talents paid dividends with regard to training the many new recruits and, after an inevitably shaky start, the captains of the fleet began working well together. Villaret wrote with some pride: '*il commence a y avoir un peu d'ensemble*' - 'things are starting to come together' - and he began to nurture hope that he could face the British with a measure of confidence.[41] Another witness clearly shared Villaret's optimism when he wrote:

> 'Never before did there exist in Brest a fleet so formidable and well disciplined, as that which is now lying there. Unanimity and discipline reign among officers and men; and all burn with desire to fight the enemies of their country, to the very banks of the Thames, and under the walls of London.'[42]

Much of our understanding of this period comes, however, from pro-Jacobin propaganda and if we look at the few other scattered sources that survive, a rather different picture emerges: one sailor claimed that the squadron was 50 per cent below strength and that many of the new recruits were completely green; the squadron was chiefly composed of elderly ships, some of which were in a terrible state and kept afloat only by manning their pumps.[43] There were so few cannon that the *Majestueux* and *Caton*, in all other respects ready for sea, could not be armed and were left behind when the fleet sailed.[44] One witness acknowledged that some of the ships were magnificent, not least the *Sans Pareil*, but with the hard-won knowledge of a canny seaman he commented, ruefully: 'But one unhandy ship can wreck a line of battle and put the finest ships on earth at the mercy of an enemy.' Worst of all, few of the officers had more than two years' experience.[45]

The ships were lacking biscuit and many were sent to sea with flour, forced to bake their own in small batches which, in turn, used up a lot of the ships' limited supply of fresh water. In fact, the dockyard was so short of food that many ships received their supplies from captured prizes. There was also a serious problem with sickness. Typhus had already ravaged the squadron at Cancale that year and 1,670 seamen were in hospital in May. At one stage, of the crew of 276 on the *Thames*, 274 were sick.[46] The fever had now spread to the Brest fleet and it was gaining hold. For all of Jeanbon's efforts, therefore, the French navy was still a shambles.

The army, by contrast, really was starting to improve. The earliest Revolutionary armies were unwieldy masses of untrained men who could not be trusted to stand and fight and who had no chance of winning an open battle without a massive numerical superiority. But by September 1793 they were already starting to see growth and progress when, and for the very first time, they defeated the allies at Hondschoote near Calais, capturing six flags, the Duke of York's entire artillery and forcing the allies to lift the siege of Dunkirk. Thereafter, political rhetoric directed at the French soldiers changed from claims that they would always win to claims that they would always win, 'provided their cavalry was reinforced'.[47] This rather important nuance could not yet be applied to the navy, however. By 1794 the army had seen constant action for almost two years and had been able to learn and gain experience against relatively weak opposition. Not so for the navy; the sailors had not yet had the chance to gauge their strengths and weaknesses in fleet battle.

In the winter of 1793, therefore, Jeanbon had managed to save the navy from itself with a Terror that, in comparison with some other areas of France, was relatively moderate,[48] but far more needed to be done if he was ever to save it from the British.

# 3.

# The First and Greatest Sea Officer

The first and greatest sea officer the world has ever produced.

Rear-Admiral Horatio Nelson of Admiral Earl Howe.[1]

You are in Bath. Cross the magnificent Pulteney Bridge and leave the Avon bubbling away behind you, tumbling down the weir. Follow the road north-east, down Great Pulteney Street toward the mansion that is now the Holborn Museum of Art. Halfway down this street of Georgian perfection, on the right-hand side, is Admiral Richard Howe's town house. This is where he came to recover from his various ailments by taking the waters at the hot springs that have eased aching bones for millennia. It is one of the most prestigious addresses in England today, just as it was in 1794.

Now you are in London, standing outside the Ritz on Piccadilly. Cross the road and head straight on into the warren of Mayfair streets that link Piccadilly with the diamond and art dealers of Bond Street. No. 2 Grafton Street is a curious red-brick building that jars with its surroundings and it is the site of Howe's London home. The surviving original buildings next door and opposite show just how grand and imposing his house, too, would once have been. Another prestigious address, in Howe's day and now.

These, then, were the homes of Admiral Richard, Earl Howe and they are almost all that remains of his private life. Taking a present-day look down Pulteney Street and Grafton Street we can get some, diluted, sense of Howe's physical perception of the world when at home, but we have very little to work from that tells us much of what he thought about in his time ashore or around his family. He was obsessively secretive and in the later years of his life destroyed most of his private correspondence. Then, in the early nineteenth century came the subsequent destruction of the Howe family papers in a fire at Westport

House in Ireland. Howe would have thoroughly approved of our ignorance. His professional correspondence contains only the carefully selected information that he considered his political masters needed to know. Nothing else was ever included: there was never any explanation, extraneous detail or emotion. Everything was impersonal. One episode, however, does throw some interesting light on Howe's character: in 1782 he challenged a man to a duel.

In the late eighteenth century, duels worked like this. The man who believed he had been wronged issued a challenge, which explained in very plain terms the reasons for the perceived slight. Each man named a friend to act as his second and a request was made for a time and location for combat. The party who had been challenged chose the weapon. If the challenge was taken seriously, and sometimes it was not, the usual weapon was the pistol which, perceived to be fairer, had taken supremacy over the sword. On the appointed day the seconds would make one final attempt to secure reconciliation. If they failed, then they would load and prime the duellists' pistols before agreeing on the terms of combat. Usually, they would shoot from a distance of twelve paces, about half the length of a cricket pitch, but sometimes it was only eight and occasionally the duellists were ordered simply to walk toward each other with the tantalising instruction to fire whenever they wanted to. Very occasionally there were unique instructions and the duel might be fought on horseback or in a dark room.

Most injuries were to the largest target i.e., to the trunk – the chest, abdomen or groin. The small lead shot and limited charge had none of the shattering effect of modern bullets fired from modern handguns, but there was still little that a surgeon could do for a man who had been critically wounded. Those who died did so over hours and sometimes days. It was a painful, miserable and, sometimes, lonely way to die. It took a particular type of man to lay down the challenge.

Duels were fought for myriad reasons, but usually over questions of honour, which was loosely defined but jealously guarded in the eighteenth century. By no means was everyone sensitive to questions of honour but Richard Howe certainly was. Although he has not been the subject of a lengthy, modern biography, it seems that, most of the time, he kept firm control of a formidable temper but, if roused, an instinctive combativeness and bravery bubbled to the surface.

The man who provoked Howe was Captain John Augustus Hervey and he did so in 1782 on the two men's return from the naval relief of the siege of Gibraltar in the dying moments of the War of American Independence. Hervey publicly criticised Howe and questioned his conduct in the presence of the enemy, claiming: 'If we had been led with the same spirit with which we should have followed, it would have been a glorious day for England.'[2]

This was too much for Howe, who had never enjoyed a comfortable relationship with his accuser, and he called Hervey out to duel for his honour. The men met at the allotted time but Hervey was there to apologise, not to fight.[3] No doubt Howe's challenge had surprised him. Howe, after all, was nearly sixty and despite his occasional explosions of bad temper, had a reputation for neither giving nor taking offence. He had had a patchy, and many would say poor, career in politics, but he had served in the navy for more than forty years with a distinguished record for bravery, ingenuity and skill in the face of the enemy. He had dedicated much of his working life to improving the quality of life on board for his crews and imposing high standards for the professional conduct of his fellow officers. Nelson, later, and in a characteristic fit of flattery, described Howe as the 'first and greatest sea officer the world has ever produced', and as 'our great master in naval tactics and bravery'. This was the man chosen to command the Channel Fleet as the noise of the French war machine drifted across the Channel and her troops cast a shadow over their massed landing craft from the high cliffs of Brittany.[4]

Howe's career began in 1739, at the start of the War of the Austrian Succession (1739–48), when he sailed with Captain Edward Legge to Lisbon on board the *Pearl*. He stayed on with Legge, who had been chosen by George Anson for his squadron that planned to round Cape Horn and attack Spanish settlements on the Pacific coast of South America. Anson's squadron subsequently suffered appalling hardship through sickness and shipwreck before capturing the treasure-laden Spanish Manila galleon. Howe was no part of this epic adventure, however, after weeks under sail in punishing conditions his ship failed to weather the Horn and was forced to return home. While many of his fellow sailors were dying in Anson's squadron Howe went on to play an active role in the Atlantic and Caribbean theatres against both Spain and France. At the age of twenty-two, Howe was appointed flag captain to Sir Charles Knowles on the West Indies station in 1748.

His career continued promisingly in the following conflict, the Seven Years' War (1756–63) and, as captain of the 60-gun *Dunkirk*, Howe fired the very first shots of the war in his successful battle against the French *Alcide* off Quebec. He spent the next few years in the Channel under the careful eye of Edward Hawke, who went on to impose the tightest blockade of Brest that had yet been achieved by the Royal Navy.

Raids were also conducted against the French coast and Howe starred in an attack against a fortification on the Isle d'Aix at the mouth of the Charente River which led to the French naval base of Rochefort. In late September 1757, Hawke sent five ships into the heavily fortified roadstead, but only Howe on board his new ship, the *Magnanime*, was able to negotiate the tricky sandbanks and get within range of a particularly strong fort that far outgunned the *Magnanime*.

In such engagements the fortification on land always held an advantage. Large warships were out of their element so close to shore and a large portion of the crew was always required for ship handling: sails would need to be set and furled, yards to be trimmed and, perhaps, anchors let go and then cables cut at very short notice. A skilled leadsman would always be needed to stand in the chains continually measuring the water depth and calling his readings back to the helm. All of this, of course, had to be conducted amid the roar of cannon. Hand signals were crucial; knowing one's job even more so. The ship's gun crews were beset by the usual problems, not least by the pitching and rolling which affected their aim, whereas those on dry land had the advantage of solid ground and the protection afforded by stout, thick walls allowing them to focus entirely on their gunnery. A well-judged shot bringing down a crucial piece of rigging could hamstring their target and leave the ship wallowing, or even aground and at the mercy of its enemy.

Nevertheless, that September Howe took the *Magnanime* steadily toward his target, and as he came within range he held his fire. He ordered his crew to lie down and only he and the helmsman stood on the quarterdeck as the ship began to taste the French bombardment. Not until he was within sixty yards, about half the length of a football pitch, and some records claim it was more like forty, did he open fire. And he did so with such accuracy and ferocity that 'the Monsenieurs said that "something more than a man must be on board that ship."' The fierceness of the broadside when it finally came was such that the French fled from their guns and the Governor was forced to surrender.[5]

Howe not only displayed excellent seamanship but also fine judgement: he had targeted the walls of the fort and the bodies of his enemy, but he had used psychology to his advantage, too. He had reasoned that the morale of those manning an isolated fort would be fragile in the face of a determined attack, and he had been correct. He had led his men into a situation of severe danger knowing that the brazen nature of this approach would, in itself, unsettle his foe. Within a generation such attacks would forever be associated with the name Nelson, who had yet to be born.

Two years later and Howe was at it again, this time at the Battle of Quiberon Bay in November 1759 when Hawke chased down a French squadron on a filthy Biscay night, his ships forcing the French against their own lee shore. Led in spirit by Hawke, the fleet was led in person by Howe who, again in the *Magnanime*, followed the French into the dangerous waters of Quiberon Bay. Howe forced the *Héros* to surrender on one of the finest days in British naval history in which the French lost seven ships of the line, captured or wrecked, a victory won by magnificent British seamanship.

In the peace that followed the Seven Years' War Howe entered the murky world of politics as MP for Dartmouth, a post which he held for the next twenty-five years. He also served as Treasurer of the Navy but when war broke out again, this time caused by the rebellion of the American colonies, Howe's experience and skill as a fighter at sea saw him afloat once more, this time in command of the entire North America station. Out of his depth amid the political manipulation from both sides of the Atlantic he nevertheless repeatedly demonstrated remarkable ability as a commander, foxing a superior French fleet with well-chosen and beautifully executed fleet manoeuvres off New York. He went on to lead a strong fleet of thirty-five of the line escorting three huge merchant convoys and supply ships to Gibraltar in 1782, then under siege by a vast Spanish and French army. Forced to negotiate strong winds and the fiendish currents of the Gibraltar Straits, Howe brought his convoy safely into Gibraltar despite a combined French and Spanish fleet snapping at his heels.

Skill at fleet manoeuvre required the type of mind that could grasp the exceptionally varied and complex scenarios it presented, and this proved a rare attribute. Few admirals in the eighteenth century demonstrated competence in fleet manoeuvre, let alone the mastery displayed by Howe. Maintaining station in a fleet was very difficult. Ships moved at different speeds under similar sail plans and all distance had to be judged by eye. The result was that any 'line' of battle was hardly ever a line as we would conceive it, but was more like several lengths of a broken chain. Three, four or five ships might keep close station with each other, but they would be in some measure disassociated from those astern or ahead, and so on.

Furthermore, the Admiral, usually in the centre of his line which was often as many as thirty-five ships long, may have been able to see clearly no farther than five ships ahead or astern of him, depending on visibility and the distance allocated for station-keeping. Even with the help of frigates passing messages up and down the fleet, most commanders of large fleets were blind to the activity of the majority of their ships. Indeed, unless they were anchored together, the term 'fleet' is misleading for this era of sail, as a single fleet was very rarely a single, united mass of ships, but rather a jumbled collection of squadrons and loose ships. Controlling fleets of sailing ships was like herding cats. Maintaining even any semblance of control could occupy all of a commander's time and energy, and getting all his ships to fight the same enemy at the same time and in a preordained way was next to impossible.

There was no official training in fleet command in this period. Those who were good at it were good at it because it came naturally to them, but competence was always relative – the trick with fleet seamanship was to be less bad at it than the enemy. Only the finest commanders could manoeuvre fleets successfully in narrow waters, as Howe did in the summer of 1782 when he took twenty-five of the line through the narrow, rock-strewn gap between Land's End and the Scillies to put his ships between a Franco-Spanish invasion fleet and the homebound Jamaican convoy.[6] The passage is the graveyard of many ships, often with engines to help them. An impressive feat, then, for a vast fleet of huge, heavy sailing men-of-war.

In battle similar problems applied to keeping track of the enemy fleet, which made them far more elusive than one might suspect. Entire squadrons could be hidden from sight by banks of fog or, once battle had commenced, by the thick gunsmoke that hung around the ships. From mere glimpses of ships in silhouette on the horizon, understanding what was happening to an enemy formation was immensely difficult and knowing how to respond required yet another level of tactical acumen. Being able to enact any plan required an efficient and effective chain of command and skilful seamanship. It was all too easy for this chain to break down at any stage, which is why fleet battle of any type was rare in this period and why comprehensive victory at sea was rarer still.

But Howe, as we've seen, was more practised and more skilled than most. He had first commanded a squadron off Normandy in 1756 and so, by 1793, he had been commanding squadrons on and off for thirty-eight years. In contrast, only one year before the British and French met at the at the Glorious First of June, Villaret was still only a lieutenant and when he sailed to face the British he had had no fleet command experience at all. In fact, he had never before been in a fleet battle.

Howe's skill as a fleet seaman and fleet leader was impressive relative to any admiral, of any nation, of any decade in the Age of Sail but what made him particularly special was that he invented and used new systems of command. From 1790, and then with an improved system in 1793, Howe conducted his fleets using numerical signal flags which could be hung on any part of the rigging and whose combined numbers referred to a range of orders laid out in a signal book.

Before this system was first tested by Howe in the 1770s, fleets were controlled by a limited number of flags that related to a limited number of vague instructions with the significance of each flag directly linked to its location in the rig. This severely restricted anything that a commander could say, and most of what a subordinate could ever hope to understand or even guess at. Howe's system changed all of this. More could be said, more could be understood and, with a little luck, more could be achieved. His popularity was crucial in achieving this because most captains were hostile to any change, as Howe's great contemporary in signal innovation, Richard Kempenfelt, found to his cost. Kempenfelt once lamented after a trial of his new system:

> 'That which I would have adopted – though most evidently the best – I could not get any of the admirals or officers of note to approve and countenance.'

Kempenfelt's solution was to use Howe's ideas so that they would be much more easily accepted by the fleet, 'he [Howe] being a popular character'.[7] We must acknowledge Howe's personal achievement in introducing his signalling system because there was no official admiralty-issue signal book until 1799. In 1793, the name Howe was synonymous with signals, tactics and fleet control.

As his popularity made the new system work, so his industry made it possible. Over and above its invention and refinement, he organised the printing of the signal books, their transportation to Portsmouth and distribution through the fleet and he oversaw the correct design and supply of all of the new flags and vanes.[8] He was instrumental, too, in formally recording much of the intricate detail about fleet seamanship, hitherto passed down through generations by word of mouth. Now, less knowledge was at risk of being lost, forgotten in the long gaps between fleet battles and, with more duties more clearly defined, it became easier to police behaviour in battle. Much more of what was expected was now written down; there were fewer places for the gun-shy captain to hide.

Howe's signal system was, however, far from perfect and no one was quicker to criticise than Richard Kempenfelt, who declared one of

Howe's innovations, in night and fog signals, to be 'extremely defective'.[9] Despite his many talents, one of the enduring paradoxes concerning Richard Howe is that he dedicated so much of his life to recording the detail of the navy and yet he was beset by a crippling inability to express himself clearly, particularly in writing, to the extent that, at times, he was rendered absolutely and resolutely beyond comprehension. Nelson received a letter from Howe that he described as a 'jumble of nonsense'[10] and with regard to successful communication on board ship Kempenfelt neatly summed up the advantage to be gained from clarity: 'When in any project for signals they appear intricate and seem difficult to comprehend, you may be sure they are faulty; what is good must be clear and simple'.[11]

While Howe largely excelled as professional seaman, he continued during times of peace to make few friends and many costly blunders, none more so than during his tenure as First Lord of the Admiralty in the peace that followed the American war. By 1793, therefore, Howe had unquestionably undergone a mixed career, but three things, all crucial to the new war against Revolutionary France, were certain: his ability to command large fleets was second to none, his personal bravery was without question and his influence over the seamen was profound. This last fact stemmed in part from the first two – the sure way to win sailors' loyalty was to excel in seamanship and to show no fear – but it can also be attributed to another aspect of Lord Howe's career: his care for the lives and health of his men.

The evidence we have for this is particularly striking. From the early 1750s, those captains concerned with their men's health and willing to make the effort to innovate and improve conditions, began to issue order books which did much the same thing for life on board as Howe's signal books and duty records did for fleet command: pertinent information and relevant expected duties were recorded and, thus, could be studied, learned, improved, amended and policed. For example, it had long been the expected duty of midshipmen on watch to climb aloft at intervals and scan the horizon for any distant shipping but Howe defined and cemented that duty in writing: 'A midshipman of the watch is to be sent up to the masthead once every half hour between the rising and setting of the sun in fair weather, to examine whether there be any strange ships in sight.' Similarly, it may appear obvious that lanterns were prepared for a night watch but by following Howe's precise written instructions, anyone would know exactly what was expected of him without having to ask: 'Six signal lights and as many false fires to be brought up every evening and kept upon the quarterdeck during the night ready for use.'[12]

A ship's order book was therefore designed to keep the crew safe and efficient. Howe was not the first captain to use this system, but his book for the *Magnanime* in 1759, the year of the Battle of Quiberon Bay, is the earliest that survives. It is a wonderful, detailed document revealing the particular concerns of a ship's captain at that specific time and in that specific location. Many aspects of Howe's order book were copied, later, by officers throughout the fleet and a little less than twenty years on Howe became the first officer to issue this type of book to an entire fleet, rather than to an individual ship. Necessarily this restricted a captain's personal influence on his ship but it instilled uniformity which made the ships under his command easier to control.[13]

It was an essential building block to progress and improvement, but it was not the only one in which Howe was directly involved. Concerns for seamen's living conditions and health led to Howe's direct involvement in the instigation of the 'divisional' system. The idea behind this was to divide a ship's company into small units, with a lieutenant allocated to each division given the responsibility of monitoring the tidiness of the messes, the cleanliness of the ship and of the sailors' clothes and bedding and the efficiency of seamanship. It was essentially devolution of responsibility and it made the whole business of life on board not only more hygienic but also fairer and less brutal. One sailor, deeply appreciative of the new system, wrote: 'By a just proportion of labour falling to the lot of each man, instead of the management of it being entrusted to the partiality and brutality of boatswains' mates, the men were kept in better temper, and were less harassed and fatigued in their spirits, as well as in their bodies'.[14] Casual violence was anathema to Howe and the fact that work could be done 'without noise, or the brutal method of driving the sailors like cattle, with sticks'[15] encouraged his early support of the divisional system. Well aware that the quality of seamanship and fighting skill was all the better for a decent quality of life on board, he took seriously the problem of scurvy among the men and appointed a physician to the fleet, as Admiral George Rodney had a decade before in the American War. Understanding of the treatment for scurvy had been growing and within two years of the outbreak of the French Revolutionary War, lemon juice was being issued routinely to ships sailing for foreign stations. Blockading squadrons at sea for long periods continued to suffer and Howe tackled this by enforcing a loose, rather than a close, blockade, thus ensuring his men access to shore supplies of fresh fruit, vegetables and meat. He, also, boosted the ships' supplies of lemon juice by commandeering any spare stocks whenever possible, such as in the spring of 1794, for example, when he heard of several hundred gallons of lemon juice lying unclaimed at Portsmouth.[16]

Howe also introduced new standards regarding hygiene and cleanliness and was particularly worried about the effects of damp on the men's health. Recognising that his rule for regular hammock-washing meant that the men often slept in wet hammocks he ordered each man to be issued with two,[17] a solution made possible because he had a powerful enough reputation to get it accepted. He was even thoughtful about disrupting the men's sleep and avoided tacking the ship or wearing his squadron during the night. When such disruption was unavoidable he gave good warning of his intention.

He could be strict when it was necessary and throughout his career he had no qualms in ordering men hanged for desertion or mutiny, but his overriding reputation for care and consideration earned him the nickname, the 'seaman's friend'.[18] The moniker is also fitting for the period because, alongside Howe, others too were actively promoting development in shipboard management, command and sailors' health.

In keeping with the general air of unrest and confusion in the year 1793, however Howe was not considered a friend by all British seamen. The inevitable and lamentable fault of his clumsy political career, Howe was associated as much with political faction as with professional naval competence. The 1770s and '80s had been notorious for political division permeating the navy. Officers were split on party lines as never before and antipathy lingered into the '90s in the aftermath of the regency crisis of 1788–9, when King George's 'madness' had been so extreme that some politicians had argued for the Prince of Wales to become regent. But George made a rapid recovery leaving those who had advocated his replacement red-faced. Political divisions seeped into the navy to the extent that, when Howe took command of the Channel Fleet in 1790, numerous officers would have little or nothing to do with him.[19] Edward Leveson-Gower, who had been Howe's second in his duel with Hervey, and who had since been appointed as Howe's first captain, resigned rather than serve alongside him. Other senior officers were, variously, unhappy about his appointment, considered him 'an unpleasant commanding officer', or simply refused to talk to him. Rear-Admiral John Jervis, a highly political man, determined to 'oppose him in everything'. Another naval officer commented simply that Howe's arrival in 1790: 'Does not serve to increase the good humour,' while another commented, as Howe drilled the fleet in expectation of war: 'It is ridiculous to see how far vanity can lead a stupid old fool eat up with the gout and various other bad humours.'[20]

Howe's natural tendency to inflame faction was exacerbated by another aspect of his character. Among close friends and family he was a quiet man, deeply loyal to his political and professional followers and charming to his inner circle, particularly those with whom he served afloat. He 'never made a friendship but at the mouth of a cannon' wrote the astute Horace Walpole.[21] But outside of this select group Howe was seen as difficult, aggressive, fractious and thoughtless or, as one contemporary put it, 'austere, morose and inaccessible'.[22] Horatio Nelson's wife, Frances, said he was the 'most silent man I ever knew' and Nelson himself thought Howe a 'strange character'.[23] Those who were not close to him had no knowledge of his kindness and warmth, and neither did they believe such a side to him could possibly exist. When the young Edward Codrington met Howe, just before joining his crew, he summed him up perfectly: 'There was a shyness and awkwardness in Lord Howe's manner', wrote Codrington, 'which made him apparently difficult of approach, and gave him a character of austerity which did not really belong to him.' As a future member of his crew, Howe went on to show the young man 'fatherly kindness' and within minutes he found himself '…at my ease with this man who was supposed to be so cold and morose'.[24]

In some respects, therefore, by 1793 Howe's time had passed. It was highly unusual to be asked to return to sea after serving as First Lord of the Admiralty. It was, in effect, a demotion and Howe had no desire to be back on board ship. At the age of sixty-seven, Howe believed he was too old for active duty, indeed, he had personally declared that no man over sixty should ever command at sea.[25] He also suffered very badly from gout, an excrutiating condition caused by the build up of uric acid leading to painful swelling, usually felt in the toes. It is one of those irritating illnesses that leaves sufferers desperate for any remedy, however alternative, and we know that Howe even tried 'electricity' to ease the discomfort. In the late eighteenth century this involved an 'electric' bath. The sufferer sat in a bath of water into which a positive electrode was submerged while the negative electrode was attached to the person's body, usually at the sternum. Howe also tried electropuncture, a painful-sounding 'cure' combining electrotherapy and acupuncture which in the eighteenth century was appropriately aquatic for a seafarer: it involved standing on a 'torpedo fish', known to us a stingray. At one point an unfounded rumour circulated that Howe had been killed while undergoing this treatment.[26]

Desperate to avoid active service, Howe claimed he was too old and too ill to command and it took a direct order from the King, to whom he was close and who insisted that having gout was no reason to stay ashore, for the reluctant Howe to hobble painfully up the gangway of the fleet's flagship, the *Queen Charlotte*.[27] There was, in any case, a well-established tradition of commanders in ill health keeping the sea. Rodney, for example, experienced most of the Moonlight Battle (1780) from his bunk with the gout. While Howe was a favourite of the King's, who called him his '*peculiar* admiral',[28] George was insistent he took command because, in 1793, there was no other choice. Of the flag officers with fighting experience from the War of American Independence, Rodney, Kempenfelt and George Darby were dead, and Edward

Hughes was fully retired and would be dead within a year. The only two senior admirals still alive were Samuel Hood, who had already been pencilled in for the Mediterranean command, and the elderly, reluctant, disliked, Howe.

It is characteristic of both Howe and the navy in 1793, however, that two of these three black marks against Howe's name could easily be forgotten or at least temporarily overlooked. Sailors had little interest in the political divisions of their superiors and they knew first hand of Howe's reputation for fairness and care. As for Howe himself, once committed, albeit by coercion, he was as focused as ever.

In 1793, therefore, not everything was quite as rosy with the English Channel Fleet as we might assume, but they did have one thing going for them. The fleet had gone through a sort of trial mobilisation three years earlier when war had threatened with Spain over claims to territory on the Pacific coast of Canada around Nootka Sound. The incompetence of the British sailors had proved quite shocking: Edward Codrington recalled how the fleet was 'composed of inferior men and of inferior ships, and commanded by officers, some of whom in the commonest evolutions betrayed a want of seamanship and of knowledge of their profession'.[29] Cuthbert Collingwood, then a captain with an impressive reputation and a great deal of experience, agreed and wrote:

> I do think (and it grieves me) that we do not manage our ships with that alacrity and promptness that used to distinguish our Navy: there is a tardiness every where in the preparations and a sluggishness in the execution that is quite new. The effect is obvious to every body and the moment the ships are put in motion they feel it. Lord Howe cou'd not get down the Channel in fine weather and the middle of summer without an accident; two ships ran foul of each other and the *Bellerophon* has lost her foremast and bowsprit and gone to Plymouth a cripple. This was not the fault of the ship nor the weather, but must ever be the case when young men are made officers who neither have skill nor attention, and there is scarce a ship in the Navy that has not an instance that political interest is a better argument for promotion than any skill...[30]

He also grumbled at the lack of available stores to repair the 90-gun *Duke* when her mainmast was struck by lightning. Collingwood was despondent, writing to a friend, '…I assure you sir, I perceive a languor in all our preparations that deprives me of many a good hour's sleep.'[31]

Nevertheless, those men gained valuable experience as Howe put them rigorously through their paces. John Jervis spoke (at that time) of the 'unparalleled exertions of every individual in the fleet', which demonstrated 'a conduct that did honour to themselves and to their country' and which, he believed, 'had never been equalled'. Jervis particularly complimented the officers who had taken their ships down the Channel '…with scarcely enough men on board to navigate the vessels, and drilling their men from sunrise to sunset with as much care and pains as were taken by a serjeant of any regiment of soldiers'. Midshipmen and mates had worked 'in the most industrious manner'; captains used their own money to rig ships; admirals did everything possible to 'promote the general activity'.[32]

For all the British incompetence in 1790 there had, at least, been a mobilisation with the chance to gain experience. A year later there followed another, minor, mobilisation and then some fleet exercises during the Ochakov crisis, when Britain sought to intimidate Russia into returning territories seized from Turkey.[33] That is not to say, however, that these crises, which anticipated the French war, solved all Britain's manning problems, either in terms of number or experience.

Very little work has been done on this embryonic stage of the navy's involvement in the war, but it does seem that, because Hood had taken so many men and quality ships to the Mediterranean, the remainder of the British fleet and the Channel Fleet in particular were left short. In February 1794 Howe was 1,000 men shy of complement. The flagship, the *Queen Charlotte,* was undermanned and the *Montagu* joined the Channel Fleet with only thirteen men able to take the helm, including the quartermasters. Worse still, the captain of the *Montagu*'s foretop had been at sea for only fifteen months.[34] From the New Year of 1794 until the spring the Admiralty received a constant stream of letters from the ships in Howe's squadron complaining about lack of crew: they were 274 men short in January and 321 short in February. That same month the

*Invincible* reported that she had no marines at quarters while Bowyer of the *Barfleur* wrote pointing out that 'Ensign Welsh', a member of the 69th Foot serving aboard, had never been in action and was so young that Bowyer thought it wholly inappropriate he should be in such a position of responsibility.[35] By April the *Caesar* remained 116 men down with the *Valiant* already fifty-four short when a typhus outbreak worsened and yet more of her crew had to be sent to hospital.[36] Pasley of the *Bellerophon* was furious and objected that the marines he had been sent were so young and weak that they were unable to carry a musket. Thirty of the 307 new marines were found to be unfit but Pasley was advised by the superintendent of the marines' barracks that they were all 'healthy growing lads' and that men were very difficult to obtain.[37] But with the French ready for war, some at least were up for the challenge. Lieutenant Byng of the *Impregnable* was so desperate to return from hospital to his ship, in case he missed anything, that he discharged himself while still, in the words of his captain, 'exceedingly ill'.[38]

The Channel Fleet was also suffering from the usual mixture of maladies that routinely disabled sailors. On 9 April the fleet physician examined every man on board: the *Montagu* had the most cases of venereal disease with fifty, the *Invincible* came a close second with forty-six and then the *Leviathan* with forty-five; there was a nasty outbreak of measles with fourteen confined to bed on board the *Arrogant*; the *Valiant* was labouring under typhus, which had also, earlier, affected the *Leviathan* crew; the *Montagu*, over and above those with venereal disease, was only just getting men back on their feet following an unnamed 'contagious disorder'[39] and the health of the *Arrogant* crew was suffering because she had lain near a swamp in ordinary for several months and there was an outbreak of measles.[40]

There were, as always, discipline problems to contend with, including a mutiny on the *Venus* over the behaviour of First Lieutenant Morgan: he had been beating the crew with his speaking trumpet, a broomstick and a treenail (a large wooden peg used to fasten planks) and pulling their ears and hair. The crew finally rose up when Morgan kicked and 'ruptured' another lieutenant who was sent to the doctor with a swollen left testicle.[41] And there was, of course, the usual run of on-board accidents. Captain William Parker of the *Audacious*, for example, was incapacitated and confined to his cabin having fallen out of his chair and cracked open his head when the ship took a big roll.[42]

Howe gave his men no time to rest idle. The early stages of the war were characterised by the Channel Fleet's frequent sorties from its base at Torbay. The French fleet was considered to represent little threat and the major concern was to prevent any privateering activity against British trade,[43] a task that still tested the British seamen thoroughly. Merchant ships continued to pour into British ports from east and west and needed protection regardless of the weather. After the summer of 1793, British sailors were repeatedly forced to take their cumbersome ships to sea and beat into the teeth of the prevailing westerlies and south-westerlies of the autumnal equinox. On one passage, Howe's fleet took eight days (28 October – 6 November) to sail from Torbay to Land's End, nearly twice as long as it would take with a fair wind. Once past the treacherous rocks off Start Point, Atlantic rollers hammered the ships' bows as they steered a safe path beyond the Scilly Islands and into the Western Approaches. Here, the fleet would look out for incoming trade convoys and provide them safe passage into England's harbours on the south-west coast or farther east to the Solent and beyond. In the first years of the war, Howe's activity in that sea area demanded consistent, top-quality seamanship.

An incident from December 1793 illustrates this particularly well. The Channel Fleet was cruising through the gap between Scilly and the Breton coast being pounded by south-westerly gales which were blowing the ships north and east, toward Scilly, the Lizard and the Start, the dangerous, rock-infested waters on England's south-western coast. The weather had been so filthy that no one on board had seen the sun, the means by which they measured longitude and thus their position, for four days. The British fleet simply did not know where they were and the weather showed no sign of improving. The conundrum was this: to remain out at sea was to endanger the fleet because sustained exposure to foul weather risked disabling any ship of any fleet, but if the fleet were to head home they would have to put themselves at the mercy of the wind. With an unknown starting point it would be all too easy to misjudge the approach and the fleet could find itself embayed – that is to say trapped by an onshore wind – to the west of the Start, from which there was no escape from the rocks.

Howe was concerned that they would be driven ashore at Whitsand Bay, immediately to the west of Plymouth. Nonetheless, his master of the fleet, James Bowen, offered to take the fleet in and Howe had sufficient confidence in Bowen's navigational skill and in the seamanship of his men that he turned the fleet north and east, toward the lee shore. Bowen's strategy was clever but simple. The fleet was led by a lugger, the *Black Joke*. Luggers were rigged with lugsails, usually on two masts. Although a descendant of the square sail, the lugsails effectively created two large fore-and-aft sails which meant that the vessel could point closer to the wind than the square-rigged warships. A lugger was also tiny in comparison with a ship of the line and therefore much handier. The *Black Joke* led the fleet because she could safer risk sailing closer to shore than the men-of-war.

A little to windward of her sailed the *Phaeton*, a 38-gun frigate commanded by Andrew Snape Douglas. Douglas had excelled in the opening months of the war in the *Phaeton* taking five enemy vessels and Howe had rewarded Douglas's ability by placing him in command of the Channel Fleet's frigates. Being a frigate, the *Phaeton* was significantly handier than a First or Second Rate. To windward of the *Phaeton* sailed Howe in the *Queen Charlotte*, using the *Phaeton* as a visible guide for coastal navigation, whose captain in turn was using the *Black Joke*. The rest of the fleet followed to windward of Howe, all using the towering masts and great sails of the fleet flagship as banners to follow. The *Black Joke* sailed close inshore and then hove to, threateningly close to the rocks of the Start where the swell broke into a churning maelstrom. Just in sight, the *Phaeton* then hove to, thereby providing the *Queen Charlotte* with a visible marker for the rocks, and allowing her to lead the rest of fleet safely around Start Point and into Torbay.[44] Soon after this, Douglas joined Howe as his flag captain aboard the *Queen Charlotte*, where he served in the Glorious First of June.

Howe's ships sighted the enemy only twice in 1793, in August and again in October, and had exchanged shots but once,[45] but many of the skills of fleet convoy, particularly those needed in rough weather, were transferable to battle. The November cruise may have been condemned by a contemporary as 'a series of vexations, disappointments and bad weather',[46] but it made no difference if a yard or mast was broken by enemy shot or by the explosive power behind a sudden squall. Either way, the crew was under pressure to repair the ship. And in battle, the ability to make repairs reliably and quickly was often the deciding factor in victory or defeat. Neither did it make much difference if a captain was struggling to maintain station in a fleet that was looking for a friendly convoy or in one looking for the enemy. All the experience gained by the fleet was useful to harden the fleet to life at sea.

No one, however, could tell how the men would react under close and sustained French fire. There had not been a fleet battle for nearly eleven years, and the last, the Battle of Cuddalore, was fought in the oppressive heat of the East Indies, so distant from decent repair facilities that fleets had tended to spar and puff out their chests rather than wrestle each other to the ground. Indecisive skirmish was not the way of Channel warfare. Squadrons were usually fresh from port and safety was a matter of hours away. More could be risked, therefore, and more was usually at stake. In the Channel, the French or British would be fighting to hold on to home soil, rather than for territory claimed in distant colonies. In addition, less could be hidden from higher authorities: the gaze of the Admiralty was considerably keener off the coast of Cornwall or Dorset than it was off southern India. It is no coincidence that most of the decisive engagements of the preceding one hundred years had all taken place in or near the Channel: Barfleur in 1692, the two battles of Finisterre in 1747, and the Battle of Quiberon Bay in 1759. And yet, in 1793 there had not been a significant battle in the Channel for fifteen years, since 1778 when the British were badly mauled by a highly trained and vigorous French fleet. There was a distant history of bloody warfare, therefore, but nothing immediate that could offer any pointers as to how Howe's men would act as the shot rained from men who refused to yield. But the British seamanship was good, their training was solid, and in battle, training and seamanship were the keys to survival; it was easier to ignore the shot if the men were acting out a routine; it was easier to be brave if there was no opportunity for thought.

How would the two fleets be brought together in action? This question vexed commanders of sailing fleets for centuries and has confused historians for almost as long. The difficulty of forcing two fleets to come to action revolved around the relative ability of a fleet to sail downwind (to leeward) or upwind (to windward). Windward sailing in any one ship, let alone a mighty fleet, was extremely difficult, particularly for the cumbersome ships of the line whose large hulls effectively acted as sails, the wind pushing the ship sideways downwind even as the ship moved forward at an angle into the wind. Wind was also usually associated with lines of swell, usually running at ninety degrees to the direction of the wind. These swell lines thumped into the ships' hulls and helped drive them farther downwind. A ship running with the wind behind, or on her stern quarter, ran with the swell. She would sail faster and had a free choice of direction in which she could manoeuvre. But a ship close-hauled, which is to say sailing as close to the wind as she possibly could, could only turn with ease downwind. She could turn her bows through the wind – known as tacking – but it was unreliable, slow, and a good deal of ground would be lost to leeward in the process. Ground to windward could be made, theoretically, by sailing close-hauled and then tacking repeatedly, but in practice for the largest ships, it was usually a matter of holding one's own against the wind until it veered or backed and began to blow in a more friendly direction.

When two fleets met at sea one would necessarily be to leeward of the other and if there was no wind or tide drifting one towards the other, that fleet would have to claw its way to windward if it wanted to attack the enemy. The fleet to windward, however, simply had to run downwind. So far so good; the basis of this scenario was that it was far easier for the fleet to windward to attack the fleet to leeward than vice versa. But in reality things were far more complex. It was very rare indeed for both fleets to want to fight to a decision. It was not, for example, like a game of football in which both sides were intent on winning in the same way, and willing to contest with each other for a given amount of time and for the same goal. Fleets represented different nations with differing strategies. One fleet commander, for example, might be intent on the wholesale destruction of the enemy, while the other could be wholly focused on survival to provide strategic protection to a convoy or port. One fleet commander could be willing to risk the lives of all of his men to secure victory, the other might only countenance the loss of a handful of men. In each case it depended who was commanding both fleets, where they were in the world, what conditions their ships and men were in, what their political masters had decreed, and, not least, whether local geography, wind and weather conditions allowed any rational choice to be made at all. Only very occasionally did two fleets meet whose commanders were prepared to slog it out until one side had won convincingly.

The problem that usually faced an aggressive fleet commander, therefore, was how to bring a reluctant enemy to battle, and how to keep him there for as long as it took to defeat him. This was *not* simply a question of somehow acquiring the windward position. Being to windward made an attack easier but in no way did it guarantee that an attack could be made, or that the enemy would even be forced to fight. What had to be borne in mind was the relative sailing abilities of the fleets. A fleet to windward might sail downwind toward an enemy to leeward, but if that enemy chose to turn and run and consisted of fast ships then there was nothing to stop him from running clean away. Exactly the same thing can be said of an attack to windward. Windward sailing took such a significant degree of quality seamanship to do well that this was often the most reliable way that a skilled fleet could catch an untrained enemy. Those sailors who could set their sails hard to the edge of the wind and then tack reliably and with precision could easily hunt down a ship crewed by men unsure of their timings, unable to execute manoeuvres well and repeatedly. The sea is a very large place; there was nowhere to hide once fleets had met in the open ocean. There were no spinneys, hedges, hills, rivers or mountains in which to find respite. Ships could cloak themselves in darkness, hide in banks of fog, or sneak in between hidden sandbars or reefs if there were any nearby, but most of the time the horizon was a good twenty miles distant. Chases could last days at a time, so long in fact that tiny percentages in seamanship made all the difference. In short, a skilled fleet could usually force an unskilled fleet to battle given enough time and decent weather conditions, regardless of its position in relation to the wind.

The next tactical problem for the aggressive commander was how to keep an enemy engaged long enough for a decision to be reached. This issue linked the question of damage with that of position in relation to the wind. It was very unusual for two ships to engage each other without one of their rigs becoming damaged in some way, and the one aspect of shiphandling that required the rig to be in top condition was sailing to windward. A ship could drift to leeward easily with broken stays and yards, split sails and cut running rigging, but all of it needed to be strong and functioning well to drive a ship to windward. The best way of preventing a damaged ship from escaping, therefore, was to assume a position to leeward of her and drift downwind as she drifted downwind, or even to make a firm stand and force the crippled ship to come alongside where she could be lashed securely in place.

These were the tactical problems that were exercising Howe at the start of the war when he issued a fleet order proposing an entirely novel form of attack, one specifically designed with an unwilling enemy in mind. He proposed an attack from the windward which began in the traditional manner with the ships of the British line gently bearing down toward the enemy. But instead of reforming at a given distance to engage in a traditional gunnery duel, Howe's ships would continue straight for the enemy and through their line, with each ship passing under the vulnerable stern of the ship opposite. The rest of the battle would then be conducted with the British ships to leeward of the French, thus preventing their escape as they became damaged. The enemy's line would not therefore be cut by a single severance, but broken at every link in its chain, causing confusion and a lack of cohesion along its entire length and trapping the French against the guns of the British. It was a tactic designed to destroy or capture as many of the enemy as possible and in 1793 it was the most aggressive tactical innovation of the sailing ship era.

Hitherto the development of sailing tactics had been very slow and confused with basic tactical ideas appearing, disappearing and then reappearing for well over a century. Most of the notably different and novel ideas were to do with manoeuvre rather than engagement and involved the complex manipulation of squadrons within fleets. But the basic science of fleet engagement had always remained the same.

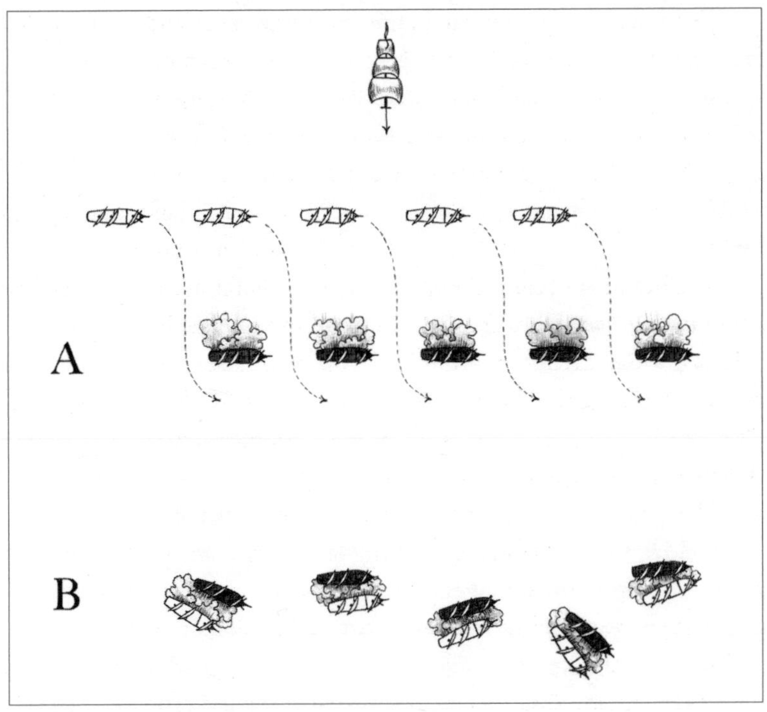


i. Howe's new mode of attack. Each ship bears down on his opponent from the windward, crosses her stern and engages from her lee.

The fleets would fight each other, broadside to broadside, in line ahead. Depending on the tactical views or boldness of their commanders, the fleets might try to stretch out to match the length of each other, van to van or rear to rear, or a commander might attempt to concentrate one part of his force on another part of the enemy, to overwhelm it. Although this became a signature of Nelson's tactics as the wars with France developed, it was by no means his alone, but an ancient doctrine of warfare that was not unique to naval actions. 'Doubling' an enemy line, that is to say engaging them from both sides at the same time, was also a well-known goal but was usually achieved by a section of the attacking fleet sailing around the van or rear of the enemy and not by deliberately passing through the line while pouring broadside after broadside into the stern of the enemy ships, as Howe now proposed.

This new tactic was not enough in itself to win any battle, of course. Howe's plan still depended on two crucial factors: first that the enemy would be both able, and far more unlikely, willing, to assume a conveniently loose formation and simply wait for the British to attack, and secondly that Howe's captains would understand what he wanted them to do, try and do it, and succeed – none of which could be guaranteed to happen.

The first point, that the enemy would be willing to receive such an attack or, indeed *any* attack, is worth considering in a little more detail, as all too often British failure in naval warfare has been considered by historians from the British perspective alone. Benbow's last fight in 1702, which was investigated in some detail in the second volume of this trilogy, is a perfect example. Benbow did his best to engage the enemy, but the French ships were led by the wily and experienced ex-privateer Admiral Du Casse, who did everything in his power to prevent Benbow from attacking in the way that he intended, van to van, centre to centre and rear to rear. Similarly at the Battle of Toulon in 1744 Admiral Matthews tried to get his fleet to draw up the full length of the enemy, van to van, but the commander of the French van cleverly stretched his ships out, stringing out the outnumbered English ships and then threatening to double them and destroy them in detail. It was so effective that the English van squadron was forced to withdraw. The history of naval tactics has been written for so long from the perspective of the 'victor' in terms of ships taken or destroyed, and with a strong focus on Nelsonian 'decisive' battle, that the complexities of tactics have simply been forgotten.

There was a wonderful art to defensive action that existed alongside the art of aggression, and the French repeatedly showed themselves to be masters at it. The Battle of Minorca in 1756 is a powerful example both of French defensive skill and the distortion of history in this way. The failure of the British to convincingly attack the French at that battle famously led to the execution of Admiral Byng, but the log books reveal that most of the time the British ships were simply unable to get anywhere near the French. Whenever the British fleet, to windward, launched an attack, the French simply drifted to leeward and out of range. Their men were skilled, their ships were fast and their commander, the Marquis de la Galissonière, was cunning. It was almost impossible to bring an enemy like that to battle.

The second crucial aspect to Howe's plan, that his officers would understand his intention, act on it and then succeed, was equally unreliable. We have already heard of Howe's inability to make himself understood and the introduction of any novel idea or instruction suffered from a heightened risk of failure through misunderstanding. Consider Sir George Rodney's attack on the French fleet at Martinique in April 1780. He tried to revive the ancient tradition of warfare that one force should concentrate its fire on a section of the enemy, thus overpowering it. He decided in this case that he would launch his entire line against the rearmost part of the enemy. Simple you might think, but once the attack was launched the leading ships of Rodney's fleet did not engage halfway down the enemy line as he desired, but stretched their way out to the van of the enemy, which is exactly what he did not want to happen.

There is also the question of physical capability. Consider the Battle of Ushant in 1778, the last great battle in the Channel before the First of June. Toward the end of this engagement the British commander, Augustus Keppel, ordered his fleet to reform in his wake to protect themselves against a supposed French attack. The attack never materialised, but a large number of ships in Sir Hugh Palliser's squadron failed to obey the instruction simply because they were too badly damaged: there was nothing they could do even if they had wanted to.

The implication of all of this was that, although Howe had impressive new ideas and an unquestioned desire to bring the enemy to battle, there was still a great deal that could go wrong. It is all too easy when considering the naval actions of the Revolutionary and Napoleonic wars to be lulled into a false sense of inevitability about British victory. The majority of the almost endless successful single-ship actions were all to come, and so too were the great fleet victories of St Vincent (1797), Camperdown (1797), The Nile (1798), Copenhagen (1801), Trafalgar (1805) and San Domingo (1806). In the previous war there had been one good victory at the Saints in 1782, and another, known as the Moonlight battle, in 1780, but these were far outnumbered by the failures. There had been five indecisive and unimpressive actions in the East Indies; a very unsatisfactory engagement in the Chesapeake in 1781 that ultimately led to the loss of Yorktown and a great deal of recrimination and bitterness between Admirals Graves and Hood; a fierce duel with the Dutch off the Dogger Bank that ended in a bruising stalemate; and the failed actions at Martinique and off Ushant already described that both caused and revealed deep bitterness within the British officer corps. Since then there had been scattered individual ship actions and privateering successes but there had also been failures. There was no lengthy and glorious tradition of victory to fall back on as there was at Trafalgar, no comfortable knowledge that the enemy had been weighed, measured and found wanting time and again in naval battle. In fact, in the spring of 1794, Howe's concern over his captains' behaviour was such that he confided to a midshipman of his flagship that he would refuse any opportunity of action at night as he needed daylight 'to see how my own captains conduct themselves'.[47]

If the capability of the British fleet was uncertain, the general strategy behind the fleet was stable. It existed to destroy French seapower and to protect and expand British commerce. In the spring of 1794 it became increasingly likely that an opportunity would arise as there were strong rumours that the French intended landings on Guernsey and Jersey using the powerful squadron and six thousand troops that had been gathered at nearby Cancale.[48] This was just one of the many rumours of French intention that circulated in the early summer of 1794. Fear of invasion was real and widespread in England. Sounds of French industry in Brest had, indeed, rung across the Channel as Jeanbon had supposed and the British fully expected that the French navy would shortly come out. For the first time in over a decade a battle seemed imminent between the British and French and for the first time in more than a century an artist was waiting to depict them in the act.

# 4.

# The First War Artist

...to obtain a most correct knowledge of the places forming the feats of war, and arranging the most essential occurrences that happened, in or near each place, for the accurate information of the public.

Circus Master Philip Astley, 1793.[1]

Imagine a line of soldiers, arms on the shoulder of the man in front, one leading another through a sea of filth, against a background of stone grey sky, patched by thick columns of black smoke. The men are following each other in a chain, physically in touch with the men in front and behind because they have all been temporarily blinded by mustard gas. Their eyes are covered by yellowing rags, their clothes and hair stained with blood and stiff with mud. This is the scene that John Singer Sargent witnessed and which he immortalised in *Gassed* (1919), one of the most powerful images to have come out of the First World War. A towering masterpiece, some six metres long and two and a half metres high, it was built for the never-constructed British hall of remembrance and now hangs in a room of its own in the Imperial War Museum in London. The image's power lies in part in his mastery of brush and oil, but it also lies in its authenticity. Sargent painted this line of soldiers when they walked past him on the Western Front in August 1918. This is not something he imagined but something he saw, from the exaggerated motion of the soldiers, one of whom is preparing to walk up an imaginary step, to the football match being played in the background. That is the power and significance of artistic witness; it leads us to a deeper and more profound perception of the event in question whether it is a modern photograph of an engagement in Afghanistan or a centuries-old oil painting of war on land or at sea. Artistic representation of modern war now ranges widely through the many mediums of contemporary art: we can interact with naval warfare in real-time video at home as easily as we can through paintings, sculptures or photographs in the world's galleries dedicated to modern art. From news clips we can see with our own eyes the tactics of Somali pirates as they stalk and then attack a merchant ship; we can see footage of submarine missile launches and fighter jets catapulted from the decks of aircraft carriers. But in 1794, what did the public know of naval warfare?

Those who had not experienced naval war first hand had very little visual reference with which to inspire their imagination. For nearly a century most battles had been fought hundreds, if not thousands, of miles from English coasts as Britain, France, Spain and the Netherlands clashed over their new colonial empires. Where naval battles had once been fought against the Dutch in the shallow waters of the North Sea, and often within sight of shore, so now the struggle for the seas was acted out under the fierce sun of the Coromandel Coast of India, above the turquoise waters of the Caribbean, around the windy sandbanks of North America, and on the great rolling swells of the Western Atlantic. News of naval warfare was devoured in the local press, but descriptions of the actual fighting were brief. Occasionally the service tore itself apart in bitter faction over conduct in battle with detailed accusation and defence published. Even the minutes of courts martial were occasionally published, but these events were relatively rare. In the ninety years between 1702 and 1792, only five controversies had really caught the public imagination in this way: the chaos of Benbow's last fight in 1702, the antipathy of Matthews and Lestock at the Battle of Toulon in 1744, the timidity of Byng at the Battle of Minorca in 1756, the political sparring of Admirals Keppel and Palliser after the Battle of Ushant in 1778, and the woolly incompetence of Graves and Hood at the Battle of the Chesapeake in 1781. Although some of these were discussed in public and in minute detail, what the public lacked was access to powerful and realistic images of the event in question.

The problem was twofold, and the first concerned public access to images of naval warfare. The vast majority of artwork was privately commissioned and privately consumed; the pictures squirrelled away to hang above the desks and dining tables, beds and lavatories, in the hallways and stairwells of private residences throughout England. Very few were ever made available for public consumption through public exhibition, a practice that had only gained momentum in the 1760s when the

Society for the Encouragement of Arts, Manufactures and Commerce in Great Britain began to hold annual exhibitions. Such public shows were still in their infancy in the 1790s. The National Gallery was not founded until 1824 and the National Gallery of Marine Painting at Greenwich Hospital would not be opened until 1829. Before 1794 the public generally had contact with naval events through the sale of engravings, taken from artwork, but this itself was a relatively new concept. Although early naval prints do survive, the first military event of any kind popularised by large numbers of prints was the Battle of Culloden in 1746, a land battle.[2]

If the means of public consumption was one major problem, the other was perhaps even more significant. The images that did exist were unreliable because the artists had neither witnessed the battle in question nor, and this was usually the case, naval warfare of any type. Some even had very limited knowledge of seafaring. The closest examples we have of trained marine artists witnessing naval operations of any type in the period immediately before the Glorious First of June are Robert Cleverley, who witnessed an amphibious assault on Rhode Island in 1776 during the American War, and Dominic Serres, later marine painter to George III, who may have witnessed the Havana campaign at the climax of the Seven Years' War (1756-63).[3] Accurate though their images may be, none of them depict fleet battle.

To muddy the waters even further, there was an explicit and long-standing tradition of the depiction of naval tactics in published treatises that bore no relation at all to the realities of naval warfare. This is an important discovery that has only recently been made and emphasised by naval historians.[4] Naval tactics in the Age of Sail were not simply professional matters for naval officers alone: the lines of battle, angles of wind and potential for intricacy transformed tactics into an intellectual challenge embraced by mathematicians and geometers who produced beautifully illustrated tracts. Thus the messiness and unpredictability of naval warfare was cleansed of complexity and gradually ignored as tactics became just another branch of the Enlightenment's mathematical crusade to bring order to the natural world. It is no coincidence that these depictions of naval battle bear a striking resemblance to the rows of trees and hedges of the landscaped gardens of the time. They represent a search for symmetry, but just as you would find no such symmetry in a naturally rambling wood, so the realities of ship manoeuvre and command control actually restricted the ability of admirals to command their fleet in such a defined way. The 'line' of battle is one of the most powerful myths of the age.

The only man who we know to have both witnessed and painted a naval action in the Age of Sail before the Glorious First of June was Willem van de Velde. A Dutchman, Van de Velde was invited to England by Charles II in 1672 and was soon commissioned at the princely sum of £100 per year 'for taking and making of draughts of seafights'.[5] Willem and his son, also called Willem and another fine artist, lived at the Queen's House in Greenwich, fittingly now the exhibition space for many of the National Maritime Museum's finest artworks, and they produced many hundreds of paintings and drawings. Their work is now scattered throughout the world in museum and private collections. The National Maritime Museum in London alone holds well over 1500 drawings. One of the Elder's images, the Battle of Scheveningen of 31 July 1653, is particularly special because he was actually there and he even painted himself into the picture. He sits in a galliot at the front left of the painting with a hat and drawing board. The man to his left may well be his son (see fig. 9). It is a valuable image because it captures the chaos of battle and the vast clouds of smoke that were an inseparable part of it. There are no formal lines of fleet battle here but endless, relatively isolated duels, reproduced like the feedback reflection of mirrors placed opposite each other. Few other images of naval warfare give such a realistic impression of bewilderment and disorientation and the conflicting and ever-changing priorities of those who fought. To left and right men jump or fall from sinking or burning ships while others rescue those swimming. Some ships fight, others avoid collision, but for the majority it is unclear exactly what they are doing, why, or even which nationality they are. This was all quite deliberate: the confusion you feel from looking at the painting is not due to artistic incompetence but quite the opposite: your perception of the sea fight is being manipulated by the hands of a master.

The image also highlights one of the significant problems of all military art: large-scale battles tended to be fought over huge expanses of land or sea. The actual battle space occupied by the Battle of Trafalgar, for example, was some 49km$^2$.[6] To depict these battles in their entirety, therefore, was very difficult unless a bird's-eye or schematic view was taken. This approach, however, so often placed the viewer an unsatisfying distance from the action. The solution was to take a single event that was representative of the whole, or to take several different events that happened at different times and in different locations and unite them in a single canvas. The canvas would therefore tell a story, but as a visual record of the event in question it would be highly misleading. It is important to realise, however, that this lack of realism in the representation of a sea battle existed alongside a correspondingly powerful desire among the public to experience reality through art. Ever increasingly, that desire was being met by the commercially aware world of theatre and spectacle that experienced a dramatic awakening in the 1790s: this was the age when the circus came to town.

The man behind this innovation was Philip Astley, a retired sergeant-major of cavalry, 'over six feet in height, with the proportions of Hercules'[7] and a highly skilled horseman who began to exploit an interest in daredevil equestrian shows in the last quarter of the eighteenth century. His first shows were conducted on a staked-out field just beyond the current site of Waterloo station, but then, as the story goes, he discovered a valuable diamond ring on Westminster Bridge. The money from the sale of the ring gave him enough capital to secure a mortgage on some fine land immediately to the south of the bridge, roughly where the London Eye stands today. There he would sit in his full military regalia and astride a white charger, directing passers-by to his shows. The shows themselves changed in both style and substance as Astley came to know his audiences better and soon the open-air, linear spectacle had become a show in a controlled, enclosed, circular space. People paid to enter, they sat around the circle, and the shape of the circle itself helped the horsemen achieve ever more impressive feats: the centrifugal force experienced by riding in a circle keeps the rider safe when otherwise he would fall. Soon Astley was filling in the gaps between the equestrian shows with clowning, tumbling or pantomime and other curiosities discovered in local fairs. In 1792 Astley included in his show 'the celebrated Mr Wildman's exhibition of bees', which consisted of the brave Mr Wildman riding around 'with a curious Swarm of Bees on his Arm' before coaxing them toward his head so that they cluster around it 'in imitation of a Bob wig'.[8] Now that's entertainment.

Astley also began to realise the potential of his horses to 'recreate' equestrian experiences or events that catered for the public thirst for reality. Fox hunting was one such example, and a promotional review from 1785 reads 'the reality of the fox and hounds divests us of every idea of its being a fiction, and therefore we receive the same entertainment as we would receive were we to be spectators of a parcel of tailors in an actual fox chase'. Whether or not this was the actual effect of the show remains highly doubtful but what matters here is that it was promoted in these terms: there was a clear commercial value attached to the reality of effect.[9]

Astley's ambition and imagination did not stop there. He soon began to put on shows with immediate contemporary relevance, regardless of the inevitably equestrian focus of his shows. In 1789, for example, he staged an elaborate recreation of the death of Captain Cook, shown as 'A Grand Equestrian Dramatic Spectacle': not a bad effort considering that horses were then unknown in the North Pacific where Cook died. But it was the French Revolution that created the most sparkling contemporary opportunity for Astley. In 1791 he staged a recreation of the flight of Louis XVI from Paris and when news of military campaigns flooded the press, Astley turned his horseflesh into ranks of cavalry. In 1793 he recreated, with a panorama of the Grand Armies, the surrender of Condé and then the Fall of Landrecies, which similarly included a panorama, this time of the Dutch army.

Astley was always keen to emphasise the authenticity of the show and he explained how he had personally travelled far and wide 'to obtain a most correct knowledge of the places forming the feats of war, and arranging the most essential occurrences that happened, in or near each place, for the accurate information of the public'.[10] With such novelty and success, Astley soon had his competitors, the most famous of whom was Charles Hughes, himself a former employee of Astley. His Royal Circus and Equestrian Philharmonic Academy was so popular that, when it was shut down for failing to have the correct licence, the Riot Act had to be read from the stage to calm the audience. Astley also faced rivalry from mainstream theatres. In the summer of 1793, for example, both Astley and the theatre at Sadler's Wells produced shows relating to the siege of Valenciennes.

While Astley was thus introducing the public to the pleasures of equestrian spectacle and circus performance, the world of theatrical entertainment was also undergoing a dramatic technological change that further extended the ability of a theatrical entrepreneur to claim an approximation to reality, and the man at the centre of this innovation, and who would have a significant role to play in the artistic celebration of the First of June was the artist Philippe de Loutherbourg.

Loutherbourg was born in Strasbourg in 1740 and was reaching a ripe maturity at the time of the French Revolution. He had come to England via several European cities, including Paris, where he had worked at the Opéra under the guidance of the talented illusionist designer Giovanni Servandoni, a specialist in *trompe l'œil*, who had himself been trained in Rome.

Loutherbourg was an artist of exceptional ability with a fine taste for dramatic events and even more dramatic representation, but he did not earn his money by producing canvases for private clients: he combined his love of art with his love of theatre and worked almost exclusively for the Drury Lane Theatre. He is often described as a 'scene painter' but that does his position a grave injustice. Loutherbourg was a scene designer, the most talented of his generation, and in the late eighteenth century he had generated a sufficient reputation to command the extraordinary fee of £500 per year, far more than the base rate of a basic naval officer's pay. He was so talented that he had been elected to the

French Royal Academy of Painting at the age of twenty-two when standing regulations prevented admission before thirty.[11]

He was obsessed with achieving realism through innovation in scenery and its presentation. He developed and extended ideas on the laws of perspective, and the use, or suggestion, of three-dimensionality with raked scenery; he invented colours and paints using his training as a chemist;[12] he used complex mechanisms to move pieces of scenery; and he introduced entirely novel ways of lighting a stage, using coloured silks and gauze to suggest fog, illuminated with hidden, shuttered and moving lights. This was all some significant way from a plain stage lit by a single, overhead candelabra and inevitably he became satirised as Mr Lanternburg.

His first known work was the *Harlequin Shepherd* at Drury Lane which recreated the exploits of an infamous prison breaker, with scenes showing both the exterior and interior of Newgate gaol and others 'all painted from the real Place of Action'.[13] He soon became hot property among the wealthy elite and one Christmas he devised a private show for a wealthy private client. Loutherbourg promised Beckford 'a mysterious something – a something that eye has not yet seen or heart of man conceived'.[14] The result was something similar to what we now know as a *son et lumière*. Loutherbourg then brought many of these new ideas together in an invention of his own, a sort of mini actor-less theatre, only eight feet deep and six feet wide, in which he staged dramatic landscape scenes. He called it his 'Eidophusikon'.[15]

Unfortunately no remains of the Eidophusikon have survived and only a handful of his working models for the theatre survive today in the Victoria and Albert Museum in London. What do survive in greater numbers are descriptions of the effects that he created and they leave one in no doubt that this was a man achieving something both entirely new and enormously exciting. Many of the techniques he used already existed in the popular Chinese and Italian shadow theatres, transparencies and the Panopticon, but it was their refinement and clever integration that made the effect so miraculous.[16] As one contemporary wrote:

> The stage on which the Eidophusikon was represented was little more than six feet wide, and about eight feet in depth; yet such was the painter's knowledge of effect and scientific arrangement, and the scenes which he described were so completely illusive, that the space appeared to recede for many miles, and his horizon seemed as palpably distant from the eye, as the extreme termination of the view would appear in nature.[17]

He was particularly inspired by the challenge of the maritime world and many of Loutherbourg's finest creations concerned the sea in one form or another. This is in part due to Loutherbourg's interest in all things maritime but it was also related to the scale of the challenge. The permanent theatres and shows in London were under constant pressure to innovate and few things posed a greater challenge than a representation of the sea or, even better, of a large ship at sea. The ship would have to be recreated as a perfect model with all the intricacy visible. Many of the audience would have had deep knowledge of maritime affairs and the ship or ships would need to be represented accurately, with appropriate motion and sail plan for the weather and sea conditions depicted.

In *Alfred* (1773) Loutherbourg created moving models of ships, an entire fleet of which took part in a mini naval review on stage. The painting of the model ships was subcontracted to none other than Dominic Serres, marine painter to George III. In *The Critic* (1779) he recreated Tilbury Fort as it appeared when facing the Spanish Armada of 1588, a production in which 'The deception of the sea was very strong, and the perspective of the ships, together with the mode of their sailing truly picturesque.'[18] He went on to work on scenes for other famous maritime subjects, not least a production of *Robinson Crusoe* in 1781 and then a very famous production called *Omai, A Voyage 'Round the World*, a fiction based on the life of a young Ra'iataen, who had been brought back to London from the Society Islands in the North Pacific by James Cook in 1773.

In one of the most celebrated set pieces of that play, Loutherbourg used no less than forty-two separate pieces of scenery to suggest a frozen ocean and the costumes were designed from studies made by John Webber, the artist who had travelled to the Pacific with Cook on his last voyage.[19] *Queen Mab* of 1775 included a representation of a full Thames Regatta, complete with barges rowed to music, their oars keeping a regular stroke. He also used the unique ability of the Eidophusikon to suggest dramatic maritime scenes, none being more successful than his depiction of the wreck of the *Halsewell*, an East Indiaman that was driven ashore at Seacombe, in Dorset in 1786. A review of the Halsewell production is eloquent testament to Loutherbourg's powers.

> The effect of a Storm at Sea, with the loss of the Halsewell Indiaman, was awful and astonishing; for the conflict of the raging elements he described with all its characteristic horrors of wind, hail, thunder, lightening, and the roaring of the waves, with such marvellous imitation of nature, that mariners have declared, whilst viewing the scene, that it amounted to reality... I can never forget the awful impression that was excited by his ingenious contrivance to produce the effect of the firing of a signal of distress, in his sea-storm.[20]

In another production his depiction of the sea was praised thus:

> The waves of his stage were carved in soft wood from models made of clay; these were coloured with great skill, and being highly varnished, reflected the lightning. Each turned on its own axis, towards the other, in a contrary direction, throwing up the foam, now at one spot, now at another, and diminishing in altitude as they receded in distance, were subdued by corresponding tints. Thus the perturbed waters appeared to cover a vast space.[21]

Loutherbourg also paid detailed attention to the noise of the sea so that more than one sense was assaulted by his artistry. Vast sheets of copper, wobbled or struck, giant tambourines, and boxes full of shells, peas and balls recreated thunder, wind and wave. In 1782 the satirist Peter Pindar summed up Loutherbourg in classic Pindar verse:

...Loutherbourg when heaven wills,
To make brass skies and golden hills,
With marble bullocks in glass pastures grazing,
Thy reputation, too, will rise,
And people, gazing with surprise,
Cry, 'Monsieur Loutherbourg is most amazing'[22]

Loutherbourg thus dragged theatre into an age in which illusion and scenic effect were an expected and predominant part of every ambitious performance.[23]

Although these glittery inventions tend to catch the eye, the more traditional art world was also caught up in this increasing commercialisation of public spectacle during this period. Among the most heavily visited attractions in London in the past few years have been the Van Gogh show at the Royal Academy and the Chinese Terracotta Army exhibition at the British Museum. Both brought art or artefacts to a new audience, and the press response was rapturous. Yet it is all too easy to forget that this public and highly commercial display of art has a heritage that can be traced to the final quarter of the eighteenth century: it is a pattern that has repeated for nearly 250 years. More specifically, it all began in 1783, the year after the end of the War of American Independence, when John Singleton Copley was commissioned to produce a rendition of the siege of Gibraltar, a defining campaign in the American War and one of the longest continuous sieges in history. The British garrison held out for three years and seven months against wave after wave of Spanish assaults launched from a combined army and navy some 70,000 strong. It was a particularly popular subject at the end of the war as it served to ease the burden of the loss of the American colonies. In the siege of Gibraltar the public had a reason to celebrate British stoicism and heroism against their traditional foe.

The way that Copley painted and exhibited his image is important in several ways. Crucially he tapped into the new tradition that emphasised the importance of historical accuracy. Hitherto artists had dealt with contemporary issues in a very roundabout allegorical way, the event usually being disguised in one form or another, such as being set in ancient Greece or Rome. It was believed that heroic themes required distance in both time and space for the heroism to be treated with the dignity that it deserved.[24] But this all changed in 1771 when Benjamin West painted *The Death of General Wolfe*, commemorating his death during the capture of Quebec in September 1759. West refused to dress James Wolfe and his entourage in togas, and instead made the bold decision to paint them in their uniform. Initially there was uproar. George III even refused to buy the painting, believing it an offence against good taste. But West stood his ground and gradually the public began to appreciate the opportunities such realism offered, not least the ability of such an image to reflect and generate a sense of patriotism. The public were proud of their soldiers and wanted them to be shown in a true light. West's search for detail, reality and authenticity in art prompted a flood of imitators.

Copley then took up the challenge in 1779 with a painting commemorating the death of William Pitt in the House of Lords in 1778. Pitt died as he rose to speak, suffering a catastrophic stroke. Copley recorded the event on a ten-foot-wide canvas. He needed the space to include portraits, taken from life, of every single one of the fifty-one members who had witnessed the event. When he took on the challenge of the siege of Gibraltar, the need for authenticity was so great that Copley even travelled to Germany to sketch a number of Hanoverian officers who had played a significant part in the defence of the Rock.[25] The work took Copley eight years to complete and it was not shown until the spring of 1791, almost a decade after the American War had ended and only two years before the outbreak of the war with France. Although it dealt with a subject held dear by a previous generation, the mode of display was still a contemporary novelty for the British public at the time of the French Revolution. And what a splendid novelty it was.

A 'magnificent Oriental tent' eighty-four feet long was pitched in the centre of Green Park, much to the disgust of those whose houses backed onto the park. For a shilling a head the public could enter to see the twenty-five-feet-long by eighteen-feet-tall image that glorified British magnanimity at the height of the battle. Copley showed British soldiers and sailors, heavily outnumbered, risking their own lives to rescue the enemy from exploding ships. The main scene was flanked by huge portraits of Admirals Howe and Barrington and was located above a separate canvas depicting the naval relief, painted by Dominic Serres. As they arrived, each viewer was given a catalogue describing the scene, which included a form to subscribe to the forthcoming engraving. Copley later claimed that more than 60,000 people passed through his tent.[26] The engraving subscriptions never materialised in the quantity desired, however. The public, it seemed, could blow cold as easily as hot in their appreciation of art. What attracted them at the time was the novelty of the size and magnificence of the tent, but when the engraving finally came out, in March 1810, twenty-seven years had passed since Howe had sailed to relieve Gibraltar. The event carried none of the contemporary relevance and excitement of the time. The world had moved on and Britain was now involved in a desperate struggle with Napoleon. Who would be interested in a distant siege when the papers were now full of contemporary campaigns? This was the final requirement of commercialised art in the 1790s: it had to be accurate, available to mass audiences who previously had not gone to exhibitions at all, and it had to be immediate. It was a mixture of reportage, idealism and theatre, and the public loved it.

Just two years after Copley's tented extravagance in Green Park, London was ready for its first travelling art exhibition and in 1793 part of the collection of the Duc d'Orléans, one of the finest ever assembled by a non-monarch, was exhibited on Pall Mall making previously unseen old masters accessible to the general public, or at least to those who could afford the shilling entrance fee. The size and rarity of this collection cannot be overestimated. There were twenty-eight Titians, twelve Raphaels, twelve Tintorettos, sixteen Veroneses and the list goes on and on, including works by Rembrandt, Van Dyck, Carracci and Correggio. Much of the collection had been privately owned by Louis XVI himself, who in turn had acquired numerous pieces from the private collections of Rudolph II, Holy Roman Emperor (1576-1612) who in turn had acquired many pieces from his predecessor, Charles V, Holy Roman Emperor (1519-1556), and from Queen Christina of Sweden, whose renowned collection had been looted from Prague Castle during the turmoil of the Thirty Years War (1618-48).

The collection is now divided among some of the world's most prestigious galleries, including the National Gallery in London, which holds twenty-five of the original collection, the Metropolitan Museum in New York, the Frick Collection in New York, the National Gallery of Art in Washington and the National Gallery of Scotland. There was as much demand to see the exhibition then as there is for its components now: we know that in the initial surge the exhibition was taking £1,000 per day.[27]

In the same year Loutherbourg himself was commissioned by the publishing brothers Valentine and Rupert Green for £500 to produce an artwork suitable for engraving of the fall of Valenciennes. With a heavy emphasis placed on authenticity, Loutherbourg obtained a special pass to travel through France and Flanders to sketch the actual locations and he took with him a famous caricaturist, James Gillray, to take the likeness of soldiers involved in the campaign. The result was hailed as a triumph for its realism. The reviewer for *The Times* commented:

> The fashionable world have now established their morning lounge at the historic Gallery, Pall Mall, where Loutherbourg's celebrated picture... attracts all who are anxious to behold an exact representation of the remarkable siege;... exact portraits of all the principal officers of the combined armies and in addition to the British troops who are represented in the trenches, the Hussars of Barco, Esterhazy, and Blankenstein, the Cuirassiers of Cavanagh, the Dragoons of Keraczy, Laudonvert and the various foreign regiments employed, are represented with an accuracy almost incredible.[28]

All of this was exciting for everyone concerned. Traditional artwork had demonstrated that it had a high commercial value and the maritime world represented as never before enraptured audiences and made good profit for theatre owners, circus masters and art-entrepreneurs. A modern survey of theatre posters from the period perfectly captures the times. The shows promised exoticism, gorgeousness, skill, novelty, magnificence, danger, display, beauty, action and spectacle, all of which in turn was promised to create sensation, delight, wonder, humour, suspense, and astonishment.[29] The country was gripped by a fever of theatrical innovation, and it was that fever that would before too long force the Glorious First of June deep into the consciousness of contemporary society, and deep into the fabric of history itself. But for now, in 1793, the one thing missing was a naval event worthy of this new type of artistic interpretation.

Depictions of the sea in the 1780s and 1790s had reflected those peaceful times; remember that the previous war, the War of American Independence, had ended in 1782, eleven years before the outbreak of war with Revolutionary France. Now consider the themes and titles of Loutherbourg's Eidophusikon productions: *Tangier at Noon*; *Sunset near Naples*; *Moonlight on the Mediterranean*; *Shipwreck*. There is nothing martial here. As the land war started to produce appropriate events to capture the public imagination, and as that commercial gap was rapidly met by artists, circus impresarios and theatrical entrepreneurs, so did pressure build behind the desire to witness a naval event. It built up steadily for sixteen months, from the declaration of war in February 1793 to the start of June 1794.

What the public wanted to hear about and also experience through art was a fleet action, a significant event that presented a fair match of English naval might with her enemy, and which marked an important turning point in British history. They wanted something to celebrate on a far greater scale than the occasional single-ship victories that made the papers. Tales of land wars in distant countries, deep in the European heartland, were well and good but did nothing to dispel the immediate concern of the British public over the threat of invasion. Nothing would change that until the French navy had been destroyed. News of a large naval battle counted for far more than news of any old military success. For the men and women in the streets, coffee shops, pubs, slums and mansions of London, only a naval victory would offer hope and provide a sense of security regained.

Only then would Britain be safe from the mistrusted ideology of the French Revolution.

The event that finally released that pressure, causing nothing less than a euphoric eruption of public interest and celebration, was the Glorious First of June, and the artist who, more than any other, met the need for authenticity in the depiction of that battle was a man called Nicholas Pocock.

Pocock knew everything there was to know about ships and shipping. He had been born and brought up in Bristol near the docks where thousands of tons of commercial shipping reached English shores from all over the world. Today the Bristol skyline is cut only by the six masts of Brunel's SS *Great Britain*, his magnificent iron passenger liner from the 1840s, and the single mast of the *Matthew*, a replica of the caravel that John Cabot sailed to North America in 1497. But in the eighteenth century when Pocock grew up, Bristol was the second most significant port in the country after London. For all of its commercial value as the country's capital, London's position so far up the Channel was a nuisance for many ship owners who preferred Bristol, which faced west, directly into the Atlantic, and which had access to fantastic inland communication up the Avon and Severn. The air was thick with the smell of tar and damp wood, the harbourside was thronged with exotic men and laden with goods arriving from or departing for, the western horizon, heading into the sunset, following it around the world to a new day. Pocock's father was a mariner and soon Pocock joined him officially as an apprentice to learn the trade. And so Pocock went to sea.

By his early twenties he was a captain and soon had sailed to the eastern seaboard of America, the Caribbean and the Mediterranean. He was not a navy man, but he sailed the waters that the navy patrolled and he thought like a seaman. Art was never far from his mind, however. Pocock's logbooks are among the finest examples of sailors' art from the eighteenth century to have survived (see fig. 14). In the centre of each day's entry is an exquisite image of a ship as she might have appeared on that day, under full sail, straining to catch every last breath of an idle wind, or groaning under reefed topsails, riding out a squall. Each image is set in a frame of detailed hourly observations of manoeuvres, sail plan, wind direction and strength, and distance run.

Aged a little over forty, Pocock left the sea and became a professional artist. He was soon much in demand among naval officers for the detailed images he produced. These seafaring scenes were painted by a man who knew the difference between the shape and texture of sailing canvas in a blustery Channel dawn and a tropical heat wave; who appreciated that the sea could be both glistening and dull, reflective and matt; whose ships were painted *in* the sea rather than mysteriously hovering on top of it, one of the most difficult of all marine artists' skills to master. The rigging was always immaculately depicted, the lines neither too taut nor too slack, unless that was exactly what he wished to depict. Pocock at his best could create a window to the sea, and to look through it was to feel the wind on your face, the sting of salt water and the heaving of the deep.

Early on in his career as an artist Pocock sent several paintings to the Royal Academy and received a most encouraging reply from its president, the famous artist Sir Joshua Reynolds. Reynolds apologised that the paintings had arrived too late for the exhibition but commented on the pieces warmly, offered some criticism and then made a number of suggestions of great interest. 'It is much beyond what I expected from a first essay in oil colours' began Reynolds before adding, 'there wants a harmony in the whole together; there is no unison between the clouds, the sea and the sails'.[30] Crucially, he advised Pocock to learn from the Dutch masters of marine art, the Van de Veldes, and also to 'paint from nature instead of drawing; to carry your palette and pencils to the waterside'. This, claimed Reynolds, was the practice of Claude-Joseph Vernet, the celebrated French marine artist.[31]

Reynolds thus encouraged Pocock to witness the scenes that he wanted to depict. Pocock seems to have taken the advice to heart and began to produce images with which he was personally familiar. Leaving his house adjacent to the harbour on Prince Street in Bristol which is still blessed with some glorious eighteenth-century architecture, Pocock began to compose views of the landscapes around Bristol, with particular emphasis on the drama of the Avon gorge. He soon received his first significant naval commission, and produced five pictures for Samuel Hood celebrating some of the successful naval actions of the American War.

With his foot firmly in the door of the world of commercial art, Pocock was quick to realise that Bristol had little to offer an ambitious marine artist. The men with the interest in art and the money to pay for it were naval officers, or perhaps high-ranking officials in the large trading companies like the East India Company. To get to them he had to be in London. Pocock moved to 12 Great George Street, no distance at all from Westminster or the Admiralty and its regular tide of wealthy naval officers looking for a piece of art to flatter their vanity. He had filled the years of peace with a number of interesting non-martial commissions, not least working up a series of drawings of John Stanley's scientific expedition to Iceland in 1789, but war provided a commercial opportunity for artists as much as it provided a gateway to honour and riches for naval officers. The two were very much intertwined and Pocock took enormous pains to ensure that a naval officer wanting to commemorate a particular action would come to him. The exact episode to be painted was then discussed at length between Pocock and his patron, and every aspect was thoroughly researched. From which angle should the scene be viewed? What flags were flown? What was the state of the sea, tide and weather? Exactly which parts of the rig had been damaged and how? How many men were visible on deck? Which gunports were open and which closed? Had any been torn off? Were any of the windows in the stern galleries open? To what degree did the ships heel under the pressure of canvas? Did the swell make the ships roll, pitch, sway or surge, and if so, to what degree?

A letter to Pocock from one of his clients offers a tantalising insight to this dialogue. It was written by Sir Harry Neal, who had captured two large French frigates in Brest Roads – in sight of the rest of the entire French fleet. Pocock had mocked up a sketch of the scene, and Neal had then added his own comments:

> The ships in Brest Harbour should be more distinct, & five sail should have their topsails hoisted ready to come out (which was the case). Mr Pocock may place the ships as they are in the sketch, or as they were during the Action. The two English engaging the *Resistance*, which perhaps would look better; either would be correct as when the *Resistance* struck, the *Nymph* directly engaged the *Constance*; and from Point St Mathews to Brest signals were flying to give information to the Port Admiral at Brest. That little spot near the Ships is intended for the Parquet Rock from which they were half a mile.[32]

Such detail was the lifeblood of naval officers and they drew a great deal of pleasure from Pocock's art that transported them back to their moment of glory. Pocock made them voyeurs of their own heroism.

Having made it so far, and with such influential men as Reynolds urging Pocock to paint from life, the next natural step was somehow to get on board a naval ship when war broke out. In the late spring of 1794, as Howe was starting to flex his muscles in the Channel hunting for French privateers and escorting inbound and outbound trade, Pocock secured a berth on HMS *Pegasus*, a 28-gun frigate. We have no idea how he did so. Perhaps through a friend; or a powerful patron such as Alexander Hood, brother of the absent Samuel Hood who we know to have already commissioned Pocock. The *Pegasus* enjoyed a role typical of frigates in larger fleets. She was used to run errands, pass written or vocal messages and repeat the commander's signals with flags. She was always busy and usually close to the beating heart of the fleet, the flagship.

Pocock did not know it then, but he had secured a berth on a ship that would take him closer to fleet battle than any artist had been for over a century. Nicholas Pocock's dream had come true and his career was about to take a dramatic step forward. Nicholas Pocock was sailing to war.

# 5.

# The First Convoy

At his peril he was not to allow the great convoy to fall into the hands of Lord Howe. If he did so, his head should answer for it under the guillotine.

Edward Brenton recalling the words of Rear-Admiral Villaret-Joyeuse.[1]

As Howe patrolled the Western Approaches, the sails of his fleet cutting the horizon like the wings of seagulls, and Pocock packed his old canvas sailor's bag, throwing in his wet weather gear, his boots, knife and marlinspike alongside the tools of his new profession, his notebook, pencils, paints and ink, the situation in Paris began to change. At first that change was imperceptible like the lapping of a new tide, but soon it rose with the full power of a flood.

By the winter of 1793, internal civil war and fighting on the boundaries of France had become less of an immediate concern, as the French armies began to produce some spirited and talented generals who had learned to manipulate their vast armies with great skill. In September Caen, Bordeaux and Nantes were won back from the Royalists and the French won victories over the British at Hondschoote and the Austrians at Wattignies. In October Lyon was reclaimed and then punished with a particularly vicious Terror. Toulon was retaken from the British in December and in the same month the Vendée rebellion was quashed at Le Mans and Savenay. With a reduced internal and external military threat, the focus of French politics began to change toward immediate social problems, such as food riots and strikes in factories, and that unrest swiftly manifested itself in political infighting. That room with the green wallpaper in the Palace of the Tuileries where the Committee of Public Safety met became the focus of violent and factional passion as the full implications of the Terror began to be understood.

On one side stood the *Hébertistes* and *enragés*. As representatives of the militant *sans-culottes*, this faction pressured the Committee to take the Terror to an even higher level. For them the blood-letting of 1793 had merely demonstrated the scale of the problem that the Jacobin enforcers faced. Everywhere there was suspicion; everywhere there was treachery; everywhere there was deceit. According to the *Hébertistes* and *enragés* the future of the Revolution could only be guaranteed by extended, prolonged and merciless intervention by the executive.

On the other side stood a faction known as the *indulgents*, grouped around the formidable figure of Georges Danton. Unpredictable, but powerful both in his extraordinary physique and rough features as much as his political clout, Danton could claim with all credit that he was one of the leading lights of the early revolution who had personally taken part in the storming of the Bastille. He went on to become the first president of the Committee of Public Safety. But Danton was well known for his clemency, even toward his bitterest enemies, and it was that clemency in an unforgiving time that gave his political enemies the opportunity they needed to bring him down: from 1793 leniency and compassion could too easily be interpreted as sedition and betrayal. Danton, moreover, had never seen eye to eye with Robespierre, and now with Robespierre in the ascendant, Danton's time was running out. Robespierre had no time for debate. Those who were not with him were against him, and outbursts such as this, published by one of Danton's followers, and possibly by Danton himself, were a sure way to the scaffold.

> You want to remove all your enemies by means of the guillotine! Has there ever been such great folly? Could you make a single man perish on the scaffold, without making ten enemies for yourself from his family of his friends? I think quite differently from those who tell you that terror must remain the order of the day.[2]

In between these two factions stood the Committee of Public Safety, increasingly identified with the dominating voices alone of Robespierre and his long-standing colleague Saint-Just. On the one hand they were unwilling to grant the *enragés* any of the power and recognition they desired and believed that they deserved as militant revolutionaries, but on the other they had become suspicious of the *indulgents*. Their calls for moderation and leniency reeked of treachery. To left and right the Committee was threatened both in the extent of its powers and in its membership. The response was as savage and swift as the very blade of the guillotine itself. In the spring of 1794, both groups were arrested and guillotined. The attack on the extremism of the *Hébertistes* was widely accepted and easily defensible, but the execution of the moderate *indulgents* posed Robespierre and Saint-Just some significant new problems. Georges Danton went to his death in that awful tumbrel that had accounted for so many perceived enemies of the Revolution as one of the Revolution's very instigators and one of its proudest and most inspirational leaders. He became a martyr for those who believed in the goodness of the Revolution, and the humanitarian ideals that had once led to such wide acceptance of it. Danton knew that Robespierre's own fate would be sealed by his death. As he went to the scaffold he shouted 'Robespierre will follow me. He is dragged down by me.' Moments before his death he urged the executioner to show his dead face to the crowd claiming 'it's well worth seeing'. Every contemporary portrait of Danton seems to agree that this was a man of striking appearance and immense charisma (see fig. 8). He would not be forgotten easily.

Both Robespierre and Saint-Just defended their decisions in the convoluted rhetoric that had already taken them so far but, by executing the moderates, they could have done nothing more powerful to strengthen the moderates' argument. Robespierre had won himself a little time, but he was unaware that he now faced a self-healing and multi-headed beast: for every head he took, another would grow back. Opposition to Robespierre grew and not only in the theatres of French politics. Assassins lurked in wait for the humourless man with those distinctive green spectacles, determined to stain that sky-blue frock-coat with his own dark blood.

Both subsequent attempts on Robespierre's life were curious in their own way and neither was planned nor executed with much zeal. On 22 May a gunman shot at him on the street with a pistol that misfired. The only injury was to a locksmith who had run to shield Collot d'Herbois, another member of the Committee who had been walking with

Robespierre. The next day the second assassin made her move. Cécile Renault, a twenty-year-old daughter of a papermaker, pretty and well presented but uneducated and apparently unpoliticised, knocked on the door of the home of Monsieur Duplay where Robespierre frequently stayed. There she asked to see Robespierre but her suspicious manner got her no farther than the front door where she was arrested and found to be carrying two small fruit knives. She later claimed that she had 'only wanted to see what a tyrant looked like'.

A real assassination attempt or not, the problem was that it mimicked in many ways the events leading to the assassination of Jean-Paul Marat in 1793. Another leading Jacobin, Marat had been murdered in his bath by a female assassin infuriated by the increasing degradation of the Republic she so believed in, and she had stabbed him in the neck with a large kitchen knife. Perhaps the scale of the threat posed by Renault was written in the diminutive size of the knives she had concealed, and under interrogation she proved nothing remotely like Charlotte Corday, the bold and brazen murderess of Marat who was proud of her crime, determined to die for it and even asked for her portrait to be taken hours before her execution. Indeed, the apparent weakness of the threat to Robespierre inspired his political enemies to claim that it was a set-up; an event that Robespierre could spin to his own advantage. Robespierre certainly made the most of the failed assassinations, savagely brandishing the stories as proof of the perceived plots and threats to France's liberty that were the lifeblood of his rhetoric and the foundation of his power.

Robespierre sent Renault to the guillotine wearing the red shirt of the parricide. He also executed her father, brother and aunt (because her mother was already dead) for good measure. This was nothing less than guilt by association and a belief in the reality of 'bad blood', both of which had been centrepieces of the *ancien régime*'s criminal system that had once been loathed and condemned by Robespierre himself. He had in fact written his first essay for the Academy of Arras against it when he was a student.

Sixty-one prisoners went to the guillotine in that ghastly procession and among their number was the beautiful Sainte-Maranthe family, a widowed mother and her two angelic daughters aged only seventeen and nineteen. At this the crowd, who had hitherto unblinkingly watched so much bloodshed, began to get restless and shouted 'no children'. But there was no interruption and all were bundled to their death. It was such a horrific sight that some claimed then, and some scholars still claim today, that the entire thing was set up by Robespierre's enemies to discredit him and brand him as a tyrant.[3] It was certainly not the only rumour to circulate in these months that discredited Robespierre. Another outlandish rumour claimed that Robespierre had visited Mme Elizabeth, the dead King's daughter, who was under arrest in the Temple prison. Elizabeth herself wrote of the meeting that was conducted under the closest security, and Robespierre's enemies were swift to claim that it was a move designed to result in marriage, to unite the blood of Robespierre with that of the Capet dynasty. She was due to be executed and it was public knowledge that Robespierre had argued against her execution. Though now considered groundless, at the time this was all plentiful food for conspiracy.

What does seem certain, however, is that Robespierre was greatly shaken by the turn of events and he could see in the shadows the gathering of his enemies and hear in the buzz of the crowd the plotting of his demise. His agitation was such that he immediately recalled his long-term ally and friend Saint-Just from the northern armies and he signed Saint-Just's recall order twice. His famous eloquence, if occasionally convoluted, lapsed into sharp slivers of rage as he roused the Convention to yet more violence against his perceived enemies. 'Slander, arson, poison, atheism, corruption, starvation and murder – they [the enemies of France] have been prodigal in every sort of crime: but there still remains assassination, assassination, assassination'. He went on in another speech, 'we swear by the daggers already reddened with the blood of the Revolution's martyrs, and recently sharpened for us too, to exterminate every single one of the criminals who want to rob us of happiness and liberty'.[4]

The assassination attempts at least made clear to Robespierre the nature of the problem he faced, if not the extent of it, and all of Robespierre's political manoeuvrings in the spring of 1794 can be seen as a quest for unity to save his leadership and to save his life. What he wanted was an end to faction and the creation of what he called '*une volonté une*', a single will.

To help provide the security he craved, Robespierre needed two things, almost as badly as each other. One was good news from the various military fronts as evidence that the extreme measures taken by the Committee in the name of the Revolution were both necessary and working. It didn't really matter exactly where this news came from as long as it was positive. Having murdered his opposition, he needed some propaganda to bolster his position and to focus the minds of the public on the present and future of the Republic. Secondly, Robespierre needed to demonstrate his ability to provide for the populace who were suffering for reasons beyond their control. He needed to demonstrate an ability to govern in the name of the people and in their interests. So much of the Revolution in the previous two years had been about armies and navies, about external and internal war, about victory, loss, massacre and retribution. Robespierre now had to secure his political support by bringing the focus of the Revolution away from the bloody iron blade of the guillotine and Danton's headless corpse, to the humanitarian ideals that lay at the Revolution's heart. The best way of doing this, and the way that would win the most friends the most quickly, was to provide food and particularly bread because, in the spring of 1794, France was starving. Robespierre was going to buy his public's forgiveness with food, in the words of the French Minister in America 'to save our *patrie* from the horrors of famine and to rid it of intriguers who would sell it to despotism'.[5]

By February 1794 meat was only distributed in Paris to the sick, and shortly after that even this had to be withdrawn. Maritime trade was at a standstill.[6] For the long-term well-being of the French national stomach, the Committee of Public Safety initiated a major programme of agricultural reform, printing and issuing pamphlets on crop care and animal husbandry. Ponds were drained, woods cleared, barren land reclaimed and peasants urged to turn their pastures into wheat fields. There was even a major political push by the Committee to encourage the consumption and cultivation of the potato, which had never known the popularity in France it had experienced in England. In the short term, however, bread flour was the only solution. A little over 70 per cent of the population relied on bread for 70–90 per cent of their calorie intake and the farms produced only a small surplus, perhaps 10 per cent, which could be used to feed the cities. Any drop in that surplus, therefore, had an immediate and profound effect on the supply of bread to the urban masses: a drop of just 5 per cent in the national harvest would translate to a drop of 50 per cent in the quantity of bread that could be produced by city bakers.[7] There was, moreover, very little storage available for excess grain, even if it could be produced, and so any shortfall could not be covered by carefully managed stockpiles. In the annual grain cycle spring was always a time of want, even in good years, and the harvest of 1793 was weak by any standards. And so the system really began to crumble. As the trees and shrubs began to bud, and the countryside blossomed, the previous year's grain supply was almost exhausted, but the new crop had yet to be harvested. Spring brought warmth and hope, but in the eighteenth century it was often a desperate hope, so much so that this time of year in France was even given a special name, *la soudeuse*, from the verb *souder*, meaning to knit together, bridge or join. For many the hope of spring was nothing more than that there would be enough grain left to survive until the new harvest was in.

In 1794 two powerful additional factors made a bad situation far worse. The first problem was the huge manpower requirements of the vastly inflated army and navy. Not only did these mobile populations require huge quantities of grain from unexpected places at very short notice, but also they sucked labour, carts and horses from the farms. Farmers became soldiers; animals became transport or food; land cultivated by generations fell into disuse. As productivity needed to increase, therefore, so did its capacity to produce decrease. Secondly, the rarity of grain drove up its price to the extent that the government was required to impose a legal maximum price for grain, which it then purchased with the almost worthless *assignats*, the Republic's new paper currency. This enforced manipulation of the market was deeply resented by the grain producers and it immediately created a lucrative black market. Very little of the country's grain actually made its way to the large markets. Grain producers began to hoard, which was then made punishable by death, and so a deeper resentment grew between the farmers, merchants and the government. The isolated resentment between farmer and government became more widespread, and as a result large numbers of hungry people directed their anger at the government. Restless, troubled and angry citizens, when roused, could swarm. Riots over bread became common; bakers became battle grounds.

Cities were the hardest hit by the civil unrest because, by their very nature, urban centres did not create the produce they consumed. They invariably bought in their grain from outlying areas but in times of want these areas took their share first. There was often little or no grain left when the carts reached the city walls. And yet it was there, in the cities, and in Paris in particular, where political fortunes were won and lost, where the crowds could be turned, where history could be shaped. The British knew this well enough and in June 1793 they declared all grain and raw materials destined to France as contraband, the first time that British seapower had been directed against an entire civil population. French trans-Atlantic commerce became severely disrupted and the situation in France worsened.[8] The want was felt particularly badly in the French naval ports and from the summer of 1793 the French navy was fed only by the victuals captured from British merchantmen by French privateers.[9] The Revolutionary government needed a quick fix if they were to retain power.

The solution to Robespierre's political problem thus lay in flour. But where was it going to come from? Who had sufficient stockpiles of flour and a willingness to defy Britain and trade with Revolutionary France? The answer was America.

Ten years previously, in the War of American Independence, the American colonies had wrenched themselves free of British control in a violent and protracted struggle that had been achieved with significant French aid. The American navy in the 1770s and '80s was extremely limited and the alliance with France allowed them to compete with the British at sea. The Franco-American coalition also caused the war to burst out of the relatively limited geographical area in which the opening years of the conflict had been fought to encompass British home waters and their distant colonies in the Caribbean and India. The British war effort everywhere had to be sustained by long maritime supply lines that brought troops and material to the armies and with French naval assistance these could be threatened. Ultimately the challenge proved too great for the British, whose navy, particularly at the start of the war, was unable to regenerate the confidence and success of the Seven Years' War (1756-63). The French navy, in contrast, was a polished unit of well-maintained and well-directed ships that in the opening years of the American War was every bit a match for the Royal Navy. By the end of that conflict the balance at sea had shifted back in favour of the British but by then the war on American soil had turned irrevocably toward the colonists and had lost all public support in Britain. In September 1783, at the Treaty of Paris, the American colonies won their independence. Now it was the turn of the French to seek help in their struggle to cast off their yoke.

The American response to the French Revolution is now widely accepted as being one of the most significant features in the formation of American culture, equal in importance to events such as the two World Wars, Vietnam and the Cold War. There was a great deal of public support for the French cause in America in the 1790s as there had been for the American cause in France in the late 1770s. In 1790 the French National Assembly even honoured the death of Benjamin Franklin, who had been ambassador to France during the American War. In America, in many of the largest cities on the eastern seaboard, public support for the French Revolution spilled out into the streets with public feasting and celebration of their 'sister republic'. In January 1793 a large crowd in Charlestown even sang the Marseillaise before sitting down to a civic feast with a revolutionary theme.[10] There were similar scenes in Philadelphia, Baltimore, Norfolk, Savannah, Boston and New York.

New political societies proudly aligning themselves with the principles of Revolutionary France sprang up in America and members started mimicking the French practice of addressing each other simply as 'citizen'. While the initial news of the French Revolution was widely approved of in America for its humanitarian ideals and the relatively bloodless nature of its initial stages, when it started to turn violent an equally vociferous political voice condemned its extremity. In a few short years from 1792 onward, the French Revolution became the most significant fulcrum in American political culture; on one side stood the great Republican leaders of the time such as Thomas Jefferson, James Madison and James Monroe, who broadly supported the Revolution in France, and on the other the great Federalist leaders, such as John Adams, Alexander Hamilton and George Washington, who opposed it.

The debate became passionate. Alexander Hamilton called the Revolution 'repugnant' and 'an unexampled dissolution of all the social and moral ties', and political societies based on revolutionary ideology were branded as dangerous to the public good, designed 'to sow sedition [and] to poison the minds of the people of this country'. On the other hand, the eloquent and fiery Madison raged that enemies of the French Revolution were 'the enemies of human nature'.[11] The divide was so wide and so deep that this issue became the origin of the two-party political system that dominates America now: the country was split in two by its perception of a revolution on the other side of the Atlantic.

The magnified significance of such a distant event in American domestic politics further helped to strengthen an already powerful ideology in America that had, in part, caused the revolution against British colonial rule, and had then been reinforced by the success of the War of Independence. At the core of that ideology was a belief that America was politically, socially, culturally and economically different from Europe; that it was exempt from the established rules of international relations; that it should stand alone, aloof from the troubles of Europe, to celebrate its distance, both physical and cultural, from the old world.[12]

Powerful voices viewed the influence of the French Revolution on American politics with distaste: what clearer evidence did one need for the malign influence of European ideas and squabbles on the health of the young American republic? This was a time for protection and nurture; no time to casually throw away its new-found independence by careless alliance with a European power. The Americans had military problems of their own, not least the Indian wars, and their army was slight as it was and could not be risked on foreign soil for foreign interests. As George Washington asked, 'Why quit our own to stand upon foreign ground?…Why, by interweaving our destiny with that of any part of Europe, entangle our peace and prosperity in the toils of European ambition, rivalship, interest, humour or caprice?'[13] In this respect, both the Americans in Philadelphia and the Jacobins in Paris were concerned with the same thing: the survival of their newly won republics. This was the voice that could be heard the loudest in the early 1790s and which ultimately led to President Washington's Proclamation of Neutrality in April 1793, by which America officially distanced itself from the troubles of Europe with an avowed intention to remain 'friendly and impartial towards the belligerent powers'.[14] This ideology ultimately led to the prolonged American withdrawal from all European affairs that was only ended by the First World War.

Regardless of this official stance, however, a general empathy existed for the Revolution in France with its concerns about education, health, food and equality, all of which are central pillars of American political life today, and that empathy existed alongside an enduring suspicion of British motives in America. The British on the other hand harboured no desire to reconquer their old colonies and were content with maintaining the flourishing post-war maritime commercial relationship with America even if they had not quite removed all British troops from American soil. In the spring of 1793, however, that Anglo-American relationship collapsed when the British war with Revolutionary France spilled into the Caribbean and began to affect the American economy. At exactly the same time the Revolutionary French first made diplomatic contact with the Americans in the guise of Edmond Genêt, sent to Charlestown to smooth existing diplomatic alliances, secure American carriage of French-bound goods and, in spite of America's nominal neutrality, raise troops and privateers. It is important to realise that this was not a 'cold call' as such: in fact a sophisticated trade infrastructure was already in place as the French had been buying from the Americans since 1792 to supply their colonies in the Antilles.[15]

The decision to target France's colonies was central to early British war planning and Henry Dundas, Secretary of State for War, intended the West Indies to be the decisive theatre. He believed it 'the first point to make perfectly certain'.[16] The principal source of coffee, sugar, rum, cotton, cocoa, ginger, indigo dye, and other luxuries, the Caribbean generated four fifths of British income from overseas and in 1793 was in the middle of a sustained period of growth that saw British annual trade with the Caribbean leap from £4,100,000 in 1781–5 to £10,200,000 in 1796–1800.[17] At the same time the West Indies were crucial to the French economy, contributing perhaps twenty per cent of her entire income. Saint Domingue in particular, the French-occupied western end of the island of Santo Domingo (modern Haiti), was then the richest colony in the world with 8,000 plantations. In the late 1780s Saint Domingue's trade was as great as the entire output of the newly independent United States. Not only was this relevant to the outcome of the Revolutionary war but the British were also keen to replace the income of the American and Caribbean colonies they had lost in the War of American Independence.

In Britain in late August 1793 a major expedition, led jointly by Vice-Admiral Sir John Jervis and Lieutenant-General Sir Charles Grey, was planned with a force that would total, once all reinforcements had arrived, an impressive 16,356 men.[18] All of the French Windward Islands as well as Saint Domingue lay in their sights. But the British already had a military presence in the West Indies, split between its bases at Jamaica, Barbados and Antigua. They lost no time in prosecuting the war against the French. Long before Jervis and Grey gathered their ships, troops and ingenious prefabricated barracks at Portsmouth, the British had already moved to cut the French out of the Caribbean.

Tobago, a tiny, French-occupied island in the deep south of the Caribbean Sea, was the first to fall. The planters there had declared loyalty to the Bourbon cause in 1792 when a false rumour spread through the Caribbean that the Prussians and Austrians had restored the French monarchy. A British colony only ten years before, it was considered likely that Tobago could be retaken with relative ease. Sir John Laforey and Major-General Cornelius Cuyler sailed from Barbados in early

April, marched across the island and assaulted the citadel guarding the island's capital, Port Louis. The citadel was stormed and taken after a fierce struggle. Tobago fell and thus the British colony at Barbados was made safe from its only French threat to windward.

The next target was Martinique, farther north and a little to leeward of Barbados. Like Tobago, Martinique had also declared for the Bourbons in 1792 and now, in the spring of 1793, was in open revolt against the Republic. But Martinique was a much more significant island than Tobago. It was a great deal larger and on the westerly, sheltered shore lay Fort Royal, the main French naval base in the West Indies. And what a naval base it was. It had an impressive arsenal and, crucially, a magnificent deep-water harbour that could shelter large numbers of ships during the hurricane season that threatened the Caribbean every year from June until November. The Royal Navy had no comparison in the Windward Islands. To take Martinique would be to control the Caribbean Sea. With no base from which to launch operations and maintain a fleet, the French would be but vassals to British seapower. The French Royalists were even happy to make this happen as they needed help in their isolated island civil war against the Republicans, and to this end they approached British forces. The British responded with food, ammunition and 1,100 troops but it was far too little to turn back the Republican tide and after a brief and muddled campaign in which Royalists succeeded in attacking each other and the scale of the challenge became clear, the British fled the island on 22 June 1793, with almost six thousand Royalist refugees. It was Toulon all over again: the opportunity to take a critical French naval base had been bungled and all the navy could do was help desperate Frenchmen scramble to safety.

Several hundred miles to leeward a similar opportunity presented itself on Saint Domingue where the white plantation owners were fighting against a confused but rising tide of white Republicans, slaves and mulattos. The Republicans were fighting for the Republic; the slaves for their freedom; and the mulattos for social equality. The civil war in France had thus created its own unique problems and divisions throughout a Caribbean that was populated by a combustive mix of white plantation owners known as *grands blancs*, poor working-class whites known as *petits blancs*, blacks who had won their freedom, mixed race 'mulattos' and black slaves. Something like 40,000 blacks per year were imported into Saint Domingue and the black population in 1794, a small percentage of which had secured manumission, numbered something in the region of half a million. White Frenchmen, by contrast, numbered no more than 40,000. As one commentator noted, the whites slept '*au pied du Vésuve*' – at the foot of Vesuvius.[19]

Fuelling this fire were the revolutionary principles of freedom and equality for all, which did not fit with the labour demands of the colony or the economic demands of France. To abolish slavery in the Caribbean would not only ruin the colonies but also the west-facing French Atlantic ports such as Nantes that depended on the slave trade. The Jacobin Republic therefore stalled on its promise of emancipation for Caribbean slaves. The issue was more clear-cut for the slaves actually living and working in the Caribbean and they had already demonstrated their power in devastating revolts both on Martinique and in Saint Domingue in 1790 and 1791. In Saint Domingue alone the revolt of 1791 left 180 sugar plantations and 900 coffee, cotton and indigo estates devastated and 200 whites and 10,000 slaves dead.[20]

Faced with such potential violence and with a growing desire to secure autonomy from France, the plantation owners of Saint Domingue sought British help. British support for the owners therefore neatly associated British interference in the French Caribbean civil war with the continuation of slavery and so the British found themselves facing not only a host of frenzied revolutionaries but also an army of blacks fighting for their freedom. And to make matters even worse, that army had found itself a natural leader in Toussaint Louverture, once a slave himself, who had been blessed with military genius.

However, the extent of the problem was not clearly understood in the autumn of 1793 when the plantation owners had first cried for help. The British responded as they had at Martinique with troops, food and ammunition. In direct contrast to the failure at Martinique, British forces under Commodore Ford were initially successful in Saint Domingue, capturing Grand Anse and St Nicholas Mole, a powerful naval station. The reports of victory were met with such delight in London that they were proclaimed by cannon from the Tower. In mid-May 1,860 more men arrived to boost British forces and they set their sights firmly on the capital, Port-au-Prince, which had the added advantage of overlooking a harbour that was then protecting a cluster of valuable merchantmen.[21] By now the main expedition from England had arrived and it quickly set about its business. The strategy was two-pronged: there would be several campaigns launched against French colonies supported by a parallel war on French trade. The French presence in the Caribbean was going to be both crushed and strangled.

The British force arrived with the trade winds in the south of the Caribbean before making their way northwards. The ongoing struggle in Saint Domingue, therefore, had to wait before any reinforcements could arrive. Piqued, and perhaps a little humiliated from the failure of the first incursion on Martinique, the new expedition fell on Fort Royal, Martinique, in early February 1794. Six weeks or so later the island was in British hands. With the window for campaigning so restricted by the sickly season of the high summer months when the mosquitoes swarmed, there was no time to lose, and the expedition moved on. St Lucia fell next and then Guadeloupe with its island-dependencies Marie-Galante and Desiderada. British victory was absolute: the French had been driven from the southerly Windward Islands. Jervis, commanding the Leeward Island station, wrote triumphantly to the Admiralty: 'I have now the greatest satisfaction informing you of the entire reduction of the French in these seas.'[22]

The French still retained a presence in the north-west Caribbean, however, and the early British successes on Saint Domingue were never consolidated. The main British force remained in the Leeward Islands to safeguard the new conquests and to make matters worse the Royalist French began to get more than a little frustrated with the behaviour of their new allies.

Everyone in England was aware of the wealth that derived from the West Indies. The capture of a mountain of treasure at Havana in 1762 was still very much within living memory and it is quite possible that many of those who sailed in current expeditions had taken part in that earlier exploit. In the American War many more English sailors made good money from the capture of St Lucia in 1778 and Tobago in 1781 and all of these campaigns were seen as part of a great tradition of British plunderers stretching back to Drake in the mid-sixteenth century. In 1793 Jervis and Grey keenly realised the opportunities and once the ball of British victory was set rolling with the capture of Martinique they did everything in their power to take as much from the West Indies as possible in the shortest period of time. The British Caribbean forces of 1793 became a systematic plundering machine to rival anything unleashed by Napoleon or the Nazis.

They staked a claim to everything that was French or even in any way connected to France. Confiscated arms, ammunition and military stores were all sold to the British government in the standard way, but Jervis and Grey took it more than one step farther. They claimed the produce of all captured French Royalist estates on the basis that they were now in Republican hands, and therefore lawful prizes. The high value of Caribbean goods ensured this alone was worth a vast fortune but they also claimed *all* property in islands surrendered to the British and all personal property of those who had raised arms against them. To get around the obviously impractical nature of such a claim, they graciously made it clear that they would accept payments in lieu. St Lucia alone was forced to pay £150,000, though Jervis and Grey granted them the benevolence of paying in three annual instalments to allow them to raise the cash. When it came to enemy shipping Jervis and Grey were equally creative and detained all French ships carrying colonial trade of any description to any location. This went far beyond any previous attempt to regulate maritime trade in time of war. One French official claimed: 'there is not an officer amongst them but studies plunder more than the art of war' and the figures that survive easily bear out this claim. One young frigate captain, Josias Rogers, made no less than £10,000 in five weeks alone in early 1794 – about seventy years of basic sea pay.

The Americans were equally enraged because a great deal of the trade that was seized by British frigate captains was actually American.

Franco-American trade was then booming as French Caribbean colonies had relaxed their own self-imposed trade isolation to boost cash flow. American merchant ships were chased down relentlessly by British frigates commanded by young, ambitious men on the make. Their goods and ships were then claimed as a prize for abetting the French in one way or another. Carrying French produce was enough to condemn a ship and its cargo. The British government was unquestionably embarrassed by the behaviour of Jervis and Grey, who never received the peerages they might well have expected for such a service. Instead they were explicitly instructed to stop the pillaging and the government even took learned advice on the legality of the impromptu prize courts that Jervis and Grey were using to rubber-stamp all seizures.

Their behaviour created a wave of bitter anger in America that swiftly found its way back to London, via the eastern seaboard ports. An American envoy was sent to Britain demanding redress and Congress started to flex its muscles by ordering its armed forces to mobilise. They made preparations to raise 80,000 men and armed two ships of 44 guns and four of 36. The British were so alarmed that they diverted precious Caribbean forces to Bermuda in case of American attack. The British consul in Virginia wrote to London with some restraint: 'the situation of this country is very critical and they are not pleased with Great Britain'[23] before going on to explain the reality of American 'neutrality' as he saw it. 'All the states are warmly attached and partial to a fault in favour of France' he wrote, 'and each state violates the neutrality declared to subsiste between it and the Belligerent powers dayly by aiding and assisting the French in every respect... they daringly insult the British flag and subjects with impunity...'[24] No doubt he had in mind the peculiar situation of Charles Knowles of the *Daedalus*, who had been effectively trapped in the Chesapeake by the arrival of a French fleet. The presence of so many French sailors, afire with revolution and armed to the teeth, emboldened the Americans. They marched through the streets sporting French-style revolutionary cockades, revolutionary flags, trees of liberty and 'with their faithful allies arm in arm'.

Both sides then spent several weeks egging each other on to bolder affronts to the trapped, outnumbered British. At one stage the *Daedalus* fired a salute to welcome aboard the Mayor of Norfolk and there were reports of shot being discovered in the town. The Member of Congress for Virginia was quick to claim that 'the dignity of the US was wounded by the British frigate at Norfolk which had wantonly fired on the town'.[25] One French captain wrote to Knowles, who refused to reply, and there was a subsequent confrontation as the French captain was pulled over to the *Daedalus* to demand an explanation for the 'insult'. Knowles said he knew nothing of any insult upon which the Frenchman appeared calmer and asked to come aboard but Knowles again refused.[26] Knowles was so cautious because he had just received fresh intelligence from the captain of another French ship, the *Ambuscade*, anchored in nearby Hampton Roads, that his captain 'could not be responsible for the conduct of his crew' if they came close to the *Daedalus*. Knowles had also received warning of a well-planned night attack which never materialised, but caused Knowles to take elaborate measures to defend his ship from boarders.

Neither Knowles nor any of his crew felt safe enough to go ashore as the French were known to have incited the Americans to violence on numerous occasions, and this state of incarceration lasted six months, from 27 November 1793 to 30 May 1794. Knowles was deeply impressed with his crew. There was 'not the least dissatisfaction on board the ship' during this period of inactivity and tension. The waters around the Chesapeake were quite bubbling with menace and intrigue.[27]

The consul concluded from all of this that: 'A watchful eye should be held over them [the Americans], for rest assured nothing but the success of the combined armies and fleets, have detered them from waging war against Great Britain, and her Allies [and] which they will most certainly do, whenever a gleam of hope for their success appears.'[28] In subsequent letters his tone became more severe and soon quite desperate. He wrote 'The people here are very much enraged threatening the British with all kinds of evils, confiscation, death &c. as they conceive the embargo to be the harbinger of that war many of them have long been desiring.' In the same letter he asked to be given early news of any hostility as 'to be a prisoner here would, of all ills, be to me the most terrible'.[29]

Overall, then, the Americans were officially neutral in their relationship with both France and England, but powerful voices were speaking out in support of the French. Robespierre had found a willing trading partner with whom he could exchange French gold for American flour, and in December he ordered Rear-Admiral Pierre-Jean Vanstabel to sail for America to bring it home. He sailed on Christmas Eve with two fast and powerful 74-gunners, ideal ships for convoy protection that combined the strength of a line-of-battle ship with good manoeuvrability and speed. They could defend against an organised enemy fleet attack; they could chase and harry fast enemy predators; they could shepherd their own convoy, patrol around it and lead the way in hostile waters.

Vanstabel was a very good choice to lead the escort. He was formerly an officer in the Compagnie des Indes, the French East India Company, who had then joined the Navy and fought with distinction in the American War of Independence as a commerce raider. Like Villaret, Vanstabel was one of the very few officers who had succeeded in retaining discipline on board his ship, the 74-gun *Tigre*, during the Brest Mutiny. He had caught the eye of Jeanbon and had been rapidly promoted from captain to rear-admiral. In November he had been given command of a squadron that sailed from Brest with instructions to intercept a British convoy with supplies for the rebel army in the Vendée. Vanstabel took eleven prizes and successfully evaded Howe.[30]

The chaos in the Caribbean, meanwhile, had also driven French West Indies ships up the eastern seaboard of America where they loitered for news of a convoy preparing to sail to France with an armed escort. When Vanstabel arrived on 12 February the displaced Indiamen flocked to the safety he offered. Meanwhile an envoy raced to Philadelphia, arriving twelve days later.[31] The convoy that would sail to France from America would carry a mixed bag of flour, grain and Caribbean wealth to boost the French war chest, feed its people and in doing so shore up Robespierre's political position. With every French and American merchantman that arrived in the Chesapeake to fill its hungry hold with flour, Robespierre felt more sure of laying the ghost of Georges Danton to rest. All he had to do now was to get the unwieldy convoy, some 156 ships strong, that Bertrand de Barère, a member of the Committee of Public Safety, described as the 'food-bearing argosy', to France.[32] But news soon reached London of the squadron's arrival, the gathering merchant ships, and of the five million livres in gold placed in the hands of Jean-Antoine Fauchet, the new French minister in America.[33] Robespierre's secret was out.

By the time that the convoy was ready to sail it was reportedly worth £1.5 million and we know from other sources that it contained 67,000 barrels of flour, hides, bacon and salt-beef, and that the holds of the Indiamen were stuffed with 11,241 barrels of coffee, 7,163 barrels of sugar, cotton, cocoa, rice and indigo. There was so much to carry that even the warships loaded trade goods. The 74-gun *Tigre* carried 672 barrels of flour.[34] The ships were also packed with military and commercial passengers and high-ranking diplomats – it is too often overlooked that this convoy was valuable for more than its trade goods alone.[35] Twelve men-of-war escorted the merchantmen.[36] The convoy was so valuable that Consul Hamilton firmly believed that Vanstabel's squadron was but the tip of the iceberg, and that 'the whole navy of France will prepare to meet and secure this convoy which must be of the highest importance to them'.[37] Knowles added to the intelligence, believing that the convoy would either keep far to the northward and aim for Cape Clear in Ireland or, as he thought more probable, they would 'keep very little to the northward of the western islands and then steer towards the bay of Biscay for the meridian of the mouth of the Garonne for Bourdeaux'.[38]

The British government's response to this intelligence was immediate and unequivocal. The capture of the convoy was considered 'an object of the most urgent importance to the success of the present war' and Howe was immediately ordered to sea. With him went a powerful squadron of six 74-gunners and three frigates under the command of Rear-Admiral George Montagu, who had served with a good measure of distinction in the American War under Howe, and who had fought with particular courage at the capture of New York.[39] Montagu was under orders to detach from the main fleet when clear of the Channel and to head south across Biscay, escorting British convoys bound for the West and East Indies. When both convoys had been shepherded clear of the threat from the French Atlantic ports, Montagu was to sail north again, to cruise in a vertical line between Cape Ortegal and the latitude of Belle Isle in an attempt to trap Vanstabel's convoy as it approached the French coast.

Howe, meanwhile, was to cruise directly off Brest to watch in case the main fleet came out to protect the inbound convoy. If they did, then Howe was to pounce. The destruction of French seapower was central to British war planning and the convoy thus presented an opportunity to attack the French on both military and economic fronts simultaneously. Because of the instability within France, British success in either respect would also cause significant political damage and thus threaten the ability of the French to continue their war.

If the general sense of the intelligence was accurate, however, it was also very vague in detail and very late. Jeanbon believed that the British knew everything: the departure date, route and arrival location, that '*tout étoit connu*,'[40] but he was wrong. The reports did not of course arrive from America for several weeks and none of them carried the type of detailed information that the British craved because no one had been able to determine either when the convoy was due to sail or where it was destined to make land. With no knowledge of the date of departure or arrival the British would be forced to cruise for an extended period of time in hostile waters and their ability to do so was limited by the quantity of food, or more importantly beer and water, that could be stowed. Four to six weeks was usually the most that could reasonably be expected. To our eyes that seems time enough to intercept a convoy, but in terms of eighteenth-century naval trans-Atlantic interception operations it was a very short period indeed. The crossing could take anywhere between six and eight weeks and convoys could easily be delayed for a fortnight or more because of foul weather or, as in the case of this convoy, iced-in harbours and then foul weather.

It was perfectly possible, therefore, that a British squadron could cruise for a full month in the knowledge that a convoy had been preparing for sea some weeks previously, but fail to intercept it and be forced home for running repairs and a fresh intake of victuals. Such a turnaround would take some time. The squadron would first have to cruise home in close formation, to protect against enemy attack, at around four knots, that is four nautical miles *per hour*, a fair average for such a fleet. Thus a voyage might easily take a week from the centre of Biscay. Another full week could then be spent in port repairing and revictualling and then another week to get back on station. So the intercepting squadron would be off station for fully three weeks, easily enough time for the enemy to sneak past. If, then, the convoy had been delayed by a fortnight, suddenly a full five weeks of uncertainty could creep into an interception operation, almost the same amount of time that it could take to make the crossing.

The second problem was destination. This was relatively easy for French fleets trying to intercept English convoys because so many of them went up-Channel, and the rest, bound for Bristol, Liverpool and Glasgow, sailed between the north coast of Cornwall and the southern coast of Ireland. In most cases a squadron cruising off Land's End would be well-placed to intercept any inward- or outward-bound British convoy. Navigation in and out of the Channel was particularly restricted because of the position of the Scilly Isles, and geographical narrowness in the Age of Sail meant predictability. Even the handiest warships were terribly restricted in their manoeuvrability and the lumbering merchantmen represented a hazard to themselves and all other shipping in confined waters. Complex manoeuvre near shore was out of the question for large convoys. Their track was determined by wind, weather and geography and therefore was in some sense predictable. What made this slightly more difficult for the Royal Navy was that the French had a choice between multiple destinations. It was out of the question that Vanstabel would head for one of the French Channel ports because none had the capacity to harbour so many merchantmen in addition to their usual shipping. The Channel ports were also subject to big tidal ranges; most dried out completely at low water. Moreover it was unlikely that a large fleet would ever get past the British guarding the Channel entrance. The Atlantic coast of France, however, is some four hundred miles from tip to toe, and there were several realistic destinations for

1. The memorial to James Montagu in Westminster Abbey, London.

2. The memorial to the *Vengeur* in the Panthéon, Paris.

3. The execution of Louis XVI.

4. Admiral Earl Howe.

5. Vice-Admiral Villaret de Joyeuse.

6. Maximilien de Robespierre.

7. Jeanbon Saint-André.

8. Georges-Jacques Danton on his way to execution. The artist clearly captures his extraordinary physique and rough features. He urged the executioner to show his head to the people.

9. The Battle of Scheveningen, 31 July 1653.

10. A view of Brest in 1794 by Jean-François Hue, an artist who produced a series of views of French dockyards.

11. The Union flag from the *Queen Charlotte*. It measures approx. 6 x 4m. Note the pre-1801 pattern of the flag: there is no St Patrick's cross. The flag can be seen in the Loutherbourg painting (fig. 16).

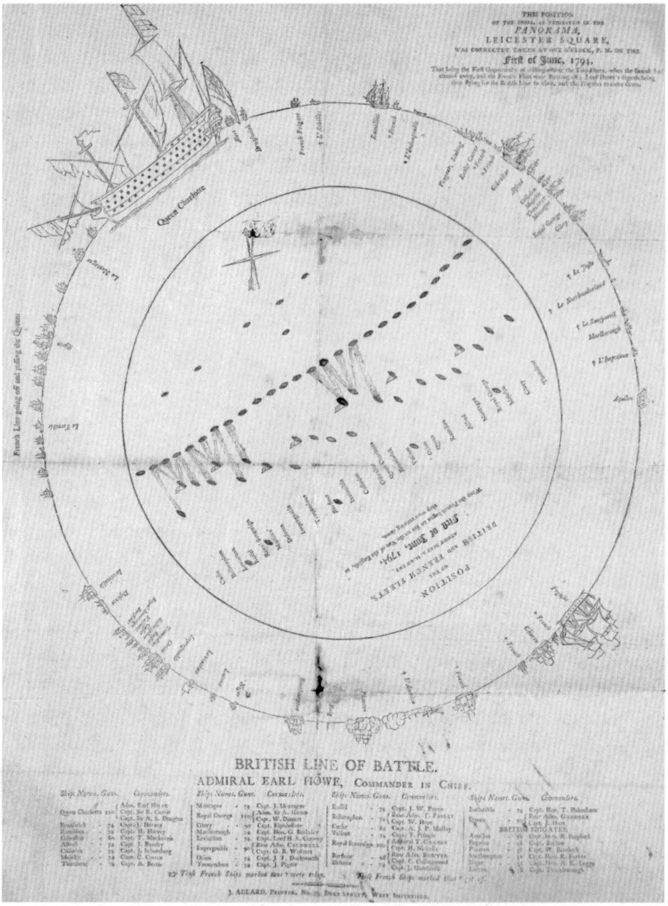

12. A schematic view of Barker's Panorama based on the position of the fleets at 1 p.m. on 1 June.

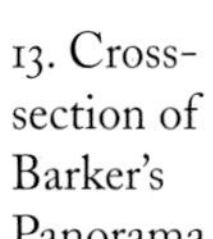

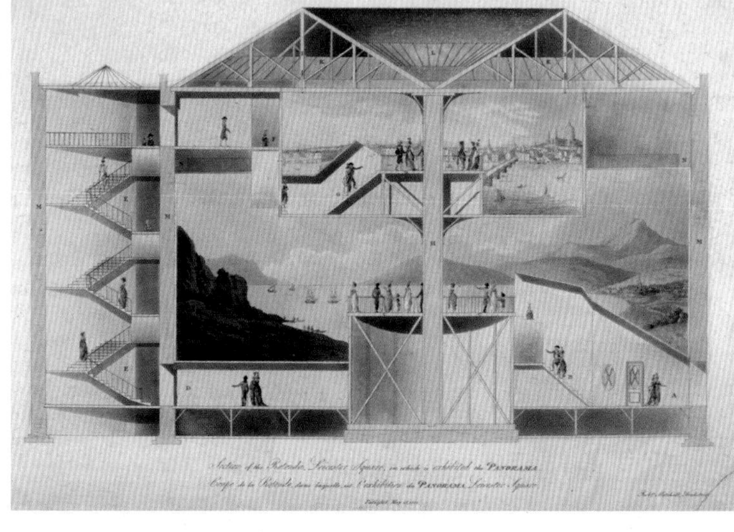

13. Cross-section of Barker's Panorama.

Vanstabel's convoy. Brest itself was an obvious choice, but so too were several other ports on the west coast such as Lorient or Rochefort with its magnificent anchorage in Aix Roads, Bordeaux and even Bayonne far to the south.

With such difficulties it is a wonder that such interception operations were ever even attempted, let alone successful. Where the nature of sailing warfare raised its own distinctive problems, however, so did it provide its own solutions. The first thing to realise is exactly how big these convoys were. Whichever estimate is taken, Vanstabel's convoy consisted of well over a hundred ships. While warships with trained and experienced captains might be able to keep station with one another at only one or two cables' lengths (two to four hundred yards) apart, no merchantman would ever risk such proximity. Even if gathered together in a 'tight' group, every merchant skipper would like to keep at least an eighth of a mile from his nearest neighbour, astern, ahead or abeam. Each ship, therefore, could easily be surrounded by half a mile square of searoom, and usually much more: 110 ships could therefore cover at least sixty square miles of searoom.

Now consider an intercepting squadron. They would spread as far out as possible to cover as much searoom as possible. Ships, using their sails, could keep in touch and communicate with each other over a distance of twenty miles on a fine day. A hunting squadron, moreover, would be sure to send ahead fast ships who could confidently relay any visual contact back to their 'mother' fleet. So too would the escorting squadron of the vulnerable convoy. One needs to see the fleets as elastic bodies whose presence could expand and contract as necessary. In between each body of ships, moreover, lay not an empty wilderness but a surprisingly highly populated stretch of water. As in the desert there are tracks, caravans, nomads, farmers and oases, so in the Atlantic are there common sea lanes, fishermen and merchants. When the French fleet left the Chesapeake, rumour spread like a blast of air before an explosion. Thus with links of ships spread out ahead, astern and abeam of both the convoy and hunting squadron, and with a good educated guess, finding a convoy in the middle of the Atlantic was not so much the search for a needle in a haystack as for a mosquito in a large sealed room. Mosquitoes may be tiny but it is not difficult to tell when one is around, whether from the bites or the high-pitched humming of their wings. Neither is it too hard to find them: one looks near the lights, windows, or on your own skin. Montagu had been set a considerable challenge, therefore, but was not by any means doomed to failure.

Just like the British, the French forces in Brest were also divided in order to play numerous hands at once, but unlike the British the French had broken their fleet into three. The main fleet was in Brest. A smaller division was at Cancale just east of St Malo for the planned invasion of England. The final detachment of five ships of the line and a number of frigates and corvettes was under the command of Rear-Admiral Joseph-Marie Nielly, who had left Rochefort on 6 May to bring in Vanstabel, just as Montagu was sent out to catch him. The strategic situation as the French convoy approached Europe, therefore, was very complicated. There were a limited number of participants but each had a magnified ability to influence events, not unlike the endgame of a chess match. There were in fact six main pieces. Just off Brest was Howe in the main British Channel Fleet; in Brest was Villaret with the main French force; in Cancale lay Rear-Admiral Pierre-François Cornic; cruising to the south were Montagu and Nielly, both hunting for the final, crucial chess piece, Vanstabel's convoy.

Mixed into this equation was a convoy of Dutch merchantmen and an English convoy, bound for Newfoundland from the Channel Islands. The way that these participants interacted with one another to produce the final showdown on 1 June is a powerful lesson in the course of naval history in the Age of Sail. These simple but dislocated elements came together with occasional skill, more frequent blunder, a scattering of both good and bad luck and a large dash of unpredictability from sea, wind and weather to create something quite extraordinary, something with the power to change history.

The starting point of it all was Howe's cruise on 2 May. The mighty Channel Fleet nosed out from St Helens, the anchorage protected by the Isle of Wight. Her primary aim was to escort a fleet of merchantmen as they left the Channel. The warships quickly formed into their predetermined order of two columns and a detached squadron of four of the fastest ships of the line. The merchant convoys, one destined for India, one for the Caribbean and one for Newfoundland, nestled in between the two columns like a shoal of anchovies and more merchantmen joined from isolated ports as the fleet moved down-Channel. A detailed and rare fleet order issued by Howe survives that carefully describes and illustrates the intended disposition of the various fleets.[41] One hundred and forty-eight ships sailed on that day; a grand armada of ninety-nine merchantmen and forty-nine warships. Howe was well aware that the French ships, class to class, were larger than the British, and so he took no 64-gunners with him, although several were available.[42] Instead, the backbone of the battlefleet was made up of sixteen powerful two-decked 74-gunners and two 80-gunners, reinforced throughout the chain by three powerful First Rates of 100 guns and three Second Rates of 98 guns.

It has long been accepted by historians of the coming battle that the French were inexperienced and perhaps poorly manned, but less research has been directed at the British fleet. Luckily, however, the muster books from the ships that fought the battle all survive in the National Archives, which means that we can get a detailed breakdown of how well manned the British ships were as they sailed to war in the spring of 1794, and the answer is surprising.

With the exception of the *Glory*, Captain John Elphinstone, *all* of the British ships were undermanned. The worst-manned ships were the frigates *Phaeton* and *Aquilon* with 78 per cent of their complement. The worst-manned First Rate was the *Royal George* (80 per cent) but the *Queen Charlotte* and *Royal Sovereign* were little better, both with 86 per cent.

All of the 74s were more than 80 per cent full, the worst being the *Valiant* at 80 per cent, the best the fast-sailing *Bellerophon* under the dashing Thomas Pasley, with 92 per cent of her complement. The *Brunswick*, though it was later claimed by one of her sailors that she was one of the most weakly manned ships,[43] was actually relatively well manned at 85 per cent. But consider it like this: nine of the ships were missing one sixth of their crew or more, and as many as twenty were missing a seventh or more. For the largest ships this meant being well over 100 men short. The *Royal Sovereign* was 128 men short; the flagship 127 short; the *Royal George* a painful 172 men short of complement. The *Queen*, which went on to fight so bravely, was 148 men short. Between them, the First and Second Rates alone were 766 men short and the Third Rates, the backbone of the fleet, and already outgunned by the French equivalents which mounted roughly ten more, heavier guns per ship, were 1,629 men short.[44]

These figures, bad as they are, in fact disguise part of the problem as some of the men mustered were in fact soldiers, drafted to make up the numbers. The *Queen*, for example, already 148 men short, actually had 151 soldiers on board. Four hundred and fifteen soldiers from the Queen's Second Royal Regiment served on board the *Queen Charlotte*, *Russell*, *Defence*, *Royal George*, and *Majestic*. More soldiers served from the 28th and 61st (later known as the Gloucester regiment) and the 29th (Worcestershire) and 69th (Welsh) regiments and those of the 69th that served on board the *Audacious* were notably young and inexperienced. 'Not above one in twenty' of the sailors on board the *Gibraltar* 'ever saw a gun fired…' before the coming battle.[45] The massive underlying manning problem was not helped by the preceding years of peace as some of the equipment had not been maintained properly, and the sailors were the ones to suffer. Aboard the *Caesar*, for example, a rotten rope snapped as a topmast was hoisted aloft and the unfortunate Alexander Kean was crushed to death.[46]

There has also been a relaxed approach from British historians concerning the level of British gunnery practice in the run-up to war: just a general assumption that the Royal Navy worked hard on their gunnery while the French navy did not. The manning figures certainly suggest that some serious practice would be required to snap the new recruits into shape and teach the crews of all of the ships – with the exception of the well-manned *Glory* – to work their guns and sails with reduced crews. Once more we are blessed, however, as the surviving ships' logs, among observations of tide and weather, recorded gunnery practice. Again, the results are surprising.

The British ships did practice, but it was by no means set in stone how regularly it was to be done. In the six weeks or so between 1 April and 14 May when the fleet left Spithead, three ships did no gunnery practice at all (the *Thunderer*, *Ramillies* and *Venus*) and six other ships only practised once. Nine of the fleet, therefore, that is just under a third, had either had no gunnery drill or had exercised just once recently, when they left to face the French. Only six ships practised more than five times: the *Marlborough*, *Impregnable*, *Pegasus*, *Queen Charlotte*, *Barfleur* and *Montagu*. The ship that practised the most, the *Marlborough*, with eleven sessions, did so on three occasions more than her nearest rival, the *Impregnable*. There were no set times for practice though there is a noticeable pattern of ships drilling on 11 and 25 April (when there was a general signal to do so which was not obeyed by all ships), and there is a notably increased pattern of practice from 25 to 30 April, two weeks before they sailed. Howe had his men practise their firing repeatedly just before they left. The entire crew of the *Queen Charlotte* were exercised on 17, 22 and 30 April, on 1 May and then, on both 7 and 9 May, those who had been identified in earlier gunnery practices as 'awkward men' were drilled once more. Ben Caldwell had his men in the *Impregnable* practise firing volleys, and when they were finished he had them double-shot every one of their broadside guns so that they were ready to meet the French.

As well as training their men at gunnery, a few, but by no means all captains, exercised their inexperienced men in the rig. The *Valiant*, *Orion*, *Royal Sovereign* and *Queen Charlotte* all did this to some degree, the *Queen Charlotte* the most, four times, no doubt to set a good example.

Unfortunately no detailed sources survive from the French navy to compare their preparation, nor has any work been done on any other eighteenth-century battle to provide us with any figures to compare. But it is clear that, while some British ships did practise, others did not, and the level of practice for all ships, with the possible exception of the flagship, is markedly less than one might suspect. By no means were the British sailors highly trained automatons when it came to war. An interesting entry in the diary of Midshipman William Dillon makes this quite clear. As the *Defence* punched through the swell on the way to Biscay the sailors filled cartridges with powder from the magazine but Midshipman Dillon was overcome with a compelling sense of dread that the ship would explode because of an accident in the magazine caused by carelessness or incompetence. He even went to oversee the operation to calm himself, much to the entertainment of the crew. Despite their jovial teasing, however, the fear of an explosion that night stayed with Dillon for the rest of his life.[47]

Howe certainly instilled in his fleet a great deal of professional pride in the sending and receiving of signals. We know that Ben Caldwell of the *Impregnable* exercised his men in both just before the fleet left Spithead, and we also know from Edward Codrington, Howe's signal lieutenant, that there was a great deal of good-natured competition amongst the fleet. At one stage, the beady-eyed and knowledgeable signal lieutenant of the repeating-frigate *Pegasus*, a man who had been trained by the exacting Codrington, repeated a signal before the *Queen Charlotte* herself had finished making it. Sir Roger Curtis, captain of the *Queen Charlotte*, exclaimed 'D— that ship, how could she know what we meant?' Codrington was nearby and simply said 'Thank you, Sir Roger'.[48]

This was also the opportunity to study the elaborate secret signalling codes that would be used to identify strange ships. Flags of differing shape and colour were hoisted at different parts of the rig to identify friend from foe and the system was changed daily with ten different permutations of flag colour and location. The codebooks themselves were kept in a lead box to be thrown overboard in case of capture.[49] Roger Curtis of the *Queen Charlotte* also took the time to survey the surgeon's stores to check he had everything necessary and to hand.[50] In some respects, therefore, the British ships were well prepared but in others they were not. If on the one hand their communication skills were impressive, on the other they were certainly undermanned, many of the crews inexperienced, and drilled neither in sail handling nor gunnery to the level that one might expect. There was not time left for any more practice, however. Once past the Lizard, the most southerly point of Britain, on 4 May Howe detached Montagu with the merchant convoys and he headed for the French coast.

Villaret, in the meantime, had been sitting tight in Brest, waiting for some spark to move him in one direction or another. He hoped that a frigate would come dashing into the Rade de Brest with news that Nielly had sighted Vanstabel and had escorted him safely to port. What he got, on 5 May, were fast, elusive British frigates sailing deep into his port to count his force and assess his strength.[51] It was a devastating blow. The British Channel Fleet darkened the horizon. The eyes of the British sailors, meanwhile, constantly scanned the southern and western horizons in the hope that the homeward-bound convoy and its escort would stumble into their path. They were exceptionally jittery. On 18 May they chased eight strange sail '& I assure you we was in a very great bustle' wrote William Dillon. The strangers turned out to be a homeward-bound British squadron under Admiral MacBride. Again on 21 May they saw several strange lights and beat to quarters to intercept some English vessels that had been captured by the French. One of the captured Englishmen was still being sailed by her captain because the French prize crew were so deficient in seamanship.[52] They saw enemy ships almost daily and gradually built up a detailed picture of what was unfolding beyond the western horizon.[53]

On 21 May, however, Howe was forced off-station by prolonged westerly winds that threatened to drive his fleet onto the rocks protecting the approaches to Brest like sharpened stakes around a castle. Howe fled to the safety of the open sea, leaving the way clear for Villaret who, now aware that the British main fleet was far out at sea, had no choice but to make sail. His orders, received directly from Robespierre, were unequivocal. Villaret confessed to an English sailor much later in life that 'At his peril he was not to allow the great convoy to fall into the hands of Lord Howe. If he did so, his head should answer for it under the guillotine.'[54]

Only the day before, the corvette *Le Papillon* had arrived in Brest from America with news that the convoy would be arriving in twelve days or so.[55] With the British at sea in strength that convoy was now clearly under great threat and so too was Nielly's force, which was greatly outnumbered by Howe. Villaret gave the order to weigh anchor and the ships of the powerful French fleet turned their bows toward the wide Atlantic.

The Committee of Public Safety was so anxious about the fleet's behaviour that Jeanbon himself sailed on board the flagship where his presence '...impassive as the law, severe as justice, indulgent to the weak but inexorable against the presumptuous... will distribute acts of authority with which it is entrusted'.[56] These were his own words and one has to admire his style. His presence was an umbilical cord running right back to the womb of Jacobin power. Few admirals in history have been subjected to such immediate political scrutiny, none with any pleasure and few with any success. Prieur du Marne, another member of the CPS, who boarded with Jeanbon and stayed on board to the last possible moment, left amid an emotional scene of nationalistic fervour. He wrote:

> You would have been enchanted by the imposing and touching spectacle presented by the departure of our squadron. Joy and impatience to measure themselves against the infamous English were painted on all faces. The most beautiful order of sailing, the voices of an immense people lining the shore at the goulet, and the thousand-times-repeated cries of 'vive la République' were the presage of our success.[57]

Prieur raced ashore, into a carriage and back to Paris to inform Robespierre and the rest of the Committee that the great Brest fleet, risen from the ashes of revolution and mutiny by the whip hand of the Jacobins, was at sea.[58] With the Brest fleet at sea, the fates of both Robespierre and the Republic had suddenly been cast off and were drifting to an unknown destination with Villaret at the helm and Jeanbon looking over his shoulder. As the sun set, the lighthouse of Saint-Mathieu ignited its flame and the ships of the French navy followed suit, each lighting a lamp before forming into three lines and heading out into the Atlantic.[59] On the very same day, thirty administrators, condemned for treachery to the Revolution and who had been imprisoned in the chateau at Brest for ten months, were taken down to the harbour and guillotined. A vast monument in the city's cemetery now recalls their fate. Nothing else demonstrates Jeanbon's style better than this piece of staged theatre. The men died to encourage the crews and to frighten those left behind, but more than anything it was a human sacrifice to the Gods of War.

Vanstabel, meanwhile, was already halfway through his voyage. He had been careful to leave behind a 40-gun frigate and a corvette to prevent Knowles in the stranded *Daedalus* from flying from the Chesapeake across the sea to warn Howe.[60] Soon the ripples of Vanstabel's presence began to be felt by the waiting squadrons.

On 15 May Montagu intercepted a French warship, *Le Maire Guitton*, in company with a number of merchantmen that soon turned out to be English. Under interrogation the captain revealed that, as part of Admiral Nielly's squadron, they had captured the British ships from the Newfoundland convoy along with their escort, HMS *Castor*, and they were now heading back to port. The Frenchmen also revealed that Nielly's purpose was to cruise for the convoy. They were 'very backward in communicating'[61] details about the strength of Vanstabel's escorting force, but they did let slip a number of crucial pieces of information. Firstly, that Nielly was under orders to cruise in a very specific location to rendezvous with Vanstabel: between 45 to 47 degrees north and 2 degrees east or west of Tenerife. Secondly, they confessed that Neilly had already been patrolling for nearly a month. Montagu, therefore, had discovered that the convoy was imminent and he even knew where to look for it. He immediately dispatched the *Venus* to Howe with this fresh intelligence and headed north toward the convoy rendezvous point.[62]

Howe, meanwhile, and still in ignorance of Montagu's new intelligence, raced back to Brest as soon as the weather improved to continue his surveillance of the French fleet. But this time the anchorage was empty. Villaret was out and the two fleets had passed each other close enough for the French to hear the bells and drums of the British fog signals.[63] On board the British fleet news that the French were out '... caused the greatest excitement... and nothing was heard but bringing the French to action'.[64]

Howe's immediate concern was Montagu. Alone, Montagu's squadron would be easy prey for Villaret. Nielly was also still out there somewhere and perhaps had even united with Vanstabel. Inexorably, however, the pieces came together and Howe swiftly realised that Villaret was close enough to be caught. Howe headed west, his frigates running ahead like hounds crossing for the scent.

Villaret by then had intercepted a Dutch convoy bound for Lisbon and made prizes of all the ships. Howe in turn intercepted them a few days later and, knowing that Villaret was at large, abandoned his practice of sending merchant prizes back to England, as he had at the start of the cruise. He simply took off the crews and burned the ships.[65] The pattern was repeated regularly over the next few days. Every merchant ship that was captured by the British was burned and every merchant ship captured by the French was sent home with a prize crew. Perhaps nothing is more indicative of the different mindsets of the fleets at this stage. Howe was unwilling to deplete his force by a single man for the benefit of monetary gain while the French fleet, already undermanned, further reduced their capability by sending sailors away on prizes.

It is unclear exactly how many prizes were destroyed in this way, but figures of fourteen,[66] fifteen[67] and eighteen[68] have all survived. Many of the British took this badly: some were destroying the fortunes they had joined the navy to make. Midshipman William Dillon saw the magnificent *Demourisque* destroyed, a sight which 'made my heart ache when I saw the flames spreading over her; in fact hurling her to destruction'.[69] The closer Howe came to the French fleet, the more ships he came across in their wake. Two French corvettes even stumbled into the midst of the British fleet.[70] It raised an interesting problem on some British ships as they were now heading toward the main French fleet with significant numbers of French prisoners on board, taking up their space, eating their food and drinking their beer. The ships' musters reveal that the *Tremendous* went into battle with forty-five prisoners on board, the *Valiant* with sixty, the *Impregnable* with fifty-five and the *Invincible* with thirty-four.[71]

As the days of May ran out so the symphony reached its crescendo. Howe closed on Villaret, Villaret and Nielly closed on Vanstabel and Montagu closed on them all. With more than 170 ships in a relatively small area of sea and with so much at stake, it was simply a matter of time before something happened.

# 6.

# The First Contact

At 9, saw a strange fleet SSE

Master's Log of the *Queen Charlotte*, 28 May 1794.

As soon as the Brest fleet weighed anchor, the men would have felt the strain on their newly acquired Jacobin-imposed confidence. Jeanbon may have made the vertical system of rank and power function once more by reinforcing respect for authority, but most officers would have been uncertain in their new roles, and that uncertainty in some cases would have led to insecurity, a deeply corrupting influence in the relationship between officers and men. At the very best of times the bloated, multi-cultural and multi-generational crews of warships required a skilled hand to manage. At the worst of times, and the spring of 1794 in the French navy counts as one of the most disturbed in all of naval history, camaraderie and trust, the sand and cement of shipboard and fleet discipline, were nothing but a thin veneer.

Even if the sailors were not prepared to admit the problems to themselves in the comfort of Brest Roads, the challenges of fleet seamanship soon left no room for doubt and, crucially, any mistake was very visible and usually noisy. This was peculiar to the sailing era. The visual spectacle was central to both fleet and battle seamanship because it was so often an indicator of skill. An engine-driven warship can speed up and slow down almost invisibly, leaving no evidence other than slight alterations to bow wave or wake. But just to make sail, the crew of a sailing warship had to man the yards, free the sails, hoist the yards and then sheet the sails home. In a light summer breeze this had to be done with as many as nine square sails, and on the largest ships thirty-seven sails in all, including the studding sails.

To maximise speed the sails then had to be trimmed to suit each ship's characteristics. There were few set rules as to how this should be done, or in what order, and even under the same sail plan no ship travelled at exactly the same speed as the others in the fleet. Manoeuvre was even more complicated because the crew would first need to take in some of the sails, before turning the yards through their horizontal plane, to force the ship through the eye of the wind. The whole palaver of setting and trimming the sails would then have to be undertaken all over again. A square sail with its clew caught would hang unattractively and awkwardly, like a sailor's limb withered by injury. A crew caught unawares by a white squall, whose presence can only be seen by a shadow passing over the sea under a clear sky, would scramble to save the sails from blowing out and the yards and masts from cracking. Even minor errors in seamanship could cause yards to snap. In every instance, the frantic bellows on deck and aloft flew across the water, like carrier pigeons with their messages of intelligence. Very little was missed. All ships in a fleet kept eyes on each other at all times. Back and forth, along and across, ahead and astern, thousands of eyes wrapped Villaret's ships in a cocoon of surveillance, every sailor witness to his compatriots' competence.

For all of the Jacobin claims of joy at their departure, Jeanbon was soon horrified at the quality of French seamanship. 'There is much enthusiasm in the fleet,' he wrote, 'and several captains are well trained; but there are three or four whose ignorance is beyond anything one could say.'[1] He went on to complain about clumsy manoeuvres, misunderstood signals, ships drifting apart, and captains running off after isolated merchantmen.[2] Part of the trouble was that some of the ships were starting to suffer from sickness as well as from scurvy and the reduction of their number to man prizes. On board the *Trajan* only forty sailors could be summoned to work the ship because she was missing a total of 240 as a result of sickness and the allocation of prize crews. There were also 150 sick on the *Sans Pareil* and the figures from Vanstabel's ship were even worse. When he had arrived in America, 600 men from the crews of the *Jean Bart* and *Tigre* alone were either dead or sick.[3] On 19 May Villaret came across the 74-gun *Le Patriote* whose captain, Jean-Jacques Lucadou, had become separated from Nielly's squadron through poor seamanship. No sooner had he joined Villaret's fleet than he collided with the corvette *La Mutine* while manoeuvring near the flagship. Villaret then spent the next seven days ignoring repeated pleas from *Le Patriote* for supplies of medicine.[4] We even have some idea of exactly what the French were bad at in terms of seamanship and shipboard life. One British midshipman revealed how an officer from a captured French corvette held aboard the British *Defiance* could not conceal his astonishment at the 'cleanliness and good order' of the British ship. He also witnessed the manoeuvres of the British fleet 'with extreme anxiety', particularly their ability to tack. The British could tack their ships within five minutes, but the Frenchman admitted they 'were always a quarter of an hour under that evolution'.[5]

By 26 May Villaret was so exasperated with the ships at the rear of the squadron that he sent a frigate with instructions to reprimand them for their behaviour, to relay new orders that sailors found to be absent from their posts were to be demoted, and to warn everyone that Jeanbon was taking careful notes for a report back to Paris.[6] This warning that everyone was being watched was a classic Jacobin solution to problems ashore. Jeanbon, rather cleverly, thus turned the surveillance inherent in sailing warfare to his own advantage. This however, could only address some of the social and cultural problems that Jeanbon perceived, or thought that he could perceive, and which manifested themselves in poor seamanship. Unfortunately for Jeanbon the men were not his only worry. Some of his ships were also inadequate, particularly in the quality of their masts.[7] By his own account the problems of the French fleet were both physical and social, the dual death knell of so many battlefleets.

The British too were far from competent, but they had enjoyed the luxury of making their mistakes weeks and months earlier. In July 1793, for example, the *Bellerophon* collided with the *Majestic*,[8] but that summer Howe issued a set of 'Additional Instructions' that dealt with many of the blunders his fleet had made. British captains were warned in writing against losing station by falling too far to leeward or astern; that the leading ships must take particular care with their evolutions; that when tacking in succession ships must put in stays before passing the wake of the ship ahead, and so on. This was all detailed stuff that has the clear mark of failure upon it: these instructions did not come to Howe suddenly in the middle of the night, but were the result of painful experience.[9]

The seamanship of the French fleet may have been significantly worse than that of the British, therefore, but the same must not be said of their desire. There was a certain shame at the way that the Mediterranean fleet had been surrendered to the British without a shot being fired and at how the Brest fleet had made itself, and France, vulnerable by mutiny. Debts were owed; reputations to be healed; personal and professional respect from sailor to sailor, ship to ship, and between the navy and the French people to be won anew. Last of all, and for many French sailors the least significant of all, was loyalty to be demonstrated to the new regime. Combined, this was a heady brew of inspiration.

The few British ships who came across French men-of-war in the winter of 1793 and new year of 1794 were all met with pride and aggression and the French resolution was never in doubt. Anchored alongside a French ship in the neutral port of Leghorn, Nelson watched the crew of a French frigate depose their captain and officers and replace them from the crew. 'What a state' he wrote to his wife, Fanny. 'They are mad enough for any undertaking... I shall be surprised at nothing they may attempt.' In the subsequent cruise Nelson soon tasted that fervour at the mouth of French cannon when his 64-gun ship, *Agamemnon*, met a French squadron off Sardinia and he engaged the leading ship, the 38-gun frigate *La Melpomène*. It did not go well for Nelson. Reading through the spin he put on the event in his subsequent letters, there is no doubting that the much smaller *La Melpomène* beat off and crippled the *Agamemnon*, and in doing so defended their smaller ship from one of the most aggressive naval officers ever to have sailed. Nelson was seriously shaken and uncharacteristically he penned a phrase from a well-known prayer in his journal: 'When I lay me down to Sleep I recommend myself to the care of Almighty God...'[10] He was profoundly affected by the ferocity of this action, which surpassed any he had experienced in the previous war. It would be dangerous to conclude that *all* French crews would fight like that of the *La Melpomène* – as Nelson so swiftly claimed, he was rather unlucky to have come across one of the best. Furthermore, the sailors on board the *Melpomène* had shown their mettle in front of the four other French ships in the squadron as well as the rest of the British squadron. The word would quickly have spread through the naval bases of France that the French could hold their own.

Nor was it an isolated event. On 24 October 1793 the British frigate *Thames* had been beaten to a standstill by the French frigate *Uranie*. In November the French had enjoyed more success when Vanstabel successfully evaded Howe in Biscay and went on to capture a British convoy from Newfoundland which he mopped up with some style, sailing back to Brest with his squadron intact and eleven prizes in tow. He later repeated the feat and took seventeen more from a convoy that John Jervis was supposed to protect.[11] In March 1794 there had been another successful raid on a merchant convoy, this time the French taking twenty-four merchantmen back to Brest. Thus by the spring of 1794, the British were somewhat uncertain about the ability of their enemy. They were clearly up and fighting again after the disaster at Toulon and mutiny at Brest and on 2 April the Admiralty received intelligence that the French were 'well manned [with] discipline pretty well established' in the crews at Brest. There were even rumours that they would use red-hot shot against the British, a terrible threat to wooden warships and something that was by no means common.[12]

There are, however, a number of very important caveats to this history of French success, which help to explain the way French sailors performed in June 1794.

In Nelson's action with *La Melpomène* the French had failed to maximise the opportunity created by their aggressive action and they had allowed Nelson to escape. They had demonstrated their desire and ability to fight, but not a desire and ability to take a battle to a decision. Nelson, unfairly, put this down to a lack of courage. There was also the matter of casualties. To consider a battle in terms of the ships alone is to miss the significance of the effect on manpower and morale that an action could have, and at no time was this as significant as it was during the Revolutionary wars. Consider Nelson's action in the *Agamemnon*. His ship had been crippled by skilful and prolonged French gunnery, but only one British sailor had been killed in the action and only six wounded. But for the state of their ship, the British could have carried on fighting and all of the men, with the exception of one unfortunate sailor, would have been able to take their expanded experience and knowledge on to the next battle. They had seen their friends withstand French fire; they had seen men stand at their guns as the air turned thick with splinters and they had been choked and blinded by gunsmoke.

The French ship and her crew, meanwhile, which had beaten off the British attack, had sustained serious damage. Twenty-four of her crew had died and fifty more were injured, many of whom would not survive the voyage back to land.[13] Those sailors were crucial to the future of the French navy because they had seen battle; they had seen how they could fight themselves clear of a British attack, but now so many of them lay dead and dying, their knowledge and experience blown away like so much spring blossom, while British success endured and grew stronger for that endurance.

This pattern was a feature throughout the Revolutionary wars but it was noticeable even by 1794. In October 1793 James Saumarez had captured the French *Réunion* in another hard-fought battle lasting two hours and ten minutes, a considerable length of time for a single-ship engagement. His frigate, the *Crescent*, much like Nelson's *Agamemnon*, had been badly damaged, but when Saumarez finally took posession of the *Réunion*, the discrepancy between casualties became clear: the French had lost 120 dead and wounded, the British, none.[14] Not a single British sailor died. Saumarez and his entire crew could learn and grow stronger, whereas half of the French crew would never fight the British again, and those that survived faced incarceration in the prison hulks and would be lucky to see another French ship before the end of the war.

The story repeated itself in November 1793 off Saint Domingue when the British *Penelope* fought the *Inconstant*. The French lost twenty-eight killed and wounded, the British only eight, a discrepancy in casualties that was matched in January 1794 when the *Résolue* and *Vengeur*, both privateers, were captured by five British Indiamen. In Sir John Warren's squadron action in April 1794, the French lost somewhere between eighty to one hundred men on *La Pomone*, but the highest casualty rate for *any* of the five British ships was one dead and twelve wounded on the *Concorde*. In May, the British *Orpheus* captured the *Duguay Trouin*, leaving eighty-one dead and wounded, to the British ten. On the very same day, the *Swiftsure* fought the *Atalante*, which suffered forty-two dead and wounded to the *Swiftsure*'s four.[15]

The reasons for this extraordinary discrepancy are diverse. Generally speaking, French warships were poorly constructed in comparison with the British. Their hulls were fastened with iron nails, which could quickly corrode, rather than durable timber treenails which fitted snugly, and they were built with light scantlings and sometimes unseasoned wood. This made their hulls particularly vulnerable to enemy fire. The British also made maximum use of a weapon that was peculiar to British service, the carronade. These short but light cannon could fire a heavy shot with an immense destructive capacity at short range and the French had no comparable weapon, the closest being their brass *obusier*.[16] We also know that the early Revolutionary government struggled to supply gunpowder to both army and navy, and what they were able to supply is likely to have been of poor quality. It was certainly a problem later in the war as proven by an experiment which demonstrated that British powder fired a shot 15.3 per cent farther than French.[17] It is also likely that the British could fire faster and keep up a sustained fire for longer than the French crews.

Even though the French had enjoyed the odd success at this stage of the war, therefore, those victories were poisoned by the reality of death and injury on board their ships. Put simply, in the summer of 1794, French sailors expected to die in battle and the British to survive. It was a mighty psychological advantage.

Finally, and perhaps most importantly for the battle that was to come, a little over a week before Howe had sailed with the Channel Fleet, news of the first action between two squadrons flashed across the Channel. A British squadron, commanded by Sir John Warren, had been ordered to protect trade between Cape Finisterre and Cherbourg, which had been regularly targeted by a powerful French squadron sailing from Havre de Grâce (modern Le Havre), Le Hay and Cherbourg.

Warren sailed with five frigates. With this many ships, any action would test more than just the fighting seamanship of individual crews. A squadron of five was susceptible to all of the problems of fleet tactics and manoeuvre, albeit on a smaller scale. The squadron had to be controlled with flag and light signals, verbal and written instruction, and the captains had to be proficient in station keeping and coordinated manoeuvre. They had to be able to tack, wear, attack and retreat together. If they did not act in unison one or more of their number might easily be picked off and overwhelmed by an enemy squadron. With so many ships, this was now a team game.

There was one other important challenge to face when fighting in a squadron of frigates. They were very nimble ships that made quick manoeuvre both possible and particularly effective because the squadron commander could respond rapidly to developments. In battle between such squadrons, everything was quicker than in fleet action: the ships sailed faster and they manoeuvred faster both individually and as a squadron. With such a small force, the dynamics of the battle also changed more rapidly. The loss of one ship to damage would, in Warren's example, instantly reduce his fighting force by a fifth, and the loss of two ships by nearly a half, more than enough to turn the course of the action. The squadron commander therefore had to have a particularly lively mind and good instincts even if the basic tactics remained the same: it was like a game of blitz chess or 20/20 cricket.

Just twenty-four miles off Guernsey, Warren came across the French squadron of four ships. They were cruising in good formation just a little ahead of Warren's own squadron. He ordered a general chase that was instantly executed by all of his ships. There was a notable difference in speed between the squadrons and Warren's ships soon caught up with the French. The British engaged as they came up but the French defence was formidable and their gunfire accurate. Within minutes Warren was driven out of his own line with shattered rigging. The British squadron's slim numerical advantage had been cut, the forces were now equal and the British commander was out of the game. In many actions throughout the Age of Sail this would have been enough to cool the attack, but Warren's captains did not falter and continued to press the French as they were overtaken and the British sailors fought until the Frenchmen struck. Only one ship, the *Résolue*, escaped and Warren brought three fine French ships into Falmouth, the *Babet* (20), *Engageante* (36) and the powerful *La Pomone* (44). Sir John Warren became a Knight of the Bath and the action launched a career rivalled by very few in the history of the Royal Navy.

Not only had a British squadron triumphed, but it had done so over the best the French had to offer: a squadron that had been sallying out regularly from the ports of Brittany and Normandy. They knew how to keep station and their considerable success at trade warfare had honed their knowledge of, and ability at, the peculiar and challenging tactics of chasing, fighting and securing prizes. They had also been resolute and had fought with great courage, stamina and considerable skill. But the British had won. Their sustained, punishing gunfire had broken the French, and only one of the French ships had escaped. With Vanstabel in America, Nielly and Villaret in Brest, this had been their *only* effective and operational squadron in the Channel and now it was defeated. More than three quarters of those skilled and experienced sailors lay dead or mutilated or were on their way to English prisons. Against all the bravura and fanaticism of the French, the British had an action they could carry in their hearts into the forbidding Atlantic as proof that their enemy could be beaten.

The most important question now facing Jeanbon and Villaret was how, exactly, they were going to fight the British. The orders that came from above are interesting in this regard. It has been too easy for naval historians to condemn the Montagnard government for a lack of reality in its dealings with the navy but Villaret's precise instructions, although a little confused and contradictory, demonstrate a good grasp of the navy's capabilities and a realistic, if pitiless, strategy. If the enemy fleet was out, Villaret was ordered to protect the convoy at all costs, its safety being 'the only rule of conduct of the commander of the fleet'. More instructions followed. 'We must not compromise our naval forces' wrote the Committee...

> ...when all our supplementary means are not yet put into execution and when the smallest failure could halt our plan of campaign against England... it is not a naval victory we need at the moment, but our convoy; it is not a battle but a proud and imposing posture which will ward off the enemy or make it to hove to. To delay our revenge is to make it more sure.[18]

The importance of the convoy at least had been made clear, though Villaret was faced with a conundrum: risk everything to secure its safety while doing everything he could to preserve the Battle fleet for the Montagnard 'revenge' – their invasion of England. And so Villaret sailed, not with the intent of defeating the British, but to avoid battle until he knew that the convoy was likely to fall prey to the British.

That was his intention, but how was he going to go about it? Complex tactics were all but useless in a fleet that could not be relied upon to keep station in line ahead or abreast, let alone change from a lozenge formation to a line of bearing, to three separate columns and then to line abreast. Villaret could just about keep his fleet together sailing in a straight line, and if any deviation of course or speed was required he could only hope that they retained their cohesion. Villaret knew that the maintenance of cohesion was essential to his survival if his ships were brought into close contact with a large enemy fleet because the line of battle was inherently stronger in defence than offence. Throughout the entire history of fleet battle in the Age of Sail, decisive results were only ever achieved through numerical superiority. Either that superiority was established when the two fleets met or it was achieved by an aggressive commander deliberately disrupting the enemy formation, or by incompetence in one fleet leading to its own disruption.

If both fleets were of a similar size at the start of the action, give or take one or two ships, the strongest and safest position was to sit tight, in close formation. This would force the enemy to attack a well-formed fleet, which was always a dangerous proposition as the attacking fleet would necessarily become vulnerable to enemy fire as it approached. Villaret may have commanded a fleet of inexperienced men, therefore, but if he could retain cohesion then he had a very good chance of inflicting enough damage on the British to force them to change priority or even rethink their strategy. Any skirmish, moreover, would take considerable time, several hours at least, which would be time enough for the convoy to pass by the British threat. This might seem basic stuff, but naval tactics in practice were far simpler than the contemporary academic treatises on tactics would have us believe. There was nothing surprising or innovative here. Villaret's mindset was transparent to Howe, who knew that he would have to disrupt the French formation or take advantage of a gap that had formed by accident.

Villaret's tactical challenge was twofold, therefore. He would have to maintain cohesion and repel any attempt to break his line. To cut the French fleet, Howe would inevitably signal his intention by assuming an intercepting course. There was no way he could do this without Villaret realising, long in advance, what was being planned. Remember that fleet battle took place at an incredibly slow pace, the ships sailing at four miles per hour or less, and any evolution took some considerable time. If, for example, a fleet had been ordered to tack in succession – that is to say that the leading ship would tack and then each succeeding ship would tack when they had reached that given point – even a well-drilled fleet would struggle to complete the manoeuvre in anything less than an hour. The very process of tacking would take a full five minutes even for the best-drilled crews on the best of ships and a full fifteen minutes for the worst. A fleet twenty-five strong, therefore, even made up of fine ships crewed by fine men, would take two hours and five minutes to perform the evolution, plus the time taken for each ship to reach the mark. Tacking all the ships together would obviously make this much faster, but it also made it far more dangerous, with collision and dislocation of formation more likely. If Howe was going to break Villaret's line without endangering the cohesion of his own line, therefore, the attack was going to be obvious long in advance.

The counter-move was just as obvious. If Howe attacked Villaret's line at an angle, Villaret only had to mimic Howe's last move to keep his fleet parallel with his enemy and thus prevent any cutting manoeuvre. Consider a game of chess on an infinitely long chess board. A pawn moves forward to attack another pawn. If the way is clear, the obvious defence is to mimic the move in exactly the same direction. That, at least, was the theory of the defensive riposte against an aggressive line-breaking manoeuvre, but in practice things tended to get messy because of the likelihood of failure to execute the manoeuvre or the discrepancy of speed between ships: two fleets could not mimic each other's manoeuvres all day long without something giving. Here, again, time was an important factor. Because such manoeuvres took so long, even a fraction of difference in speed would make a significant difference: a discrepancy of only one mile per hour translated to a mile gained or lost every hour. In the process of manoeuvring, therefore, the fastest ships of one fleet would be able to bring themselves up with the slowest ships of the other and thereby force a partial engagement. The commander of the fleet on the defensive would then have to decide whether he should bring about a full engagement by sailing to support his hard-pressed ships.

This all seems a little vague and unscientific; a system of exceptions rather than rules, but that is exactly the nature of sailing warfare. Each commander knew what the other would try to do, and would be able to see him do it, but in the process unpredictable events would happen and it was the job of the commanders to react appropriately; in Villaret's case to maintain the status quo, and in Howe's case to alter it. That is how fleet battle in the Age of Sail unfolded: a tumbling and unpredictable series of events. The very best any commander could do was to act according to the capability of his fleet. If he tried something too difficult it was likely to fail, and fleet battle was far easier to lose than it was to win. Viewed from this perspective, Howe's highly innovative tactics issued to his fleet in the homely comfort of Portsmouth carried with them a very great risk. If the tactics failed, his fleet could rapidly find itself vulnerable, a scattering of snowflakes instead of a snowball.

What Howe could rely on and Jeanbon could not, however, was the experience of his captains. Experience alone was by no means a guarantee that they would behave as he might wish but at least the British fleet's captains knew what to expect in battle at sea. They were well aware that communication systems, however innovative, were likely to fail at some stage as signal flags became invisible behind gunsmoke or were shot down; they knew that they would have no choice *but* to act on their own initiative as the shape of the battle shifted in their immediate location which, for many of the captains, could be a mile or more from the fleet commander; they knew that the identity of the combatants could easily become confused and that friendly fire was a very real possibility; they knew that their priorities would be torn at times between attacking the enemy and maintaining their position in relation to other ships within their own fleet; they knew that any and all of these factors would create unforeseen scenarios, moral, physical and professional conundrums that could only be solved, or at least negotiated, on a case by case basis, and with no recourse to higher authority.

Howe's captains knew that fleet battle was the ultimate test of fighting seamanship and there is no doubt that his captains were more experienced than the French, but it is worth considering exactly how big that difference was. Of the twenty-three highest-ranking British officers from Howe's fleet of twenty-five ships of the line (74- to 100-gunners) on whom we have information, all had seen fleet action, seventeen of them more than twice, and six of them more than four times and all had considerable experience of single ship action. The most experienced had fought in three wars, the War of the Austrian Succession (1739–58), the Seven Years' War (1755–62) and the War of American Independence (1775–83). Of the seventeen commanding officers for whom dates concerning their career survive, all had served for at least twenty years, nine of them for at least thirty years, six for at least forty years and two for more than fifty years, Howe being the longest-serving and most experienced, having joined the navy fifty-five years earlier. Nine had fought at the most decisive actions of the previous fifty years: the two battles of Finisterre (1747), the battles of Lagos and Quiberon Bay (1759) and the Battle of the Saints (1782).

In contrast, only *one* of all the twenty-five French fleet captains or admirals had ever commanded a ship in fleet battle and he, Rear-Admiral François Joseph Bouvet of the 110-gun *Terrible*, had fought only once before, in the American War, at the indecisive Battle of Sadras in April 1782. Of the three flag officers in the Brest fleet, two, including Villaret, had only recently been promoted from lieutenant and the third from sub-lieutenant. Three of the captains had been lieutenants, eleven had been sub-lieutenants, nine had been captains, or even mates, of merchant ships, one had been a boatswain, one a seaman and the remaining captain was so insignificant that the written records contain no trace of any previous career for him of any description.[19] It is not too harsh to say that, as it reads on paper at least, these men simply did not know what they were doing.

Howe also had unreserved faith in his vessels. Strong and built to withstand the strains of fleet battle, all his ships of the line were British-built with one exception, HMS *Gibraltar*, which was originally the Spanish warship *Fénix*, flagship of Admiral Juan de Lángara, captured by the British at the Moonlight Battle in January 1780. Using the unmatched resources of their colonial empire the Spanish built very fine ships out of tropical hardwood, which made them almost impervious to rot, and the *Fénix* was a magnificent example. She was built in 1749 and not broken up until 1836 – that is eighty-seven years later – having served in the Spanish navy for thirty-one years and actively in the Royal Navy for thirty-three years before she was hulked in 1813. Of all Howe's other ships the oldest was HMS *Valiant*, built at Chatham and launched in 1759, and she had benefited from a substantial rebuild in 1775. The next oldest, the *Defence*, was launched in 1763; too late for the Seven Years' War, she remained uncommissioned throughout the next war and did not begin her service life until 1782, a mere twelve years before the Glorious First of June. More than half of Howe's ships were less than ten years old including four that were under five years old. The newest, moreover, had benefited from a significant change in ship design in the 1780s which increased the hull length. The 80-gun Third Rate *Caesar*, for example, launched only the year before (November 1793), was only three feet shorter than Thomas Graves's flagship, the 100-gun First Rate *Royal Sovereign*, and was three feet longer than the previous generation of First Rates.

The British had acquired good, recent inside knowledge of French warships when they captured fifteen of them at the surrender of Toulon. The largest, the *Commerce de Marseille* was a massive ship of 120 guns and 2,747 tons but she sailed beautifully with 'lines uncommonly fine' and 'notwithstanding her immense size, she worked and sailed like a frigate'. One of her British captains had reported that she was 'kind, safe and easy ... steers remarkably well, never known to miss stays'. This was all music to the ears of any sailor and said a great deal about the French shipwrights' skilful ability, but the speed and manoeuvrability of these ships was won at a cost as, to achieve it, their hulls were made light and their rigs loose. Indeed, the *Commerce de Marseille*, when analysed by the cool heads of British shipwrights, was considered so structurally weak that she was deemed fit for use only as a prison ship. Gabriel Snodgrass, a significant voice in British ship design, condemned the captured French ships he surveyed as 'ridiculous' for their slight construction and excessive tumblehome, that distinctive wine-glass shape of ship's hulls that varied from country to country and from period to period.[20] By the 1790s excessive tumblehome had been outmoded in British shipbuilding for a century or more.

The relative capabilities of the French and British fleets were mixed, therefore, and were exceptionally complex. This was not a clear-cut contest between a flawless unit of skilled men and a ragtag collection of hoodlums. There were strengths and weaknesses on both sides. What the French lacked in experience of fleet warfare they made up for in their enthusiasm for a scrap, a fact acknowledged by Jeanbon himself when he encouraged his captains to 'disdain evolutions and attempt to board'.[21] Villaret was under direct instructions to avoid battle unless it was essential to save the convoy. His was a weakened fleet, certainly, but one with realistic instructions. Villaret knew his own weakness, which made his fleet highly dangerous and a tough nut to crack. Howe would be stretched to his absolute limit to bring the French ships to battle, let alone to win convincingly. But if he could bring about an action the French were more likely to make mistakes than the British, and the British were more likely to be able to seize an opportunity that presented itself. The British fleet had some very fine officers and some not so fine, but the history of fleet warfare over the preceding century made it absolutely clear that even a handful of the very best officers was often enough to make the difference between victory and defeat.

The fleets now stumbled blindly onward, ever farther out into the Atlantic. The only squadron no longer part of this extraordinary dance was Montagu's; he had already exceeded by six days his orders to hunt for Vanstabel's convoy and had been unable to find Howe. According to the wording of his orders, therefore, and even with explicit intelligence that the French were to hand, Montagu returned to Plymouth.

In the other squadrons, eyes strained toward the horizon, the seamen blinking away the wind-tears in their eyes. Who would see whom first? How would they react? Crews stood braced between mast and shroud, yard and footrope, hour after hour, as the unwavering seam between sea and sky refused to give up its secrets, then: Is that the hull of a ship or cloud-cast shadow on the water? Is that a glimpse of sail or the surge of spray at the top of the swell? A string of questions then rattled forth, each demanding instant attention. Is that the sail of a warship or merchantman? If she's a warship how big is she? A frigate? A two- or three-decker? Is she larger or smaller than us? Is she English, French, Spanish, American or Dutch? Is she a threat or target? What course is she sailing? The sail looks square, but are we sailing toward or away from her, or are we on the same heading? The sail appears at an angle now, but how has she changed course? What course must we steer to intercept or escape? Are we gaining or losing ground? And then, the most important question of all for a lone ship or a small squadron: are there any other ships? Is this the van of a fleet, a roving lookout, or the sternmost ship? Have we blundered into the midst of the enemy fleet?

Nothing was simple. Observation, interpretation, analysis and action all required significant skill, knowledge and experience. At every stage a mistake could be made that might prove fatal and at any time the circumstances could change. The swell could rise or fall, sandbanks, headlands, islands and estuaries could all come into play as time wore on. Fog could fall or lift and squalls disrupt everything for a brief time, like a tornado tearing through a battle field. With far more subtlety but a potentially deeper impact on the outcome of events, the wind could simply change direction. A comforting, gentle breeze caressing a ship's quarter then veering or backing by as little as two or three points could prove disastrous or miraculous. All ships had their own best point of sailing, the point at which they sailed fastest, but they also had their own best point of sailing in relation to other ships, which was rarely the same. Some could be swift as a dolphin with the wind on the quarter but sluggish as a hippo with it abeam; others could be generally slow but able to hold their own in a headwind better than any other. The first sight of an enemy sail therefore created so much uncertainty and unpredictability that had to be negotiated before any two ships or fleets could meet.

On board Howe's flagship, the signal lieutenant was Edward Codrington. Codrington was well known for his skill as a lookout because he was unusually long-sighted and, as a result, 'much practised in the use of his strong vision by observing signals &c.c. Howe was so dependent on Codrington that the poor man was forced to spend many hours at a stretch at the masthead or on deck, to the extent that Howe would allow him a chair on the quarterdeck in which to rest. He went below only for meals and then was so tired that he would fall asleep between mouthfuls, to the hilarity of his messmates who would do everything in their power to wake him up but without success. It is a reminder of the variety of skills and specialists aboard a sailing ship. Codrington was a dedicated specialist look-out, adding immense value in exactly this situation.[22]

It is important to remember that the lookout on a flagship would be scanning for some of their own ships as well as the enemy's; in Codrington's case, one of the frigates or part of the flying squadron[23] that was scouting far ahead of the main fleet. These were the ships that would see the enemy first, but that did not make the flagship lookout's job any easier. On the contrary, he must both observe and translate. When a scout spotted a strange sail, her captain would signal his intelligence rather than sail back to deliver it in person: not only would this waste valuable time but, also, to lose sight of a vessel was to increase greatly the likelihood of its escape. Any ship which had been seen would also have spotted her discoverer and, if allowed out of sight, could easily shake them off.

Look-out ships therefore used their sails as signal flags which, combined with the course they set, served as both a statement of intent and a report on the activities of the ship they had found. This was necessarily a simple process because of the considerable distance between scout and flagship, but it was very effective. First, the scout would usually point her bows in the direction of her find and immediately assume the same course. Then, she might raise and lower her topgallant sails to identify the number of vessels sighted. Thus, while much too far away to be able to discern any information from normal, small signal flags, the flagship's lookout could glean immediately that a ship or ships had been seen and in which direction they were sailing.

On the morning of 28 May, Codrington spied what he knew beyond any doubt was the enemy fleet. He counted twenty-seven of the line, one frigate and another vessel that he could not identify, which turned out to be a *razée* – a two-decked ship cut down to make a very large single-decker; the *razée* later became a stalwart of the French navy but it was entirely novel in 1794.[24] There was no mistaking that this was the enemy, and yet because he was on the flagship, he was by no means the first British sailor to set eyes on the enemy fleet. That privilege went to the un-named look-out of the frigate *Phaeton*, 429 miles west of Ushant and five miles away from the *Queen Charlotte*: who saw a strange fleet-several miles to the *Phaeton*'s south-west shortly after half-past seven that same morning.

The crew of the *Phaeton* were busy interrogating the crew of a Scottish brig they had intercepted bound from Cadiz to London. But as soon as the French fleet was sighted the *Phaeton* abandoned the brig and raced to get into station, all the while watching the enemy fleet running down toward them. Isaac Schomberg, captain of the *Culloden*, thought that the French had mistaken the British fleet for another because they came down in confused order, and he seems to have been correct.[25] The French confusion can be explained partly by a lack of telescopes, something that plagued their fleet, but there was no such confusion on the decks of the *Phaeton*.[26] Her captain was so desperate to get to safety and his appointed position that he carried away her foretopsail yard. He didn't stop to rerig but simply ordered it cut clear and thrown overboard along with everything else the crew were chucking into the sea to clear the decks for action: a hen-coop, a binnacle, a pantry and a bulkhead were reduced to flotsam. Three hours later and the enemy were forming their line of battle, three and a half miles away from the *Phaeton*, which was still a mile and a half from Howe.[27] By now it was clear that the French fleet actually consisted of twenty-six of the line, exactly the same size as the British and a remarkable coincidence given the numerous and readily available forces of both sides.

The numerical equilibrium was not auspicious for a decisive battle. The *Phaeton* signalled to Howe, who then signalled to Pasley to reconnoitre, and so Pasley's 74-gun *Bellerophon* stretched away from the comfort of the main fleet and sailed toward the enemy.

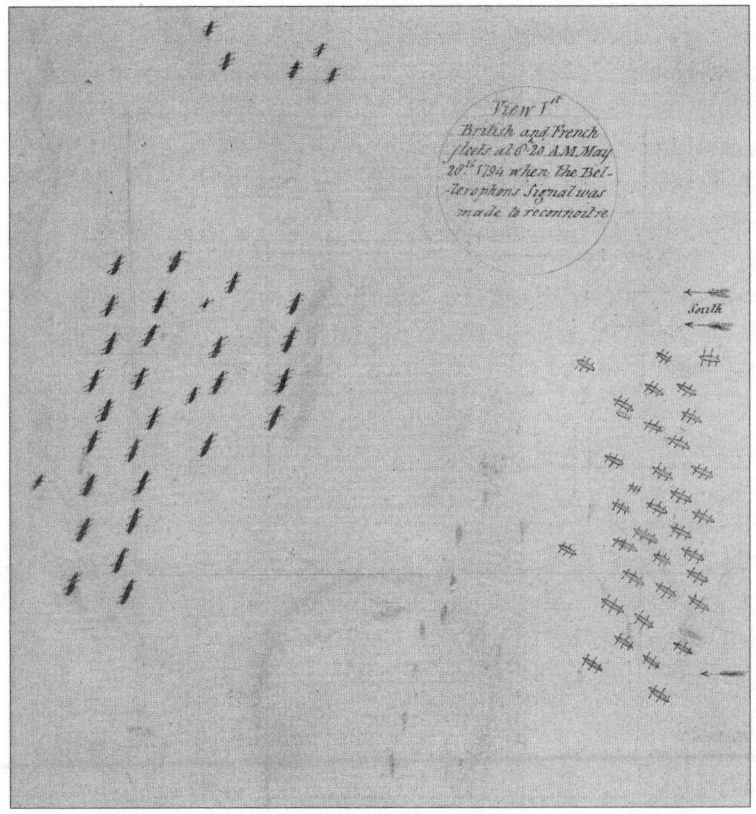


ii. Battle plan made by Matthew Flinders, then a midshipman of the *Bellerophon*. This shows the fleets on the morning of 28 May. The British fleet is to the right. The French are in a rough group, seemingly awaiting a British attack.

The young Matthew Flinders, a future Royal Navy star of hydrography and exploration, was on the *Bellerophon* and noted how an enemy ship broke away from the main fleet and sailed toward them to reconnoitre the British just as they were reconnoitring the French.[28] Howe looked on anxiously three or four miles to leeward. Unprepared to take any risks with Pasley and his fine ship, Howe soon ordered him to shorten sail, a firm tug on the leash of his gundog.

There they all remained, for several hours, the *Phaeton* and *Bellerophon,* sharp pinpricks between two vast fleets cutting the horizon with a forest of masts. The French then hove to and, while at rest in this way, three replaced their main topsails and one a maintopsail yard while a three-decker sailed the length of the French line, perhaps relaying verbal instructions. Visibly struggling with the challenges of fleet seamanship, the French took several hours to form into a line of battle and all the while they were being blown down toward the British fleet.[29] And so the fleets came together, the French like a shoal of fish drifting on wind and tide toward the British net. The British, meantime, took the opportunity to have lunch. At thirteen minutes past eleven Admiral Howe signalled rather politely that: 'The people may have time to dine.'[30]

Once their line had been formed the French altered their course, which so clearly would have brought the two fleets to battle, by hauling their wind and steering away from the British; this was a strategic, not a cowardly, move. Villaret was carefully leading the British away from Vanstabel's arrival point. Now fortified by food, Howe ordered a general chase when it became clear that it was up to the British fleet to force the French hand. All the British ships cleared for action. When cruising, the gundecks were littered with the jumble of everyday life and the decks divided up by temporary screens to afford the officers some privacy. These screens were now removed and stowed away in various dark corners of the ship but, occasionally, items of furniture were hoisted into the rig, out of the way of the gun crews, to take their chance against enemy fire. Splinter netting was hung over the quarterdeck to receive the blocks that might be shot away, and a cask of water was lifted into the main top, in case of fire.[31]

Anything else that was in the way went overboard including, on the *Queen Charlotte*, a total of twelve butts. All of this had to be done in the face of squalls and a big swell, with the ships heeling dramatically as another gust of wind caught the sails or the hulls plunged into the deep trough of a wave. The sailors on the weather deck would have been able to brace themselves against wind and waves but those below were blind to whatever was coming next, forced to react as the ship heaved and rolled. The sea was so rough that it tore off part of the *Thunderer*'s figurehead and head-gratings.[32] In these conditions, moving around anything heavy below deck was dangerous but it was especially so with the crew all rushing to their tasks, arming the ship and themselves. Amid the chaos a woman on board the *Tremendous* chose her moment to give birth.[33]

As the two fleets closed, Howe made the signal to attack the enemy's rear with the specific intention of bringing about a general action, a tried and tested tactic.[34] The British fleet, under as much sail as they could bear in the conditions, steadily closed with the French. The long wait was nearly over. Eight hours had passed since the French were first sighted. The scent of pain and glory was now as powerful as it ever could be, the men of both fleets had readied themselves for battle, physically and psychologically. In the French fleet, a cry of: '"*Vive la République*" arose from our ships and carried to the English a challenge and a proof of our devotion to the cause we were about to defend.'[35] A similar aggressive exuberance rose up in the British fleet. As soon as the signal was made to prepare for battle and the frigates of Howe's flying squadron were unleashed, according to Midshipman Dillon of the *Defence*

> ...a state of excitement was manifested totally beyond my powers of description. No one thought of anything else than to exert himself to his utmost ability in overcoming the enemy. It was also very satisfactory to observe the change of disposition in the ship's company of the *Defence*. All animation and alacrity pervaded these men: no more sulky looks. The enemy was near, and all hands were determined to support their Captain. The ships when

> near each other were cheered by their crews in succession. Death or Victory was evidently the prevailing feeling.[36]

The leading British ships now reached out to catch the rearmost of the French ships, to drag them down and tear them apart. But the French were far from willing victims cowering from attack. The ships in the van of Howe's fleet were as strung out as those at the rear of Villaret's, and the closest of them all to the British was no weak frigate but *La Révolutionnaire*, a mighty 110-gun three-decker longer than any ships in the British fleet. At half past two in the afternoon on 28 May 1794, with the range between the leading British and sternmost French no more than a mile, *La Révolutionnaire* turned to fight.

# 7.

# The First Blood

We tacked before the rear ship got on [our] beam, which enabled us to bring them to action a considerable time before the other ships could get up to our assistance.

Master's Log of the *Bellerophon*, 28 May 1794.

As the fleets closed, the British ship closest to the *Révolutionnaire* was the 74-gun *Russell* which, through vagaries of ship performance, course and wind, was more than a mile closer to the French than any other British ship. Her captain, John Payne, had fought with Howe at Sandy Hook in the American War. She was the first ship in the British fleet to open fire. It was a little after 2:30 p.m. The ships were however in no position for a prolonged engagement. The *Russell* was still some distance astern of the French and although they returned fire there is no evidence that the guns of either ship had any effect on its enemy. In mid-afternoon the weather became yet more squally and the *Russell* was forced to take in three reefs in her topsails and haul up her courses.

By now the difference in speed between the greyhound 74-gunners that led the British chase and the rearmost of the French ships had begun to tell and several of Howe's 74-gunners had closed with the *Révolutionnaire*. Her captain was so keen to fight that, contrary to his orders, he had even shortened sail.[1] The French fleet, meanwhile, had tacked, and while the *Russell* and *Thunderer* now manoeuvred into their wake, Rear-Admiral Pasley of the *Bellerophon* had anticipated their manoeuvre and new course and had tacked early, thus bringing his ship into contact with the rearmost of the French far earlier than the others. Bold as this was, Pasley now found himself up against a much larger and more powerful ship than his own, and with no hope of early support. He gave them 'a very warm & fierce reception which the enemy returned with great vivacity'.[2]

Howe, vigilant as ever, immediately saw the danger and ordered the *Russell*, *Audacious* and *Marlborough* to the *Bellerophon*'s assistance, but in the ninety minutes it took for help to arrive the *Bellerophon* was mauled, 'having received sundry shot in different places, the main cap disabled and the mast likely to fall over the side'. She was forced to stop fighting to repair as a matter of self-preservation. If the weather changed for the worse, the *Bellerophon* could quickly find herself in difficulty but, more importantly, if a bold Frenchman chose to fight, the crippled *Bellerophon* could have been taken.

Meanwhile the entire British fleet had set every stitch of canvas to get into action. As other British ships caught up they passed the drifting *Bellerophon* and continued to attack the *Révolutionnaire*: the fire from the *Leviathan* and *Thunderer* was particularly impressive in its accuracy.[3] The *Audacious* also engaged from 8:03 p.m. until 9:50 p.m., two hours of sustained gunfire and 'never exceeding the distance of half a cable's length [100 yards]'. Half an hour into this new stage of the battle, two and a half hours after the *Bellerophon* had first engaged her, the *Révolutionnaire*'s mizzen mast caught fire and was lost overboard, probably cut and sent into the sea by her crew to prevent the fire from spreading. But, still, she carried on firing for another ninety minutes, when she eventually fell across the bows of *Audacious* and *Thunderer*, and by now her foreyard, mainyard and main topsail yard had all been shot away. The light had been failing rapidly for the past hour, to such an extent that the rest of the British fleet saw 'a grand and awful sight from the flash of the guns'.[4]

The *Audacious* was now so badly damaged, 'every brace, bowling, most of her standing rigging, and all her running rigging shot away',[5] that she, much like the *Bellerophon*, was forced to heave to and attend to repairs instead of securing the Frenchman as a prize. Her log records that she was 'entirely ungovernable'. Nineteen British sailors were out of action, dead or wounded, and the masts and rigging so cut up that it took her crew all night to make her serviceable. The *Thunderer*, at least, was not so badly damaged and her captain, Albemarle Bertie, was anxious about the status of the *Révolutionnaire*. He hailed William Parker, captain of the *Audacious*, and asked if the Frenchman had struck. Parker said he did not know,[6] and so Bertie sailed up to the ship and asked her captain direct. Captain Vandongen replied in English that he had struck,

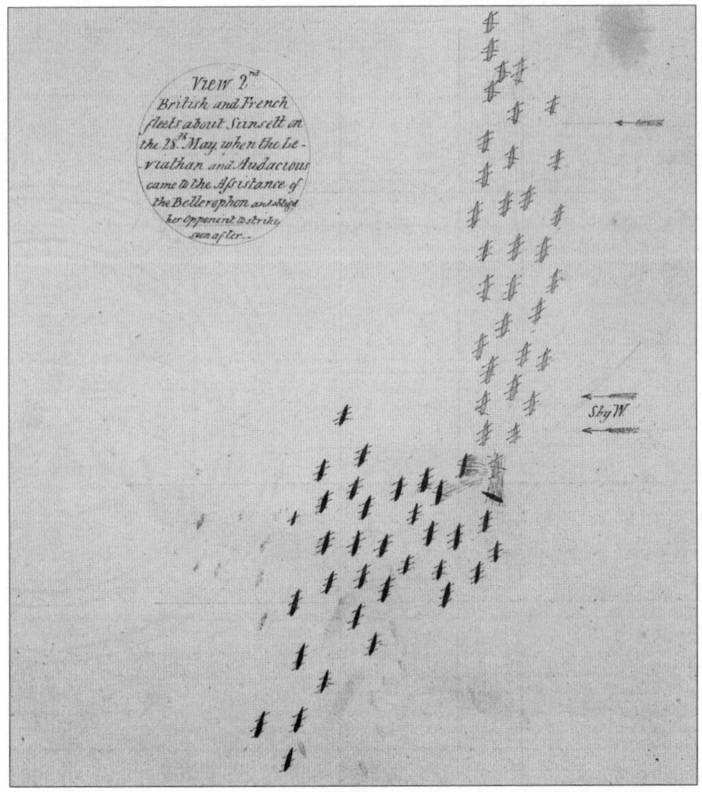


iii. Battle plan made by Matthew Flinders. This shows the fleets at sunset on 28 May. By now the French have set all sail, drawing the British away from the convoy rendezvous point. The rearmost ships engage.

and would follow the British ships during the night. Bertie then went about his business, speaking to a British frigate, perhaps to inform her captain of the events which could be passed on to Howe. He then wore ship to join the main fleet, according to a signal, made considerably earlier, at 7:40 p.m., for all British ships to leave off the chase. He did not put any crew aboard the *Révolutionnaire*, nor did he take her in tow.

Captain Berkeley of the *Marlborough* believed that the *Révolutionnaire* had struck and had been secured by the *Audacious*. The masters of the *Niger* frigate and *Latona* were under the same impression and this is the message that the *Niger* relayed back to Howe.[7] The master of the *Culloden* even thought she had been boarded.[8] The captain of the *Audacious* was 'certain' the Frenchman was beaten because: 'His fire slackened towards the latter part of the action, and the last broadside, (the ships sides almost touching each other) he sustain'd without returning more than the fire of two or three guns'. But Parker was unaware that everyone else thought that he had officially accepted the Frenchman's surrender. By 10 p.m. the unsecured prize had already drifted a mile east-north-east. The wind now blew hard and the sea became too rough to continue firing, which according to one frustrated British sailor 'much dissatisfied our officers & the ships company'.[9]

And so the first engagement ended. A French three-decker, much larger than any British three-decker, had been beaten to a standstill, but so had two British 74s. Alone, the *Révolutionnaire* had fought for nearly four hours against six British ships, an extraordinary achievement for any ship of any nation in the entire Age of Sail, and she had inflicted severe damage on her enemies without being able to fire any of her guns from the lowest deck because of the heavy swell.[10] There had also been significant confusion among the British ships. Some thought the *Révolutionnaire* had surrendered, others were not so sure, and the leading, chasing ships had either not seen, in the coming of night and hazy weather, or had chosen to ignore, Howe's signal for recall made at 7:40 p.m., more than two hours before the fighting ceased.

In spite of the lengthy chase and the fact that the rearmost of the French and headmost ships of the British fleets had stopped to engage for more than four hours, the British fleet was still strung out as the sun set on 28 May. At 11 p.m. the *Venus* was still 'four or five miles' from the rear of the British fleet.[11] Making repairs meant that night did not bring any rest for the sailors aboard the damaged ships. Their disability and location was cloaked by dark but with the dawn that security would disappear. There was no way of knowing what had happened during the night to either of the main fleets.

Station keeping by day was difficult, but by night it was almost impossible. The best a captain could hope for was to stay in touch, somehow, without endangering his officers and men or blundering into the enemy. To make it easier Howe had ordered all ships to carry a light, and he had wisely made this signal in the middle of the afternoon when visibility was still good. This was classic Howe, a methodical man planning ahead. Thirteen minutes after that signal he made exactly the same one to the *Valiant* alone, naming her specifically. At first glance, this seems a curious thing for Howe to do, but we know from her log that in the evening she was a full two miles distant from the *Queen Charlotte*, so perhaps Howe was anxious that the *Valiant* might not be recognised if she approached the fleet in the dark and without a light. If we take the evidence of a single ship as representative of the whole fleet, the British recognised each other by three lights hoisted in a triangular formation. At one stage there were so many British lanterns swinging in the night sky that the captain of the *Leviathan* was frustrated in his attempts to signal the enemy's movements to Howe.[12]

Lookouts now strained to follow the blinking and bobbing lights of the ships ahead and astern and the race to repair was run against the rising of the sun. By daybreak, the ships needed to be as manoeuvrable as possible or their security could not be guaranteed. Sailors on the *Audacious* were up all night splicing and reeving new running rigging, no small challenge on a thick Atlantic night in a 'tumbling swell'. Her captain was fretful because he had no idea where he was in relation to the French. The only guide he had to his safety was the absolute silence surrounding his ship. Every preparation was made to renew the action in the night but no opportunity came.[13] The sailors burned up nervous energy waiting, crouching, listening. But nothing came out of the darkness.

Howe made his first signal the next morning at 3:55 a.m., long before sunrise but with flags that would be visible in the first grey light of an Atlantic dawn. He ordered his ships to form line of battle ahead or astern of the Admiral and to leave off chase.[14] The British fleet responded well but one ship was missing: the battered *Audacious* had drifted far away from the main fleet and when dawn broke her sailors' night-time fears materialised into the solid shape of nine French ships bearing down from windward, which her captain witnessed 'to our utmost chagrin and astonishment'.[15]

The *Audacious* fled under the pitiful canvas her broken rig could hold;

a main topmast staysail and a fore topmast staysail, those small triangular sails rigged fore and aft between the towering masts whose damaged square sails had been removed. Her standing rigging, that is to say the rigging that holds up the masts, was poorly secured. With great fortune, however, a bank of fog almost immediately hid her from those prying French eyes. Meanwhile every officer and man in the ship worked relentlessly to bend the foresail and main topsail, but before they succeeded the fog lifted and they saw two Frenchmen bearing down fast. Only when they set the main topgallant and the mainmast studding sails did they begin to preserve their distance from the Frenchmen.[16] Then three more French ships came from the east, an entirely different direction and perhaps from Nielly's squadron, but the *Audacious* could do nothing to change course because of the damage sustained to her rig: any change would mean amending the set of the sails, and though they could withstand the pressure on their current course, such an alteration in direction was unsupportable. The sails would split and the weak masts would come crashing down. The *Audacious* was going to have to fight.

The French ships eased across the British bows and opened fire but they did not sustain it; this was nothing more than a cheap shot against a weakened enemy. Two attempts at boarding were fought off by the *Audacious* and eventually she was left alone. Another French frigate then approached from astern and engaged with a few long shots but she, too, did nothing to press her attack home, perhaps because the ships were anxious to rejoin the main body of the French fleet. By 12:30 p.m. the ordeal was over. Some French shot had damaged one of the studding sails which had to be cut away and cast into the sea but, for now, the ship's safety was assured. The respite gave the sailors a chance to survey the rest of the rigging. The chase had been so intense and the rig so damaged at the start that the foremast was found to be both wounded and sprung.

The *Audacious* had survived, though she had run twenty-four leagues to leeward.[17] At 5:15 p.m. she passed the *Révolutionnaire* adrift with none of her masts left standing and, according to one source, 400 of her crew killed or wounded.[18] The *Audacious* and *Révolutionnaire* then rapidly drifted apart and within only fifteen minutes they were well over a mile distant. In her shattered state the captain of the *Audacious* decided to take her home. She arrived in Plymouth at three o'clock in the afternoon of 4 June, the first firm evidence for those ashore that, far out of sight, two nations were letting each other's blood.

The *Révolutionnaire* enjoyed a similarly lucky escape. Jeanbon and Villaret appear to have had very little detailed knowledge of the previous evening's engagement and both were surprised to find the *Révolutionnaire* missing the next morning. This may explain the curious fact that no French ships came to the assistance of the *Révolutionnaire*, in direct contrast to the concerted British support for the hard-pressed *Bellerophon*. With no British ship keen to or capable of taking her as a prize she had drifted until she was discovered by a 74-gunner from Nielly's squadron, *L'Audacieux*, which towed her back to Rochefort. There, and in true Jacobin style, all of the ship's officers, who had so bravely withstood the fire of so many British ships and for so long, were imprisoned.[19]

As the *Audacious* and *Révolutionnaire* were making their escapes, the two main battle fleets closed once more in the early morning of 29 May. Unlike the previous day, the French now formed up quickly and well, having impressively maintained their cohesion through the blustery night.[20] The sky was a leaden grey, the wind still gusting from the south-west with a heavy swell that thumped into the bows of both fleets, covering the exposed weather decks in heavy sheets of salt rain. The French lay on the western horizon heading south, close-hauled against the south-westerly, their blood-red hulls appearing as black dots to the British sailors still several miles to the east. Howe's challenge, therefore, was to force a battle from leeward, a difficult task that would require his fleet to tack, perhaps several times, within gunshot of the enemy.

Before this attempt could even begin, Howe had to make certain that his fleet was well up with the centre, or even van, of the enemy before tacking. That way, when his fleet had tacked, they would still be able to engage some of the enemy and would not sail ineffectually past their rear. The French, it must be remembered, were not going to lie-to and just wait for Howe's attack, but would continue on their southerly course. Howe therefore had to hit a moving target, a task that required a significant degree of skilful anticipation; everything had to be timed to perfection and then executed without fault. It was a challenge not unlike trying to shoot a clay pigeon with a shotgun. The pellets in the cartridge will spread once fired, but the spread will only be so wide and to stand any chance of success the gunman has to sweep past the target and fire at thin air in the hope that the target and shot collide. In this example, however, the distance and time frame are short and the speed of both shot and clay fast. The extra problem Howe had was that the fleets were six miles apart and only moving at perhaps four or five miles per hour, and not toward each other. The large time frame involved made the likelihood of error far greater as his ships would be vulnerable to enemy gunfire or other accident. There was a great deal of opportunity for things to go wrong.

Just before 7 a.m. the British fleet tacked, the leading ship first and then every other ship in succession, so that they retained their linear formation. Now the British were heading toward the enemy rear at an angle and with the specific intention of cutting through their line. But there was a problem. The manoeuvre had been misjudged. Either the French fleet were moving too quickly, the British too slowly, or the manoeuvre was initiated too early. Whatever the cause, the leading British ships were now on a course that would take them harmlessly past the rear of the French. The initial aim of severing the French fleet had failed, but all was not yet lost. The British now found themselves in a similar position to that of the day before when, by harassing the enemy rear, they had hoped to bring about a general engagement by forcing the main French fleet to come to the support of its hard-pressed ships (see fig. iv). In spite of their best intentions, this had manifestly failed to happen when the *Révolutionnaire* had fought in total isolation against the leading British ships. But this time the lure worked, and far to the west the French van wore round on to the same tack as the British and headed for the battleground.

The French fleet, led 'with great gallantry by a beautiful 80-gun ship',[21] now edged down toward their enemy. The British centre engaged first as the French slowly crept along, parallel to the British fleet. Once the vans of both fleets and some of the centre ships were engaged, the battle formations remained static for an hour and a half before Howe decided once more to attempt to break the enemy line. At 11:27 a.m. he ordered the fleet to tack in succession, but only eight minutes later he annulled the signal. He waited a further forty minutes before he, again, made the signal to tack in succession. But nothing happened.

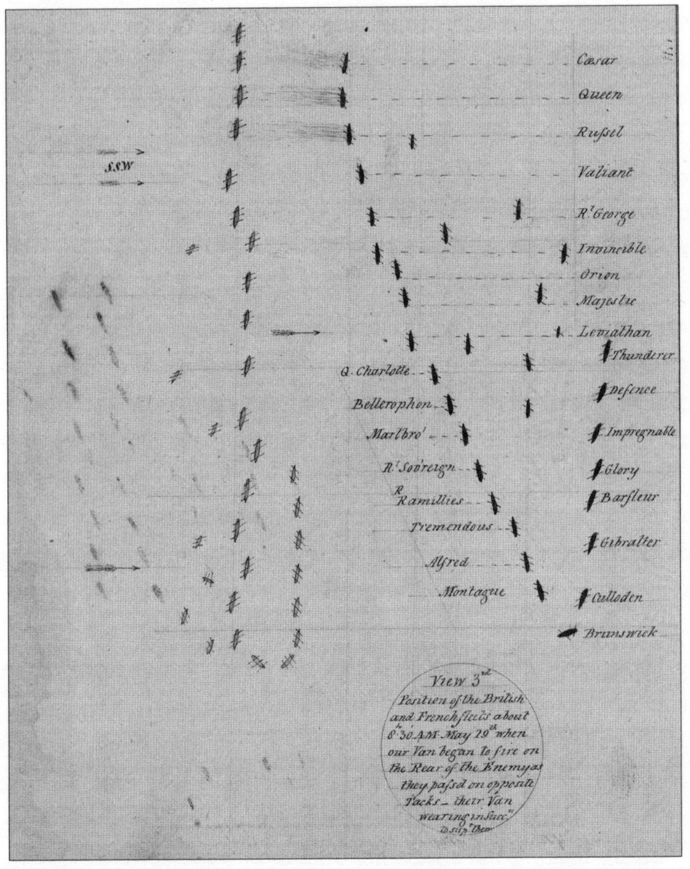


iv. Battle plan made by Matthew Flinders. This shows the fleets at 8:30 a.m on 29 May. The French fleet is to the left. Most of the ships are sailing from top to bottom, but the leading ships are now sailing to support their rear. The British fleet is to the right, heading in the opposite direction to the majority of the French. The British van, therefore, is at the top of the page, engaging the French rear. Howe decided that he would tack the *Queen Charlotte* in an attempt to break the French line when the French completed their manoeuvre.

Howe, at this stage, was still at least five ships away from those engaged at the greatest distance and nine ships distant from the van, where the fighting was closest. Despite the distance and clouds of smoke that we know made the flagship intermittently invisible,[22] Howe's signal was clearly picked up by the headmost ship, the *Caesar*, and her next astern, the *Queen*. It is possible that this was seen from a repeating frigate which is shown to leeward of the main engagement in Nicholas Pocock's eye-witness sketch of this stage in the engagement (see Appendix III, fig. 27). The unnamed frigate [13] has a clear eye-line directly to Howe in the *Queen Charlotte* (K). The *Russell* did not pick up the signal to tack until 1 p.m.[23] The next ship astern, the *Valiant*, undoubtedly saw the signal when it was first made, shortly after noon. None of those ships, indeed none of the entire fleet, tacked immediately and it was not until 1:13 p.m. that the leading ships were seen from the flagship to have manoeuvred, and they did so only once the leading ship, the *Caesar*, had moved.

It is apparent from their logs that the ships were all suffering from varying degrees of damage, and none of them actually tacked, but wore ship. This had the effect of getting them on to the opposite tack but, initially, far to leeward: it did not allow them to sail aggressively to windward and to cut the enemy fleet as Howe had intended. The *Caesar*, in particular, assumed a new course some distance from the French. The *Queen* also began her new course some distance to leeward but eventually hauled her wind to a position between the French and British lines and then sailed down the entire length of the French line, receiving the fire of every enemy ship that she passed, an experience shared by the *Royal George*.

Howe was left with a conundrum. With the exception of the ships already engaged in the van, his fleet was well poised to tack and cut through the enemy who were close enough for this manoeuvre to work well, but his leading ships were too damaged to execute such a plan: he had by now made the signal four times to tack in succession and nothing like that had happened.[24] As the time to take advantage of the relative fleets' positions slowly ebbed away, Howe resorted to a tried and tested technique of fleet leadership: he began the manoeuvre himself, in the belief that his captains would follow their admiral. Howe, in the middle of the fleet, tacked out of line and headed straight for the enemy. He was immediately followed by his 'seconds', the ships ahead and astern of the flagship, the *Bellerophon* and *Leviathan*.

It was a bold manoeuvre, executed 'in the midst of a very heavy fire or cannonade', and the rest of the fleet followed his example as best they could. Howe, still some distance from the enemy, was out of the range of gunshot but the ships ahead of him had moved closer still and several were forced to run the gauntlet of numerous French ships' broadsides. At the same time, those British ships now descending on the French were hammered by a violent squall, 'accompanied by a thick mist and rain, during which no object could be distinguished at 100 yards' distance'. The fleet was thrown into disorder and strength instantly turned into vulnerability. One midshipman noted that, when the mist eventually cleared: 'Scarcely any two ships were on the same tack, and many were near running on board each other … Nothing but confusion was visible in our Fleet, whilst the enemy's line was in perfect order.' He added, ruefully, 'Had the enemy availed himself of the opportunity thus offered, not intentionally, of attacking our broken line, who knows what might have been the result?'[25]

Soon, however, Howe came up with the French fleet, six ships from the rear, and there he ranged alongside the 74-gunner *L'Eole* before cutting through the enemy line across her stern. The *Queen Charlotte* had closed all of her lowest gunports for fear of shipping water as they passed through the line, which made it impossible for the gunners on the lowest deck to glean any sense of what was going on. By now Lieutenant Codrington had descended from his masthead and was in charge of seven guns on the lowest deck, and because he had not received the order he had expected to open fire, he decided to take matters into his own hands. He opened a port, peeked out and saw that they were passing a Frenchman. He then ran to the other six ports of his guns, hauled them up and ordered his seven windward guns to fire before running across to leeward and repeating the attack from the port side. Later, anxious that he had overstepped his authority, he spoke to the ship's master, James Bowen, who admitted that on deck they had been so preoccupied avoiding a collision as they passed through the line that they had forgotten to give the order to fire. And as for Codrington taking the initiative, Bowen was unequivocal: 'I could have kissed you for it!' he told the beaming Codrington.[26]

Shortly after they had passed through the French, however, Codrington was victim to one of the numerous accidents that befall every warship's crew in the heat of action. With decks slippery with blood and water, and sailors' senses numb from the percussion of their own cannon fire, a warship's crew was often as vunerable to self-harm as it was to wounds inflicted by the enemy. Nearby, and unseen by Codrington, an injured sailor was crawling along the deck to get help when he caught the trigger-line of a cannon. The resulting explosion and recoil of the gun caught Codrington off-guard, hurled him the width of the deck into the lee scuppers and thoroughly soaked him in the pool of water that had collected there. The water was so deep that, according to Codrington, 'on leaning on my left arm I could just raise my head out of the water.' He came to, flat on his back, looking at the deck timbers and thought, mistakenly, that he had been mortally wounded. He was only stunned, and was soon up on his feet commanding the guns in his division. Now aware of the quantity of water that they had shipped, the lee gunports which were no more than eighteen inches above the water line, were opened to drain it.[27]

The *Bellerophon* also made it through the French line at a point two ships down from the *Queen Charlotte* and so too the *Orion*, although it is not clear exactly where. As she broke the line her animated crew 'gave three hearty cheers' while 'shot passed thick everywhere'. Several hammocks that had been brought up on deck for protection caught fire.[28] Earlier in the day some members of this high-spirited crew had 'jumped up in the rigging to huzza, & Captn Duckworth hauled them down by their legs'.[29] Captain Harvey of the *Brunswick* struggled to find a spot for his ship but insisted that he '*would* have a berth somewhere'. Having tried already to get in between several British ships he was forced to signal the *Culloden* and ask her captain to shorten sail to make space for the *Brunswick*, which she did; an excellent example of British cooperation and camaraderie in the heat of the action.[30] The *Leviathan*, whose rig was shattered, whose wheel had been shot away and who was now forced to steer with cumbersome relieving tackles, still managed to cut through the French line, and in doing so she left two French ships, the *Tyrannicide* and

*Indomptable*, completely isolated at the rear of the French fleet. Not all British ships were able to do as they hoped, however, as the French were well formed and some of the British were too damaged to force their way through. The heavily damaged *Queen*, for example, failed to cut through the French line on each of her four separate attempts.[31]

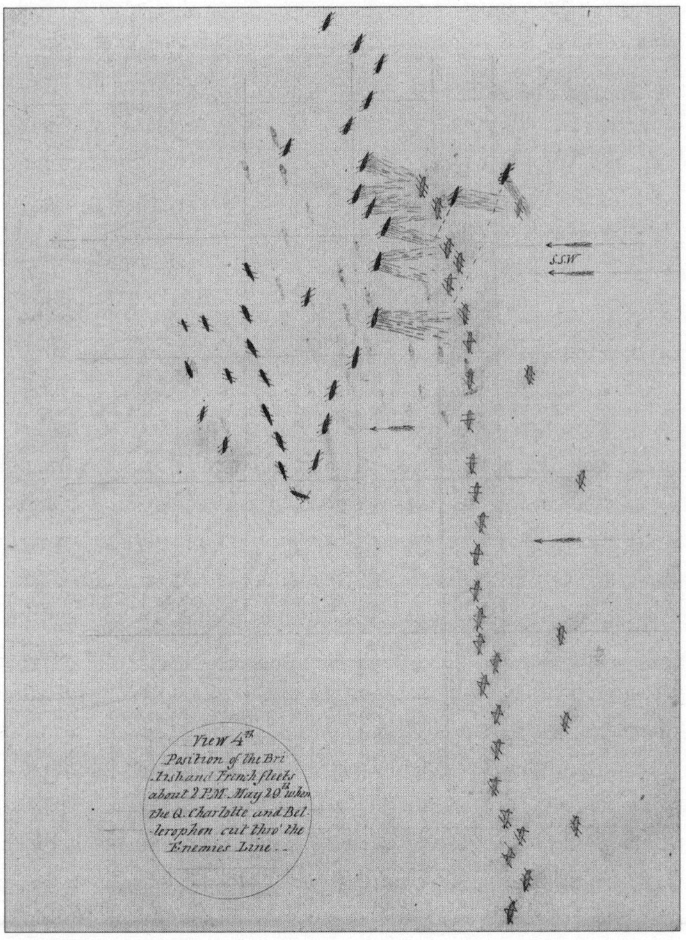


v. Battle plan made by Matthew Flinders. The entire French fleet has now changed direction, but the orientation of the image has changed from fig. iv, and the fleet is now heading towards the bottom of the page. Two British ships, the *Queen Charlotte* and *Bellerophon* have cut through the French line. The rearmost five ships of the French fleet are now severely threatened.

Howe's manoeuvre had cut off five French ships from the main fleet and he was determined to make as much as he could of this advantage. He had little luck, however. Once through the French line he immediately tacked on to the port tack, the same tack as the French fleet, and chased the *Terrible*, but his bold move went unrewarded as the damage sustained by the *Queen Charlotte* together with the large quantities of water she had shipped into her lower deck diverted the men and made her unhandy. The pumps were kept constantly at work while she was in action and there was so much water aboard that they were kept going all that night.[32] The *Bellerophon* and *Leviathan* were likewise shattered and unable to make anything of the advantage they had created. The *Defence*, relatively undamaged at this stage of the action, caught in stays as she attempted to tack after cutting through the French line. Left hanging, immobile and vulnerable, the French poured their fire into her. The shots flew and the sailors died. One was struck on the crown of his head by a splinter of wood 'and when he fell the blood and brains came out, flowing over the deck'. Faced with such carnage, and remember that this was a new experience for so many of the British crews, 'some of the men could not help showing symptoms of alarm' wrote one midshipman. To calm them, the captain, James Gambier, walked the decks encouraging his men and showing that he could master his own fear. At one stage 'one or two shots passed so close to the Captain that I thought he was hit. He clapped both hands upon his thighs with some emotion: then, recovering himself, he took out of his pocket a piece of biscuit, and began eating it as if nothing had happened'.[33]

The difficulties continued for the British. In the middle of the action a gun on the *Caesar* burst, killing or wounding eighteen men. The sails of the *Queen* and *Royal George* were 'literally torn into shreds' and the *Leviathan* was so shattered that the *Queen Charlotte* immediately came to her assistance to draw fire from the enemy ships. Her captain, Hugh Seymour, was deeply touched by this act of selflessness.[34] This was another example of British teamwork at its best in close, chaotic and disorientating action but such examples were matched by numerous others of accidental friendly fire. Pasley of the *Bellerophon* admitted that 'it was difficult to know who was French or who was English, we was all firing through one another'. At one stage the *Culloden* stopped firing so that she would not shoot into the *Orion*'s decks; and that morning the *Caesar* had been struck by British shot and was forced to stop firing so that the smoke might clear and allow her confused antagonist to see her colours.[35]

At the very end of the French line the *Tyrannicide* and *Indomptable*, severed from the main body of their fleet by the British assault, now prepared to face a series of attacks from British ships whose crews had been frustrated in the actions of that morning and the day before when their ships had been too distant to engage. Just as the bloodthirsty British bore down on the isolated Frenchmen, however, Villaret, and for the second time that day, refused to abandon any of his ships and turned the rest of his fleet around and sailed to their support.

This time, however, there were other factors at play. In the morning the British fleet had been in perfect formation, with all of its ships in excellent fighting condition, but now as the French ships wore, numerous British ships, already crippled from the morning's engagement, came within their range. The French bore down, in the words of one sailor 'in a very Gallant Manner & in Good Order towards Our Fleet', a manoeuvre that was also later admired by Collingwood.[36] According to one source Villaret hoisted the signal 'Who loves me follows me' before bearing down. 'The power of the example was irresistible' wrote the same witness. Those captains farthest away obeyed so promptly that they arrived in time to form up at close intervals and within half gunshot of the enemy.[37] The dynamics of the exchange had therefore suddenly shifted. Howe was as good as adrift in his shattered flagship while the French flag, in pristine condition, was now bearing down to attack the confused and damaged British.

As Villaret approached, the British could do nothing to prevent him from gathering his damaged ships into the warm embrace of the main fleet. There was no significant engagement apart from a distant cannonade and the single exception of the British 98-gun *Glory* which passed close enough to three Frenchmen to fire at their rigs. She shot down topmasts on two of them.[38] When the disabled *Queen* was obviously threatened by Villaret's fleet and in danger of being completely cut off from the British, four British ships, the *Royal Sovereign*, *Barfleur*, *Impregnable* and *Glory*, immediately sailed to her assistance and the French backed off. Howe, meanwhile, formed his ships into a line on the starboard tack and kept to windward.

The day thus ended with Villaret shepherding his damaged ships away from the British, who were too incapacitated to interfere. There were also several damaged ships in the French fleet, not least the *América*, which the *Leviathan* had fought until 'there was not one Gun returned, or man to be seen, nor a word to be heard on board [her]'. Another witness recorded how the rammers and sponges had been left in the guns and the ship was totally silent.[39]

The tactical lessons of the engagement on 29 May were surprising: Howe had attacked Villaret's rear twice, and both times Villaret had manoeuvred with skill and precision to come to its defence. This was not the action of a man avoiding battle, but of one refusing to be bullied by British aggression. His ability to get his inexperienced fleet to respond to his directions was impressive, the only example of indiscipline being the failure of the *Montagnard* to obey his signal to wear in the afternoon (though we do know that she was damaged and had an excuse, if not permission, to leave the French line).[40] The manoeuvres were not executed faultlessly by every ship in the French fleet but few fleet manoeuvres in the midst of battle ever were and, more importantly, the manoeuvres were executed well enough and by enough of his captains to be effective. The British were certainly impressed by Villaret's manoeuvres, which says a great deal about their conception and execution.[41] The steadfastness of Villaret's sailors had also been demonstrated once again, as it had been the day before by the crew of the *Révolutionnaire*. This time it was the crews of the *Indomptable* and *Tyrannicide* who had endured more gunfire without surrendering than a great many other ships had in the Age of Sail.

After more than nine hours of engagement and several opportunities to capture French warships on 29 May, the British failed to capture any. It had unquestionably been a good day for the French, who had fought with endurance and aggression and had manoeuvred their ships with skill under the guidance of astute leadership. They had been effective. Jeanbon later described the French behaviour that day as 'eminently glorious'.[42]

Throughout the day the French had demonstrated the tactical value of being passive and reacting to an enemy attack, and the British had demonstrated the difficulty of forcing an engagement from Leeward. Only three of the twenty-six ships in Howe's fleet had actually made it through the enemy line as he had desired. Many were simply unable to get close, being too disabled to manoeuvre in the strong groundswell. The *Alfred*, *Barfleur*, *Culloden* and *Tremendous* all missed stays, which caused the *Alfred* and *Tremendous* to collide, carrying away the starboard and stern galleries of the *Tremendous* 'with other sundry damages'. The *Alfred* lost her cat head, top timber and plank sheer and broke her bower anchor.[43] In the long-standing tradition of collisions at sea, the masters of both vessels were quite certain that the other was to blame.[44]

The British failure to break the line as Howe had ordered was caused by the intrinsic logistical difficulties of attacking from the leeward position. This was part of the nature of sailing warfare. A commander could make a good decision and transmit it successfully to his captains, his captains could all understand and be keen to enact the instruction yet be unable, logistically, to do so. In this specific case, it is very impressive that Howe managed to break through the French line at all, and it is also important to realise that Howe did not accuse any of his captains of indiscipline.[45] Rather, once he saw that the *Caesar*, the leading ship that should have started the tacking manoeuvre, had failed to do so, it was simply 'supposed that some undefined circumstances must have happened in the Van, to render the compliance with the signal impracticable at the moment; and it was therefore annulled'.[46]

The damage reports of the British ships tell a tale of powerful French aggression, though this is in stark contrast with another, particularly vivid, account. One of the most famous eye-witness accounts of the battle comes from the pen of William Parker, a midshipman on HMS *Orion*, and the nephew of Sir John Jervis, later Earl St Vincent. Parker recorded, in a letter to his father characterised by its entertaining prose, how, when the *Orion* opened fire on one of the isolated rearmost ships of the French fleet, the British broadside was so effective 'that it made the Frenchmen according to custom race from their quarters and huddle together down below'. Parker added that 'the enemy fired chiefly at our rigging trying to dismast us & we at their hulls'.[47] These statements have too often been taken at face value to argue for French cowardice and an inappropriate gunnery tactic but we know from Parker's own hand, as well as from numerous other reports, that both of these statements are manifestly false.

Parker was only thirteen years old when he wrote his account. He came from a naval family and would have been indoctrinated in certain myths of naval battle, some of which he writes in his diary, clear to see as he so often repeats the phrase 'according to custom'. Not only did the French flee their stations 'according to custom' but so too did Admiral Gardner of the *Queen* break through the enemy line 'according to custom'. Parker was young, impressionable and inexperienced. This 'custom' is behaviour he had been told about, not something that he had witnessed himself. We know that it was common for sailors to weave stories of enemy cowardice to bolster themselves psychologically for battle and we also know that, although the idea of breaking the line had existed for some time, it was by no means 'customary' for it to be done.

Parker's reference to French gunnery is also interesting. That the French always fired high and the British fired low is a myth that endures to the present day. Parker went on to admit that a broadside from the French ship killed and wounded several men on the *Orion*'s lower gundeck, and that very early on in the action he saw a French broadside cut a man's head in two 'and wound five youngsters, the sight of which "I must confess did not help to raise my spirits".'[48] All of this is evident proof of the French firing low. We also know that Villaret thought that the British gunners had been trained to fire high because so many of his ships were dismasted after the main battle.

The damage figures agree and tell an altogether different story from Parker's: thirteen French ships were dismasted and only four British.[49] The *Caesar*, *Queen*, *Russell* and *Royal George* all complained of hulls leaking from shot holes. The *Caesar* was so badly holed that 'it was with difficulty we could keep her free, for until we had stopped some of the principal shot holes, the leaks gained on the pumps'. The *Royal George* had so many holes between wind and water that two of her pumps were constantly at work. The British fleet also suffered sixty-seven dead and 128 wounded on 29 May.[50] These are not the casualty figures of a fleet that has been targeted only in the rig. Parker's claim that the French were driven from their stations is contradicted by his assertion elsewhere that the French gunners fired into the *Orion*'s hull and there are numerous other sources testifying to French endurance, not least the refusal to strike of *Révolutionnaire*, *Tyrannicide* and *Indomptable*. The master of the *Bellerophon* was particularly impressed that these two-decked ships withstood repeated broadsides from British three-deckers.[51] Perhaps Parker saw some Frenchmen on the weather deck flee; he certainly would not have been able to see inside the French ship's gundecks where the main batteries were housed.

The boy does offer one particularly interesting observation that is so specific that it lets us clean the cobwebs off a Jacobin myth. Soon after the *Orion* had fired a destructive broadside, Parker claims that 'the French Captain was the only person seen upon deck which he walked very resolutely & put every one of his men to sword whom he saw fly'. Obviously the captain cannot have been the only person on deck if he was murdering his fellow sailors left and right, but there is reason to give this shocking observation some credence. We know that Jeanbon had threatened the captains with death if they failed to follow Villaret's orders, and there is every reason to believe that such an unforgiving approach would have filtered its way down through the ranks. There are also a number of references, from the battle on 1 June, of French ships deliberately firing on other French ships that appeared to be on the verge of striking.[52] Although Parker's account may have been subject to some youthful exaggeration, there is every reason to believe that the French tenacity was, in some cases, not the result of harmonious passion for the Revolution as later Jacobin propaganda would have us believe, but was enforced at the barrel of a pistol or the point of a cutlass.

By sunset on 29 May the fleets were ten miles apart. Naval historians have tended to gloss over the events of that night and the following two days but to do so is to ignore some of the most important aspects of sailing warfare and to do a great disservice to the sailors of both fleets: this was no aside to the battle but an integral part of the fight.

As much as the ability to fire, the ability to repair was a decisive factor in battle because these ships were extremely difficult to sink. All canvas and timber could be replaced or repaired, given the necessary manpower and time to do it. In the immediate aftermath of battle, as the wounded lay moaning below decks, or screaming as the surgeons amputated limbs and dug out splinters, the lucky but exhausted sailors who had survived unscathed were given no time to relax, or even celebrate their survival, but were driven to concerted effort to repair their ship. As the two fleets drifted apart on the evening of 29 May, therefore, the battle continued as a test of British versus French seamanship. Which could splice and knot rope, fish wounded masts or yards, patch canvas or rebend sails the most efficiently? Which crews could demonstrate the necessary innovation that would make their ships manoeuvrable by first light?

A system of exchange existed to distribute supplies among the damaged ships. The frigates *Phaeton* and *Aquilon* thus launched their cutters to ship to the *Invincible* '1 and a half coils of different sized rope, some matches, tallow, elm boards [perhaps for plugging shot holes], nails and spare anchor stocks'.[53] Mutual assistance and generosity was one form of currency and ingenuity was another. The sailors of the *Queen* had been in action since eight o'clock that morning but now they needed to replace their foreyard, mizzen topmast and mizzen topsail yard. With no dedicated spares for those parts of the rig they made do with what they had, shifting cumbersome lengths of timber weighing many tons about the rig of their battle-damaged ship. They used a maintopsail yard for a foreyard, a foretopgallant mast for the damaged mizzen topmast and a foretopgallant yard for a mizzen topsail yard. In a little less than an hour they had prepared a foretopmast to step as a jury mainmast. They also bent a complete new set of square sails, and all of this was completed before dark. This was the kind of seamanship that could turn a battle. The next day the *Queen* was not isolated and vulnerable but sailing in company, and at 8:45 a.m. they made the signal that they were ready to renew battle.[54] The *Queen* may have been patched, and with a mismatched rig, but French eyes would have counted the British fleet at dawn and found it one ship stronger than they would have hoped. The psychological impact of such hard work would have been profound. It was the most powerful signal possible that the British were difficult to beat: if you knocked them down, they simply got back up again. Alongside the close battle between men armed with cannon another was played out in parallel and at a distance: the battle of resolve and ingenuity which relied upon sheer hard work and the ability to withstand exhaustion.

The situation in the French fleet is not so clear. Written accounts by Jeanbon tell of some very poor seamanship among the French. The frigate *Brutus*, which Jeanbon complained about regularly, lost a main topmast at 7 p.m. but the stump of the old mast was not removed until ten o'clock the following morning and then the replacement maintopsail yard was not hung until eight o'clock on the morning after that.[55] It is surely worth remembering, however, that Jeanbon recorded this example because it stood out as a particularly bad one. In direct contrast, the British sailors seem to have been deeply impressed by the condition of the French fleet on 30 and 31 May and 1 June.[56] At this stage, the French fleet was improved, in part, by the return of the damaged *Indomptable* to Brest and the arrival of Admiral Nielly and three pristine ships of the line which effectively erased the French losses of the previous two days' fighting.[57] Nevertheless, the French were as mauled as the British in the action of 29 May and they seem to have repaired their ships with sufficient skill to affect the way in which they were perceived by the British sailors – an impressive achievement and a valuable advantage.

The actual impact of battle damage was also far more varied than simply damage to the hull and rig or injuries to men. It is too easy to forget, when reading narratives of battles, that the ships were also the sailors' homes. Even when cleared for battle, the decks remained to some extent encumbered by the essentials for daily life. Foremost were casks of food and drink, which would have been located strategically around the ship, and they were as vulnerable to 'injury' as the sailors. The logs reveal time and again that butts and leaguers were shattered by enemy fire and the broken carcasses later thrown overboard. The *Tremendous* is a fine example: in the action of 29 May, two leaguers and twenty butts were destroyed. Significant enough in terms of piles of splintered timber that would hamper the men, but consider also the fate of those barrels' contents: aboard the *Tremendous*, in the heat of battle, three tons of water or beer would have been sloshing around the decks, dripping through the deck planks on to the heads of those working below. The *Tremendous* would have smelled like a brewery.[58]

Nightfall posed particular challenges. Officers had to pay more than a little attention to the conduct of the crew. With the enemy so close, those aboard any ship isolated from the fleet invested great effort in remaining as invisible or as silent as possible, something which was very difficult on a sailing warship. With as many as 900 men on the biggest ships, the vessels hummed with the sound of constant human activity, and sails flapped and masts creaked, all of which are telling noises in mid-ocean. And it was surprisingly difficult to keep the ships dark as sailors on watch passed with lanterns whose light could be glimpsed through partially open gunports as well as cabin and ward-room windows. Warships simply leaked light and noise.[59]

The lull in proceedings on the night of 29/30 May also provided the opportunity to call a muster, the first time that the ship's company would have discovered the full impact of the day's action. The recently deceased, men who had been injured in the earlier fighting but who had lingered into the night, would be buried.[60] Perhaps unsurprisingly, the stress of the battle was too much for some and the constant apprehension and exhaustion they laboured under posed a threat to internal order throughout the fleet. That tension spilled into violence on board the *Culloden* where Richard Alfred and Dan Malone were given eighteen lashes each for fighting. Another sailor, Pat Sullivan, was given the same punishment for striking the ship's corporal.[61] With these underlying issues surfacing during such moments of tension it is not surprising that the *Culloden* went on to mutiny in December 1794.

Such immediate problems of physical disability and internal distraction were the uncomfortable realities faced by every ship that had seen action on 29 May, but Howe's problem on the morning of 30th was to establish some idea of the fighting capabilities of his fleet as a whole: he could not order the fleet into aggressive battle until he had accurate intelligence on each ship's ability to fight. Another important aspect of the events of 30–31 May, therefore, was the construction of a dialogue between Howe and his fleet. The frigates hovered around Howe and were hailed in turn to be given specific orders to sail through the fleet and determine the location and assess the condition of each ship.

Fog made the operation more difficult but the frigates flew a compass signal showing the direction in which the flagship could be found.[62] The frigates therefore played a dual role – a mix between sheep dog and messenger – both herding the British fleet toward Howe and relaying the secrets of the night. Who was nearby? Who had become separated? And most important, who was fit to fight? By mid-morning the fog had lifted to reveal both fleets, with the enemy on Howe's horizon. Immediately, Howe signalled his ships to form a line, a standard defensive measure in the presence of any fleet. Once the line was formed he hoisted signal number eleven with an interrogatory pennant: 'are you ready for action?' This was no rousing call to arms, but a specific question that needed a specific answer from each ship in the fleet. Much of the information he had received earlier from the frigates concerned work in progress, such as carpenters plugging shot-holes or sailors repairing broken masts. He knew, for example, that the *Royal George* was leaking but he did not know if those leaks had been stopped.[63] Now, at 10:34 a.m., he needed to know precisely the battle-readiness of each ship in the fleet.

The response of the *Invincible* is pertinent in that there was a big difference between being able to fight, and being able to manoeuvre and fight. The *Invincible* hailed the frigate *Niger* to take a message to Howe: her crew had stopped the leaks but her foremast, fore and main yards and mizzen topmast were still wounded. She was 'in every other respect fit to go into action',[64] but this was not good enough for Howe. He could not risk such a weak link in his line. To sail in line without leaving a gap that the enemy could exploit and to be capable of avoiding collision required a ship to be fully manoeuvrable. In Howe's eyes, the *Invincible* was not and, therefore, she could not be allowed to fight. In spite of our perception of sailing warships lining up neatly at close quarters and pounding each other where they stood, the tactics of fighting in fleets were all about motion and manoeuvrability; the ability to fire one's guns was a secondary consideration. Howe ordered the *Invincible* to quit the line. Otherwise, the British sailors' response to the battles of 28 and 29 May was such that only the *Caesar*, the headmost ship of the fleet the day signalled an inability to fight.

Once more, therefore, and for the third time in three days, the two fleets sailed towards each other on the morning of 30 May. Because Howe had found his way through the French line on 29 May, the British now held the weather gage. The contest by now was well advanced. Injured masts creaked as they strained to bear the weight of the sails, fault lines in the timber opened and closed as the ships pitched and rolled, but the spider's web of rigging that supported each mast gave them the support that they needed, even if their captains could not set as much sail as they would have liked. The mizzen mast of the *Majestic* still stood even after a 42-pound shot, from the largest of the French cannon, had passed right through it.[65] The uninjured sailors were tired, the walking wounded uncomfortable, the injured in extreme discomfort, panicking muscles around the injured body parts seizing into spasm as the ships lurched with the swell.

By noon on 30 May, that is a full twenty-four hours after the *Queen Charlotte* had opened fire on the French, her sailmakers were released from mending sails to start making cots for the wounded. They were still at it ten hours later, though by then they had been joined by the ship's carpenters who had stopped plugging the holes in her hull and were now making frames for the cots.[66] The work was endless for everyone. Even the sea was feeling the effects of more than fifty ships clearing decks, fighting and repairing over three days. Isaac Schomberg, captain of the *Culloden* and future naval historian of distinction, laconically noted several English gun carriages floating past his ship on the morning of 30 May.

The rising of the fog had given both fleets sufficient time to organise themselves and assess their capabilities, but just as their gaze turned toward the enemy, so the fog descended once more. It was so thick that one British ship, the *Defence*, was unable to see any other ships at all. The crews, who moments before had found themselves in the centre of a crowded seascape now fought their own demons in the isolation of dense fog. The air filled with the haunting noise of ships' bells.[67] The shipboard posture and routine therefore changed from battle preparation to the gentle rhythms of station keeping in fog, when, like blind men, the sailors navigated by sound. Bells and guns identified ships both distant and nearby, the pattern of the sounds identifying their nationality. This, however, was far from an exact science: at 5 p.m. on 30 May a midshipman of the *Defence* heard a gun which he 'supposed' was from Howe. Battles have been won and lost for such assumptions. The fog never lifted again that day and at 7:43 p.m. Howe abandoned any attempt to find the enemy or even maintain station and simply ordered his ships to close around the flagship.[68]

By midnight the situation had become alarming. No other British ship could be seen or even heard from the decks of the *Queen Charlotte* and by four o'clock only two were visible. Howe therefore spent the early hours of 31 May frantically searching for his own fleet. Once again it was the frigates that acted as shepherds. At nine o'clock in the morning the *Latona* hailed the *Queen Charlotte* and informed Howe that his fleet bore east by south, in the opposite direction to that in which he was going.[69] It was not until one o'clock that afternoon that another frigate, the *Pegasus*, informed Howe that his own fleet was in company. Forty-five minutes later and the French were sighted from the decks of the flagship, a very close call indeed. If the British frigates had not been so effective at herding their fleet, Howe could easily have found himself isolated in the face of the enemy.

There were still several hours of daylight left and the fog had now cleared. Howe gradually edged his fleet down toward the French and ordered his van to engage the enemy van, his centre their centre, and his rear their rear and there followed a distant engagement for a few hours.[70] Shortly before seven he called his ships off from the attack.

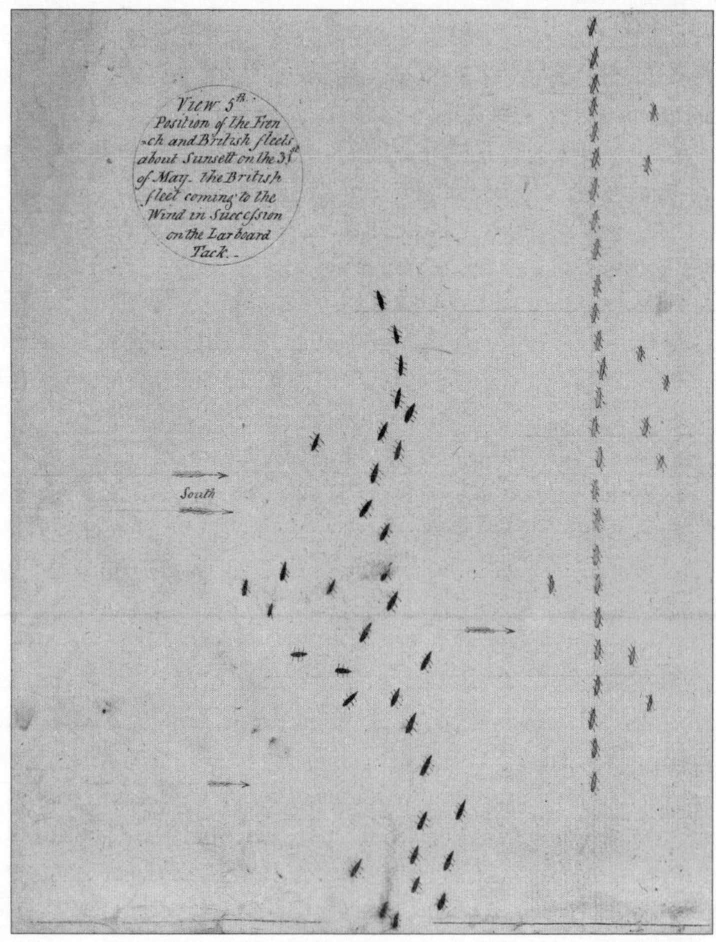


vi. Battle plan made by Matthew Flinders. This shows the fleets at sunset on 31 May, the British to the left and the French to the right. Howe's challenge was to maintain cohesion and contact with the French during the coming night to make sure that no time would be lost in forming up or bringing the enemy to battle the following day. British seamanship on the night of 31 May was therefore crucial to the subsequent battle. Not only did Howe bring the enemy to action on 1 June but he did so with sufficient time remaining in the day to make it decisive.

This was very defensive behaviour. There was no attempt to concentrate the British force on any particular part of the French line or even to force a close engagement. At least one French captain made the mistake of identifying the British behaviour as cowardice but in fact it was a tactic chosen for the time of day.[71] We know that Howe was against night-time action of any sort, and we also know from the pen of a British midshipman that 'Lord Howe always likes to begin in the morning & let us have a whole day at it.'[72] It was in many respects, therefore, a preparatory action for the next day. He was anxious not to lose the weather gage, which would have been the likely result if he had committed his fleet to a full-scale action, and he knew from his experience of the previous four days of contact that the French were not trying to escape. As long as the two fleets kept in touch during the night, he had a very good chance of bringing about an action the following day in the way that he wanted and at the time that he wanted. It is the tactic of a man brimming with confidence in his own ability.

Howe's use of a defensive tactic should not lead us to condemn him for negativity or the system of tactics for being too restrictive but should be celebrated as a wise decision by an experienced admiral with an impressive variety of plans from which to choose. It is significant that Edward Codrington, the young lieutenant aboard the *Queen Charlotte*, spoke much later in life with deep admiration of Howe's ability to pause when others might have rushed. Another British sailor at the battle considered his deliberate delaying tactics on 31 May 'very prudent'.[73] In direct contrast, we know from the scholarship surrounding Nelson that he favoured a far more direct approach, but the context of Nelsonic victory must never be overlooked. Nelson knew his enemy and so did Howe, and those enemies were very different. The French fleet that faced Howe on 31 May 1794 had demonstrated over the previous days that they were both resilient and boldly led, whereas the fleets that Nelson faced at the battles of the Nile (1798) or Trafalgar (1805) had demonstrated in previous contact that they were neither resilient nor boldly led. Nelson knew that their skill was no match for the British. Howe's decision to delay action on 31 May, therefore, was sound.

The night of 31 May was going to be very different from the previous two and Howe needed a good deal of time to make the necessary preparations for the coming day. There was no fog and there was a fresh wind. Both fleets were in good order, the British a little to windward, though a little astern of the French as night fell. Whereas the challenge of the previous night was for the British to keep station as close as possible to the flagship, now their seamanship was to be tested in a different way. They were required not only to keep station and retain the windward position but also to catch up with the French by dawn. With the French already ahead, and showing no sign of stopping as Villaret cunningly continued to lead the British as far away as possible from Vanstabel's fleet, Howe was in danger of finding himself some distance from the French in the morning. That would then lead to the loss of yet another day in manoeuvre as the British attempted to bring their enemy to action before dark. It was a pattern that Howe had to break and he did so by issuing some very specific instructions to his fleet.

We know that Howe spoke personally with six ships, the *Caesar*, *Gibraltar*, *Latona*, *Phaeton*, *Venus* and *Southampton*, outlining his intentions for the coming night.[74] Howe ordered the British to chase through the night and he gave details of his intended sail plan, so that the rest of the fleet could gauge his speed, and therefore retain cohesion, even though he would be invisible. He told everyone that the *Queen Charlotte* would carry: 'foresail, single reef'd topsail, jib, and main topmast staysail during the night if the weather would admit of it'.[75] Every British ship was expected to sail as quickly as possible without disrupting the formation. He then ordered the frigates to patrol in the no-man's-land between the two main fleets, a mile distant from the British flagship, to ensure that the British kept well up with the French. Howe did not just want to be in touch with his enemy at daylight but 'right abreast' of them and in order; he was particularly concerned that they were trying to pinch back the weather gage by getting far enough ahead for the entire enemy fleet to tack to windward of his own.[76]

Thus the anxiety and tension continued for yet another night, but the thoughts of one man strayed from the impending battle to the home where his daughter was enjoying her second birthday. The proud father was Cuthbert Collingwood and his mind was filled with love and apprehension. 'Many a blessing did I send forth to my Sarah, lest I should never bless her more,' he wrote.[77] And so the crews of both fleets stood by their guns for another troubled night, asking themselves what the morning would bring. The answer was destruction on a scale that few sailors on either fleet had witnessed before. On board the *Jemappes*, one French sailor looked back ruefully on that evening and his experience of the distant action of 31 May. He wrote 'We received some twenty [shot] aboard the *Jemappes*, without counting those through our canvas; and in the evening those among us whose first experience of naval engagement this was spoke extremely scornfully of naval warfare, and considered the sunken roads of Brittany and the brushwood of the Vendée a great deal more dangerous.' He then added rather dryly, 'Experience acquired twenty-four hours later caused us to alter this opinion.'[78] The storm of war was coming. Just three weeks from the summer solstice, there were only six hours or so of night before the sun once more lit the stage. None of the sailors were allowed to sling their hammocks but one exhausted British midshipman still grasped the opportunity to nod off. The sky was quite clear and beautifully starlit so he made his way on deck, chose an empty topsail halyard tub, curled up inside and fell fast asleep.[79] The ship rocked and groaned beneath him, the sails cracked to the wind like whips, and his mind whirled with the promise of tomorrow.

# 8.

# The First of June

English sailors never like to fight with empty stomachs: I see the signal flying for all hands to breakfast; after which take my word for it, they will pay you a visit.

Captain Thomas Troubridge to the French crew holding him prisoner aboard the *Sans Pareil*.[1]

Howe had enjoyed the luxury of postponing the action on the evening of 31 May because he had carefully judged from the French behaviour of the previous three days that Villaret was quite content to meet the British in battle. Only once, on the very first day, did the French run and even when the British closed the gap, the *Révolutionnaire* demonstrated a desire to fight. At no stage since then had the French tried to escape and there had been ample opportunity to do so: on the nights of the 28th and 29th and most of the day and all night of the foggy 30th. Their behaviour, rather, had been circumspect, cautious and patient. Only when stung by British attack had they responded fiercely. Villaret had never been ambitious. They had made no attempts at elaborate manoeuvre or formation and Howe would have expected much the same as the two fleets approached each other on 1 June. The security of the French lay in cohesion and both commanders knew it.

Villaret's perspective was a little more clouded. The British had chased him with success on the 28th and had attacked the rear of his fleet with aggression. On the 29th they had attempted and partially succeeded in breaking the French line. On the 31st they had begun a formal van-to-van and rear-to-rear engagement. Three days had produced three very different actions, testament to Howe's tactical acumen and British skill in its implementation. But what would 1 June bring? The variety of attack already ensured that Villaret would have been uncertain of the answer. While Howe had a good idea of what to expect from his enemy, therefore, Villaret had no such comfort. Everything he would do would be reactive. The initiative lay with Howe, not just because he held the weather gage but because he held all the cards.

The creation of such uncertainty was a valuable tool in its own right, later exemplified by Nelson at Trafalgar who made it an integral part of his tactical plan.[2] On the morning of 1 June 1794, therefore, Howe found himself in a very powerful position because he had created uncertainty in the mind of his enemy, not by a feint but by several days of sustained tactical variety: Villaret did not know what Howe was going to do because he thought that Howe could do anything. Would he break the line at a single point or at multiple points? Would he attack in the traditional fashion, van to van and rear to rear? Or would he concentrate at van or rear? The only clue to what was going through Villaret's mind was that the gunports on the lee side of his flagship, the *Montagne*, were shut when Howe broke the line, perhaps indicating that Villaret was only prepared to withstand an enemy attack on his windward side, although there are several other explanations for such a tactic.[3]*

When the fleets sighted each other in the spectral dawn of 1 June, the French were some five miles to the north and in very good order on the larboard tack, indeed they were in such good order that several British sailors later mentioned it in their letters home.[4] Howe, directly to the south, and with the wind behind him, began to form his line almost as soon as there was any hint of light. Aboard the French ship *Trajan* was a fifteen-year-old British sailor called Nathaniel Pearce, who had been captured three weeks previously on a British packet ship bound for Newfoundland. On the morning of 1 June he was sitting on the bowsprit of the French ship, the sea surging beneath him, as her bows forced their way through the swell. The sight of the British ships, so distinctive with their bright yellow sides, was a wonderful tonic for the young Pearce.[5] If only he could survive the battle there was a chance that he could get home. The French sailors immediately began boasting of their martial prowess but the bold young Englishman 'got myself

*Villaret may have been anxious about shipping water through his lee gunports. To open the lee gunports may also have been a tacit admission that he did not expect to be able to keep the British at bay, thus sowing a lack of confidence in the minds of his crewmen.

some good hard thumps for telling some of them they would change their tune before sunset'. On the *Jemappes*, the frustration caused by the inactivity of the previous three days which had 'weighed heavily on everybody' burst with a 'shout of joy' as the British were seen on the horizon.[6]

There is similar evidence of good-natured banter on the British fleet. One sailor recorded that 'The best joke was that the French Commander-in-Chief had the impudence to say to those ships who had joined him that he had thrashed us on the 29th completely & that he only wanted to have another little dust with us before he would carry us all into Brest'.[7] In a brief moment of quiet another young sailor was admiring what he later described as 'A scene of magnificence and importance, not of common occurrence, and not often equalled on the ocean – upwards of 50 sail of the line viewing each other, and preparing to pour out their thunder destructive of the human species, which would decide the fate of either fleet, and probably that of the Nation'.[8] Howe himself, in the words of one more witness, 'seemed to contemplate the result as one of unbounded satisfaction'.[9]

Howe's first signal was made at 3:45 a.m., to speak with the frigate *Venus*, and thereafter he unleashed a flurry of signals as he shepherded his fleet into the formation and on to the course that he wanted. He had made seven signals before he was even happy to form his fleet into battle order. By 7:25 a.m., however, everything was ready but for one minor adjustment that could only be made with the enemy line in sight and abreast: several British ships changed places so that they would be matched against ships of similar firepower in the French line.[10] A frigate was then allocated to each of the three flagships as a dedicated repeating frigate, the *Pegasus* (with the artist Nicholas Pocock aboard) to Howe's *Queen Charlotte*, the *Niger* to Graves' *Royal Sovereign* and the *Aquilon* to Hood's *Royal George*.

Howe hoisted signal no. 34 accompanied with the discharge of a signal gun requiring all of his captains to break through the enemy line. He then turned to his officers, saying: 'And now, gentlemen, no more book, no more signals. I look to you to do the duty of the *Queen Charlotte* in engaging the French Admiral. I do not wish the ships to be bilge to bilge, but if you can lock the yard arms so much the better, the battle will be sooner decided.'[11]

His chosen method of attack first required each ship to steer for its opposite number in the enemy line, which was no mean logistical feat. Fully extended, the fleets were at least two miles long. While it was easy, therefore to work out your position if you were near one end of the line, if you were in the middle it was very difficult indeed. The captain of the *Valiant* was so unsure of his position, and so keen to get his attack right, that he sent a responsible officer aloft to count their position accurately. It certainly was a tricky one: they were ten ships from the rear of the line. The *Queen* and *Orion* were also confused by the challenge and they hailed each other to work out whose opponent was whose. Just as they had sorted it out, the enemy made sail, which confused everything again and the *Orion* ended up taking the seventh ship of the enemy fleet and not the tenth as they had previously agreed with the *Valiant* and *Queen*.[12]

Before the attack was launched, time was made on both fleets for the men to eat. The French thought the British pause was a display of cowardice and aboard the *Sans Pareil* the captured Thomas Troubridge was goaded. 'Wait a little,' he replied, 'English sailors never like to fight with empty stomachs: I see the signal flying for all hands to breakfast; after which take my word for it, they will pay you a visit.'[13] His confidence was shared by other Englishmen aboard French ships, one of whom, incarcerated on board the *Trajan*, claimed that 'there was scarcely an English prisoner on board that could eat for joy'.[14] Those few sources that have survived from both fleets and which mention breakfast complain about it. A young British midshipman said that it 'was a sorry meal, scarcely deserving the name'.[15] The central problem at this stage in the battle was not a scarcity of food but an absence of facilities to prepare and then enjoy it in comfort. The ships had transformed themselves into battle-machines. Tables, benches, stools and cutlery were cleared and, crucially, the stoves had not been lit for some time. The stove of the British *Defence* had not been lit since the fleets had first made contact on 28 May. Nothing was now to be seen on her decks 'but powder, shot, ramrods and instruments of destruction'. It is reasonable to assume that this was the common experience in both fleets. One French sailor aboard the *Jemappes* said that from 29 May onward they existed on nothing but cheese and biscuit, and he added rather sorrowfully 'It is asking a lot to expect men who have fasted for a week to fight to the death when called upon'. On the morning of the 1 June he again complained that their breakfast was 'frugal and hurried'.[16] We can assume that the meal was brief, cold and dry for everyone; this was no hearty and warming stew to fortify the sailors for the trial and torment ahead but it gave them some energy, something to concentrate on and complain about, which, in the words of one British midshipman, 'kept their minds calm'.[17] This was a meal for the mind, and not the stomach.

After breakfast the prisoners of the *Trajan* were ushered into the ship's hold where they would be unable to threaten the security of the ship. Unfortunately for the sailors they would also be unable to see any of the events unfold, something that struck them as particularly unfair.[18] On the *Defence* time was set aside for prayer. James Gambier was one of a few evangelical officers in the navy and he made the time and, more impressively, found the space, to gather all of his officers together. In the words of one midshipman aboard, prayer 'was offered to the Almighty for protection against the impending event'.[19]

As on 29 May, Howe was instrumental in giving the attack momentum, and the centre of the British fleet, with Howe's *Queen Charlotte* at its heart, surged toward the centre of the French 'in a manner that would have animated the coldest heart, and struck terror into the most intrepid enemy'. Collingwood, his mind so often back home with his wife and two-year-old daughter, observed to his Rear-Admiral, George Bowyer, as the two fleets prepared to open fire that it was 'about that time our wives were going to church, but that I thought the peal we should ring about the Frenchmen's ears would outdo their parish bells'.[20]

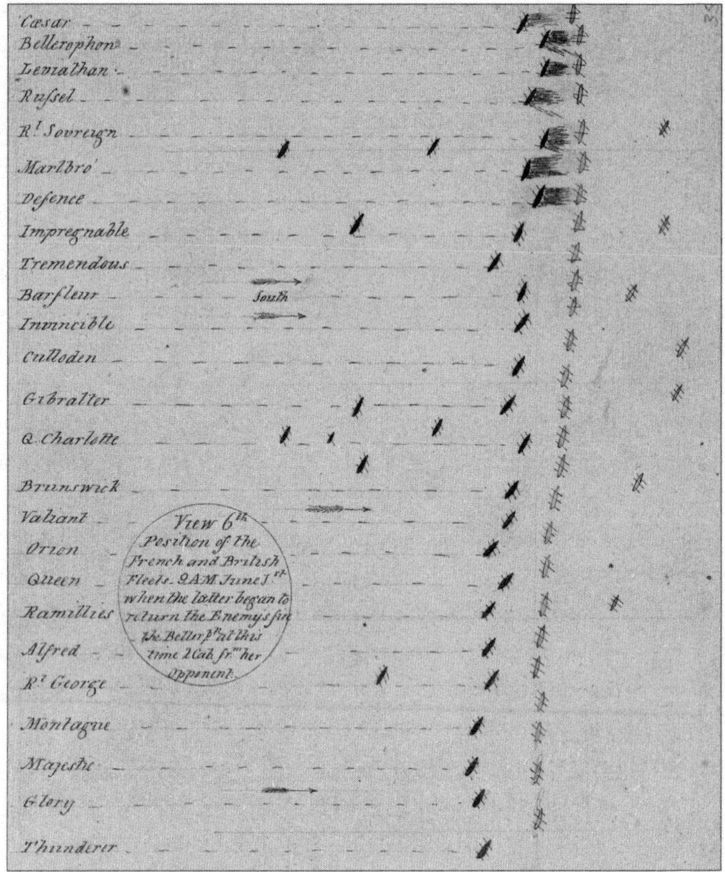


vii. Battle plan made by Matthew Flinders. The morning of 1 June. The British fleet to the left bear down on the French to the right, each ship for her chosen opponent. Moments after this the *Queen Charlotte* broke the French line under the stern of the *Montagne* and the *Brunswick* crashed into the *Vengeur*.

But it wasn't Bowyer and Collingwood on the *Barfleur* or even Howe on the *Queen Charlotte* who reached the French line first, but Gambier on the *Defence* who broke the line between the seventh and eighth ship of the enemy's van.[21] Howe was impressed. 'Look at the *Defence*,' he said to the officers around him. 'See how nobly she is going into action!' Gambier had made rounds of the ship as they bore down. One midshipman noted how he

> … spoke to all the men at their guns in terms of encouragement, to fight for their country. The replies he received were gratifying in the highest degree. The noblest feelings of patriotism were proclaimed, with expressions of the warmest enthusiasm: in short, a determination to conquer prevailed throughout the ship – and, I may as well say, throughout the British fleet.[22]

A similar atmosphere pervaded the French fleet and in the words of Collingwood, 'a more furious onset was never or more obstinately resisted'.[23] Looking back on that battle from 1799, the contemporary author of Howe's first biography simply said 'never had two fleets met in those, or indeed in any seas, more resolutely determined to conquer, or to die …'[24]

The battle began at the van but the engagement soon spread to the very tips of both lines, and for the first time in these five days of sporadic engagement the battle became general. Every captain now had an opportunity to fight. Howe headed directly for the French flagship, which took him on a slightly slanting course toward the French line and, like many other British ships, he was forced to withstand the fire of several French ships as he approached. As they passed the *Vengeur*, three ships astern of the flagship, Howe's crew withheld their fire, saving their first broadside for the line-cutting manoeuvre that would take them across the vulnerable stern of the *Montagne*. The exact timing of that first salvo, however, seems to have varied between gun crews. We know from Lieutenant Codrington, stationed on the lower deck, that he was given 'permission' to fire, something explicitly different from being 'ordered' to fire, a point that Codrington checked before ordering his crew to lie down and wait 'so that we should keep our fire for our opponents – while the men at the next quarters were firing, and my men cheering them'. He only fired his first double-shotted gun when he saw the *Montagne*'s rudder pass the *Queen Charlotte*'s bow port. He then did exactly the same thing with each of the seven guns for which he was responsible, as he saw the rudder pass each port. Once engaged the gun crews of the *Queen Charlotte* were unrelenting and the guns became so hot that they nearly kicked the upper deck beams when fired.* Codrington was forced to reduce the quantity of powder and allow longer gaps between each volley.[25]

The classic British gunnery tactic of withholding fire, so that the British gun crews were fresh when combat started and their initial broadside could be devastating both physically and psychologically, was also repeated on other ships. The *Barfleur* received broadsides from three ships two or three times before they even fired a gun and two British sailors died on the *Orion* before any gun crew had opened fire. On that ship, at least, British sailors believed the French gunners were skilled at long-range fire. Nevertheless, *Orion*'s gunners were resolved to withhold their fire until Howe had opened fire and, as one sailor said, 'he is not in the habit of firing soon'. The untimely deaths of the two British sailors:

> ... so exasperated our men that they kept singing out – 'For God's sake Brave Captain let us fire! Consider Sir two pour souls are slaughtered already' – but Captn Duckworth would not let them fire till we came abrest of the ship we were to engage.[26]

The *Orion*'s sailors therefore lay down by their guns and waited for the order to fire. Like everything else on a sailing warship, there was a skill to waiting. Keep focused. Keep still. Keep flat. Keep calm.

Breaking the line was not easy. The first problem was actually getting to the French line. The French admiral sailed so much faster than the *Queen Charlotte* that Howe, who had initially matched the Frenchman's sail plan, then had to set the mainsail and topgallant sails to get anywhere near him.[27] The French ships crowded close astern of their

*A hot gun recoiled more violently because it caused a far higher-pressure explosion by improving the efficiency of the propellant burn. The hot barrel brought the propellant to temperature faster and ensured there was little wastage: cold barrels had to be cleaned out more due to caking caused by unburnt propellant.[28]

flagship and it was only a mistake from the *Jacobin*, the *Montagne*'s second astern, that let Howe through the line. In the French fleet 'Everybody understood the consequences of this decisive act, and the most hearty curses were heaped on the head of the captain who had allowed the line to be broken ahead of his ship'.[29] Even then, there was little room as the *Jacobin* now ran ahead, immediately to leeward of the *Montagne*. Howe did not think there was sufficient room to place himself alongside the *Montagne* but his master, the larger-than-life James Bowen, responded 'My Lord, the *Queen Charlotte* will make room for herself'.[30] And she did so, firing hard into the great French flagship's stern and across her decks.

So close did she go in breaking the line that the Frenchman's flagstaff brushed the *Queen Charlotte's* main and mizzen shrouds, and the *Charlotte's* guns tore into the stern of the French flagship with great destruction. They were met with equal force.[31] Remember that both admirals were men of immense pride and aggression: we have seen how Villaret ran away to sea in 1765 after killing his opponent in a duel and that Howe was no stranger to duelling. For a brief moment, therefore, the battle between the two great fleets, even between the two great nations, was fought in microcosm between the two admirals. This was not just the *Queen Charlotte* fighting the *Montagne* and Howe fighting Villaret, it was George III against Robespierre, Britain against France, revolution against continuity but, above all, and this is what made the subsequent battle quite so ferocious, it was freedom against freedom – the difference lying only in the sailors' perception of their enemy and the identity of their oppressors.

The *Queen Charlotte* had been badly damaged as she bore down and broke through the line. Then, as soon as she finally broke through, at exactly the same time that she became isolated from the rest of her own fleet, her fore and main topmasts fell as she hauled her wind onto the same tack as the French, a manoeuvre that put a great deal of strain on the damaged rig. These were the masts that were used to maintain one's position in battle. Amazingly, the captains of the foretop and maintop survived even though they fell with the masts when they collapsed. It is unclear how the captain of the foretop did so, but the captain of the maintop was thrown into the water, managed to swim alongside and then climb up the broken rigging hanging over the side of the ship.[32]

Directly to leeward of the *Montagne*, the *Jacobin*, the 80-gun *Juste* and the 110-gun three-decker *La Républicaine* now began to engage the *Queen Charlotte* on her starboard side. The action had only just begun, but the *Queen Charlotte* was already crippled, isolated, and had been doubled. Her sailors on the gundecks were fighting on both sides of the ship while her sailors on deck and aloft were forced to cut away the fallen rigging that encumbered the rest of the rig and threatened to maim or kill any that became trapped in its unpredictable path. Heavy blocks, easily capable of killing or breaking a limb, whistled down cut ropes before finally unreeving themselves and falling to deck or into the sea. Yards, designed to be slung horizontally but broken at one end now swung to the deck like the sails of a giant windmill. As the French cannon fire came horizontally into the ship, therefore, the *Queen Charlotte*'s own rig became an enemy in the sky. The threat was three-dimensional, the likelihood of being injured by part of one's own ship as real as that of enemy cannon or musket fire. The *Queen Charlotte* was in such visible distress that Captain Thomas Pakenham of the *Invincible* sent a boat to Howe offering his ship if Howe wanted to transfer his flag.[33]

Howe had been very lucky in his attack. His ship had not become too badly crippled until he had already passed through the French line and he had been able to break through a gap that had suddenly opened astern of the *Montagne*. Numerous other British ships were not so fortunate on either count. Several were so badly damaged on their approach to the French line that they were simply unable to bear down. The *Caesar* was one such ship: a lucky French shot jammed her rudder and left her unable to control her direction. The weakness, perhaps incompetence in the French line that had let Howe through, was not repeated elsewhere in their line and several ships found themselves forced to sail parallel to the French on their windward side. Captain Pringle of the *Valiant* was simply unable to get his ship through the French line. The *Brunswick* was another ship that could not initially find her way through. She had enjoyed the 'honour' of covering the *Queen Charlotte* from much of the fire of the French centre and rear as she had approached. Now, already damaged, her captain John Harvey searched desperately for a gap through which to lead his ship.[34]

Harvey thought he saw a sufficient gap between *Le Patriote* and *Le Vengeur* but the captain of the *Vengeur*, spotting Harvey's intention, trimmed his sails to catch more wind and instantly increased his speed to close the gap. The *Brunswick*, therefore, did not break clean through the French line but crashed with such force into the side of the *Vengeur* that both ships became locked together as the three starboard anchors of the *Brunswick* caught in the larboard fore-channels and fore-shrouds of the *Vengeur*. Mr Stewart, the *Brunswick's* master, then asked Captain Harvey if he should cut the ship clear, and Harvey replied 'No; we have got her, and we will keep her'.[35] British sailors kept his word and later in the action carefully shot any Frenchman trying to cut the ships apart. At the start of the battle, however, the sailors of the *Vengeur* were not prepared to accept this violent imposition and her men fought with sustained ferocity. Eventually the momentum of the British attack seems to have turned both ships, and together they sailed off to leeward, directly downwind, leaving the rest of the battle behind. This battle within a battle was caught in one of the Age of Sail's most evocative images by Pocock, who was watching the battle from the decks of the *Pegasus* (see fig. 17).

We have a good record of this fight because several detailed sources have survived, one of them written by a woman named Mary Anne Talbot who was serving aboard in disguise as John Taylor. Mary was stationed at the second gun on the vulnerable quarter deck, responsible for handing fresh cartridges to the men. It was not long before she, like so many of the sailors on the weather deck of the *Brunswick*, was injured by a piece of grapeshot that took her in the ankle. She wrote: 'I attempted to rise three times, but without effect, and in the last effort part of the bone projected through the skin in such a manner as wholly to prevent my standing'. She was then shot by a musket ball straight through her thigh. She was taken down to the surgeon who was unable to remove the grapeshot from her ankle because it was so close to the tendons. She survived the battle but the lead pellet remained in her ankle for the rest of her life.[36]

The *Brunswick*'s second lieutenant, Rowland Bevan, described the fight in a letter to a friend. The ships were locked together, he wrote, 'sometimes their guns running into our ports, at other times ours into theirs'.[37] One British sailor even saw the foot of a Frenchman on the sill of his gunport and, in the act of reloading his gun, instead of loading the shot into his cannon, he simply threw it as hard as he could at the Frenchman's head which knocked him off his perch and to certain death between the two ships.[38] At the start of the action, the *Brunswick* was crushed so close to the *Vengeur* that the British gunners were unable to open the nine sternmost gunports on the starboard-side lower deck. Desperate to start the fight they fired their cannon anyway, blowing off their own gunport lids. As the battle continued, the *Brunswick*'s figure-head, a carving of the Duke of Brunswick (George III's brother-in-law) had his hat shot off. This rather upset the sailors who:

> not feeling satisfied that their great leader should continue uncovered in the face of his enemies, sent a deputation, in form, to the quarter-deck, to request that their captain would be pleased to order his servant to give them his *laced cocked hat* to supply the loss. The captain, of course, immediately complied; and the hat, *nailed* upon the head of the figure, remained there the rest of the action ...[39]

Meanwhile sharpshooters on both ships swept the decks with sniper fire and one young midshipman from Sandwich was said to have brought down no fewer than fifteen enemy sailors alone, never missing his man. It was claimed by another sailor that the French sharpshooters were so much more effective than their gun crews that they accounted for most of the British casualties, an entirely plausible claim backed up by eye-witness reports of the *Vengeur*'s gun crews abandoning their station in the midst of battle.[40] Among the *Brunswick*'s crew of sharpshooters was a Dutchman who, 'seeing a hat fall, clapped it on his own head, shot the fellow on the main Yrd to whom it belonged, and seeing him come down, gave him a cheer *en passant*'.[41] The dead of both ships were cast out of the gunports or over the side so that corpses became trapped between the two vessels. Bevan noted how: 'The British and *Sans-culottes* lay on each other till the ships wind [*sic*] and separate a little, which gave the bodies to the Deep…'[42]

Her hatless captain, John Harvey, was then wounded three times. First, a piece of langridge took off three fingers from his right hand, a wound he kept hidden from his officers, before a large splinter, breaking clear of the ship's hull, struck him on the right arm. Moments later he was struck on the head and forced to go below for medical attention. Still he refused help and shouted that 'he would have no man leave his quarters, he had two legs left yet, to go down to the Doctor.' Before disappearing he is alleged to have said in a classic apocryphal tale: 'Persevere my brave lads, in your duty. Continue the action with spirit, for the honour of our king and country; and remember my last words, "The colours of the Brunswick shall never be struck".' A proud sailor from the *Brunswick* then recorded that his captain 'suffered amputation about sunset, on the same day, with the most intrepid resolution, not a groan or sigh escaped him'.[43]

Harvey was just one on the the *Brunswick*'s casualty list, the longest in the British fleet with forty dead and 113 wounded. Another of the casualties was Bevan himself, who appears to have had a lucky escape, being wounded in 'my left eye, my breast and both legs'. When he wrote his letter he was still very anxious about the fate of his left leg. At one stage the *Brunswick* was on fire in four different places, and the *Vengeur* alight twice. When the ships finally pulled apart, the *Vengeur* tearing the *Brunswick*'s anchors from her bows, the *Brunswick* was so shattered that Bevan wrote 'we were left to the mercy of the sea'.[44] Her mizzen mast had been shot down, her other masts were all crippled, all of the ship's boats were destroyed and she had twenty-three guns dismounted. Her damage report records that gunports 1, 2, 3, 4, 5, 6, 7, 8, 10 and 13 on the starboard side lower deck had all been 'shot and carr'd away'.[45] The *Brunswick* by now was some considerable distance from the main British fleet and far closer to the French who had reformed after Howe's initial attack. The *Brunswick* was so damaged that she could do nothing but sail in one direction: downwind. Sailors aboard the *Orion* who could see this all unfold 'were very much afraid she would have been taken'.[46]

It remains unclear exactly how many other British ships actually broke through the French line as Howe had intended. Certainly the line was broken in four places and possibly five or six,[47] but no more than that. Even at the most generous estimate three-quarters of the British line could not, or chose not to, break that of the French. Nevertheless, the few that did make it through caused sufficient disruption in the French line to break the battle into an unstructured mêlée as Howe had intended. Howe's tactics had not been executed perfectly, but he had still achieved his aim: the battle would now be decided by superior seamanship, gunnery and the degree of support between the ships of each fleet.

The *Queen Charlotte*, meanwhile, was rather stuck. As soon as her masts had fallen, she stopped almost dead in the water and, instead of the *Montagne* reducing sail to stay abreast of the British Admiral, she shot forward and then increased sail to get away. Howe's attack had been bold, but he was now so crippled that he had allowed Villaret to escape. This was a major problem. For all of the structural weaknesses of the French ships, the *Montagne* was simply enormous. With 120 guns and a length and breadth significantly greater than any of the British First Rates, she dwarfed all of the British ships in the line ahead of Howe, including the only other First Rate ahead of him, the 100-gun *Royal Sovereign*. In fact the *Montagne* displaced 500 tonnes more than the *Royal Sovereign* and was very nearly ten metres longer. Her lower deck was armed with 36-pounder guns, measured in French pounds which were significantly heavier than British pounds (a French 36-pounder weighing slightly over 39 British pounds). The lowest deck of the *Royal Sovereign*, by contrast, was armed with British 32-pounders. And now Villaret in the *Montagne* moved up toward the French van, shadowed by his seconds, and together they poured their fire into any British ship that they passed.

The *Royal Sovereign*, flagship of the British van, was already heavily engaged with the equivalent French flagship, the three-decker 110-gun *Terrible*, when the *Montagne* and the 74-gun *Jacobin* ranged up on her stern. They opened fire before moving on and targeting the 74-gun *Marlborough* with great success, severely injuring Captain Berkeley, carrying away all three of her masts and causing 'other considerable damage'. The only way that the *Marlborough* could now make headway was, rather cleverly, to set the sails of the ship's boats stored on the spare booms in the centre of the weather deck.[48] Even so, the destructive power of the *Montagne* ensured that the *Marlborough* had become an easy target for several French ships that passed by. She soon had to be towed to safety by the *Aquilon* frigate. The *Marlborough* suffered the second highest casualty figures of the British fleet with 119 killed or wounded. A significant job of the First-Rate three-deckers was to keep the enemy three-deckers occupied. Capturing them, of course, was ideal, but these vessels were primarily there to prevent their enemy's equivalent from roaming the battle, badly disrupting the balance of firepower where they chose to engage. This is what Howe had failed to do.

When Villaret had engaged all of the British ships nearby he then cast his eye over the battle to see where next he could influence events, and his eyes settled on the *Queen*, flagship of Rear-Admiral Alan Gardner. She was adrift some distance to leeward of the main action, in the words of one of her lieutenants '... unmanageable, all her after yards and sails shot away'.[49] When the French line had been broken the French captains nearby had automatically, and with some skill, regrouped around their Admiral. Villaret, now with a line of French ships eleven strong and well formed in his wake, headed for the *Queen*. Howe saw all of this play out in slow motion from the decks of the drifting *Queen Charlotte*. Codrington saw him watching anxiously from the poop and as soon as he realised Villaret's intentions he shouted to Roger Curtis, 'Go down to the "*Queen*", Sir; go down to the "*Queen*".'[50]

This was the ship that had so distinguished herself on 29 May that she had been cheered throughout the fleet. On 1 June she also made certain that she was in the thick of things and fought with immense skill and power. Pocock witnessed her in full flow, '... though it may be improper to particularise where Clouds of smoke kept the chief part of the Fleet totally covered' he wrote, 'yet there appeared something so superior in her fire to that of the Enemy that I cannot desist mentioning Her.' Jonathan Wilkinson, an almost-literate sailor on board the *Queen,* recorded that action in the most wonderfully eccentric letter to a former employer. He wrote: 'Sir in the time of the action you would of thort the Ellement ad bene all on fire and the Shot flying a bought hower Eds 42pr. And Case Shot and dubbel eded Shot it was all the same as a hale Storme a bought the Ship.'[51] Wilkinson continued: 'hower ship ad to run the gantlet twice throw the french lins and we ad no les than three ships uppon us at one time.' The tracks of some of the British ships are a little uncertain but Wilkinson's claim that the *Queen* actually broke the French line twice is supported by another eyewitness.[52]

As she was so obviously in trouble, several other British ships also headed for the *Queen*, led by the *Pegasus* frigate whose captain planned to tow her to safety. The *Queen*'s sailors were realistic. A journal entry records laconically, 'our fleet so much disabled to windward, no hopes of relief from them. Beat to arms'.[53] They braced themselves to receive the French attack. The French fired heavily on her but the formidable fire the *Queen* returned, and the sight of the British ships coming down to her support, was enough to discourage the French from making a bold move to capture her or even any attempt to renew the action. With no yards or sails to occupy the sailors the crew of the *Queen* could focus solely on their gunnery, and to devastating effect.

The battle drew to a close. Villaret was still well formed to the north-east with eleven of the line but the original British attack had isolated seven French ships. All had been beaten to silence though none had surrendered. This enraged Thomas Pakenham, captain of the *Invincible*, who hailed one French ship to ask if she had struck. Her captain replied that they had not, upon which Pakenham 'hallooed out, in great rage, "Then d—n ye, why do you not fire?"'[54] This was clearly a new situation for Pakenham. A man of great experience, he understood that a ship beaten to silence would necessarily surrender, but not this crew and not in this fleet. This was the difference between the French navy of old and that which had been whipped into shape by Jeanbon. This is why the Glorious First of June became known as the hardest-fought battle in the Age of Sail. The British ships, all disabled to a greater or lesser degree, surrounded those beaten Frenchmen in no sort of order.[55]

A little to the south were two disabled French ships being closed by the *Culloden* and *Thunderer* as quickly as they could in their own shattered states. The *Thunderer*'s fore and mizzen masts were wounded and the shrouds of the mainmast, which gave it the support it needed to stand and carry sail, had been shot away. She was also leaking from a large hole in her bow.[56] As they were beginning to close, however, Howe, possibly at the instigation of Roger Curtis, ordered the chasing ships back to the British fleet, perhaps in the belief that the French ships had already been secured as prizes. When it became clear that they had not, and Isaac Schomberg, captain of the *Culloden*, was careful to signal directly to Howe that the prizes had yet to be secured, Howe amended his signal and ordered the *Culloden* and *Thunderer* to take their prizes. But it was too late. The French ships had been towed to the heart of the French line. In fact Villaret managed to rescue five crippled ships in this way,[57] three without a mast standing apart from the bowsprit and all of which might have been secured as British prizes. Every effort was then made to secure those French ships still surrounded by the main British fleet, yet it was only when Villaret had clearly demonstrated no intention of offering them any assistance that these ships submitted to British capture.[58]

Because the *Brunswick* was too disabled to secure her own prize, two of the closest British ships, the *Culloden* and the *Alfred*, raced to the *Vengeur* to claim her. Unsurprisingly, the *Culloden*, a magnificent ship, reached her first. A British officer boarded the ship but soon took himself off again:[59] far from a glorious prize, the *Vengeur* was in dire need of humanitarian aid. She was rolling very low in the water, already with great quantities of water aboard, and now more poured through her lowest ports, many with no lids left to close. Precious time had been lost because no British boat had dared go alongside until the French had clearly demonstrated their submission by hoisting the British Union flag above the Republican colours.[60] As well as the *Culloden*, the *Alfred* and an unidentified cutter were close by and they all began to take off those men who could move. It was profoundly shocking to many who witnessed it. 'You could plainly perceive the poor wretches climbing over to windward & crying most dreadfully' wrote one witness, and another described how 'the most piteous and loud lamentations were uttered'. Boats from the *Alfred* took off 213 and the *Culloden* about 300. The crew of the *Orion* quite deliberately did not send her boat to help, 'because they would have sunk her by too many poor souls getting into her at once'. The crew of the *Brunswick* also declined to offer any help, deliberately withholding their charity.[61]

A few more of her crew of 723 would have scrambled to safety, but a figure of 356 dead and injured has been claimed by one French historian.[62] We do know that her captain, Jean François Renaudin, together with his twelve-year-old son, did survive, though neither realised the other was alive until they were reunited in Portsmouth several days later.[63] Nothing could be done to save the *Vengeur*. As William Parker of the *Orion* said:

> Our own men even were a great many of them in tears & groaning. They said, God bless them, Oh that we had come into a thousand engagements sooner than so many poor souls should be at once destroyed in that shocking manner. I really think it would have rent the hardest of hearts.[64]

Suddenly, the stricken ship righted a little, as if to see the world for the last time, before she sank by the stern. Her foundering was hailed by jubilant cheering from the sailors of the nearby *Barfleur*.[65] So ended one of the most remarkable fights in the Age of Sail. The sinking of the *Venguer* was no fortuitous combination of circumstance, her fate sealed by a large wave or strong gust of wind; she sank for no other reason than sustained gunfire. Her destruction is a unique event in British and French naval history.

The French now left the scene of battle, with a handful of ships left to monitor Howe's fleet. Villaret was out of sight by 6:15 p.m. and the battle was over.

British experiences of the first stage of the battle shared several important characteristics. All of the British ships engaged in close action were very damaged in both rig and hull. Masts went overboard, hulls splintered under French gunfire and shot holes let water in by the ton. Several British ships were so damaged that they had to be towed clear of the action by frigates for fear that they would easily be taken by the French: the *Bellerophon* by the *Latona;* the *Marlborough* by the *Aquilon* and the *Defence* by the *Phaeton*. At one stage the *Orion* signalled to the *Gibraltar* and *Culloden* to cover her from enemy fire because she was too disabled to extract herself.[66] The *Defence* was so damaged that her crew even had to lash some oars to the stump of the mainmast to provide a flagpole from which they could signal for assistance. When Thomas Pakenham, 'a rattling good-humoured Irishman', saw the stricken *Defence* he cried over to her captain, James Gambier, a man of deep faith, 'whom the Lord Loveth he chasteneth!'[67]

Eleven British ships were totally or partially dismasted. All of the French ships had put up a strong fight and none, even the most damaged, surrendered until the battle was over and they were certain that any last chance of help from the remainder of their fleet had gone. Even then, some of them resisted the British boarding parties. Collingwood wrote, 'we understand their orders were to give no quarter; and indeed, they fought as if they expected none'.[68] Aboard the beaten *Jemappes* hope of an end to their suffering was lost when her captain refused to surrender to a British three-decker: '…and calling a signalman he said, "My lad, go aloft and show our colours to the admiral."' The boy scurried up the mizzen ratlines and spread out the limp flag. A French sailor reported that 'the English admiral sent us to the devil with an oath and gave the order to open fire'.[69]

Several British ships, just as they had in the actions of 28 and 29 May, fired into ships of their own fleet: the *Royal Sovereign* into the *Defence*;

the *Gibraltar* into the *Queen Charlotte* and *Marlborough*; the *Culloden* also into the *Marlborough*; the *Queen Charlotte* into the *Invincible*; the *Tremendous* into the *Barfleur*.[70] Nine British battleships, out of a fleet of only twenty-five – that is more than a third – were involved, one way or another, in a 'blue on blue' action on 1 June. Then, if one adds in the *Caesar, Orion*, *Bellerophon* and *Culloden* (again), which were all caught up in friendly fire incidents on the 28 and 29 May, the total climbs to twelve – very nearly half the British fleet. And these are only the ones that we know about; with so many recorded in the few sources that survive it is more than sensible to suspect that the real figure is higher still. The evidence, therefore, suggests that sailors on board British ships of the line faced at best a fifty per cent chance of being targeted by another British ship. The high incidence of this type of self-inflicted damage was a unique characteristic of naval warfare in this period.

In an effort to stop themselves from firing at their own ships, the British admirals all hoisted distinguishing flags and every British ship flew a red ensign, although it does not seem to have worked very well and there are good examples of confusion over flags.[71] In the French fleet, only the flagship flew the tricolour, the newly adopted flag of the Republic, while every other ship flew the flag created much earlier in the Revolution, which was white with a small tricolour in the upper quarter (see Appendix III, p. 363). The flagship's tricolour had a profound effect on one French sailor who described it as 'the square three-coloured flag which as yet knew neither victory nor the ocean, but which this day was to be consecrated immemorially by our blood'.[72]

It is certain that flags were mistakenly identified but, also, at sea and in battle factors such as fog and smoke from the guns could render visibility simply too poor to see even the nearest ship, never mind its flag. Nicholas Pocock's sketches and paintings of the battle scenes give a realistic impression of how debilitating and disorientating the smoke could be, a feature that is missing from so many images of naval action (see figs. 17, 31–32, 38). Over and above Pocock's images, we are fortunate that one French sailor, who appears to have been fascinated by the smoke, took the trouble to write a detailed description of it. Battle smoke was no uniform, single-coloured, single-textured cloud, like a fog bank, but an evolving, dynamic, shifting thing that hurt the lungs and stung the eyes, becoming more and less dense and in ever-changing colours and locations. The Frenchman who described it left us one of the most evocative descriptions of a battle seascape to have survived:

> The cloud which enveloped us was produced by the burning of a hundred thousand barrels of gunpowder; it did not in any way resemble the sea fog of previous days; instead of a uniform grey colour it carried not only in tint but in intensity according to the circumstances. Sometimes it was a thick sooty black, gleaming with sparks and suddenly stabbed with ruddy flame; then again it was transparent, giving to the light of day the appearance of moonlight and blotting out objects by a fantastic sort of mirage. It was frequently sown with brownish circles, floating upwards horizontally, which recalled those traced by medieval painters above the heads of saints.[73]

The smoke was so thick around the *Defence* that the sailors on her gundeck could not see each other. It is no surprise, then, that several British sailors mistakenly believed they had sunk their opponents when, in reality, the enemy ship had simply been swallowed by smoke.[74]

The British experience was also distinctly coloured by the way that the French fought. Howe was convinced that, compared with any other navy he had fought, the French showed a greater willingness to engage close, but once so engaged they were markedly inferior to British sailors. Villaret agreed and suggested that the difference lay in the ability to keep one's head under fire. He later wrote: 'Give command of ships of the line to experienced men who have proved themselves. Courage is innate no doubt in French Republicans, but the man accustomed to gunfire has great advantages.'[75]

There is, also, an evident perception on the part of the British that the French were not fighting 'fair'. Lieutenant Smith of the *Royal George*, for example, describing his experience of the battle claimed that the French fought with 'desperate behaviour and great rascality'. Smith reported that one French ship was seen firing into another for striking and he complained that both the *Phaeton* and *Royal George* were targeted 'in a rascally manner'.[76] The attack on the *Phaeton* was 'rascally' because it was a long-established convention of sailing warfare that ships of the line would not fire into frigates unless the frigates were engaging the enemy. In the instance Smith refers to, we know from her log that the *Phaeton* – a frigate – passed an unidentified French 74-gunner but deliberately chose not to engage 'she being dismasted'. Moments later the Frenchman opened fire, killing two and wounding five of the *Phaeton*'s crew. 'This villainous behaviour disgraces the gallant and desperate spirit with which they fought,' wrote Smith.[77]

There is also good evidence that the French used red-hot shot, as British sailors had feared they would, as well as other curious forms of ammunition. One witness claimed four French ships were supplied with furnaces for heating shot, though he admitted he had not heard that they had done 'any mischief in any part of the fleet'.[78] The 80-gun *Scipion* was without doubt so equipped and at one stage her furnaces were 'knocked down' and the shot that had been heating in them was scattered about the deck'.[79] The *Leviathan* received some red-hot shot, possibly from the *América*, *Trajan* or *Eole*, and so did the *Orion*. The shot burst into the captain's cabin and 'kept rolling about & burning every body, when gallant Mears our first Lieutenant took it up in his speaker-trumpet & threw it overboard'.[80] On the *Brunswick*, British sailors complained that the French used 'raw ore' and sulphur pots that 'scalded our people so miserably that they wished for death to end their agony'. Another source from the same action spoke of 'stink pots' and 'hot shot'.[81]

Contrary to the impression one might get from reading previous narratives of this battle there were a number of examples of British cowardice and incompetence. It is difficult to ascertain how widespread this was because the logs and letters were understandably more concerned about recording 'glorious', amusing or courageous events, but there is more than enough evidence to suggest that a vision of the British fleet all working in harmony is a flawed one.

Aboard the *Defence* a Swedish sailor began to show 'backwardness' as the fighting grew thick and later deserted his quarters. A lieutenant, again on the *Defence*, resorted to drawing his sword and 'flourishing it about with threats that he would cut the first man down that did not do his duty' when he suspected a 'disinclination on the part of the seamen to exert themselves'. And, yet again on the *Defence*, the second lieutenant was so drunk that he fired his guns through the ship's own wreckage hanging over the side, which promptly set it alight.[82] Even aboard the *Brunswick*, that ship usually associated with tales of nothing but of valour and heroism, we know that her captain was forced to go down to the main deck prompted by 'the people's conduct not pleasing him'.[83] Aboard the *Marlborough*, having been shattered by attacks from the *Sans Pareil*, *Mucius* and *Montagne*, whispers of surrender were heard as she lay completely dismasted with her captain and a lieutenant severely wounded. Her crew were raised from despondency by Lieutenant Monkton who roared that he would be 'd—d if she should surrender, and that he would naile her colours to the mast.' A cockerel that had scrambled to freedom from its splintered coop and fluttered on to the stump of the mainmast then clapped its wings and crowed, energising the sailors who cheered in response and there was 'no more talk of surrender'. The cockerel was cared for thereafter with great tenderness by the sailors and eventually given his liberty ashore where he lived with the Governor of Plymouth and was frequently visited by members of the *Marlborough*'s crew.[84]

The French shared many of these experiences. Their British opponents fought with resolve and great effectiveness. All the French ships who were closely engaged were severely damaged and thirteen were totally or partially dismasted. They were as encumbered by the smoke as the British, Jeanbon recording that they were forced to rally to the sound, and not the sight, of their friends. Several French ships, also, fell victim to friendly fire; the *Jacobin* even fired into the fleet flagship.[85]

Significantly, however, the French experience was on a different scale in terms of damage to manpower. There is evidence that the British gunpowder proved less effective than had been hoped, and certainly less effective than it was later on in the war,[86] but, still, *thousands* more French than British sailors died. This discrepancy can be partly explained by inferior gunpowder – even less effective than that of the British – and the French ships' design which rendered the vessels light but inherently weaker. Many of the British ships were targeted in their hulls but some, despite hundreds of shot in their hulls, had relatively low numbers of casualties. On the *Culloden*, for example, with a 'vast number' of shot in her hull, the figure was astonishingly low: two British sailors died and fourteen were wounded, only five of whom were unable to return to their duty.[87] On the French ships hundreds died at a time. Several sources have estimated that perhaps 350 lay dead in the gun-decks of the *Montagne* alone, which also had some 250 shot in her starboard side having received fire from at least six British ships. Villaret had a very lucky escape when, during the action, his chair was shot from beneath him. The *Trajan* was raked repeatedly by British ships and her gun crews stationed on the forecastle suffered particularly horribly. The crews of those guns had to be replaced *five* times: the station was a death trap.[88]

In at least one case, the huge number of dead or wounded on one French ship made it impossible for her remaining crew to take advantage of an opportunity to inflict severe casualties on their enemy. A French three-decker passed by the vulnerable stern of the helpless *Defence*, whose sailors were ordered to lie down to receive the fatal fire they all knew would come. Midshipman Dillon wrote of it:

> This was, to me the most awful part of the battle ... we could not defend ourselves from the stern, and here was an immense overpowering ship of upwards of 100 guns going to pour in her broadside into the weakest and most exposed part of the ship. It was a moment of extreme anxiety. As there was the chance of our being sunk ... we waited the coming event with a silent suspense not easily described.[89]

But to the crew's astonishment and relief, the hail of death never materialised; only a few cannon were let off, randomly, which did no more than bring down the *Defence*'s already disabled foremast. British gunfire had already taken its toll aboard the French ship. With most dead and injured, what was left of her gun crews were at the pumps or desperately trying to secure the rigging: there was no one left at their quarters to fire shot. In such fleeting opportunities lay the seeds of victory. Had the French had enough gunners, as they did at the start of the action, they would have been able to seize this kind of chance, as they did, for example, when they raked the foredecks of the *Defence* with grapeshot, killing the master, boatswain, captain of the forecastle and 'nearly the whole party of the Queen's 2nd regiment stationed forward …'[90] As the battle progressed, however, the discrepancy between the effectiveness of British and French gunfire took its toll on French manpower. The British powder was stronger and their ships' hulls were stronger, thus British crews were much less likely to be driven from their station by an enemy broadside. Ultimately, British gun crews were not only able to maintain their fire longer than the French but, also, their fire was more effective in the first place.

It appears British gunners had new technology that allowed them to reload with the gunport lids shut. The tools used to clean and reload the guns were usually long, straight instruments called spoons, sponges, rammers and 'worms' – so named for its corkscrew tip for cleaning the gun. The British had recently introduced flexible handles for these tools, which made it easier to reload the guns from farther inboard. Sailors with traditional rigid-handled tools, by contrast, were compelled to 'expose their persons, even to climbing half-way out of the ports'.[91] The ability of the British to lower their gunports if they desired 'was a great casualty-preventer, and proved a considerable advantage to the British'. The same witness claimed that he distinctly saw a Frenchman 'riding upon a lower deck gun, loading it'.[92]

Aboard the *Marlborough* the captain was trialling a new method of securing the guns to the ship's sides. Pioneered by a carpenter disabled in an action long past and who had since dedicated his energy to innovation, it involved securing the cannon by one tackle, not the traditional two. The advantages of this were considerable: it ensured the gun was run out and recoiled through the centre of the gunport every time, it needed men on only one side of the gun to move it around, leaving the other side clear for men to load it, and the gun could be worked with fewer men. The ship's captain, George Berkeley, wrote to the admiralty singing the praises of the new method, though it remains unclear if it was more widely adopted.[93]

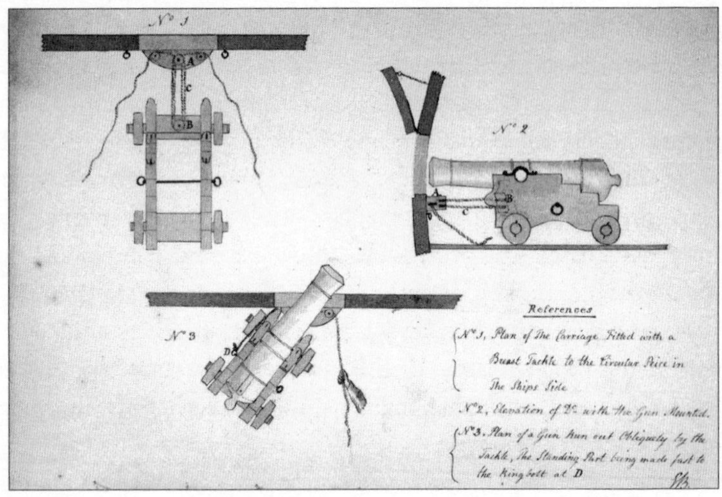


viii. The new gun tackles trialled aboard the *Marlborough*, devised by a disabled carpenter, James Hooper. The lower image shows how the new system allowed those manoeuvring the gun to work on one side only when the gun was set at an extreme angle, leaving more space for the rest of the crew to clean, load and fire the gun.

There is also the issue of gunlocks to consider, the flintlock firing mechanism for cannon. This very important device had not been introduced to the French navy. British guns, by contrast, had been equipped with gunlocks from as early as 1745, their gunners were skilled at using them and the British benefited greatly from their advantages over the linstock – a length of burning match secured to the end of a stick. When using a linstock, the man who fired the gun had to be to the side of the gun, he could not sight along its length to aid his aim as he could with a long lanyard attached to a gunlock. Another advantage was that the gun was ignited without any loose priming powder. When using a linstock, loose powder was poured down a touch-hole which fed into the pierced cartridge, a process which worked but was neither wholly reliable nor safe. The gunlock, in contrast, was used with a quill or tin tube filled with powder that was injected directly into the cartridge.[94] The gunlock therefore made gunnery safer, more reliable and more accurate and it is highly significant that, in Mather Brown's celebrated contemporary painting of the *Queen Charlotte* after the battle, not only does he give a gunlock a prime place in the painting but Howe is gesturing toward it and Roger Curtis's hand is resting right next to it: Brown meant the gunlock to be noticed (see fig. 19).

Another factor regarding the discrepancy between each side's gunnery is that the French cannon were much larger and heavier than those of the British which, on the French ships, made the whole process more tiring and more time-consuming, a devastating burden on their depleted crews. One final reason for the overriding effectiveness of British gunnery lies, perhaps, in the tactics used. There are two reports from this battle claiming that, when engaged close, the guns of the British ships were aimed alternately, high then low, firing up through the enemy's decks and then down through the hull, effectively trapping the sailors in a deadly diagonal crossfire from which there was nowhere to hide.[95] A middle-deck gun on a British ship, therefore, was able to fire at the gundeck directly opposite but also on those decks above and below it.

A further difference in the French experience during this battle was in the level of support that ships from the respective sides gave each other. There were examples of French ships coming to one another's aid, but they were very rare and often the rescuer was so crippled by British gunfire that they, too, were forced clear. As a rule, French ships did not support each other as the British did.[96] Consider the engagement between the *Brunswick* and the *Vengeur*. Driven to leeward, they continued their fight for more than an hour and a half, until Henry Harvey, captain of the *Ramillies* and brother of John Harvey, the *Brunswick*'s captain, bore down to his brother's assistance: 'Word was instantly passed, that the brave Captain Harvey was come to the support of his gallant brother. The cheering again became raging, the seamen lying out of the ports, to see her, as she was coming up on our larboard quarter.' As the *Ramillies* arrived, the *Brunswick*'s crew managed finally to free themselves from the *Vengeur* and as the Frenchman bore away, the gunners of the *Brunswick* 'split her rudder, [and] stove her stern post into shivers; we saw the water pouring into her counter by tons'. At this point the *Ramillies* opened fire, her gunners having carefully laid their cannon so they did not fire into the *Brunswick*. 'Such a tremendous fire, in my life, I never saw or could have believed,' wrote one witness ... 'I verily think every shot struck her, and as she was within pistol distance, the effect must have been terribly severe'.[97] Thomas Pakenham of the *Invincible* similarly appreciated, via a 'cordial and grateful Acknowledgement', the support he had received in the heat of the battle from the *Royal George*, *Orion*, *Barfleur* and the *Queen Charlotte* that effectively drew fire from the *Invincible* when she broke the enemy line on 1 June.[98] This pattern seems to have been repeated numerous times and the abiding lesson of the battle is that a French ship which had enjoyed success against a British opponent soon found herself facing one, two or three more British ships. With the single exception of Villaret's flagship, which appears to have acted as a particularly powerful magnet, the same could not be said for the other French ships, a fact that Villaret himself acknowledged: 'if all captains had done their duty, if without consulting tactics they had consulted the sentiment of nature to fly to the rescue of one's brother, 13 Prairial [1 June] would never have been made infamous to the French navy.'[99]

The British had captured six French ships and sunk another. The French had neither captured nor sunk any British ships. The sources do not agree, but that 1,098 British sailors were killed or injured is a reasonable estimate. In the wars of 1793–1815 only the Battle of Trafalgar had higher British casualty figures.[100] Sixty-two of those dead and injured were officers, and many of those were both experienced and high-ranking. The luck of Rear-Admiral Pasley, who had so bravely fought his *Bellerophon* on 28 and 29 May and then again on 1 June, finally ran out when he lost a leg from a shot which came through the barricading around the quarter deck.[101] Rear-Admiral Bowyer was also injured and so too were Vice-Admiral Hood and Captains Hutt, Montagu and Harvey. Collingwood emphasised that a 'great number' of lieutenants, the future of British naval command, had been killed or wounded and five midshipmen, all teenage boys, died.[102] The Royal Navy also lost four of its masters, each a seaman of vast experience and authority. One master's mate also died. The French, by contrast, lost 1,590 killed or injured on the six captured French prizes and the sunk *Vengeur* alone. It has been estimated that, in total, somewhere between 5,000 and 7,000 Frenchmen were killed, wounded or taken prisoner, though only four captains died or were injured.[103]

Could it have been better for the British? Almost from the moment that news of the battle reached England Howe has been criticised for failing to capture more ships.[104] Certainly, in the latter stages of the battle there was a mistake in recalling the *Culloden* and *Thunderer* from their near-capture of two disabled prizes, but the majority of the British fleet were simply unable to launch any sort of renewed attack against the French who were, at the end of the battle, already in good formation. The sailors were all exhausted after five days of action, not least the 68-year-old Howe. Howe did not go to bed once during the three-day chase leading up to the action, let alone the ensuing five days of contact. From the morning of 28 May his only resting place had been an armchair in his dismantled 'cabin' where his only privacy from the crew had been behind a hastily erected canvas screen. It had been so cold that Howe spent the few quiet moments available wrapped up in his greatcoat and huddled into his armchair. Unsurprisingly, at the end of it all, he collapsed. Codrington wrote:

> On such occasions one is enabled familiarly to approach a man in his situation. We all got round Lord Howe indeed, I saved him a tumble; he was so weak that from a roll of the ship he was nearly falling into the waist. 'Why, you hold me as if I were a child' he said to me good-humouredly.[105]

Jonathan Wilkinson of the *Queen* recorded how 'we lay upon the Decks at hower guns all night for two nights and three days'.[106] This was no short, sharp battle but a campaign of unremitting tension over five full days and five full nights, and even then there was still much work to be done on every British ship and prize to make all secure against the elements. Collingwood, a truly dedicated correspondent, was too tired and busy after the battle to write more than a few lines to his wife.[107]

There was desperate and imaginative repair, just as there had been on 28 and 29 May, but now there were more ships affected, the men were more tired, there were fewer spares to make good those repairs and fewer men to carry them out. On 2 June many British ships had to go through the same dispiriting rigmarole of 29 and 30 May, when the musters were taken to ascertain exactly who had died or been injured in the preceding day's battle. Crews were sent on to prize ships and more were required to transport and then guard the prisoners, a task shared throughout the fleet and one of no small responsibility. Sailors of the captured *Juste* got drunk, rioted and threatened to blow up the ship, thereby requiring a considerable armed presence from the *Latona* and some time-consuming reallocation of the *Juste*'s captured crew. The captain of the *Latona* was so concerned that he signalled for 'boats manned and armed' to come to his assistance, a signal studiously ignored by the entire British fleet. Eventually the *Invincible* took sixty troublemakers off the *Juste*,[108] and this was a relatively small number: the *Royal Sovereign* took no fewer than 348 prisoners and even after some redistribution among other ships, she took 239 back to England. The *Majestic* carried 270 prisoners, the *Culloden* 221 and the *Orion* 209; only one ship, the *Marlborough*, carried none, and for such a large ship the *Queen Charlotte* had surprisingly few – only eighty-eight, and they had all been transferred to another ship by 16 June.[109] That there were at first so few prisoners aboard the *Queen Charlotte* before they were swiftly moved, must be interpreted as a remarkable perk of the flag officer. Howe's ship was no more damaged than any other, it was one of the largest in the fleet and yet it sailed back to England with not one extra man aboard while the *Latona,* a small frigate, took 140 prisoners when her full complement of men was only 290 – so she had to find space for nearly 50 per cent more men than she was designed to carry.[110]

Space had to be found for the prisoners, along with food, water and medical relief for the most desperate among them, and then British crewmen who were sufficiently alert and physically fit were posted as guards. Empty casks were all heaved overboard to make room for the prisoners. The *Queen Charlotte* alone threw away eighty-nine butts with '890 hoops' which they entered into their log to ease the investigations of dockyard officers on their return to port. Similarly, the log of the *Ramillies* recorded 70 butts of beer destroyed or dismantled and the cooper of the *Orion* was employed for the entire day following the battle.[111]All prisoners were fed at two-thirds the seamen's allowance.[112] If the British were anxious to contain their prisoners, the French were keen to put theirs to work. Unfortunately for Nathaniel Pearce, a young prisoner on the French ship *Trajan*, he and his fellow captives were hauled out of the hold and, having been given a double allowance of wine, ordered to help the surviving Frenchmen repair the ship.[113]

Spare masts and rigging had to be sent throughout the fleet and it is far too easy to overlook the logistical challenge this posed. The first problem was the variety of items needed for repair. The *Invincible*, for example, received help from four different ships: two fishes from the *Aquilon*, two carpenters from the *Latona*, and wads, grease, spikes, oakum, cordage and sails from the *Venus* and *Phaeton*.[114] The next problem was the sheer scale of some of the parts and equipment that needed to be moved. The *Southampton*, for example, sent the *Royal George* a main topmast, main topsail, topsail yard, main topgallant mast, topgallant yard, main topmast cap and cross trees, a vast amount of rigging and timber.[115] Each spare mast and yard was unwieldy and heavy and needed to be floated or shipped over in small open boats in a heavy swell by exhausted sailors, who then had to come alongside the towering hulks of dismasted battleships rolling uncertainly and deeply. The spares then had to be hoisted aboard, in many instances without any of the functioning masts or rigging that would, normally, have provided the height and leverage of a natural crane, something that would have made the whole process relatively manageable and safe given a calm sea and a fit crew. With little or none of this in place it was a formidable and extremely dangerous struggle even to raise spare yards from the sea on to a warship's weather deck, let alone to swing them aloft. Only then could the lengthy and dangerous process of rigging a jury mast even begin.

The conditions for such repair were atrocious. Even walking around one's own ship was at times compromised – aboard the *Defence* no one could access the quarter deck because the splinter netting had collapsed, effectively turning it into a giant cage.[116] Stray cannon fire had affected repair during the action. The British *Impregnable* was in a terrible state:

> … our own ship nearly unmanageable, expecting the Fore mast and mizzen mast to go overboard, both shot through and otherwise damaged. The forestay cut through – most of the fore shrouds and lanyards of others, gone most of the Topmast Rigging and Backstays cut; maintopmast shot through, and cut in other places – Fore and MainYards shot through and Mizen Yard down …[117]

Her sailors, meanwhile, were repairing her split mizzen mast with a fish. An appropriately sized piece of timber was found, prepared and carried to the mizzen mast and then, just before it was secured into place, it was damaged by a stray shot and they had to start all over again. In other examples, the crew of the *Phaeton* frigate lost overboard a 150-fathom 'deep sea line', dropped while being lowered into a boat and the hawser they were using to tow the *Defence* broke and only ten fathoms were saved. There would have been innumerable, similar accidents as the fleet struggled with broken ships and exhausted, broken men but there was neither time nor desire to record mistakes.[118]

Thus the spirit of these men was tested relentlessly and in more ways than we might suspect. The best crews just got on with what needed doing with a wry smile or a hail of expletives. Aboard the *Queen* there even seems to have been a sense of competition between the officers 'to vie with each other for distinction' in the refitting of the ship, an activity in which the entire crew demonstrated an 'unequalled zeal & activity'.[118] The weak sailors on damaged ships, by contrast, could face it no more and they waited for anyone, of any nationality, to come and take charge. Several days after the battle a sermon was preached aboard the *Bellerophon* to help the crew through this trying time. We are particularly lucky in this instance – we know what was said because the sermon was printed and then sold to raise money for injured sailors and their dependants. The relatively small number of dead and the perception that the British had defied great odds, which was claimed to have been of an inferiority of 360 guns and 8,370 men, was seen as proof of God's support for the British cause.[120]

Conditions below deck were grim. With the prisoners aboard, the lower decks were more crowded than usual and the water seeping through holes in the hull and split seams made everything wet. Many of the men had been soaked for hours. William Dillon had peeked out of a gunport early on in the action and was drenched when the sea poured in, an event which greatly cheered those who witnessed it. One wag said, 'We hope, Sir, you will not receive further injury. It is rather warm work here below: the salt water will keep you cool.'[121] His clothes were still wet and, by now, covered in blood. This was no laughing matter for a shocked and fatigued teenage boy on a cold, damp ship and with night approaching fast.

Some ships, like the *Brunswick*, had no gunport lids to keep the sea at bay, having deliberately blown them off in their enthusiasm to fire at the *Vengeur*. Other ships were able to close their lids but had already shipped great quantities of water. Dismounted cannon, loose cannonballs and wet blood made conditions treacherous for the sure-footed and a nightmare for those injured favouring one limb over another. It was also very cold aboard; the wind would have whistled right through the ships until repairs were made. The master of the *Culloden* estimated that 200 panes of glass had been broken on his vessel and the windows of the *Arethusa* were 'all smashed'.[122] Even if a moment could be spared for sleep it would have to be taken rough, and for some it would stay that way for the foreseeable future – when the masts of the *Marlborough* and the *Defence* went overboard they took with them all the sailors' hammocks which had been lashed to the railings as part of the ship's routine for clearing for action. Midshipman William Parker's cot[123] survived the French onslaught, and peppered with case shot it became a treasured possession of a very proud young man.[124]

As they were on 29 May, the men's victuals had again been incidental targets of enemy fire. Food and water was damaged and now, with everyone quivering with nervous energy, would have been the worst possible time for the sailors of the *Russell* to discover a barrel of pork to be inedible. Some of the *Defence*'s huge water barrels had been polluted when bags of salt, hanging over the barrels, had been shot. The *Queen Charlotte* lost a cask of pork, and the *Tremendous* lost a pipe of wine and two puncheons of rum.[125] But these were all minor losses compared with the French *Jemappes*. She had been so badly damaged by 150 shot-holes on or just above the waterline that, when the sailors listened at the hatchways, they 'could hear the sea washing in through the shot-holes on the waterline and cascading into the body of the ship'; surely enough, the entire forward biscuit-room was flooded. A young French sailor on the *Jemappes* stated explicitly that the suffering of the injured was increased by the destruction of the ship's stores. He, relatively uninjured, could find nothing to drink, a serious problem because battle at sea created an intense thirst and debilitating dehydration.

The recollections of that same boy give us a wonderful insight into the effect of battle on a young mind and body. He went to the surgeon to have a large splinter removed from his face but when he saw the surgeon 'get out his knives, all bloody and splintered by the work to which he had been putting them, in order to open my face' he thanked the surgeon for his 'polite intentions' and ran away. He then went to the lower battery and was shocked once more:

> I was filled with a sense of horror which no amount of reasoning could conquer, at the aspect of the charnel-house which once had been the lower battery. To start with it had been necessary to put the wounded there, for whom there was no room in the hospital on the orlop deck; then, when the orlop deck had to be abandoned owing to the water, we had to haul up these wretched creatures, mostly dangerously or even mortally wounded, and put them side by side in two lines in the battery. The luckiest were those who had a friend or brother to give them what little attention our appalling situation permitted. They at least got something to drink, whereas the others vainly prayed or cursed for water.[126]

He fled from the decks and their 'terrible stench of carnage' until, on the weather deck, and in the fresh air of day, an old helmsman rolled him in a flag and laid him to sleep on the corner of the poop deck. The boy was 'devoured by thirst' and when the ship's captain came up and offered him a sip of water, it was all finally too much and he burst into tears. Over the next few days the rest of his watch took turns offering to take his place and the ship's officers sent him food from their table.[127]

There are several examples of men showing no apparent effects of their experience of battle, such as Mr Ritchie from the *Defence* of whom it was reckoned 'had it not been for the bloody marks upon him, one might have supposed he had been at a merry and jovial party instead of a destructive battle.'[128] Nevertheless, many battle-weary sailors would have suffered from some form of psychological shock, just like the French boy nursed by his crewmates. While the subject might be physically unscathed, psychological shock could cause a range of physical symptoms from paralysis, uncontrollable shivering and nausea to exhaustion, light-headedness and confusion. It was all too much for Jonathan Wilkinson of the heavily damaged *Queen*, who wrote home soon after the action. He was barely literate and this letter now reads as a desperate attempt to get home:

> I have bene this three years at seea and as but ad my foot on shore 5 times pleas to be so good as to give my respects to Salley Barrows … I hope this whar will not be long and then I meane to Cum down to See you plas God to Setel at home witch I make no doupt but what you wood be glad to see your old Servant once more all thos it is so long Since I lived with you as a boy you may of forgoot me …[129]

Seven months later, in January 1795, he deserted, and it is nice to think that he may have received a reply to his letter and that he made it back home. Other British sailors reacted to the horror of battle in an all too predictable but nevertheless understandable way: they got drunk, and drunkenness led to rioting. The behaviour of Abraham Bible of the

*Orion* was so bad that time was set aside to punish him in front of the whole crew.[130]

Some sailors were forced to deal with medical emergencies of unimaginable horror: Andre Ure, captain of one of the *Queen Charlotte*'s fighting tops, had a leg shot off while he was aloft and had no choice but to remain there for the rest of the action.[131] One wonders how he was recovered to deck. William Dillon witnessed some shocking sights. As he stood at his gun enjoying a little banter with his gun crew, one particularly short sailor, John Polloy, commented with confidence that he was so small that the shot would all pass over him but, 'the words had not been long out of his mouth when a shot cut his head right in two, leaving the top of each ear remaining on the lower part of the cheek... The head of this unfortunate seaman was cut so horizontally that anyone looking at it would have supposed it had been done by the blow of an axe'. Dillon himself had been blown across the entire width of the deck by the wind of a passing shot and had to be revived and his limbs rubbed back into life.[132] On the *Jemappes* the continual uncertainty of living under fire was rendered even more disturbing when her foremast brought down her mainmast and 'the shock was so violent that in the lower battery we all thought the ship was splitting in two.'[133] It was not just sights that could be shocking, but sounds too.

In the aftermath of action injured sailors now had to endure the attention of the surgeon. To make this rite of passage easier aboard the *Queen* and *Invincible*, sailors who had undergone amputation on 28 and 29 May came to assist the surgeon in the blood-soaked cockpit by encouraging those men destined for the saw, declaring, one suspects with a little bravado, that 'it was much less painful than it appeared to be, that they felt no pain from the wounds'.[134] The butcher's bill for the *Royal George* was exceptionally shocking as five of their twelve young midshipmen, boys all in their teens, suffered amputation, three at the thigh, one of the leg and one of the arm. The rest of the surgeon's list makes difficult reading. There are compound fractures, lacerations and other miscellaneous wounds all over the body: front, back, throat, thigh, foot, abdomen, head and brain, and poor old Sam Wainwright lost his left eye.[135]

Their task was mountainous. Each ship had a surgeon assisted by a number of mates. The surgeons of the largest ships had as many as five official mates, smaller ships had fewer. On British ships they set up on the orlop deck, the lowest deck, where there was little space, light or ventilation; terrible conditions for surgery, but at least in relative safety from the enemy's guns. There was no system of triage as we would know it now, when casualties are initially assessed and prioritised. This posed a major problem for naval surgeons because they were so close to the source of the action. Army surgeons rarely met with the most severe cases as they had to be transported some distance to reach medical help and they tended to die on the way. On naval ships the surgeon was never more than a matter of minutes away. As a result the most serious, hopeless cases could take up the surgeon's and other patients' valuable time, according to the unwritten rule that the injured were treated in the order in which they arrived, perhaps a system devised to avoid disputes over whose injury was worse. The injured had to sit in their own blood and just wait their turn while the surgeon became increasingly exhausted. Many simply bled to death, in spite of a good supply of tourniquets and as much as ten per cent of the ship's company being proficient in first aid. There is little information about surgery in any naval battle, but we do know that, at the Battle of Camperdown in 1797, one surgeon worked non-stop from one o'clock in the afternoon until four o'clock the following morning, operating on no fewer than ninety patients. Throughout that entire period 'melancholy cries of assistance were addressed to me from every side by wounded and dying, and piteous moans and bewailing from pain and despair'. The surgeons became exhausted and not all could cope with their allotted task on 1 June 1794. James Malcolm, surgeon of the *Defence*, was too nervous to perform a single amputation and left the ship as soon as it returned home. One of the surgeon's three mates, William Yowell, was forced to take charge throughout the battle.[136]

When considering the question of whether or not Howe should have renewed the action, it is clear that at least some, and perhaps all of the debate, should be focused on capability, on whether he was or was not able to renew the action considering the shattered state of both his ships and their crews. There is, furthermore, the experience of the previous days' fighting to consider, together with Howe's perception of Villaret's intentions. As the battle ended, Villaret was well formed up, and Howe was not, with his ships surrounding several disabled Frenchmen. On 29 May, when a similar situation presented itself on three occasions, Villaret had immediately attacked the British to secure his disabled ships, and with great skill and success on each occasion. Everything that had happened on 29 May suggested that this was what Villaret was now going to repeat. Howe's decision to form around the *Queen Charlotte* at the end of the battle, rather than go haring off in damaged ships after a well-formed enemy, was not excessively timid but sensible, made on the strength of his current capability and the accumulated experience of the previous days' contact. It is not a decision for which Howe should be criticised.

Howe's fleet was so seriously shattered that it was not until 5 p.m. on 3 June, a full forty-eight hours after the battle had ended, that he set sail for England. And so both fleets returned home, all of the sailors cold, hungry, thirsty and in many cases terrified that their ships would sink beneath them. Hundreds of men were suffering from a multitude of injuries: fractures, dislocated bones, loss of limbs, burns, blindness, deafness, deep cuts and splinters inches long embedded beneath their flesh. The sea was equally brutalised, littered with debris and bloated corpses, food for hungry fish and sharks. One French sailor was convinced that 'these terrible creatures swam alongside in veritable flocks waiting for the bodies to be thrown over; they counted on this to such an extent that they did not leave us until we were off Ushant'.[137]

The immediate strategic situation, meanwhile, had still not been resolved, and in that respect Villaret had conducted his fleet magnificently. Over five days of fighting he had continually lured Howe away from the rendezvous zone for Vanstabel and the grain convoy, and in battle he had disabled the British ships sufficiently to render them incapable of renewing their hunt for it. But the British still had a card to play: Rear-Admiral George Montagu, the man who had been sent out originally in order to hunt for the convoy, could still influence events.

On 31 May Montagu had returned to Plymouth. He had not intercepted the grain convoy and, although he had been aware that Howe was hunting the main enemy fleet from Brest, had not attempted to find him. All of this was appropriate behaviour according to the strict wording of his Admiralty orders. He had, in fact, already far exceeded them by staying out as long as he did; the initial orders had given him authority to cruise for the convoy only until 15 May. The holds of his ships were now empty and echoing. By then the Admiralty knew that Villaret had left Brest and that Montagu could now become the decisive factor in the campaign. If he could rendezvous with Howe the British could create a numerical advantage. On the other hand, if Howe could occupy Villaret, Montagu would then be free to intercept the convoy. Montagu's squadron was therefore enlarged and he was given sufficient ships to outnumber Vanstabel and Nielly combined.

On 2 June, too late to influence the battle, new orders were penned in London for Montagu making it clear that it was 'of very great importance that you should return to sea as soon as possible'. He was given four more 74-gunners, one more 64-gunner and five more frigates, making his squadron now 20-strong – a formidable force of rapid ships. His official orders gave equal weight to the importance of Howe and the convoy: Montagu would have to go where the intelligence led him. But a private letter from the First Lord himself made it clear that the convoy was to be his priority.[138] He did not receive his new orders until 4 June, by which time news of the battle was already starting to drift into Plymouth. News of the convoy, however, came a little later, when Montagu's sails were already clear of the horizon. It had been sighted by a Bristol merchantman, but in Plymouth there was no one to tell.

As soon as Montagu was on station, just off Ushant, he saw a small squadron of French ships, all in excellent condition. This was the squadron that had been based at Cancale, finally released by the politicians in Paris to join Villaret in Brest but now too late to influence the battle. Montagu chased them close inshore before resuming his station. The next morning more ships were in sight but these looked altogether different. To begin with there were far more of them, twenty-four in all. Some were shattered, four completely dismasted and they were all heading for Brest. This was unmistakably Villaret returning home from battle. Montagu's squadron was lightweight by comparison, his frigates were no match for the French ships of the line, even with their cargo of dead and injured. And once again Villaret's captains worked well together. Montagu reported how they 'kept so closely connected and guarded with so much care their disabled ships that it was not in my power to take any step that was likely to contribute to His Majesty's Service'.[139] He was also acutely aware of the squadron of fresh ships he had just chased into Brest. Montagu edged away and the French ignored him, heading for Brest. When it became clear that Howe was not in pursuit, and without the least scrap of new information regarding the grain convoy, Montagu, once more, headed back to Plymouth.

Not far to the west and south, meanwhile, Vanstabel was approaching Brest with his convoy. He had been very cautious. He had sailed to the Azores before sending out a corvette to scout ahead. On 29 May the corvette heard gunfire and the action was confirmed when Vanstabel came across the dismasted *Montagnard* being towed home. Vanstabel had been so close that he passed through the site of the action of 29 May the very next day.[140] Fearful that the British were still in the area, Vanstabel chose to head toward Brest by the hazardous southern approach, the Raz de Seine, a narrow gulley of water with hidden rocks and vicious currents that can reach six knots. This would be an extraordinary feat of seamanship for any fleet commander but, even more remarkably, Vanstabel passed through at night, a stunning achievement that has been celebrated by one French historian but has been shamefully ignored by everyone else.[141] With no little thanks to Vanstabel's skill and judgment as much as to Villaret's manoeuvres and his sailors' sacrifice, on the morning of 14 June, Villaret, with his mangled fleet, and Vanstabel, with his convoy intact and even enlarged – he had captured no fewer than sixteen prizes en route – were finally united. Together they sailed into Brest roads, triumphant, their arrival beamed though the gloom by the lighthouse keeper on the Penmarc'h.[142]

Thus the fleet campaign of May and June 1794 fizzled out. The convoy the British had been so desperate to stop reached France; the French fleet had suffered severely in keeping the British at bay; and the British had been prevented by French stoicism and perseverance from making the battle as overwhelming a British victory as it might have been. Such a confused picture was bound to have a complex aftermath in both Britain and France as the political machines of both countries embraced this major event. The first thing to do was to proclaim victory, and both sides did it with gusto. Victory was celebrated equally in Brest and Portsmouth, Toulon and Plymouth, Paris and London. Artists awoke from their slumber and took up their palettes; politicians rose to their feet, words bubbling up inside them like geysers ready to blow; mobs afire with energy moved restlessly through large cities; captains who had not behaved as was expected shifted uncomfortably in their cots; captains who had done their duty thrust out their chests, raised their chins and urged their ships forward ever faster to claim their due rewards. The battle, fought so far from land, was now coming ashore with the irresistible force of a tsunami.

# 9.

# The First Reaction: Honour and Glory

Oh! Give me Pocock's Pencil
And give me Pocock's art!

John Betjeman on Nicholas Pocock.[1]

Naval battles are complex events that defy simple description or characterisation: fought over large areas, ships hidden in wreaths of smoke, captains unable to act as they want or unwilling to behave as expected. It is important, therefore, to retain a sense of that confusion and dislocation when considering the aftermath of battle as well as the battle itself. Throughout the eighteenth century, many sailors believed that to question the behaviour of the fleet under such trying circumstances was entirely inappropriate, and there was usually a parallel political imperative to support the navy. These underlying beliefs create a trap for the unwary historian. The battle fought on 1 June is one of the strongest examples of this because of the 'glorious' title attached to it. This suggests that the battle was glorious, and without exception; it suggests that it was *so* glorious that it deserved the title more than any other battle; and finally, it suggests that what was 'glorious' for one side was necessarily not 'glorious' for the other. All of these implications and assumptions are demonstrably false. The impact of the battle and its fallout are far more complex than one might suspect.

But let us begin with the reports and celebrations of the battle in Britain, where the pressure for naval victory had been building since the start of the war, where Howe now returned with his prizes in tow and his holds full of enemy prisoners. This was the ultimate sign of military victory. The battle could and would be measured in any number of subtle ways by politicians and historians on both sides, and they would not all come up with the same result. For the French sailors lying squashed together in the darkness, however, the identity of the victor was never in doubt. They now faced years in the grim squalor of the

British prison hulks, those leviathans of misery that blotted the British coastline, proclaiming victory through the visible and symbolic incarceration of her enemies at the gates of her maritime empire.

Howe arrived in Spithead at eleven o'clock on the morning of 13 June, having sent half of his fleet[2] on to Plymouth to repair there. The shipyards were ready for them and quickly rushed out boats full of fresh beef and beer; surveyors came on board to assess the damage and shipwrights to begin repair. At the same time, shipwrights and caulkers were ordered to travel from Chatham to Portsmouth and Plymouth to get the fleet back to sea as soon as possible. Tons of stores including hemp, cables, spars and varnish came with them and a separate order was made for 12,000 hammocks and 2,000 sets of bedding.[3]

Reduced as the fleet was, the spectacle of the ships arriving in Portsmouth was impressive and 'crowds of eager spectators lined the ramparts and beech [*sic*]'. A salute was fired from the town when the *Queen Charlotte* anchored and another when Howe landed at Sally Port. In the words of one witness, he was then received with 'military honours and reiterated shouts of applause, the band of the Gloucester regiment playing, *See the Conquering Hero Comes*! It was a scene that baffles description!'[4]

By then London was already alight, quite literally, with celebration. The artist and diarist Joseph Farrington recorded that, at two o'clock in the morning on 12 June, he was woken amid something of a riot in which many windows of known war-opponents were broken. The family home of Thomas Hardy, political activist and open sympathiser of the French Revolution, was viciously attacked and his wife, pregnant with his sixth child, only escaped with the help of her neighbours.[5] A mob demanded every house 'put out lights'. Soon the illuminations 'became general', lights flickering in the summer dawn as far as the eye could see. The following night lights were lit again and Farrington took a walk to admire them with his friend and fellow artist Johann Fuseli. By then the fever of the previous night had dissipated, 'the streets undisturbed by mobs and no windows broke'.[6] *The Times* thought the illuminations the greatest since Culloden – the final confrontation in the Jacobite rising of 1745.

News of the British fleet's success had, in fact, arrived three days before Londoners first lit their lamps. Howe had sent Roger Curtis ahead with dispatches and he landed at Plymouth on 9 June before travelling directly to London, guarding his news with the utmost secrecy. The First Lord of the Admiralty, the Earl of Chatham, took the dispatch to the King, who immediately wrote back to Curtis a personal and hearty letter of congratulation and thanks. George was delighted. In another letter he wrote, 'I cannot refrain from… expressing, on the return of the dispatch from Lord Howe, the joy I feel at the signal success of the Channel Fleet…' He was so excited that he forgot to remind Chatham to send a frigate to Ostend to bring over his son, Ernest.[7]

Even before Curtis arrived in London with the dispatches, word was out that there had been an action, albeit the result unknown. Montagu wrote a letter to the Admiralty on 3 June having fallen in with the *Audacious* on her return to Plymouth. The *Audacious* herself arrived on 4 June, and on 9 June the Prince of Wales had heard from the Admiralty that a merchant captain had witnessed the action on 31 May and reported the French fleet 'extremely shattered & disordered'.[8] On Tuesday 10 June an initial report was published in London, though perhaps not until late in the day, because the news broke that evening in a theatre in London.[9] The MP George Canning wrote:

> We had not been there above half an hour when we perceived a degree of bustle and hurry in the lower boxes – presently the Opera stopped – people stood up, some knowing, but the greater part wondering for what reason – and Boringdon came dancing into the box where I was with the news of Lord Howe's victory. I never saw a finer or more affecting spectacle than the almost electric and universal sensation that seemed to pervade every part of the House – the transport and triumph which burst forth as soon as their astonishment subsided.[10]

News of victory brought Lady Chatham to town and she visited 'both the Playhouses' to witness the exuberant celebrations. The response and instinctive outpouring of joy was so impressive that it made headlines in *The Times*:

> The colours were brought on the stage, and the House, as if inspired with one sentiment, joined in those noblest of all choruses, 'Rule Britannia' – 'Britons strike home' – and 'God save the King'. All next morning the bells of London 'pealed merrily' amide constant discharges of cannon, and 'every FLAG, excepting those bearing the THIRTEEN STRIPES [of the USA], were hoisted in compliment to Lord Howe.'[11]

The earliest reports were coloured by rumour of heavy casualties among the officer corps: the Duke of Portland celebrated the victory but considered it dearly bought.[12] Nevertheless, the capital was energised by lights, flags, songs, explosions and rioting – a British way of celebrating now as much as it was then. Imagine the streets of London the day after England finally win the football World Cup again, and you have a fair idea of the wave of emotion and public interaction that marked this victory. Sport is also a useful analogy because of the contrasting levels of celebration and types of behaviour associated with different games. The celebrations after the Glorious First of June were distinctive and of a notably excessive level because it was a *naval* victory, in the same way that the celebrations should England win a football world cup would be far greater, longer and louder, affecting and involving a far greater percentage of the population, than if England won a rugby or cricket world cup. In a similar way, the style and scale of the battle's celebration was considered vulgar or uncivilised by those with what they considered to be more refined tastes. Among those quarters the illuminations and public celebrations were described as a 'plebeian wave'.[13]

There are several reasons for this. First, the army had never enjoyed a reputation among the British public to rival that of the navy. It has even been argued that the army was feared by the public – because of its long-held association with absolutist government it was perceived as an alien imposition.[14] Its role in policing and controlling crowds, often with violence, did nothing to improve that reputation, nor did its campaigns on mainland Europe, however glorious they may have been. The navy, in contrast, was an institution that was seen to defend Britain from her enemies abroad; it was intricately linked with perceptions of national security. This view of the navy was always particularly strong in times of fear of invasion, as in 1794, and was all neatly summed up in an article in the *St James's Chronicle*, a popular London newspaper of the time:

> The extacy of joy displayed by the public on receiving the news of Lord Howe's glorious victory, proves how much more Britons are delighted by success at sea than on land. The sea is our protecting element, and as long as *Britannia* rules the waves nothing can hurt us. A victory at sea must ever give us more heart-felt pleasure than twenty victories on the Continent.[15]

Thomas Erskine, MP for Portsmouth, shared this view. He wrote to Captain Payne of the *Russell*: 'Would to God I were to look nowhere else than to the ocean for the military occurrences of Great Britain. We might then encrease [*sic*] every day the enthusiasm of Englishmen for their country & its Constitution ...'[16]

Naval victory, as opposed to army victory, was what most of the British public wanted, and naval victory is what Howe had given them. For some it was also a victory for monarchy and for monarchists. The public revelled in rumours that the *Brunswick,* the ship with the name of the German duchy ruled by the House of Hanover and linked directly to George and his wife Charlotte, had single-handedly fought and sunk the *Jacobin*. Entirely untrue, it nevertheless beautifully distilled the complexities of the battle to a clash between tradition and revolution, between monarchy and republic. Another rumour circulated that, of all the sovereigns depicted in the figureheads of British warships, 'not *one* crown was either shot or even scathed'.[17]

The scale of the victory itself was another factor in the wildness of the celebrations. Although it is easy to belittle the Glorious First of June as a minor victory in comparison with the scale of the later victories of the Revolutionary and Napoleonic wars, it was at that time the greatest naval victory in anyone's memory. In the Battle of Camperdown in 1797 nine enemy ships were taken or destroyed; at the Nile in 1798 it was eleven; and at Trafalgar in 1805 it was twenty-two: all very impressive. But from the perspective of 1794 and the aftermath of the Glorious First of June in which 'only' seven were captured or destroyed, one has to go back 102 years, to the Battle of Barfleur in 1692, to find a battle in which more French ships were captured or destroyed, and even that comparison is false in some respects as the destruction actually happened in the bay of La Hogue the day after the battle.

As the purveyor and deliverer of this wondrous new level of victory, Howe was showered with awards: a diamond hilt and diamond sword valued at 3,000 guineas; the thanks of both houses of Parliament; the thanks of the common council of London; the Freedom of London (presented in a gold box); the Freedom of the Skinners' Livery Company (in two gold boxes, valued at £100 each); and the Freedom of the Goldsmith's company.[18]

The battle also became the platform for the launch of a new system of military honours, described by the issue of a medal. We automatically associate exceptional battle performance with the issue of medals, but this only began in 1794 with the Glorious First of June. The flag officers received a gold chain which suspended a gold medal of neoclassical design, showing Britannia on an ancient galley being crowned by winged Victory. Those captains worthy of particular praise also received a gold medal, but to be worn suspended from the button-hole by a blue-and-white ribbon, not from a gold chain. Official symbolic rewards were given purely to the officer corps until the second half of the nineteenth century, when Queen Victoria took up the cause of the ordinary sailor and issued a Naval General Service Medal to veterans of numerous naval battles, including the few surviving sailors from the Glorious First of June.[19] There is some suggestion that the hundreds of junior officers who found no recognition in the official rewards system made their own medals. In the collection of the National Maritime Museum in London there is an oval gilt plate, shoulder-mounted, that celebrates the wearer's presence on the *Queen Charlotte* at the First of June, a fine example of a non-regulation uniform accessory. There is also some suggestion that elaborate badges in the shape of anchors were made and presented as part of this unofficial rewards system (see fig. 25 and chapter openers).[20]

Vice-Admirals Graves and Hood were created Irish peers, Vice-Admiral Gardner and Rear-Admirals Pasley, Curtis and Bowyer were created baronets. Pasley and Bowyer, who both lost a leg, received a pension of £1,000 a year. All first lieutenants and some junior lieutenants aboard flagships were promoted to commander. James Gambier and Hugh Seymour were appointed colonels of the Marines. Sir Roger Curtis, captain of the *Queen Charlotte*, Thomas Pringle of the *Valiant*, Henry Harvey of the *Ramillies*, William Parker of the *Audacious*, James Pigott of the *Tremendous* and Thomas Mackenzie of the *Gibraltar* were all awarded flag rank through a timely promotion in order of seniority on 3 July 1794.[21]

James Bowen, Master of the *Queen Charlotte,* was made prize agent, a position that secured him a fortune, and was then given an officer's commission.[22] Bowen thus made that particularly difficult jump from warrant to commissioned officer, a step up the ranks that had been pioneered by men such as John Benbow.[23] Like Benbow, Bowen progressed right up to flag rank. Lieutenant Codrington, signal lieutenant of the *Queen Charlotte*, was given his first command, the *Comet* fireship. By April 1795 he was in command of a frigate and by the end of the war was a rear-admiral and knight of the Bath.[24] Howe even took the opportunity to play a little trick on one of his lieutenants, Thomas Larcom. At one stage in the action, Larcom had been a little free in his observation of the behaviour of Captain Molloy in the *Caesar*. Howe had rebuked him for speaking out against a superior but, nevertheless, advised him to keep his eyes open. Now, with honours to be distributed, he summoned Larcom to his cabin and told him that his conduct in the action was such that he had to leave the ship. Larcom was horrified, until Howe explained that he had to leave because he had been promoted to commander.[25]

At Lloyd's, liberal subscriptions were established by merchants for relief of the wounded as well as women widowed and children orphaned by the battle. By 2 July they had raised an impressive £10,000. The cities of London, Edinburgh, Dublin and the seamen's charity Trinity House all contributed 'very largely', though our understanding of how much difference it made in the aftermath of battles such as this remains woefully incomplete.[26] A successful theatrical production at Drury Lane, inspired by the battle, also contributed to the relief fund for the sailors. Written by the famous playwright Richard Sheridan, the play was performed free for one night, with voluntary contributions going directly to the relief fund for injured sailors and their families. It was repeated seven times in all, with the first show raising £1,526 11s. This was the first time in British history that this type of charitable performance had ever been made and the sum would not be matched by any other charitable performance in the eighteenth century.[27]

Personal donations were also made to aid suffering dependants. Midshipman William Parker asked his father to set up a subscription for the wife and children of one seaman, George Graham, 'who was slaughtered in the engagement on the first of June in a manner too shocking to mention to a tender hearted parent', and Parker did this because Graham had taken him under his wing and had taught him a great deal.[28] A certain Mr Devaynes, along with an unknown number of other generous individuals, also raised a 'vast sum' of money for relief. The fleet physican Thomas Trotter thought all this benevolence tremendous: 'such are the blessed effects of a naval triumph!' he gushed.[29] Slightly less philanthropically, merchants and trading companies who despised the war for its effects on commerce now used the opportunity for naval victory to heap pressure on the government to bring the war to a swift end, even advancing large sums to pay for naval equipment and setting up funds to be used to encourage men to join the navy. In one case £10,000 was raised in the naïve hope that it would lessen the fleet's dependence on impressment.[30] As always, the Navy also provided its own support, via the Chatham Chest, for the bereaved. John Harvey's family, for example, received £74 4s 6d for expenses incurred after his death.[31]

As was the rule the prize money was shared out, with striking unfairness, throughout the fleet. The pool of prize money totalled £201,096, 13s od., the captains received £1,400 each, warrant officers £25, petty officers £10, and each seaman, marine or soldier the princely sum of £2 2s but, as a gesture of goodwill and thanks to the fleet, the money was advanced directly by the King so the deserving sailors did not have to wait for their reward. The sailors received their prize money as early as 4 July and, to ease the pain a little more, the legislature repealed the duty of 5 per cent on all prizes awarded and warrant officers, petty officers, foremastmen, marines and soldiers all received an advance on theirs. The prize court was also generous in its judgement of the *Castor* as a valid prize, as she had been retaken by the *Carysfort* only days after the French had first captured her from the British: had the British recaptured a British vessel or taken a French one? It could have been decided either way because the new French captain of the *Castor* had not actually taken his prize back to port to be formally commissioned by the French navy. In the end, Sir James Marriot, Judge of the High Court of the Admiralty, awarded the whole value of the *Castor* to her British captors.[32]

The officers who received such a large proportion of the prize money do at least seem to have been generous with it. The fleet physician Thomas Trotter noted how the officers 'cheerfully resigned' their personal supplies of fresh food to the wounded, both on board and ashore. As soon as they heard rumour that the diet at Haslar naval hospital was inadequate they sent funds so it could be improved. That diet certainly was bad: Trotter criticised it for a lack of livestock, vegetables, fruit, pickles, eggs, porter and milk.[33] The diet on offer at Haslar was probably making men even sicker than they were when they arrived there. For those who were well enough, a Grand Ball was held on 16 June and the highlight of the night was Admiral Gardner leading the dance with Mary Howe, Admiral Howe's daughter.[34]

Howe's most glittering awards and the officers' gold chains were all presented in person by the King, who came graciously to Portsmouth with his family amid great pomp and ceremony – though the idea for this symbolic royal visit had, in fact, been cooked up by the politicians Pitt, Chatham and Dundas. With news that the King was coming to see the fleet, together with the attraction of the battered ships themselves, 'all the world' descended on Portsmouth, wrote Canning. The House of Commons was adjourned for ten days, from 20 to 30 June, as an 'enabling measure' and Canning was so anxious to beat the crowds that he set out for Portsmouth a week before the royal review was due to begin. The journey from London was particularly miserable for Lord Mulgrave who, in the middle of Putney Common, was set upon by bandits preying on the crowds of people heading south. Mulgrave, never a man to be messed with, fought the blackguards off and continued on his way.[35]

When the naval gala got under way, to maximise his wife's pleasure (she was, of course, Queen Charlotte) and his sailors' pride, the King appointed sailors of the *Queen Charlotte*, instead of his royal servants, to row the royal party out to the ship. On board, King George inspected the ship's company, which had a profound effect on Mary, who thought the world of her father: 'nothing during the day was more pleasing to me than this walk through these brave fellows, every one of whom I am certain would attend my father to a cannon's mouth, and all of whom have exposed their lives for him'. This sentiment was shared and publicised by Howe's earliest biographer, who believed that the attachment of the sailors to Howe was 'unexampled'. Mary went on to enjoy a little chitchat with the sailors, discussing good-naturedly which title George might bestow on Howe. It was suggested that he might become Duke de La Montagne for his attack on the French flagship, which Mary reckoned would make her Lady Molly Molehill. After the inspection, the King made a donation from his privy purse to the entire crew of the *Queen Charlotte* and all the men were invited to touch Howe's new diamond-hilted sword, a gift from the King, which then toured the fleet.[36]

The wounded admirals Bowyer and Pasley were unable to attend the festivities but everyone else who could, did, and 'the cheering of the multitude in honour of the Royal Visitants, wherever they appeared, made the air ring, and bands of music continued playing in the yard, and on board the ships and yachts in the harbour'. There were cries of 'God Save the King, and Lord Howe to defend him ...' The Royal Family dined with the captains after the awards ceremony, an event which Collingwood considered impressively relaxed, writing the King was 'cheerful and good humoured to all, and there was as little ceremony as at the table of a private gentleman'. The Royal Family had also dined privately with Howe's family, giving Mary the chance to meet the three princesses, a truly thrilling experience for her.[37]

The next day King, Queen, Prince and Princesses reviewed the Gloucester Regiment and heard a sermon[38] before the entire royal party trooped off to the launch of a magnificent new 98-gunner, the *Prince of Wales*, and George let his son (the Prince of Wales) perform the naming ceremony. There, at the yard, King George made donations from his privy purse to the dockyard artificers, workmen and labourers and the victualling and ordnance departments, and he ordered £100 to be distributed to the poor of the parishes of Portsmouth and Portsea, £50 to the poor of Gosport and £50 to the debtors in Portsmouth Gaol.[39]

The visit ended with George and the Royal Family embarking on the frigate *Aquilon* for a trip into the Solent. Seven magnificent barges belonging to the King, the Admiralty and five flag officers, snaked out in procession from shore to the *Aquilon*'s anchorage at Spithead. There was a cacophony of celebration as they neared, the *Queen Charlotte* fired two guns then the entire fleet fired twenty-one. Crews cheered and ships' bands played 'martial symphonies' as the barges passed. With the royal party aboard, the *Aquilon* then circled the fleet before making a round trip, via the Needles (on the Isle of Wight), on which she was followed by a straggling flotilla of pleasure boats of every kind. Just off the Needles she was met with more cheering by a convoy bound for Newfoundland. The weather was beautiful and the Hampshire coast looked magnificent. Even when the *Aquilon*, rather embarrassingly, ran aground off the Isle of Wight, her passengers didn't seem to mind and the King and his party, cheerfully, stayed aboard until the tide was high enough for the ship to float, which was at ten o'clock that night. George made another donation from his privy purse, this time to the crew of the *Aquilon*.[40] After yet more salutes and fireworks, King and entourage departed Portsmouth, leaving the fleet aglow with pride and Howe's daughter Mary to return home with her family 'perhaps the happiest mortals breathing'.[41] All were right to feel privileged because, while no one could have known it then, this was the only time in the eighteenth century that the monarch would visit the fleet in the aftermath of a battle.

It was a visit of extraordinary benevolence and would have lived long in the minds of the crew and dockyard workers. George had reminded them that their navy was his navy. It was not the British navy, it was the *Royal* Navy. The King was clearly proud of his navy and, as if it were one of his own, he had embraced it with symbolic displays of patriarchy. He had rewarded sailors and yard-workers from his own pocket. His family, too, had taken the navy to heart – the Prince of Wales had launched the *Prince of Wales*; Queen Charlotte had visited the *Queen Charlotte*. In return for those displays of royal attention, the sailors loved their King and the Royal Family. It is not insignificant that George III was the first Hanoverian monarch who chose not to visit Hanover:[42] exactly eighty years after the death of Queen Anne and the succession of George I, the British monarchy was starting to become British and to be perceived as such.

George III's visit to Portsmouth was, in itself, a significant result of the battle. The British had fought well and had been rewarded and praised by their King, in person. That praise and personal attention was undoubtedly influential in inspiring the continued devotion to duty displayed by the Royal Navy in the ensuing years. The fact that the Royal Family's sojourn at Portsmouth was driven by political motives – the idea was nurtured and implemented by Pitt, Dundas and Chatham – is an important reminder that those crucial links between king and Navy and between Navy and public were deliberately strengthened by politicians. Those links that had such a profound influence on the great wars with France through sustained public and political support for the Royal Navy were not the result of some kind of 'natural' spring of good will of an island race, but were, in part at least, a calculated political move.

The only dampeners on the events in Portsmouth were the deaths of both John Harvey of the *Brunswick* and John Hutt of the *Queen*, who had fought their ships with such distinction. They had travelled together from London in the same post chaise before the fleet left for war; they both lost limbs; they both died on the same day. The medal honour system was so new that no one had yet thought of posthumous awards, and thus Harvey and Hutt were not decorated. They were, however, buried together, and given a truly magnificent memorial.[43] The Abbey also became the final resting place of James Montagu, who was given that magnificent memorial where this book began. Numerous other memorials of men who fought but did not necessarily die at the First of June can be found scattered around England: Roger Curtis at St James's Church in Clanfield, Hampshire; Andrew Snape Douglas in Fulham, London; and Lieutenant Francis Ross in Topsham, Devon. Ross's memorial features a poem written by his son:

> One vengeful ball by battle sped
> A gallant spirit flies;
> Blue surges close above his head,
> In ocean's depths he lies.
> A severed trunk – no warning given,
> One moment warm with life;
> Buoyant with hope, and trust in heaven,
> The next past mortal strife.
>
> Wield up – yield up – thou mighty sea,
> Restore thy prey to light;
> Death has been vanquished, souls are free,
> Stand forth, redeem'd in might.[44]

The captains of the British ships seem to have been, almost without exception, happy with the performance of their men, especially on those ships that were undermanned or manned by inexperienced sailors or soldiers. Thomas Mackenzie of the *Gibraltar* commended the performance of his men, 'which far surpass'd my most sanguine expectations as I may venture to say not above one in twenty ever saw a gun fired prior to the later periods' and William Parker of the *Audacious* declared that the conduct of his crew 'exceeded every possible expectation' even though the majority had never before served in the navy, let alone been in an action.[45] Howe was careful to thank those who had fought for him, praising 'the highly distinguished examples of resolution, spirit, and perseverance, which have been testified by every description of officers, seamen and military corps in the ships of the fleet'.[46] When his own crew petitioned Bowen for an audience with Howe, Bowen arranged for him to come to the quarterdeck with the crew massed below. They thanked him 'for leading them so gloriously' then Howe, deeply moved, said: 'No, no, I thank *you*; it is *you*, my brave lads – it is you, not I, that have conquered.'[47]

Some sailors were lucky and enjoyed a well-earned taste of kindness and comfort when they returned to Britain covered in glory. When the *Orion* arrived in Plymouth, and Midshipman Lane's father came to take his son home, he ended up with three of the lad's friends, too, one of whom was William Parker. Parker later wrote effusively of the kindness of Miss Lane, probably his friend's sister, and a Miss Collins who Parker honoured as 'a very pleasant amiable girl'. She was the daughter of a naval widow and no doubt Parker and his friends regaled the young ladies with tales of heroism. Parker was so grateful that he wrote home telling his father it 'would be very proper for my sisters to make Miss Lane a present'.[48] I bet his sisters loved that.

In France, the main fleet was welcomed into Berthaume roadstead 'with the jubilation of a revolutionary festival',[49] the loss of seven ships easily masked in the enormous body of shipping that flooded the outer harbour as Villaret, Nielly, the Cancale fleet, plus Vanstabel's convoy and his sixteen prizes, arrived all at once. Brest harbour, so recently full of only hopes and fears, was now full of masts and hulls, cheers of welcome and tears of relief. Ten days later and still in a convulsion of Revolutionary fervour, the main streets of Brest were all renamed, just as the ships had been. The Grande Rue became the Rue de la République; the Rue du Château became the Rue de L'Egalité; the Rue Guyot became the Rue des Vétérans; and the Place des Septs-Saints became the Place du 31 Mai after the popular 1793 *journée* in Paris that saw the end of the Girondin opposition to Jacobin politics.[50]

In his report to the National Convention Jeanbon did his best to put a victorious spin on events, describing the battle as '*glorieux*'. His report was full of examples of bravery on the part of men such as Captain Bazire of the *Montagne* whose single dying wish was the 'triumph of the Republic' and another who, as he was carried to the surgeon, said 'they want to take our ship, but they never will'. Men like this, wrote Jeanbon, saved France from the 'sharp tooth of the English leopard'. He ended by requesting a pension of 650 livres for the sailors.[51] The officers then joined a celebratory parade from Brest to Paris. Villaret remained very much in favour. He retained his command and ten years later was promoted to become Governor of Martinique, France's most important West Indian possession, when it was returned to France in the 1802 Peace of Amiens. The other flag officers, Nielly, Bouvet and Vanstabel had all acted with skill and intelligence and were considered beyond reproach.[52]

In Paris, the positive spin continued when the full details of the battle became known and Bertrand Barère, that high-ranking zealous Montagnard, seized upon the sinking of the *Vengeur* as an example of undaunted Republican virtue and courage, an event to be cherished.[53] What finer example of Republican zeal than sailors accepting certain death rather than surrender? What finer example than men shouting '*Vive la République*' before their lungs filled with cold salt water? He stood up in the convention and declared:

> Calm resolution succeeded to the heat of combat. Imagine that ship, the *Vengeur*, riddled by cannon-balls and cracking at every seam, surrounded by the English tigers and leopards, a crew now composed of the dead and dying, struggling against waves and cannons both; suddenly the tumult of combat, the cries of the suffering wounded cease; they all go or are carried to the deck. Every flag and pennant flies out; on every side rise cries of *Vive la République! Vivent la liberté et la France!*; all the animation and feeling of a civic festival, in the terrible last moments of a shipwreck.[54]

A new three-decker on the stocks was to be named *Vengeur* to immortalise this spirit in the French navy,[55] and an ivory model of the ship was commissioned to be hung above the heads of the politicians in the Salon de Liberté. As always the men of the provincial Jacobin clubs, who had their ears so carefully tuned into the ever-changing sympathies of their Parisian masters, quickly took up Barère's cry and spread the story of the *Vengeur* throughout France.[56] A glorious myth of the *Vengeur* thus rose from the grim reality of her demise. As one contemporary British commentator put it, 'such an account but ill accords with the squallid [*sic*] and melancholy figures of the poor wretches, who were rescued from a watery grave by British humanity. If they uttered any shout it was to thank their deliverers'. Another British diarist reckoned 'there was no truth of the report of the French having in that situation called out "Vive la République" – on the contrary they were earnestly soliciting aid from our ships'.[57]

Captain Renaudin, whose heroic death with his ship and so many of his crew was rather central to the entire myth, was not, in fact, floating face down in the mid-Atlantic, but having a rather civilised time as a prisoner on parole in the charming English West Country town of Tavistock, having been picked from the sea by a British boat.[58] His official report would soon blow the lid off this Montagnard propaganda but, for now, the word of those few men who controlled the Committee of Public Safety was law, and they were leading the festivities in the typically macabre and topsy-turvy style of the Terror by celebrating the deaths of their countrymen. The myth they generated was in fact so powerful that, in spite of the clear evidence to the contrary, the Jacobin version of events survived as a powerful artistic tradition in the late nineteenth century and then well into the twentieth as a popular Breton *chanson*. Sailors who died on the *Vengeur* also received impressive memorials and examples survive in the villages of Cozes and La Tremblade near Rochefort.[59]

In America the earliest reports wildly celebrated the 'glorious news' of French victory with false claims that three British warships, including one First Rate, had been sunk, that half the British fleet had been disabled and they had last been seen retreating up the Channel in disarray.

'We are now masters of the sea' proclaimed one newspaper along with the customary '*Vive la République*' and the interesting addendum, 'Our Sailors like our Soldiers Triumphant' – the author of this article must have been aware of a public perception of French naval underachievement. The American response to news of this French victory was, unsurprisingly, joyous. The news was proclaimed through Norfolk, Virginia by the Bell Man and the town was illuminated.[60]

Tellingly, these spurious claims of glorious French victory were never represented by French contemporary artists on any significant scale. Nicholas Ozanne created a pictorial equivalent of Barère's speech celebrating the *Vengeur* but it stands as the only example of a finished work in response to the battle by any French artist of the time. Louis Lafitte began, but never finished, a sketch that could have become something truly magnificent (see fig. 18). This absence of contemporaneous French paintings concerning the battle is not, however, particularly surprising. In terms of the representation of military victory, the visual arts of Revolutionary France in the early years of the new Republic had become sterile ground. It was not until Napoleon consciously encouraged artists to depict heroism and military victory in the early nineteenth century that French artists once more turned their minds to military subjects, as they had under the reign of Louis XIV.[61] In the early 1870s there was another unprecedented upsurge in such topics as the French art world sought to negotiate the ideology of the newly founded Third Republic, but in 1794 next to nothing was produced in France.

In Britain things were very different. An immense number of oil paintings, watercolours, prints and drawings commemorated different aspects of the battle in different ways. Together, they created a canon of work hitherto unmatched in naval history. At London's National Maritime Museum the print collection alone, which is not quite a complete record of naval prints, features as many as thirty-three different views of the action on 1 June; more than four times as many as the most significant British victory of the previous war, the Battle of the Saints (1782).[62]

As we have seen, in 1794 Britain was in thrall to innovations in art and theatre, and a central ingredient stimulating the public thirst for military works of art was the demand for historical accuracy. The artists who suddenly found themselves in a powerful position to profit from and direct this underfed wave of enthusiasm were Nicholas Pocock and Philippe de Loutherbourg; Pocock because he was an experienced sailor and had witnessed the battle first-hand, and Loutherbourg because of his innovative mind and exceptional artistic talent. Pocock feverishly drew and sketched everything he had seen (see Appendix III) while Loutherbourg raced to Portsmouth from London, his satchels bulging with blank sketchbooks. One artist, Thomas Rowlandson, was already there and had witnessed then depicted the arrival of the fleet (see fig. 20). Pocock and Loutherbourg were the outstanding favourites to produce something magnificent but there was going to be a lot of competition.

Public demand was insatiable. The first print purporting to represent the battle appeared on 21 June, only eleven days after news of victory broke. It is such an impressive feat that scholars now suspect the picture may have been rehashed from an image of an unidentified battle from the previous war.[63] At this early stage quality did not matter as much as the subject matter; any picture of the battle would increase broadsheet sales. But the more established artists knew there was real money to be made if they played the long game and they set their minds to capturing the essence of the moment, each in his unique style and medium.

Among the many artists flocking to the scene were the Englishmen Robert Dodd and Robert Cleveley and the American Mather Brown. All enjoyed success in very distinct ways. Dodd, a Londoner who had achieved some renown from his depictions of the American War, produced a series of aquatints showing different aspects of the battle but his prize piece was the vast canvas that he painted in situ, in his local pub on Commercial Road in Stepney, London. The original George Tavern has since been knocked down, twice, but a pub of the same name stands on exactly that spot today and, appropriately, it is now also an arts centre and music venue. Dodd's painting *The Battle of the First of June, 1794* is 3.4 metres (just over 11 feet) long and 1.94 metres (6 feet 4 inches) high and its subject is the moment that so many grasped as the decisive point of the battle, the sinking of the *Vengeur*. In contrast to Ozanne's painting of the wrecked *Vengeur* which shows French sailors merrily waving their hats as towering British battleships crush it with cannon from all sides, Dodd has focused on the British rescue of the French crew in a celebration of both British victory and compassion. The *Alfred* which led the rescue operation grabs the spotlight and the tiny cutter *Rattler*, easily recognised by her distinctive rig, features in the centre of the canvas, astern of the *Alfred*. The painting was clearly cherished as it was safely stored and rehung when the pub was rebuilt in 1833. Only in 1932 when the building was demolished for the second time was it removed and bought by Sir James Caird, that well-known benefactor of maritime heritage and endeavour, and it is now in the British National Maritime Museum's collection.[64] Dodd also produced two other magnificent canvases of the action which were recently sold at Sotheby's.

Robert Cleveley, another Londoner and, again, a marine artist with sound knowledge of naval matters, took up the challenge to paint the battle and, like Dodd, went large. Cleveley did not paint one giant canvas, but two, and one of them was fractionally larger than Dodd's at 3.43 metres (11 feet 3 inches) long and 2.28 metres (7 feet 6 inches) wide. He produced them very quickly, too. The first was finished in 1794 and the second the following year. They showed two scenes from the battle: one in the morning, shortly after the *Queen Charlotte* was dismasted when Villaret crowded off toward the van, and the other in the early afternoon with Villaret moving to protect his damaged ships. The originals were lost and then rediscovered in a London store room in 1981, after which they were quickly sold, separately, at Sotheby's. Both paintings then vanished again and their present location is unknown. Perhaps they hang in a (large) dining room, a framed window into maritime history to be appreciated over dinner; perhaps they are back in storage, thick with dust and never seen; perhaps they have been destroyed by fire or flood. Prints and good descriptions of the originals survive, however, and we know the works were described for sale as 'strictly historical'.[65]

Cleveley gave his public the reality and accuracy they sought. People didn't just want to see a picture of the battle, they wanted to know what it was like to be there.

The next artist with a novel take on the events was the Boston-born American Mather Brown, who did something quite extraordinary. Artists of naval warfare traditionally painted scenes from the perspective of a witness looking out over the field of battle, but Brown defied convention and painted a deck scene from the *Queen Charlotte* that contained a portrait of Howe in uniform. This representation of the hero in context had never before been seen in the genre of marine art and only recently in military art of any description. It was first essayed by Benjamin West in his *The Death of General Wolfe* of 1770 and then twelve years later by John Singleton Copley in *The Death of Major Peirson*. Artists, therefore, were enjoying the liberation of painting their subjects free of the burdensome and often bizarre necessities of the traditional classical background and context.[66] But Brown took it one step further. In *The Death of General Wolfe* West had shown no interest in the accurate depiction of his human subjects but Brown, by training and profession, was a portrait painter, and he decided to use West's approach, but to paint true-to-life portraits of the people he featured. The result was, in the words of the reviewer from the *Britannic Magazine*, 'entirely *Novel*, and perfectly distinct from any other nautical engagement hitherto executed; there has never yet been *even* attempted the introduction of portraits into a naval picture …'[67] Brown gained access to the *Queen Charlotte* and Howe sat for his portrait, as did many of the principal officers on board included in Brown's picture. Howe appears centre left, and to his left is Lieutenant Neville of the Queen's Regiment, dying from a wound by a cannon ball that drove the hilt of his sword deep into his side (see fig. 19). Much of the detail of the costume is accurate, if its presence at the battle is questionable. For example, in the battle, Howe may not have worn the uniform of an admiral, but have been dressed 'like a sailor in a blue jacket and fur cap, and … when the action was over Lord Howe was in appearance like a chimney sweep with gunpowder'.[68] Nonetheless, Brown's accurate attention to detail is impressive and his painting heralded a new era of naval art which began to feature deck scenes and led, directly, to the numerous famous depictions of Nelson's death at Trafalgar. The damaged warships of the battle became famous in their own right and several intricately detailed sketches, aquatints and engravings were made of them by artists of repute such as Richard Livesay and Dominic Serres (see figs. 22, 23).

Dodd, Cleveley, Brown, Livesay and Serres had already painted impressive and different scenes of the battle and its aftermath. Would Loutherbourg and Pocock now rise to the substantial challenge of their rivals?

With his unequalled skill as a draughtsman and his interest in movement and light, Loutherbourg sought to create a canvas that would have a profound physical effect on its audience, so that the viewer would feel the wind, hear the noise of battle, shiver with cold and cower under the constant threat of death. He was going to create a piece of theatre. He was, nevertheless, still interested in a degree of historical accuracy, and when he visited Portsmouth, Loutherbourg made some magnificent sketches of the British, and captured French, warships (see fig. 24). In his surviving sketchbooks, held in the British Museum in London, we see rigging drawn in magnificent detail, the sway and hang of the sails caught by a master. We also have damaged ships, intact ships and even sailors. Loutherbourg is well known for his sketches of sailors from the Battle of Cape St Vincent (1797), but it is not so well known that he sketched some of those from the Glorious First of June and his images are an important addition to the extremely small number of surviving pictures of common sailors at that time. Where Brown made portraits the principal focus of his picture, Loutherbourg's sailors occupied the lower reaches of an image dominated by a clash between the two flagships, the *Queen Charlotte* and *Montagne*, encapsulating the battle between Britain and France in a personal duel between the fleets' commanders (see fig. 16). The artist concentrates a great deal of attention on British sailors saving Frenchmen, realising their struggles magnificently. The ships' rigging is full of the movement of war as the structured order of the square sails suddenly falls in a frantic jumble of disassociated, tangled, ropes, canvas and blocks.

Loutherbourg's painting was commissioned for the handsome sum of £500 as a companion piece to the large canvas he had recently completed of the Siege of Valenciennes, and it was advertised in the same way, with due regard to historical accuracy:

> The Proprietors, in submitting the above subject to the public, respectfully assure them that the same care and attention will be shown in collecting the material from nature, and the most authentic information, and every exertion will be made to render the picture as correct as that of the Grand Attack on Valenciennes, painted by Mr Loutherbourg, which has already given such universal satisfaction.[69]

Loutherbourg's *The Glorious First of June* was exhibited at Orme's gallery in Old Bond Street and was initially very well received and reviewed as 'one of the boldest and most successful efforts of the artist who produced it ...The sea performance before us is the strongest effort at individuality that was ever before attempted'. A reviewer for *The Times* told of its 'uncommon merit' and revelled in the variety of people, from all ranks of life, who came to view it. We know that Prince William V, Stadholder of the Netherlands went to see it three times.[70]

Gradually, however, despite such a promising start, the image fell into disfavour and eventually fell so far that it was sold to cover a debt. The problem was, and quite contrary to the claims of the publicists, that Loutherbourg had created a work accurate in the detail of the men and the ships but wholly inaccurate in its depiction of the scene. In reality, the *Queen Charlotte* was never in the position Loutherbourg suggests, as she was dismasted the moment she swung to leeward of the *Montagne*. The immediate implication from the painting, therefore, was that Howe should never have let the Frenchman escape and thus the image was, in effect, a slight against Howe and the crew of the *Queen Charlotte* and was condemned as such. Perhaps unsurprisingly neither Howe nor Bowen, the ship's master, liked the picture. One contemporary wrote: 'Mr Loutherbourg's picture on this popular subject is too licentious in the points of historic fact to please any nautical observer'. Another problem, though minor when considered alongside the incorrect juxtaposition of the main contestants, was that Loutherbourg's canvas also showed the sinking of the *Vengeur*, and that happened several hours after the first clash between the flagships.[71]

And so one of the most theatrical depictions of war at sea lost its audience. The canvas was taken from its frame, rolled up and stored away. The British public appreciated great artistic talent but they wanted fact and accuracy above all else and it was not until the 1840s that the culture had changed sufficiently to accept romantic interpretations of historical events, the period when J. M. W. Turner's symbolic and poetic image *The Fighting Temeraire* was so well received. Loutherbourg was in this respect an important precursor of Turner and a man whose artistic vision was ahead of his time. His painting of the First of June lay hidden until 1823 when St James's Palace in London was being redecorated. By then it had become long disassociated from its original companion piece, *The Siege of Valenciennes*, which had been sold privately to Lord Hesketh. This dislocation directly led to one of those curious quirks of fate that generate benefit from disaster. In the early 1820s, the new King, George IV, a naval enthusiast, decided to commission a new partner for Loutherbourg's now resurrected image and the result was Turner's magnificent *The Battle of Trafalgar* (1824), an example of artistic theatre equal to Loutherbourg's canvas of the First of June and a perfectly fitting companion piece. Yet again, however, the artist's emotional, romantic take on naval events found little favour; Turner's image, along with Loutherbourg's, was banished to the Hospital for Seamen at Greenwich in London where they still hang.

Pocock's response to the battle was more sober. He had the supreme advantage over all his rivals that he had actually been there. He was the first naval artist to witness fleet battle for well over a century and he relished the challenge of creating a journalistic record of the battle in pictures. He exhibited three large canvases in the immediate aftermath of the battle and then another seventeen years later, in 1811. He issued several prints and was later commissioned to illustrate the opening article in the first edition of the *Naval Chronicle*, a regularly published journal of naval news and events. Pocock's sketches in the *Naval Chronicle* were printed alongside lengthy descriptions, written by him, that encapsulate his thoroughness and rigour. His first sketch was described as:

> ... The *Queen Charlotte*, on the 29th of May 1794, upon the starboard tack, under double-reefed topsails, after having led through the French line of battle. This view is supposed to be taken from the eastward, in order to show the extent of the enemy's line, which is on the larboard tack. The manner of passing through it is exemplified by the Bellerophon, Rear-Admiral Pasley, which ship is firing on both sides, as she passes.[72]

Together with the images Pocock published, sold and exhibited, numerous sketches survive in the National Maritime Museum archives including four separate bird's-eye views of different stages in the battles (see Appendix III, pp. 353–6). His finest achievement was the oil of the *Brunswick* engaging the *Vengeur* (see fig. 17) which is full of movement and smoke and a sense of the drastic which is very different from most images of naval war, but far closer to reality. On the day, the fight was conducted in its own heroic isolation some distance from the main battle, but Pocock, ever anxious to get things right, received and carefully preserved a lengthy and detailed first-hand account of the contest from a midshipman of the *Brunswick* which he used in conjunction with his own lengthy journal of the battle. The painting shows the *Brunswick* in the centre, the *Vengeur* to the right and the French *L'Achille* to the left, at the moment the *Brunswick*'s gunners, while in serious danger of being assaulted on both sides, brought down the masts of *L'Achille*. The image shows how all the ships were subject to dramatic and unpredictable roll. Note how the *Vengeur* is to leeward, and therefore one might expect her to be heeled over to starboard with the pressure of the wind, but she has in fact rolled heavily to port, as has *L'Achille*. The *Brunswick*, meanwhile, is righting herself. This is exactly how three ships would appear if a large wave was passing from left to right, at right angles to the wind which we can discern from the ships' ensigns. The ships on the left and right are in the trough of the swell and the *Brunswick* in the centre, rising at its crest.

In direct contrast to Loutherbourg's elaborate fantasies, Pocock's work is a triumph of deadpan realism that makes his images as valuable to the historian as written sources. His numerous watercolours and sketches (see Appendix III) show the battle area as it must have looked, with numerous scattered, dismasted ships appearing to be lost, drifting this way and that in a woolly haze of concussion. Together, Pocock's renderings of the battle form a unique record of fleet warfare in the Age of Sail; they are the most realistic images ever created. His work was immediately well received and that success rapidly accelerated his career. Soon established as one of the leading naval artists of his generation, a stream of private commissions followed and he counted among his patrons Admiral Lord Hood and the Admiral's brother Lord Bridport, Lord Gambier, Sir Richard Strachan, Lord Barham and Admiral Byam Martin. By the age of eighty Pocock had exhibited 113 pictures at the Royal Academy and 183 at the Old Water-Colour Society and from these a vast number of engravings were produced. He was also commissioned to illustrate a book, *The Shipwreck* by William Falconer, that was one of the publishing phenomena of the age and, by 1830, had been reprinted twenty-four times. During the first fourteen years of the *Naval Chronicle* Pocock produced more than sixty illustrations, images that have become inextricably linked with our contemporary perception of the era. Pocock not only recorded naval events, but shaped them in the mind of future generations.

The public's insight to the battle was further enhanced by bird's-eye-plans of the action showing how it unfolded. Several such works were created of which three were published, including an unreliable schematic version, printed on 28 June in the *Morning Herald* newspaper. A large fold-out plan by Robert Cleveley was included in A. C. de Poggi's 1796 narrative of the battle, alongside the Cleveley prints. Cleveley's plan is valuable because it marks his viewpoint for the prints, giving us an immediate sense of the battle's geography. The third of these published works was a magnificent print by Livesay showing the arrangement of the fleets and the course they plotted from 19 May when

Howe discovered that Villaret had left Brest. Its value lies in the fact that it was taken from an original chart supplied by none other than James Bowen, Master of the *Queen Charlotte*. No other battle chart produced in the Age of Sail can claim such authority.*

There was yet one more novel way that the battle was presented to the public. Robert Barker's innovative Panoramic Theatre aimed to give its audience an insider's view of the action. An artist from Edinburgh, Barker had only recently patented his panorama idea: a painting was copied in such a way that it could be displayed right around the wall of a circular room and then viewed from the centre, to give the impression of being 'in' the painting. By lighting the image from above and by masking out the space above and below it, Barker made the picture appear as if 'floating' (see fig. 13). The viewing platform for Barker's presentation of the First of June was designed to look like the quarterdeck of a frigate. So realistic was the overall effect of his show that, when Queen Charlotte visited, it made her feel seasick.[73] A broadsheet published a guide to the Panorama showing exactly where the viewer stood: in the centre of both fleets, close to the *Queen Charlotte* at 1 p.m. as the French fleet, now reformed, was bearing down on the helpless *Queen* (see fig. 12).[74]

Barker had shown various panoramas in his theatre just off Leicester Square, but this was the first time that he had presented a naval subject. He was challenged at every stage. The essential difficulty lay in painting on a flat surface something that would appear straight when curved, while at the same time achieving a sense of proportion, distance and perspective within the fleet. The final canvas was 10,000 feet square: 283 feet (86.3 metres) long and 35 feet (10.7 metres) high. A copy survives in the National Maritime Museum but its glory remains hidden without an appropriate building in which to display it. There is, however, a miniature recreation of the theatre in the Victoria & Albert Museum in London. One visitor prepared to pay the pricey one shilling entrance fee

*The track chart of the fleets in map 1 is based on this source.

to Barker's show proclaimed: 'nothing can be seen but sky and water, and the beholder thinks himself on the Ocean surrounded by ships of war in action. The whole thing has a fine effect and exceeds any idea I had formed of painting.'[75] It was yet one more way in which the Glorious First of June broke boundaries.

These, then, were the basic ingredients of the celebrations in England, France and America and a sheen of glory became attached to the battle both subconsciously and quite deliberately. On the very same day that news of the victory broke in London, a newspaper published an advertisement for a stage production celebrating the battle, describing it as 'glorious'. The battle was described as such in the House of Lords on the same date, and within a month a theatre company was promoting a new show called *The Glorious First of June*.[76] This shiny interpretation has been remembered and celebrated for generations but the thanks bestowed upon the officers and their men and the ways in which their victory was absorbed by the British general public were much more complex than this simple exchange of awards and peacock-like display of art and theatre suggests. The baubles of state, the purses of coin, the illuminated cities and the gaudy banquets that so easily catch the eye lead us away from a viperous nest of anxiety, discontent, partisanship and social tension, where the grinding of teeth is more audible than the cheers of joy.

# 10.

# The Second Reaction: Acrimony and Disgrace

The language of conciliation and respect produces no other effect on your mind than increased irritation.

Naval historian Edward Brenton to Admiral George Montagu.[1]

The battle and its aftermath proved extremely traumatic for some of its observers and participants. Those related to flag officers were fortunate as they found out very early on, usually in the first dispatch, about the fate of their loved ones. This is why Howe's sister could appear in public and be on such excellent form so soon after the battle: she had been informed that her brother had survived unscathed. Until that moment, however, Howe's daughter Mary, had still had to endure some days of uncertainty. She was with a friend when they heard that the British had been in action. Mary later admitted that in the subsequent days 'I have contrived lately not to look well nor be very strong' and her friend, also called Mary, 'was so much struck, when she first heard of my father's glorious victory, that it made her as yellow as saffron.' Howe's wife was particularly lucky: the King wrote to her in person telling her that her husband was safe.[2]

The relatives of ordinary sailors and officers found it much more difficult to get news of loved ones and a network of friendship and family contacts mobilised as soon as reports of the battle arrived. A man whose son was serving aboard the *Russell* contacted a man called Ebenezer Fisher who had previously met the *Russell*'s captain, John Payne, for news of his boy.[3] The MP George Canning, who experienced the outburst of joy at the London theatre, must have been consumed by worry because he immediately set to work the next morning in an attempt to find news of Easley Smith, presumably a close friend or relation, who was serving aboard Hood's flagship, the *Royal George*. It was a full four days before he received any word of Easley's safety.[4] This whole problem is wonderfully encapsulated in a series of letters between a Mr and Mrs Baker who hunted desperately for their son, Ned, a young midshipman on board the *Orion.* As soon as the fleet had returned, Ned's father, William, rushed to Portsmouth to hear news of his son. A lack of horses frustrated his journey and he arrived late and already upset, only to find out that the *Orion* was not in Portsmouth at all, but Plymouth. Eventually he heard news of Ned's gallant behaviour from Admiral Gardner himself, but the tales of his conduct merely made William's desire even stronger to see his son and still he had no news of his actual wellbeing. All he discovered was bad news, that 'one or two of the youngsters on board have been slightly touched'. He then wrestled with his internal demons in a letter to his wife, trying to explain that he had no real information but that 'I am shocked at myself for having even seemed to suppose that there was the least reason to think or to leave you in the least degree of doubt about our Dear Boy's safety … Adieu! Adieu! My ever dearest …' William then tried to get to Plymouth but was frustrated time and again by weather, wind or a lack of shipping. After several days of waiting he wrote: 'My heart yearns after our dear boy, & every moment employed on any other subject is an age & waste of time'. Several days later he finally arrived in Plymouth, but by then 'dearest' Ned had made his own way home.[5]

This was of course a two-way process. Sailors on board ship but unable to secure leave were anxious on behalf of their relatives, eager to ease their worried minds. Thus Midshipman William Parker wrote to his mother in something of a panic as he only had five minutes to scribble a letter before the boat left for shore. He wrote 'you will hear by the newspaper of the engagement we have been in, and to tell you not to alarm yourself about me, as I am sound, well, and happy as a king'. He did, however, take the opportunity to set his mother's pulse racing by declaring that 'the engagement was the severest that ever was fought in the whole world' before telling her in another letter to 'never be the least alarmed at hearing the winds sound and play a little tune, as there is, I assure you, no danger…' He also kindly wrote another rushed letter to the father of a friend he had seen that morning alive and well 'lest your son should not have leisure'.[6]

James Maxwell, a Royal Marine from the *Leviathan*, also wrote a hasty letter, probably to catch the same post as Parker. Maxwell was a little more refined than the overexcited Parker and began his letter: 'Thank God Almighty my dear mother I am in the greatest good health and spirits', before spending the rest of the time available writing quite a long letter about why he could not write a long letter.[7] This scribbling of hasty lines of reassurance was mirrored throughout the fleet as sons and fathers wrote to soothe anxious parents, brothers, sisters, lovers, wives and close friends.[8]

As far as fleet discipline was concerned, victory was often as hard to cope with as defeat, and the sailors of HMS *Orion* mutinied. Midshipman Parker had gone ashore for leave and when he heard the news of the mutiny it made him 'so uneasy & almost broke our brave Captain's heart'. On their return the ship's company had smuggled aboard a large quantity of spirits and had got drunk before demanding leave to go ashore and the release of shipmates who had been put in irons, presumably for a similar offence. The officers were summoned and they kept watch throughout the night before rousing the crew at 4 a.m. and rounding up seven ringleaders. 'Most of our brave boys have undone all the good they ever did,' wrote Parker. The mutineers were lashed and the leaders put in irons. Court martial could so easily have led to the death sentence but her captain, John Duckworth, 'had them before him to-day & said that as he was of a forgiving nature he gave them into the hands of the ships company, that he restores them with love for the services they had done him'.[9] Sometimes coping with the excesses of victory required a gentle hand.

Things started to go wrong for some of the British captains as soon as Howe's report was published in the *London Gazette Extraordinary* of 11 June. Howe covered the basic details of the battle but he studiously failed to comment on the behaviour, good or bad, of any of his captains or flag officers. The only men whose names were included were those who had been severely wounded: 'Admiral Graves has received a wound in the arm ... Rear-Admirals Bowyer and Pasley and Captain Hutt of the *Queen,* have each had a leg taken off.' The implication of such wounds was one of bravery or heroism, but in omitting to name any specific examples of good conduct, Howe was breaking an established tradition, as well as disappointing Parliament, the public and, of course, the officers concerned.

Howe was still exhausted and very conscious of the difficulty he faced. There was no chance that he could comment, from personal experience, on the behaviour of all twenty-six of his captains. The battle had been fought over too large an area and for too long a time to achieve any accurate overview of all events so soon afterwards. Gun smoke and mist had obscured whole sections of both fleets for lengthy periods. The overriding sense of the battle was one of confusion and uncertainty. In several phases it was unclear what had happened, let alone why it had happened, but the news-hungry public wanted specifics, and they wanted them now: they wanted to know who were the heroes and who the villains, they wanted tales of sacrifice and of cowardice. The man who insisted that Howe should provide a list of names was Lord Chatham, First Lord of the Admiralty.[10]

Grudgingly, Howe complied, sending requests to his flag officers for more information on the conduct of their officers. To a man they appreciated the problem which Howe now faced. They were all concerned that they would cause offence by failing to name someone simply because they had not been seen.[11] When Howe finally committed himself to naming several officers who he believed had performed well and deserved a medal, he did so having made it quite clear that: 'The commander of a fleet, their Lordships know, is unavoidably so confined in his view of the occurrences in time of battle, as to be little capable of rendering personal testimony to the meritorious service of officers...' He then named:

> Admiral Graves and Sir Alexander Hood; the Rear-Admirals Bowyer, Gardner and Pasley; the Captains Lord Hugh Seymour, Pakenham, Berkeley, Gambier, John Harvey, Payne, Parker, Henry Harvey, Pringle, Duckworth, and Elphinstone ... Captains Nichols of the *Sovereign* and Hope of the *Bellerophon* ... Lieutenants Monkton of the *Marlborough*, and Donnelly of the *Montagu*.

He then wrote in a private letter that he feared his naming of names 'may be followed by disagreeable consequences'.[12] He was right: one contemporary soon wrote that 'hotter actions have since been fought at Spithead than on the First of June'.[13]

Those mentioned glowed with pride as the congratulations came in. Thomas Erskine, a leading politician, wrote to Captain Payne of the *Russell*: 'I saw your name with great satisfaction amongst the list of captains distinguished by Lord Howe upon the late glorious occasion',[14] but others found themselves facing unpleasant implication and insinuation because they had been left out. The list certainly left some glaring gaps. Where was Captain Collingwood of the *Barfleur*? Schomberg of the *Culloden*? Bazeley of the *Alfred*? Where on earth was Rear-Admiral Ben Caldwell of the *Impregnable*? There is no hint from the logs and correspondence that any of these men had done anything wrong and we know that several of them had been conspicuously and repeatedly brave.

Howe, of course, realised that there were gaps and he wrote after his list of names: 'These selections, however, should not be construed to the disadvantage of other Commanders, who may have been equally deserving of the approbation of the Lords Commissioners of the Admiralty, although I am not enabled to make a particular statement of their merits.' It was a clear commitment that no slight was intended; simply that those who were named were those whom Howe had noted himself or had been informed of by others. It is typical, bumbling, Howe: a rambling and contradictory statement that could confuse as easily as clarify, but always with the best of intentions. In hoping not to create offence he created the opportunity for offence to be taken. He even made it awkward for those who were supposed to be awarding the medals. The King and Dundas got in a terrible muddle as they planned the awards ceremony in Portsmouth because Ben Caldwell, one of Howe's flag officers, had not been named in the list though he had already been thanked in Parliament. No one knew if he had been deliberately omitted or accidentally overlooked. The King wrote grumpily: 'if Lord Howe is dissatisfied with Rear-Admiral Caldwell he ought to speak out and then I will omit him' before agreeing to take a spare chain to Portsmouth in case. Caldwell had not been given the cold shoulder, and took comfort from the fact that none of the chains had been allocated to specific officers. Dundas also grumbled in a letter to the King that it was regretful that Sir Roger Curtis [Howe's flag captain] 'had not been instructed to inform your majesty's servants confidentially of Lord Howe's sentiments respecting individual officers'.[15] It is an important reminder that naval victories posed their own unique problems to the administration of the time and that the management of victory itself was an art that had yet to be mastered.

No doubt all of the captains named were disappointed that the medals did not materialise for two years,[16] but one captain, destined to play a very significant role in the forthcoming wars with France, did take particular offence to his omission and complained in writing. His name was Cuthbert Collingwood. Collingwood had been captain of Rear-Admiral Bowyer's flagship *Barfleur* and Howe's attention had rather skipped Collingwood and settled on Bowyer, even though Collingwood had fought in sole command on 1 June from just after 10 a.m., when Bowyer was wounded.[17] Howe's technique, if insensitive, was at least evenly applied to every other flagship. Pasley was mentioned, but not his captain, Hope; Graves was mentioned but not his captain, Nicholls; Gardner was mentioned but not his captain, Hutt;[18] and Hood was mentioned and not his captain, Domett. In this, the second letter, Howe's own captain, Curtis, was not even mentioned. Collingwood, a curious character at the best of times and an insufferable moaner, moaned as he had never moaned before. 'The appearance of that letter had nearly broke my heart,' he wrote. His disappointment soon turned to anger.

Collingwood quickly realised that there was a link between the scale of damage the ships had received and the names of the officers on the list. When later venting his anger at Sir Roger Curtis he claimed:

> I considered the conduct of the *Barfleur* had merited commendation when commendation was given to zeal and activity and that an insinuation that either had been wanting was injurious and unjust, nor do I believe any ship was more warmly or effectively

> engaged than the *Barfleur* from the beginning of the action to the end of it. That the Frenchmen did not knock our masts away was not my fault.[19]

He was right to notice the link between damage and reward as Hood had written to Howe explaining how difficult it was to judge the performance of other ships and had actually suggested that 'the best testimony that can be given to Your Lordship, of the Meritorious conduct of the ships in the Divisions of the Fleet, is the Report that each Captain may make, of the Real Damage his ship has sustained together with the number of killed and wounded in each particular ship'.[20] Collingwood demanded an explanation from both Curtis and Howe but received no sense of satisfaction from either meeting.

His subsequent letters are filled with loathing toward Curtis, who Collingwood described as 'an artful, sneaking creature, whose fawning insinuating manners creeps into the confidence of whoever he attacks'. Collingwood banged on to anyone who would listen that he was 'sick with mortification' that there was any shadow of suspicion concerning his behaviour and it seemed to him, at least, that '… while all England was rejoicing in a great victory, the hearts of those who won it were sinking with disappointment'. In another letter he wrote that the victors were 'dejected and sad' and that the confusion caused by Howe's letter had 'soured the minds of every body'. He even claimed that the officers who *had* received a medal were 'almost as much offended at the manner [in which the letter was written] as those who were omitted'.[21]

If his claims to universal dejection appear a little over-zealous, Collingwood was personally deeply hurt by the snub. Already hypersensitive, he even took offence when the Royal Family visited the fleet at Spithead because the King's time and space were occupied by the flag officers. He wrote in yet another grumpy letter: 'nothing cou'd have been more gratifying to them [the fleet captains] than to witness the honours conferred to *him* [Howe] … while officers of inferior rank in other corps had been received into his ship, they were positively excluded, and he knew of no honour the officers of the Navy had received by his presence unless sitting in a boat four hours was an honour'.[22]

Collingwood and several other officers had fought as well as they could but had not received the professional and public recognition that they believed was their due. Although ignored in Howe's letter, Collingwood was actually rewarded with the command of the relatively new 74-gunner HMS *Excellent*. He now, therefore, had an independent command, a significant professional advance.[23] This was not enough for Collingwood, however. He did not just want or hope to be mentioned in the press by his superiors after such an action; he expected it. The collapse of that expectation was crushing and it highlights quite how badly Howe had bungled the entire affair. It is quite clear that many of the officers not named in Howe's list were obviously deserving candidates: their names had not been withheld as a deliberate snub but because Howe had bungled his letter. This is a very important distinction as historians have used the absence of certain names in the list to suggest a significant degree of professional malpractice in the fleet, using the flawed logic that Collingwood so feared and argued against so strongly.[24]

The Admiralty eventually relented in 1797 when he was awarded a medal for fighting with great distinction at the Battle of Cape St Vincent, one which he actually refused until he was awarded another for his conduct on 1 June. There does however remain a small question mark over the entire affair because there is some suggestion that Howe really *was* displeased with Collingwood. In the margin of Collingwood's own report of the battle Howe has scribbled a note. At the point where Collingwood describes opening some secret instructions, Howe has underlined the passage and scribbled in the margin: 'no such signal made in the *Queen Charlotte*. But appeared to have been made by the captain of the *Barfleur* [Collingwood] when Rear-Admiral Bowyer was wounded'. Howe then noted that Collingwood had made the error 'through inattention to the tenor and words of the instructions'.[25] This is certainly strong criticism, and it comes from a man obsessive about correct signalling procedure. For all of Collingwood's outbursts, it remains quite possible that Howe was indeed dissatisfied with his behaviour.

Another piece of evidence that has been used to suggest poor British performance among Howe's captains was their failure to break through the French line as Howe had ordered, and there is some suggestion that this perception of failure did exist in the public mind at the time.[26] The numbers are certainly quite striking: Howe led twenty-five ships of the line into battle and ordered all of them to cut through the French line and engage from leeward. But how many did as he ordered and followed his bold example? The answer is five: the *Defence*, *Marlborough*, *Royal George*, *Queen* and the *Brunswick*.[27] If judged in these most narrow of terms, therefore, only five of his captains actually did what he had asked of them. The result is that the Glorious First of June and Howe himself have suffered in some of our history books with the unfair burden of a tainted reputation. Most recently it has been argued that Howe's inability to express himself was responsible for this tactical failure[28] but there is only one, minor, example of confusion in the voluminous written evidence surrounding the battle. Edward Codrington, the young lieutenant aboard the *Queen Charlotte,* spoke after the battle to an old friend called Floyd who had been serving aboard the 80-gun *Gibraltar*. 'Our captain [Thomas Mackenzie] is about the stupidest man possible,' Floyd opined. In the run up to the battle Floyd, the signalling lieutenant, had carefully presented Howe's tactical intentions, explaining what he meant by 'each ship to take her opponent' and 'engage to leeward'. After the action Mackenzie asked Floyd if either signal had ever been made.[29] The *Gibraltar's* log records no such confusion. With the exception of this young sailor's possibly unfair jibe against his captain, there appears to have been no confusion among Howe's captains regarding his intention. The explanation for the failure to break the French line must lie elsewhere.

It must never be overlooked exactly how difficult it was to break a well-kept enemy line. Howe himself in the *Queen Charlotte* was only able to break through because of a mistake in the French line, a mistake for which the French commander responsible was held criminally responsible. Where the French did not make such mistakes the British were simply unable to break through. The *Brunswick*, which went on to fight her lonely duel with the *Vengeur*, was ensnared in the rigging of the *Vengeur* because her captain had been unable, at first, to break through the French line. All he could do was crash broadside to broadside into the ship opposite him in the line. Collingwood on the *Barfleur* found it impossible to break the line because there were too many British ships in the way that would inevitably fire into him if he tried.[30] Even brave Admiral Pasley of the *Bellerophon*, who had fought with such sustained courage and ferocity on both 28 and 29 May, did not get through the French line. Many of the British ships by this stage were severely damaged and simply unable to make the necessary adjustments to take them through a narrow gap in a moving fleet.

We also know that Howe was well aware that this might happen and when he ordered his fleet to break through the enemy line, he did so with the very important addendum:

> The different captains and commanders not being able to effect the specified intention in either case [the signal applying to the passage through a line to windward or to leeward], are at liberty to act as circumstances require.[31]

Howe therefore only expected some of his captains to be able to break the line. In fact, the only thing that Howe really cared about was that the British engaged the French closely, something which was achieved by all of those who were not disabled.[32]

Most importantly, however, when Howe had asked his flag officers to comment on the performance of their divisions, all of them had showered praise on their captains.[33] The only exception was Pasley, who queried the behaviour of Molloy of the *Caesar* and Pigott of the *Tremendous*. He reported of Molloy 'it gives me great pain in being obliged to report that Admiral Graves made *Caesar*'s signal to make more sail when we were going down to the attack, and, that I felt myself under the disagreeable necessity of throwing out her pendant twice for close action, while in battle… at which times she was lying near half a mile to windward …'[34] Pasley was also concerned about the behaviour of the *Tremendous*, which 'did not appear to be damaged either in masts sails or yards'.[35] In a private letter, Collingwood shared Pasley's dim view of Molloy but was generous toward everyone else. He wrote: 'Except Molloy's there was not a cool heart in the fleet, all seemed satisfied, there did not appear a doubt, that all had not exerted their utmost ability to do justice to their country's cause on the first of June.'[36] Others felt the same way about Molloy.[37] What, then, must we make of Anthony Molloy and his conduct in the *Caesar*?

The Molloy case is a very interesting one. There were two main areas of concern. Firstly, that he did not break the line as Howe ordered on the 28 May but kept well away from the French fleet, and secondly that he failed to assume his station properly on 1 June.[38] The defence at his court martial argued convincingly that, on both occasions, the ship was too damaged to fulfil the Admiral's orders, with a shattered rig on the 29 May and a jammed rudder on 1 June, and that, whenever it had been possible, Molloy had fought the French as well as he could.[39] He was also the victim of malfunctioning ordnance: by the end of the battle he had one 24-pounder cannon burst and two split, one 32-pounder, two 24-pounders, five 12-pounders and one 12-pounder carronade 'wounded'. In total that is eleven cannon and one carronade out of action, a 12.5 per cent reduction in her potential firepower.[40]

The prosecution based their case simply on numerous observations by high-ranking officers of the *Caesar*'s position in relation to other ships in the fleet and yet Molloy was found guilty. Either the judges thought that he was lying about the damage he had sustained or they simply chose to take the opportunity to rid the service of an unpleasant officer. Both explanations are possible but one gets the sense that everyone was waiting to see the worst in Molloy given the slightest opportunity, and that Molloy simply had no idea of the range or depth of feeling against him. We know, for example, that Howe was so cross with Molloy during the battle that he removed his nephew from Molloy's ship in the heat of the action and had him transferred to the flagship.[41]

Molloy was incandescent after the sentence was passed and clearly thought he was the victim of a set-up. He later wrote: 'Prejudice Sir once born grows rapidly to maturity… the glance of prejudice is never absorb'd, but reflecting from it's object back upon itself, spreads into a Glare.'[42] He went on to rage against the techniques of the prosecution, particularly how his words had been twisted and turned against him. He fingered Roger Curtis in particular for his 'crafty catalogue' of questions.[43]

The first thing to realise is that Molloy himself had demanded the court martial because he was so confident that his actions were honourable and that he would be acquitted. He went on to explain, at length, how his ship was disabled and how he later could not 'express the pain and anxiety of mind I labourd under all the time'. Howe, ever anxious to keep a public impression of unity in the fleet, did his utmost to prevent Molloy from seeking a court martial, even though we know Howe to have been long frustrated with Molloy for taking too-frequent leave on unexplained family business and that Molloy had a reputation for policing his ship with an uncomfortable mix of harsh discipline and incompetence.[44]

The outcome of the trial is a powerful reminder of the professional, political and personal faction that so buzzed around the fleet in 1794. Molloy was found guilty but, importantly, the court acknowledged that his personal courage had been unimpeachable in the actions of 29 May and 1 June 'as well as on many former occasions', a sentence clearly designed to appease as many as possible.[45] Before the sentence was declared, moreover, the savvy Howe predicted how each member of the jury would vote, according to their prejudices or interests, and he got it exactly right.[46] The King, for one, was delighted that Molloy had been dismissed from his command but believed that his previous good service record was enough to prevent him from being dismissed the service altogether.[47] Even the King seemed to realise that Molloy was an exception to the rule in the height of the confusion over who had been named in Howe's honours list.[48] Collingwood was also scathing of Molloy, saying that this conduct 'was past defence' but otherwise he declared with great pride that 'there was not, I believe, a suspicion in the mind of any man that all had not done their duty well'.[49]

Nothing more was heard of Pasley's concern over the behaviour of the *Tremendous* and it later came to light that, contrary to his original observation, the *Tremendous* had been behaving oddly because her standing rigging was shattered. Her hull was also so holed that the pumps had been constantly at work.[50]

Thus, with the single exception of Molloy, there does seem to have been a strong sense of unity and dedication to duty in Howe's fleet that has not been properly recognised. In fact one of his most recent biographers condemned Howe in the shadow of Nelson as 'never likely to have a "Band of Brothers"',[51] but the evidence suggests otherwise. Certainly he did not have the charisma of a man like Nelson, but fleets are drawn together by more than charisma alone. The ferocity of the French threat and the strength, or at least ideological fervour, of their hostility helped to knit the British fleet together, but Howe also played his part. The words of Horace Walpole have often been quoted, usually as supporting evidence for Howe's shambolic political career, that Howe 'never made a friend but at the mouth of the cannon',[52] but the flip side of this quote is too easily overlooked – that he *did* make friends at the mouth of a cannon and that he *could* inspire loyalty and devotion at sea in his own steady and unflamboyant way.

Howe himself seems to have got so fed up with the broiling acrimony spread by men like Collingwood that he threatened to resign, saying 'he wou'd remain no longer in the fleet than he cou'd give general satisfaction'.[53] We also know that he discussed the idea of resigning in private with Vice-Admiral Alan Gardner, a close friend. Gardner argued against the idea strongly.[54] Howe was even attacked in the press, which he took to heart. One might assume that naval victory was so important to the national interest as to rise above partisanship but of course the opposite was true: it was *so* important that it became political currency. Howe had won a great victory but for all the accolades he received he now found himself sandwiched between a dissatisfied officer corps and a scheming press who intended to use him for their higher political aims.[55] The aftermath of the battle, therefore, saw Howe, under siege both personally and professionally rather than basking in glory. Upset, he wrote to the First Lord of the Admiralty: 'I cannot be insensible to the flattering distinction of being thought capable of rendering public service, while I most sincerely lament the disappointment I have to apprehend in that desirable pursuit ...'[56] Unfortunately for Howe, obstacles to his happiness were very highly placed.

Just before Howe fought his battle, William Pitt had realised that to wage a convincing and sustained war against France, a cross-party government of 'patriotic unity' would be required to reduce partisan bickering over finance, aims and strategy: he wanted to create 'one Great Family' to face the Jacobin danger.[57] The key man Pitt needed to woo was the Duke of Portland, a leading member of the opposition Whig party, and one of Pitt's enticements was to make Portland a Knight of the Garter, the pinnacle of the British honours system. Unfortunately, the King had already promised the award to Howe, during the Royal visit to Portsmouth, and membership of the Order of the Garter was strictly limited in number. It was impossible to make both Howe and Portland a Knight of the Garter.

When Howe's victory was celebrated in the middle of June the political situation had still not been resolved, and Portland, much to the King's and Howe's disgust, received the Garter. Pitt offered Howe a marquisate as some form of compensation, telling him haughtily that 'it would be for the advantage of the public service that he should forego the King's promise of it'. Howe lowered his head, forwent the King's promise but proudly refused the marquisate.[58] Pitt won over Portland and the coalition was confirmed in the summer of 1795 with six members of the opposition in a new thirteen-strong cabinet.

The timing of Howe's victory was therefore unfortunate: an ageing, frequently sick admiral whose future active service could be counted in months rather than years carried little political weight at a time of great political uncertainty when so much loyalty, cooperation and confidence was for sale. It is more than likely that Howe's largely unsuccessful political career, so blighted by poor judgement and lack of wisdom, had now come back to haunt him. He had been broadly independent as a Member of Parliament and was a friend of the King but was now no friend of the ministers.

Even with Pitt and Portland moving toward a new coalition in May and June 1794 there was still much vocal opposition to the British war effort: it was this very diversity of opinion that had first led Pitt to seek a coalition government. A host of principles was at stake: should Britain be at war at all? If so, what should be her aim? Was it to protect other European powers from French aggression and achieve some kind of stability in France or was it nothing less than the re-establishment of the French monarchy? The war, moreover, had brought with it a number of distinct problems: an economic crisis as the British government sought to fund her armed forces and social problems as the Government tried to man them. The poor weather that had so crippled France had caused similar agricultural problems in Britain.[59] It is notable that, when the news of the victory was celebrated in one London theatre, the riotous celebration was not quite as widespread as some sources lead us to believe. As the MP and dedicated diarist George Canning recorded

> The effect to an impartial observer was not a little heightened by the contrast between the feeling *generally* apparent, and that which was discoverable in one or two boxes – the *Bouverie* box* (to which I sat nearly opposite in particular. Not a breath appeared to be stirring there… and when the Opera was permitted to proceed, the attention which they paid to the stage (rather than look about them to see rejoicing faces) was highly entertaining.[60]

There were riots and other demonstrations against the war but the most vicious and direct attacks came in the form of caricatures. Fox's Libel Act of 1792 had ensured that insinuations against character or competence could not be made in printed text but the law was significantly more tolerant of cartoons, and this is where Howe found himself under the most direct attack.[61] Both Howe and his flag captain, Curtis, were targeted on the anniversary of the battle in a cartoon playing to the public rumour that the latter was responsible for the advice that led to the admiral calling off the action when several disabled French ships

*The Hon. Edward Bouverie (1738–1810) and the Bouverie brothers – Hon. Edward and Hon. William Henry, all Foxite whigs and hostile to the war.

were still in his grasp (see fig. 21). Howe was mortified at this public ridicule, not for his reputation with the public, but for how he was perceived by the seamen.[62]

The other artistic medium that hijacked the First of June to make political headway was the theatre. The battle was the subject of four significant plays, each of which told the tale of the battle in its own way and for its own ends. That old wizard of the stage spectacular, Mr Astley himself, had visited Portsmouth to see the ships arrive and, within a fortnight of the news being announced, a naval gala was held at Vauxhall, probably in the pleasure gardens. The subsequent and varied stage shows produced some memorable songs, not least this from Sheridan's *The Glorious First of June*:

> Our line was form'd, the French lay to,
> One sigh I gave to Poll on shore,
> Too cold I thought our last Adieu –
> Our parting kisses seem'd too few,
> If we should meet no more.
> But love, avast! My heart is oak
> Howe's darling Signal floats on high;
> I see through roaring cannon's smoke –
> Their awful line subdued and broke
> They strike, they sink, they fly.
> Now (danger past) we'll drink and Joke,
> Sing 'Rule Britannia'; 'Hearts of Oak!'
> And Toast before each martial tune –
> Howe and the Glorious first of June.[63]

Sheridan's script was enhanced by some ingenious special effects with the entire stage at the Theatre Royal in Drury Lane turned into a sea. One happy theatregoer described it thus:

> Nothing can surpass the enchantment of this exhibition – It is

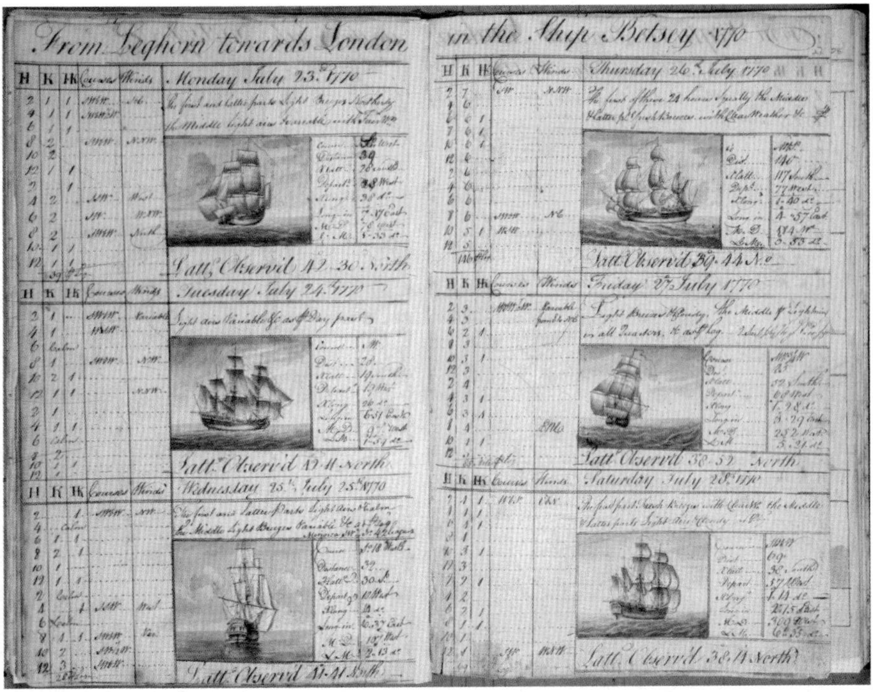

14. Nicholas Pocock's logbook of the *Betsey* 1766–7.

15. Boarding flag from the French 74-gun *L'America* captured by the British *Leviathan*. It reads 'Sailors, the Republic or Death'.

16. The Battle of the First of June.
The *Queen Charlotte* is to the left, the *Montagne* to the right.

17. The *Brunswick* and *Vengeur*. Notice how the ships roll as the swell passes by. The *Vengeur* is to the right, the *Brunswick* in the centre and to the left is the French *L'Achille*, caught at the moment she loses her last remaining mast.

18. Louis Lafite's dramatic unfinished sketch of the sinking of the *Vengeur*.

19. A portrait of Howe on the quarterdeck of the *Queen Charlotte*. One witness claimed that Howe was actually dressed as a sailor 'in a blue jacket and fur cap' and that his face was blackened with gunpowder. Lieutenant Neville dies to the right. Sir Roger Curtis stands at the far left of the image.

20. A contemporary cartoon by Thomas Rowlandson capturing the carnival atmosphere of the fleet's return.

21. Caricature of Howe published on 9 June 1795, just after the battle's anniversary. Roger Curtis, Howe's flag captain, is depicted as his dog.

22–3. Views of captured French ships at Portsmouth. The ships at the top are *Le Juste* (80) and *L'America* (74) and below is the finest of the French prizes, the *Sans Pareil* (74). Notice how thin are the masts: these are temporary 'jury' masts, rigged to replace those lost in battle. The stumps of some of the original masts are still visible.

24. One of Loutherbourg's many sketches taken in situ when the triumphant fleet returned. This shows the damaged sterns of the captured French warships. Notice how high they are riding out of the water without the weight of their masts and yards, crew, stores, cannon and shot.

25. One of many unofficial medals and uniform accessories created after the battle. This oval gilt plate would have been worn on the shoulder of a junior officer's uniform.

> not the usual mockery of pasteboard Ships. The vessels are large, perfect models of the ships they represent, and made with such minute beauty, as to be worthy of a place in the most curious collection. All the manoeuvres of the day are executed with nautical skill, – the lines are formed; they bear down on each other; the firing is well managed, and kept up warmly for some time on both sides; at length, the French line is broken, several of their ships dismasted – boarded – taken ... the expanse of sea affords a variety, which it is not easy for the mind to conceive possible for mere scenic representation.[64]

The underlying message all the plays carried was as important as the visual spectacle and was far more complex than a simple celebration of British heroism, character and victory. The theatre afforded a way to communicate with the masses, to inform and influence public opinion: it was a mouthpiece for political propaganda that reflected and even incited social, cultural and political conflict. This was achieved by exploring themes central to contemporary society, many of which had naval aspects. Opposition to impressment, for example, was a central theme of Whiggish ideology and it is no coincidence that the Whiggish Sheridan explored impressment and civil liberties in *The Glorious First of June*. Sheridan's plot revolved around William, who was employed on the farm of a deceased shipmate's family. The farm could not be worked without him but William was still taken by the press gang. Sheridan thus made the conflict between state impressment and personal loyalties clear to the masses. Other playwrights explored an anti-war stance or were critical of aspects of British victory culture.[65] By no means were these plays a platform for naval veneration. Quite to the contrary, they explored the conflicts inherent in the whole business of naval victory and revelled in the discomfort that it caused.

George Montagu was another who began to feel the heat as the detail of the campaign became known. He had, without doubt, followed his instructions to the word and in some cases used his initiative to exceed them. Yet it seemed to many that he still had not done quite enough. Critics could point to two particular episodes in the campaign that might have had a profound impact on its outcome if Montagu had made different decisions. First, when Montagu returned to Plymouth once he knew that both Howe and Villaret were out, hunting for each other in the misty Atlantic; and secondly, when Montagu returned to Brest and bumped into Villaret's crippled fleet with the American convoy a matter of hours to the south-west. In both instances Montagu had acceptable explanations. On the first occasion he had gone back to Plymouth because his ships had run out of water and on the second he had found himself substantially outnumbered by Villaret's force and the Cancale squadron, now in Brest, and he had no knowledge of the location of the American convoy.

As the events unfolded Montagu even received explicit approval of his action in letters from the Admiralty.[66] Support for Montagu gradually turned, however, as the King waded in. In the words of one contemporary, George III was 'was apt to take very strong disliking, very often without any good grounds, and who, when once he conceived a dislike, could not easily be brought to abandon it'.[67] The King had taken a personal interest in Montagu's role as the campaign unfolded and now began to see Montagu as a significant limiting factor.[68] The victory still had a rather bitter, lingering aftertaste: the successful arrival of the convoy. Its capture, after all, was the reason that Howe had first been sent out. In the most clinical of terms, therefore, by failing to stop the arrival of the convoy, Howe had failed to do his duty. Therein lay the conundrum. No one could possibly claim that Howe or any of his other flag officers had failed to do their duty because they had won the greatest naval victory in over a century and several of them had lost limbs, but it was also well known that the French had invested a great deal of political capital in the convoy. To stop the convoy would have been an opportunity to destabilise Robespierre and the Terror, perhaps fatally.

It is an interesting paradox because it identifies a tacit assumption about the battle. The politicians wanted the convoy captured; they wanted a strategic and subtle victory with significant consequences but what they got was a cumbersome, shiny, loud, awkward fleet battle with all of the whistles and bells associated with it. Of course it advanced the British war effort but it did so in a way that was not quite what they had hoped. The instrument was blunter, more unwieldy and less effective: they had asked for a spade and, at great cost, they had received a shovel.

Howe of course had to be thanked, if through gritted teeth, but Montagu was another matter entirely. Although he could not be criticised directly, sideways glances and tutting made at the time can still be perceived all these years later. When he returned to Plymouth, Montagu requested leave on grounds of ill health – it is important to remember that Montagu was forced to make all of his crucial command decisions on limited information but also burdened with sickness – but he never received another sea-going command.[69] He was offered the post of port admiral at the Nore which, disgusted, he turned down. St Vincent wanted him to serve afloat in 1800 but his request to the Admiralty was ignored. Montagu then applied again in 1801 only to receive the chastening reply from St Vincent: 'My dear Sir – I am extremely concerned to acquaint you, that there is an insuperable bar to your being employed in any way'.[70] The insuperable bar was none other than the Earl of Chatham, now a member of Addington's Cabinet and in 1794 the First Lord of the Admiralty.[71] Montagu's failure to intercept Villaret or the grain convoy, therefore, had robbed Chatham of the glory he believed was in his grasp and the job security he deserved: Chatham was ousted from his position as First Lord in the autumn of 1794. It is likely that Chatham blamed Montagu for his fall from grace. Perhaps feeling sorry for Montagu, two years later the Admiralty offered him the post of shore command at Portsmouth, the most prestigious of all shore commands. Montagu, realising what he was up against, took this olive branch and worked there until his retirement, no doubt cursing the poor cards he had been dealt.

Unfortunately for Montagu, things did not end there, with a wrecked career. A full fifteen years into his retirement he found himself having to deal with one of those ghastly people who feel that they can make or break someone's reputation long after the event – Montagu came up against a historian, one Edward Brenton, a man with naval blood in his veins and a willingness to judge those of whom he wrote.

The second son of Rear-Admiral Jahleel Brenton, Edward had served in the navy and, rather awkwardly for Montagu, he had served aboard the *Bellona* on the very cruise that had ruined Montagu's career.

Once he had achieved the rank of captain, Brenton rose no higher in the service and then took to writing a substantial multi-volume history of the Royal Navy that was published in 1823. One certainly feels for Montagu. It is easy to imagine him full of trepidation at the publication of such a work. He would surely feature, having played such a significant role in such a significant event, but how would he be portrayed? In what light would he be cast to his contemporaries and then remembered by generations ahead? This was his shot at history and it was totally out of his hands. Unfortunately for Montagu it was in the hands of Brenton, whose latest biographer has described him as 'incapable of sifting his evidence, and to have been guided more by prejudice than judgement'.[72] And then Montagu opened the book. Perhaps he flicked through to the index or went straight to the chapter dealing with the opening stages of the Revolutionary War. He would have scanned the pages, found his name, and his heart would have sunk.

Two brief passages particularly concerned Montagu. Brenton described how he had met with Villaret in his damaged fleet but had failed to engage, before commenting: '*all* in the British squadron anxiously expected the signal to engage'. He then added: 'We do not mean to say that the Rear-Admiral was bound, with his disparity of force, to bring on a general action, *although many officers, under similar circumstances, might have so done*'.[73] Finally, Brenton described how the Admiralty ordered Montagu to strike his flag after the battle. Taken together the unwary reader was left with no doubt as to Brenton's perception of Montagu: that he had failed to engage when he should have done so, and that he was punished by the Admiralty for his failure. The reality of the situation was far more complex, however, as Montagu explained to Brenton in a series of ferocious and lengthy letters, urging him to change the text. Montagu had these published in an attempt to put public pressure on the historian and he even wrote to the King.[74] Montagu's position was quite clear. He wrote: 'It is out of his [Brenton's] power to make me an atonement for the distress his book has produced on my mind, and the disquiet he has given to all my family; he has wantonly broken in upon my happiness, and ruffled the repose of my few remaining days.'[75] He was so concerned about how he would be perceived after his death that he deposited all the relevant correspondence with a lawyer at Lincoln's Inn.

Brenton withstood a barrage of personal and professional abuse. Montagu, for example, wrote: 'being present there are some things you should have known better; and of *all* you should have procured more correct information'.[76] In subsequent letters he ordered Brenton, in increasingly biblical language, 'to tell the public the truth, the whole truth, and nothing but the truth, so help you God'. He then warned Brenton to 'Judge not, lest ye be judged … I have not that [power] of forgiving as I hope to be forgiven'.[77] Brenton, to his credit, was immediately apologetic, but he was not sufficiently repentant to calm Montagu:

> My Dear Admiral
> I am extremely hurt and grieved at the contents of your's, *because I think you have expressed yourself in terms to me, which I have deserved*; and because I find I have wounded your feelings, – the very last thing in the world which I would have done, or ever intended. In speaking of your meeting with Villaret, I *never attempted, or meant, any censure on your conduct …*[78]

Brenton offered to change the text in the second and third editions and even to remove the offending passage in the first volume, but Montagu wanted the chance to give a full explanation of events from his perspective, which Brenton refused to allow. The exchange between the two men swiftly collapsed into bitterness and petty squabbling. Brenton suggested they end the correspondence as 'the language of conciliation and respect produces no other effect on your mind, than increased irritation', but Montagu could not even offer him that, explaining: 'I cannot concede to you the power of putting a stop to it'.[79]

Gradually the row fizzled out and Montagu's time ran out. He died on Christmas Eve, 1829. With Montagu out of the picture, Brenton, seemingly incapable of letting things rest, picked up his pen once more for the latest edition of his naval history. He started, at least, rather well: 'It is due to his memory to add that a more honourable and gallant officer never lived; that he was as amiable in private life as he was esteemed in public', before going on to explain how magnanimous he, himself, had been during the public spat: 'I bore everything,' wrote Brenton, 'with more patience than I thought I possessed'. He had already taken back a number of statements that Montagu had disagreed with, particularly the claim that the Admiralty had ordered him to strike his flag. But he still stood by his basic claim that Montagu had made an error of judgement, adding, perhaps for the benefit of Montagu's surviving relatives if not for the ghost of the man himself, that it was an error 'from which the greatest warriors have not been exempt'.[80] The publicity surrounding the correspondence, however, had at least attracted some sympathy in the press. One article explained that there 'is but one opinion in the navy on this point', that if Montagu had attacked Villaret's force, his ships would inevitably have become crippled and 'the whole of his little force must have been carried into a French port'.[81]

This whole episode, a full twenty-nine years after the event, had been nothing less than a nightmare for Montagu, though he did manage to extract an apology from Brenton and raise some support for his cause in the press. Naval historians now consider Montagu to have been unlucky rather than incompetent, the victim of events and logistics beyond his control and the wrath of an unkindly king.

From the British perspective, therefore, the aftermath of the battle generated some significant discord, but it is important to realise that, certainly where Howe's relationships with his captains was concerned, the result was the exact opposite of the intention. As Howe wrote to the Admiralty:

> Conscious, my Lord that almost every advantage to be derived from our late good fortune, would be dependent on the general impression made of it; and the idea of perfect harmony subsisting in the fleet, as well as concurrent opinion of unexceptionable good conduct [he seems to mean good conduct without exception] of every person having part in the late engagement; I wished

> to confine my reports to such general statement as I have given of our transactions ...[82]

Translated, from Howe's bewildering syntax, this statement says three important things. First, that upon the return of the fleet, the British public believed that every captain in Howe's fleet had performed admirably; secondly, that Howe understood that the political significance of the victory was very important and rested on an assumption of professional naval excellence; and thirdly that Howe made a conscious effort to encourage such a public perception of the victory.

The contemporary British reaction that Howe alludes to is important because it is so different from that of the French. There was certainly some explaining to do in both Brest and Paris. As Nathaniel Pearce, still a prisoner of a French man-of-war, commented of the French fleet's return, 'a pretty sight, for the Frenchmen to see their lame ducks come in a line!'[83] When Villaret initially arrived off Ushant without the convoy there was absolute consternation, followed by immense relief when it finally arrived, principally one suspects from Villaret whose head was at stake.[84]

Where Howe wanted to encourage a perception of unity, Jeanbon, in classic Jacobin style, conducted a public witch-hunt for 'traitors'. He was furious about the poor seamanship of the fleet and chose to interpret several examples of modest or poor behaviour as evidence of traitorous crimes rather than of practical incompetence.[85] On 23 June Jeanbon issued an *arête* – a decree – calling for the dismissal of captains Tardy, Langlois, Barrade, Keranguen, Allary, Dumoutier, Gassin and Bompard and Lieutenant Benoît of *L'Eole*, who had taken command of that ship after the death of her captain.[86] Allary, Dumoutier, Gassin and Bompard were all sent before the Revolutionary Tribunal, the dull shadow of the guillotine blade hanging over their necks. The rest were dismissed. Jeanbon saved his most vicious ire for Gassin of *Le Jacobin*, who had failed to close a gap in the line immediately astern of the French flagship and thus let Howe break the line. In an attempt to prevent something similar reoccurring, in classic Jeanbon style he immediately passed a new resolution threatening death for any captain who allowed the line to be broken.[87]

More widely, Jeanbon condemned his fleet for 'a lack of practical knowledge … slowness of manoeuvres, continual mistakes, small means when large ones should have been conceived and daringly executed'. He further complained about the conduct of the frigates, especially *La Seine* and *Le Brutus*.[88] All of these failures were not described in terms of experience, injury or damage and never, of course, in terms of leadership failure, but as failure of courage, honour or duty; as a lack of loyalty to the Revolution, to the Jacobins and to Jeanbon himself. The crimes were described and investigated as multi-tiered, complex and political.

The truth must lie somewhere between the two. On the one hand, fog, confusion and battle damage all played their part but we know that, in spite of Jeanbon's vigorous attempts to unify the French fleet, it was still riven with bitterness and faction. It has been argued strongly that his impressive use of the Terror to revitalise the fleet came at significant cost by worsening the pre-existing social and political divisions among the officers and men.[89] Jeanbon's cries of treachery, therefore, may not have been too wide of the mark. Crucially, however, this political tension in France in the aftermath of the battle did not flow in just one direction. Jeanbon and the Jacobins held the whip hand but there was a growing sense of confidence and unity in their opposition that began to have serious implications for the way that the battle was perceived and for the future of the Revolution itself.

Jeanbon left for Paris on 24 June, the day after the issue of his *arête*, and from there he was sent to Toulon. He was not immediately replaced by a representative of the Committee of Public Safety and his absence left a vacuum in Brest, where the navy was particularly agitated after the battle. Hundreds of sailors had died for the Revolution just as the Jacobins had asked. They had withstood sickness and horrific injury but returned only to find the Jacobin ways of old – purge, imprisonment and threat – still in operation. A strong anti-Jacobin contingent in the navy had had enough. One of the finest officers in the French fleet, Captain Genteaume of *Le Trente-et-un Mai*, had written to Jeanbon as early as 15 June, arguing with some boldness for the arrested officers to be tried by naval court martial and not by Revolutionary tribunal because 'it is a question of the facts of manoeuvre and tactics, and not of conspiracy or counter-Revolution ...'[90] It was a letter with hidden meaning, written by a man with the security of clearly demonstrated professional competence, a warning that the politicisation of the navy was damaging and loathed. Only six days later and Villaret wrote to Jeanbon in some distress that, through his alliance with Jeanbon, he was becoming increasingly isolated by a powerful anti-Jacobin cabal who 'tormented him cruelly'. 'One must not mince words, my dear Jeanbon, all goes badly here and worsens day by day,' he wrote. 'Subordination is still maintained in the roadstead, but this is by awarding more punishments in a day than I inflicted in a week.'[91]

In Paris also, Jeanbon's attempts to paint a pretty picture of what was, in reality, a significant defeat did not wash with the Jacobin's political opponents. The Prairial campaign gave them an opportunity to raise their voices, particularly because Jeanbon even made a conscious effort in the Convention to make it a political, rather than a military issue, declaring: 'Perhaps you will see like me a great political victory in a military reverse.'[92] Significantly, this declaration was not met with bowed heads by everyone, but with mockery and anger by a significant contingent. In France, the battle was, in the words of one French historian, '*très diversement jugée*'.[93] One contemporary commented:

> The most disgraceful defeat was transformed into a genuine triumph. We proclaimed a victory, after having lost seven fine ships, that mounted upwards of 500 pieces of cannon. We gave to the commander-in-chief the rank of vice-admiral and threw flowers in the way of the representative that had embarked the fleet, on his return to Brest.[94]

Just as Jeanbon hunted in the navy for traitors, so too did some politicians now claim that he himself, and Villaret with him, were traitors. Rumours that Jeanbon had not acted particularly well in the battle began to circulate. When the *Montagne* first tasted the full force of the *Queen Charlotte*'s broadside, it was reported by some that Jeanbon took the opportunity to go below, out of harm's way. Detailed denunciations of Jeanbon soon followed.[95] His apparent cowardice even produced a poem:

Poor Jean was a gallant Captain.
In battles much delighting:
He fled full soon
At the First of June
But he bade the rest keep fighting.[96]

He was later defended by some, such as the French historian Rouvier, who claimed that he had gone below to encourage the sailors,[97] but the significance of the event is not necessarily about the truth of the matter, but that the rumour even existed and was then allowed to persist: it is evidence of the growing influence of anti-Jacobin propaganda in and around the French navy.

This battle, therefore, claimed by both sides simply as 'glorious', was in reality, far more complex. Howe and several of his captains were upset and angry; Jeanbon and several of his captains were upset and angry; and Villaret was caught between what his political masters had expected of him and his naval capability. In London the continuing uncertainty regarding the progress of the war pushed Pitt and Portland quickly toward agreeing the terms of a coalition to present a united front to the nation. In Paris, meanwhile, the increasing volume of political dissent, nourished by the result of the battle, had the exact opposite effect. Increasingly isolated, Robespierre did not open his arms or mind to alternative perspectives but became increasingly aggressive and, with the tools of tyranny already at his disposal, increasingly violent. The Terror, which had begun as a weapon to unite France against internal and external military threat, was now used to crush internal political dissent and to wage a social war. The Revolution's journey from liberty to tyranny was complete.

# II.

# The Second Terror

Monster, spewed from hell. The thought of your punishment intoxicates me with joy.

A French woman cursing Robespierre as he went to the guillotine.[1]

The Glorious First of June was one of the many factors in the summer of 1794, each with its own social, political, cultural or military dynamic, that ultimately led to Robespierre's downfall, the end of the Terror and a bright new dawn for the Revolution. To understand the impact of the battle, therefore, we must view it in context and consider a number of other significant changes that occurred at the same time.

A distinguishing feature of that spring had been the increase in paranoia among the men who had masterminded and nurtured the Terror over the previous year. The assassination attempts on Robespierre had filled many of the other high-ranking Jacobins with dread. Jean Tallien carried a dagger everywhere; Jean-Baptiste Amar armed himself with a sword-stick in the style of a *grand seigneur*; the public prosecutor Fouquier-Tinville lived in constant fear behind locked doors; Joseph Fouché slept at different addresses every night; Robespierre set spies on both Jacques Thuriot and François Bourdon; and Marc Vadier, president of the Committee of General Security, a new and powerful rival to the Committee of Public Safety, set a spy on Robespierre*. The spy was so terrified of Robespierre that he became a double agent and actually reported to him on Vadier's movements.

In early April both Louis Legendre and François Bourdon had brought documents to the attention of the Convention outlining plans to murder Saint-Just, Robespierre 'and others' and to lead a popular revolt that would massacre the judges of the Revolutionary Tribunal. Bourdon left a new will with his lawyer and made it clear that he

*Brief biographies of all these men can be read in Appendix IV.

intended to murder Robespierre himself with a bloodstained sword that had seen service at the fall of the Bastille.[2]

The biggest threat to Robespierre, however, did not come from the pens of violent fantasists or from the wayward gunshots of crazed assassins but from his political opponents: Robespierre himself had set up the necessary infrastructure to guarantee that a political coup could end in legalised violence. His enemies, therefore, could achieve the bloody public end that so many wanted for the man associated with personal tyranny and despotic ambition, but they could do so without any blood on their hands. To retain a level of legitimacy, however, it was important that Robespierre was removed from power *before* he was executed.

The root of Robespierre's problem was that the execution of Danton and Hébert had driven his political opponents underground rather than destroying them, and there they plotted in back rooms and bars. By killing some of his political opponents Robespierre had clearly demonstrated how far he would go to retain political power. This extreme behaviour also served to unite his enemies. The vivid sparks of the two botched assassination attempts were nothing more than firecrackers. The real explosion was brewing out of sight, where his political opponents were simply waiting for the right moment to stage a legitimate political coup rather than another bloody *journée*.[3] That moment arrived in June, gathered momentum in July and was at full flood in August.

The first factor was the arrival of the grain convoy, so carefully planned by politicians in Paris and America, and so well executed by seamen from Brest. Some of the ships had great difficulty unloading their cargoes in the already crowded harbour at Brest, and were forced to wait for several weeks, but by the end of June most of the grain had been dispersed.[4] Brest had such poor inland transport links that the cargoes were transhipped to ports such as Nantes and Bordeaux that enjoyed river and canal communication with Paris. Even then it took between three and eight weeks for grain to travel from Brest to the capital; but arrive it did. The relief was only temporary and slight but the suffering at the time was such that any respite from hunger was a reason to celebrate and a boost to morale.[5]

The second factor was an increased pattern of French military victory. For all of the cynicism surrounding Jeanbon's report of the 'victory' at sea, two things were very obvious. The French navy, a matter of weeks before an undisciplined mess, had apparently discovered sufficient unity to sail boldly into the Atlantic, confront the British and then return triumphantly, albeit in poor shape. Nobody in France was comparing the French navy to the British, we must remember, rather the Brest fleet to the Toulon fleet, which had so recently handed itself over to the British without so much as a shot being fired. In those terms, the Glorious First of June was a clear and surprising success.

The French themselves were in no position to take advantage of this new situation but it did mean that their trade and their valuable food convoys were no longer under immediate threat. The food was going to get through; the Revolution would not be destroyed in the foreseeable future simply by starvation. This French naval 'victory', therefore, must not be underestimated for its role in shifting French morale from insecurity to confidence, from besieged to besieger, from defence to attack.

Several significant victories for French armies followed in the subsequent weeks and France soon found herself secure on land as well as more confident about the seaward threat. Hitherto, the offensive aim of the French armies had been to secure the natural borders of France, the Pyrenees and the Rhine. By late July 1794, that had been achieved. General Dugommier crossed the Pyrenees in May and a matter of weeks later the great Austrian army that had threatened France for two years was defeated decisively at the Battle of Fleurus (26 June). The French then took their fight deep into enemy territory. Dugommier rampaged through Catalonia on the other side of the Pyrenees, and only two weeks after Fleurus the French army took Brussels and all of Belgium lay at their feet. These military triumphs demonstrated that France was no longer under military threat from foreign powers and they allowed the politicians more time, space and opportunity to be introspective, to question the political crisis at the heart of French government. The tensions and uncertainties of early 1794 did not disappear, therefore, they just changed character and focus. External military insecurity became internal political tension.

That spring, the political differences between Robespierre and his enemies had become more clear-cut and numerous. The *sans-culottes*, a significant section of Robespierre's power base, had turned against him by midsummer. A body consisting mainly of artisans, they were hit particularly badly by Robespierre's imposition of a wage maximum in mid-July in an attempt to curb inflation. It effectively capped the figure that anyone could be paid as a salary, which meant in turn that workers' income could not keep pace with the over-inflated price of food. The result was increased hunger and bitterness directed personally at Robespierre.[6]

In the aftermath of the execution of Hébert and Danton, one of the ways in which Robespierre's search for unity had manifested itself was in a change of state religion. The Cult of the Supreme Being was effectively launched with its inaugural festival on 8 June. In part this was a simple way of bringing Revolutionary ideology to the question of religion, but on another level it was designed to provide a shared focus for a troubled and divided population. As the recently elected president of the Convention, Robespierre himself acted as a sort of high priest for this new religion and presided over the festival. The ceremonies were enacted with great symbolism and natural joy: women paraded with posies of flowers, men with sheaves of corn, and Robespierre dominated everything in his sky-blue frock-coat and giant tricolour sash. After a rambling speech he burned a monstrous cardboard representation of atheism, complete with donkey's ears.

Always in the background, however, and occasionally over the laughter and fun, could be heard growing growls of discontent, sarcastic slander, and derisive sniggers. It was an unrivalled chance to laugh at Robespierre and mock him for his personal ambition but it was also a valuable opportunity to strike a telling political blow. The new cult badly irritated deputies who represented the passionate Catholic departments of west and south, particularly from the Midi. Not only was his posturing regarded as self-serving, they also saw his new cult as insulting and, more importantly, as narrow-minded; it was a single belief system applied unfairly to all. The ideology of the Revolution in reality was far more fractured and diverse among the masses than it was in the idealist utopia of Robespierre's mind. His reaction to the ongoing tension between religion and the Revolution revealed him as unworldly and impractical. Men and women of diverse religious beliefs had taken on a king and won, but they were not prepared to take on God. It is one of the most significant shifts in this period. When Robespierre stood there on that day, dressed so splendidly, he did nothing less than highlight and worsen the pre-existing fractures in the politics of France that are still clear today, the divisions between city and country, north and south, Protestant, atheist and Catholic. His remaining political support abandoned him as rapidly and completely as rats from a sinking ship.

These issues were so far-reaching that the cohesion of the Committee of Public Safety fractured. Robespierre's imposition of the Law of 22 Prairial on 10 June then made those existing tensions even worse. It ranks as one of the most threatening and tyrannical laws ever imposed on its subjects by any national government, and Robespierre imposed it without even consulting the Committee of Public Safety.[7] It greatly expanded the tools of political repression by expanding the definition of enemies of the Revolution. It read in part: 'The following are deemed enemies of the people: those who ... have sought to disparage or dissolve the national Convention ... have sought to inspire discouragement ... have sought to mislead opinion ... to impair the energy and the purity of revolutionary and republican principles.'[8] The penalty for all of this was death. The law also increased the tempo of the Revolutionary Tribunal by making it even more difficult to offer a defence. After 22 Prairial, defending counsel was not allowed, witnesses were virtually dispensed with and jurors could use their 'conscience' to come to a verdict where material evidence was lacking. The conviction rate of the Revolutionary Tribunal quickly topped 80 per cent.[9]

The new law also further centralised the Terror. All conspiracy cases were now tried in Paris, under the eyes of the politicians and the mob. The official execution figures demonstrate a clear division between the Terror before the spring of 1794 and after, and in particular they highlight a distinct period in June and July. This was the Terror energised, the Terror centralised, the Terror as a machine. In the six months between March and August 1794, over half of its victims died in June and July alone and in those same months, more were executed in six weeks than in the previous fifteen months.[10] A new record of sixty-one deaths was set on 17 June when those who had attempted to kill Robespierre together with many others 'implicated' in the crime were taken to the guillotine. That record was then broken on 7 July when sixty-seven died: that is a fraction over eleven executions an hour for six hours, non-stop, or roughly one every five minutes. Only two days later sixty more were executed, followed by a further sixty on 9 July. The identity of the victims also changed: 38 per cent of all the nobles executed under the Terror were executed during this spell, a fourfold increase, and the clergy suffered particularly badly. The Terror thus became more of a weapon of social, as opposed to political, war than it had been before.[11]

The increase in the Terror created its own political problems. The Terror, it must be remembered, was instigated by the Jacobins to secure the fragile new Republic from both internal and external military threat, but by late June, when the Terror was obviously increasing, there was no longer any legitimate moral authority to defend its continuation. The Republic was now secure from military threat. In fact, the Republican armies had been so successful that the Republic itself had vastly expanded. With that success the Jacobins found themselves both morally bankrupt and trapped in a logical cul-de-sac: the foundation of their authority was justified by a military threat that no longer existed.

In sponsoring the Terror, moreover, the Jacobins had become tainted with the blood spilled by the many zealots they had unleashed on the provinces. Now fearful of being held to account and violent reprisal, those who once were friends of Jacobin extremism became its enemies and they joined in the clamour to topple Robespierre. As the foundations of the Terror crumbled, so friends as well as enemies pointed the finger at the Jacobin leadership, to shift the blame away from those who had wielded the swords, fired the guns and let the guillotines drop; people such as Fouché, Collot d'Herbois, Fréron, Barras – loyal Jacobins who had been instrumental in the shockingly violent suppression of the Federalists – now proclaimed Robespierre, Saint-Just and his fellow Committee Members as tyrants to mask their own culpability. Both friends and enemies turned against Robespierre with the desperation of men fighting for their lives.

The result of these changes was that pressure began to build up on Robespierre to such an extent that something had to give. It is easy with hindsight to see what happened as somehow inevitable, a result of Robespierre having pushed the boundaries too far, but that was not the case at the time. He still commanded some support in the powerful Jacobin clubs and from some members of the Committee of Public Safety, notably Jeanbon Saint-André. But as had been demonstrated time and again in the swirling changes of loyalty and faction in the early years of the Revolution, one did not actually need a large body of support to claim a mandate to govern, and Robespierre himself had made certain that the infrastructure of tyranny now in place could be used to bolster such a minority position.

It was in this period of heightened tension that the meeting room of the Committee of Public Safety was moved to a top floor in the Tuileries Palace where passers-by would be unable to hear the heated arguments that had replaced the muted industry of the Committee's work. One of those arguments, perhaps between Vadier and Robespierre, and possibly because Vadier called Robespierre a tyrant, was so severe that Robespierre refused to come to any of the Committee's meetings or even attend the Convention. He continued to work, but did so from home. It was political suicide because it reinforced the impression that he was attempting to control things by himself. The fact that he appeared to be doing so furtively, further fuelled the fires of conspiracy and paranoia.

Robespierre's silence and privacy particularly alarmed his political enemies, who believed that he was preparing to move against them with the same lightning speed and ruthlessness he had shown against Hébert and Danton. Their concerns seemed to be validated on 26 July when

Robespierre finally broke his silence and gave a wild and rambling speech at the Convention and then later at the Jacobin Club. It was both an accusation and a call to arms but it lacked one crucial ingredient: Robespierre failed to name any of the enemies and conspirators who he claimed were plotting to bring down the Revolution. The speech, in effect, was an opening gambit, to be followed by careful manoeuvres to secure the Jacobin grip on power and realise his own personal ambition. But it was all that his enemies needed to act – it was proof that their time had come. The pressure that had been building since late May, in which the result of the Glorious First of June played an integral part, burst out on 27 July.

Robespierre and Saint-Just had decided to take their case directly before the Convention, away from the intrigue of the Committee rooms, but those plotting their downfall had already decided upon a subtle means of achieving what they so desperately sought. There would be no Brutus moment, no flashing knife or concealed gun: the Convention had simply decided to prevent Robespierre and Saint-Just from speaking. They had both won and secured their power with words; their speech was both the means by which they had won their authority and its sustenance. To deny them this was to sentence them to a lingering death.

Saint-Just was the first to try to speak, but was interrupted by Tallien on a point of order, followed by Billaud. They both claimed that neither Saint-Just nor Robespierre spoke with the sanction of the Committees, that they had gone rogue and did not respect the authority or integrity of the Convention. It was all too much for Saint-Just, who had ironically prepared a speech advocating widespread reform, one he would never get the chance to deliver. Shocked and exhausted, he simply stood there, unable to reply, unable to defend or argue his case. Robespierre immediately sprang to the defence of his friend but the weakness of Saint-Just was so visible he was howled down: the Convention smelled blood. 'Down with the tyrant' came the cry. The debate then meandered a little before Robespierre tried to speak again but his words were drowned in a cacophony of catcalls. 'The blood of Danton chokes him,' cried one. An insignificant member of the

Convention then proposed the arrest of Robespierre and the motion was carried. Saint-Just, Couthon, Le Bas and Robespierre's brother were also all arrested. But so much was still uncertain.

The jailer of the Luxembourg prison refused to receive Robespierre and the others were all released. They gathered in the Hôtel de Ville in the hope of gathering support and forcing a stand-off. The Convention then took a decisive step by declaring them all outlaws, which meant that they could be executed without trial. Some came to support Robespierre but his authority had evaporated. The Convention, meanwhile, had taken control and raised troops which now marched on the Hôtel de Ville, securing it without a struggle. Robespierre's brother tried to escape out of an upper-floor window, edging his way along a parapet until he slipped and fell in a hideous tangle of broken bones. Some claimed he fell onto the sabre of a passing soldier. François Hanriot, leader of the Parisian armed forces, also fell from a window, though it is possible that he was pushed. He escaped into the sewer system but was later arrested covered in excrement and crippled. The disabled Georges Couthon, another member of the Committee of Public Safety, threw himself down a flight of stone steps in an attempt at suicide but only knocked himself unconscious and gashed his head. It is rumoured that he was taken to the Convention to hear his fate in a wheelbarrow. Lebas shot himself and Robespierre tried to do the same but only succeeded in blowing off a section of his lower jaw. Saint-Just simply gave himself up. They were swiftly tried by the Revolutionary Tribunal while the tumbrels were drawn up outside and the guillotine moved back to its most symbolic location – the Place de la Révolution.

Huge crowds gathered and many bayed at the fate of their tyrant. Twenty-two men filled the carts, all committed Robespierrists. Robespierre himself was the penultimate prisoner to die. His face had been bandaged tight by a surgeon after his failed suicide attempt and now the executioner ripped the bandage off, perhaps so that it wouldn't snag the blade. Robespierre screamed, the crowd held their breath, the blade fell, the jawless head rolled. It was 28 July: only six weeks since Robespierre had appointed himself high priest of a new religion; only five weeks since news of the fleet battle had reached Paris; only three weeks since news had arrived of victory at Fleurus. France was basking in a new security from foreign threat and the men who had achieved it were dead.

The impact of naval battles is always full of contradictions and paradox, and in this case the consequences for Britain were not what one might expect from a famous naval victory. Indeed, the argument is quite compelling that some of the long-term results of the battle were not in British interests at all. A case can be made that it even served to lengthen the war.

The Glorious First of June helped to expose contradictions in the logic behind the Terror and it provided an opportunity for both pre-existing and new enemies to marshal support and begin to make their move to unseat Robespierre. But what happened next? The execution of the Jacobins did not stop with those of Robespierre and his immediate supporters on 28 July. Eighty-three more died in the subsequent three days (the bloodiest of the Terror), sixty of whom were guillotined in less than an hour and a half: that is three every two minutes. The Irish political exile Hamilton Rowland watched it and, from more than a hundred paces away, the blood streamed beneath his feet. There was then a vicious backlash against the Jacobins in both Paris and the provinces. A spate of illegal and brutal murders accounted for many notable Jacobins all over France in what became known as the 'White Terror', most notably in Languedoc and Provence, regions with powerful and ancient traditions of vendetta and which had suffered so badly in the Terror.[12]

Many of those who escaped the death squads and punishment beatings were imprisoned for their loyalty to the Jacobins, and one of those men was Jeanbon Saint-André. Gradually, meanwhile, the machinery of the Terror began to be dismantled. The political prisoners were released and the extremism and excesses of 1794 disappeared. Only three days after Robespierre's death, the Law of 22 Prairial was repealed and eleven days after that the Committee of Public Safety was denied its superintending role in government. By the end of August some 3,500 prisoners had been released.[13] Denunciations stopped; French men and women resumed referring to each as monsieur and mademoiselle; novels began to be published again; political songs disappeared. The Terror and everything associated with it vanished as quickly as it had arisen. But life was still very hard. Inflation rose sky-high as Robespierre's hated maximum was abolished, the Assignat reaching its lowest ebb of 7.5 per cent of its face value in 1795, when prices were 750 per cent above the levels of 1790. A cold, hard winter caused untold suffering, racketeers controlled certain parts of the economy and there was the occasional outburst of rebel activity, but there was no escaping the fact that the Republic was still very much alive.[14]

In June 1795 the young Louis XVII, son of the beheaded King, died in prison, probably from neglect, possibly even because his cell had been walled up to prevent his escape or any communication with the outside world – an Edward V for his age. His uncle declared himself Louis XVIII from Verona but there was no momentum behind the Royalist campaign, even after the excesses of 1794. Passion for the Republic still abounded. The second anniversary of the Revolution was celebrated with wild abandon on 10 August. It was as if the downfall of the Jacobins had made the Republic inclusive again, a project with broad appeal and passionate support, a project reinvigorated. The two extremes had now been experienced: the unfairness of the *ancien régime* on the one hand, and the political extremism of the Jacobins on the other. Everything that followed was an attempt to occupy the middle ground.

Those allied against France, meanwhile, though privately considering peace, had been loudly boasting about returning French boundaries to their *pre*-Louis XIV borders, a shameful and insulting prospect for all Frenchmen, regardless of their political or religious beliefs.[15] Moreover territory had been taken from France in the West Indies. In short, the war was already far enough advanced to give ample cause for the French to unite. To make matters worse for the allies, the significant military victories of the summer of 1794, including holding their own against the British at the Glorious First of June, did much to reassure the French that, despite earlier reverses in fortune, they were now masters of their own destiny. And those victories just kept on coming. From 1795 the French annexed Belgium, the Rhineland and Piedmont, increasing French territory by 20 per cent, creating further wealth, military and industrial resources, and further legacies of success. This was military achievement greater than Louis XIV's in his prime.[16] Even the civil war in the Vendée and the Federalist revolt had been snuffed out. The soldiers and military resources that had been tied up there could now be thrown into battles beyond France's borders. The rhetoric of war changed from protection to expansion in the name of '*La Grande Nation*' and there was no room for weakness. The men at the helm in Paris were not inexperienced daydreamers but men hardened in the fire of Jacobinism. They were strong men; they were survivors.[17]

Several factors, moreover, were easing the way forward to a military dictatorship. The Jacobins had left behind a political infrastructure geared toward autocracy, and had proved in some measure that attaining economic stability with the Revolutionary platform in place required a strong hand. The French were proud of their armed forces, particularly the army. The navy had saved some face at the Glorious First of June but the shame of capitulation at Toulon was too severe and too recent to disappear. The acceptable naval performance against Howe was nothing when compared to the scale and number of crushing land victories that the army was regularly producing and, more significantly, was becoming dependent upon for its survival. The French armies had become voracious machines and their very existence depended upon the continuation of conquest. All the while, their leaders became wealthier and more influential.

The exasperation with French politicians also increased and in September 1796 a body of moderates and Royalists who had come to power were forced out in a Republican coup. The men who replaced them were cynical and corrupt. By the end of 1796, therefore, the entire system and political environment was geared toward a high-ranking army officer seizing both political and military control of France. A young man who had witnessed the potential of such power as a close friend of Robespierre was Napoleon Bonaparte, General of Artillery of the Army of Italy. He had, in fact, been so close to Robespierre that he had been briefly placed under house arrest after Robespierre's fall, and had witnessed first hand the potential of, and for, personal ambition in the new France, born by the Revolution.[18]

The coalition of European allies, formed with such energy in the aftermath of Louis XVI's execution, collapsed in 1795 having aroused more jealousies than it had created unity. Prussia, Holland and Spain all made peace with France in 1795. By 1797, when the Austrians finally made peace, the First Coalition had ceased to exist. Britain now faced France alone. The early British success of the war, of which the Glorious First of June was an important part, had come to nothing. British influence in European affairs slipped through Pitt's fingers. Glory had turned swiftly to frustration and soon the fleets of both countries were back at sea locked in that curious maritime dance across the world's oceans that would characterise the next twenty-one years of incessant warfare between Britain and France.

Claims made in the British press, in the aftermath of the First of June, that the French navy had been destroyed were nonsense, and no one knew this better than the Navy. The correspondence to and from the British naval dockyards rings with a sense of urgency as men were drafted in to make the ships ready for sea as quickly as possible. The ships that could be repaired quickly were prioritised to maintain British naval strength.[19] The French fleet stayed in Brest and certainly did very little for the rest of the summer. In the absence of Jeanbon dockyard activity slowed, but by no means did French seapower dissipate. As early as August a frigate squadron was making repeated captures off Cape Clear and in November Admiral Nielly took a squadron into the Western Approaches and captured the British 74-gun *Alexander*.

On 22 December the French *Prudence* and *Cybèle* fought magnificently off the Île de France and forced her two British opponents to flee.[20] On 31 December the main fleet left Brest, and then remained at sea entirely unmolested for thirty-one days, and although the sailors suffered terribly from a lack of food and their own inexperience, which resulted in five ships of the line being lost, they still captured over 100

British prizes.[21] In spite of concerted British efforts which met with some striking successes, convoys from America to France continued. If measured from the day after the departure of Vanstabel to October 1794, France acquired 123,000 barrels of flour, 1,500 hundredweight of rice and vast quantities of leather, salted beef, bacon and potassium carbonate (for making saltpetre for gunpowder). The French navy also played a significant role in the recapture of Guadeloupe in 1794 by transporting the troops that retook the island.[22]

In the summer of 1795, the French Brest fleet was at sea once more, still under the command of Villaret, and this time determined to fox a British attempt to send troops to the Vendée to aid the remaining glimmer of Royalism in that shattered province. A fleet under Admiral William Cornwallis was very nearly overwhelmed in June by the French, and only saved by the admiral's cunning ruse of signalling to imaginary ships over the horizon to give the impression that he was but part of a larger force. Six days later and this time Villaret encountered Alexander Hood's larger fleet and fled for Lorient, losing three ships of the line in the process. The men may have been less than competent, the crews sick and the ships dirty, but they were still at sea. The French Mediterranean squadron had also risen from the ashes of the destruction of Toulon, and was effective once more.

In the following summer, French maritime strategy became even bolder. Cruising again in late December 1796, this time the fleet had a serious objective: they were escorting some 15,000 troops in an attempt to invade Ireland. The fleet was vast, some seventeen of the line and thirteen frigates, but they were beaten back by foul weather when they reached their intended landing spot at Bantry Bay. Two months later, in February 1797, the French navy even managed to get 1,500 troops ashore in Fishguard, Wales, though the men were the dregs of the army and were quickly arrested. All of this time, moreover, French privateers cruised the Channel and Western Approaches with success, though actively and successfully hunted by British frigate squadrons. In spite of the heroics of their commanders such as Edward Pellew and John Borlase Warren, French privateers took some 5,600 British merchant ships between 1793 and 1801.[23]

The revolutionary zeal that had done so much to bolster French crews at the First of June also persisted. On 12 July a small British merchant ship was taken off Algiers and every member of her crew was executed according to the law of 7 Prairial which insisted that no British prisoners would be taken. Then, in late summer 1794 the British *Gorgon* sailed to Gibraltar with forty-seven French prisoners aboard and one morning one of them struck up *La Marseillaise* on the forecastle. Midshipman Gardner recalled:

> ... when he came to that part 'Aux armes, Citoyens, formez vos battalions,' etc., he seemed inspired; he threw up his violin half way up the fore mast, caught it again, pressed it to his breast, and sung out 'Bon Ça Ira,' in which he was joined by his comrades ... and seemed ready and willing for any mischief. But our soldiers were called up and the French were sent below, and not so many allowed to be on deck at a time.[24]

The size of the French navy certainly dipped in this period. The battleship strength increased from a displacement of 231,000 tonnes in 1790 to 180,000 in 1795, compared with a steady 312,000 in Britain, but the relative frigate strength of France grew, expanding in the same period from 73,000 to 78,000 tons. France had enjoyed such success on land that, in 1795, they conquered the Netherlands and took control of its powerful navy. Then, in 1796, Spain changed sides, adding the formidable Spanish navy to that of the French and Dutch. The Royal Navy was faced by such an overwhelming disparity that the British abandoned the entire Mediterranean to concentrate their forces on the defence of home waters. Without British naval support, Venice, the Ionian Islands and Malta swiftly fell and Napoleon began eyeing up the crumbling Ottoman Empire. To make matters worse, France and her allies continued to out-build the Royal Navy. In the years 1791–1810 the French alone built 441,000 tons to Britain's 397,000.[25] That discrepancy was made up for only by the continuous British capture of French ships, but the high tonnage of French output kept their navy in the game.

This constant manufacture of French warships was critical to the continuation of the war. The Royal Navy existed to defeat its enemy at sea but the French navy just needed to endure while France conducted territorial expansion on land. As long as it existed in sufficient numbers to trouble the British then it continued to influence the outcome of the war, which is exactly what happened: in spite of victories like the Glorious First of June, which set back the operational capability of the French navy, the numbers of ships built continued to rise. Losses were quickly replaced and even if it was inferior to the Royal Navy the French navy remained a continued threat and represented a potent strategic component of the French war machine.[26]

The immediate impact on British manpower was also far more serious than we might suspect, for two main reasons. Firstly, a significant number of senior officers had been killed or wounded in the battle and even those unscathed physically were shattered by their exertions: both Howe and Hood were sent straight home to recover.[27] Of greater importance for British crews, however, was the poor health of the thousands of French prisoners that now shared their ships, many of whom carried typhus. The British fleet had remained healthy throughout their cruise, even though Howe had been forced to sail without the thousands of gallons[28] of lemon juice he had ordered on 23 April. So proud was he of his men's wellbeing and confident that sickness could be kept at bay that he wrote to the Admiralty after the battle celebrating their 'permanent' good health.[29] Howe had not, however, allowed for their exposure to typhus. Thomas Trotter, physician of the Channel Fleet, inspected the captured French ships and was horrified: he described them as 'dirty to an extreme degree' and the surgeon of the *Majestic* noted how humid they were. It was clear that a 'contagious fever' had already claimed many lives. He was told by one sailor that the lower decks' ports had not been opened from the day that they had left Brest until the day of battle, somewhere between twelve and fifteen days, depending on the engagement.

The sickness soon began to have a serious effect on the already inadequate pool of manpower available to the Royal Navy. Three men from the *Majestic*, a lieutenant and two midshipmen, were the first to be infected. They had survived the cannon, splinters and falling rigging, the snipers' bullets and the grapeshot, only to be infected by their enemy in their own harbour. The unlucky victims had been superintending the French prisoners cleaning the lower deck where the sick and wounded lay. As soon as they showed signs of sickness they were transferred to Haslar Hospital, the Royal Naval hospital in Portsmouth, but nothing could be done for them and they died. Aboard the *Valiant* the marines who had looked after the prisoners fell sick as well as a quartermaster who had slept near the hatchway that led to the hold where the prisoners were kept. Men from the *Castor* who had been captured and held aboard the *Sans Pareil* had also become infected and their captain, Thomas Troubridge, had cared for them himself. The crew of the *Southampton* suffered and, although her physician showed in the words of his superior, 'singular address and ability' by separating those who showed any sign of fever, fifty sailors still became sick. The staff at the hospital also started to be infected: nurses, attendants and guards.

To get a grip on the unfolding crisis, Trotter personally inspected every ship in the fleet and ordered reports from each ship's surgeon. It soon became clear that the *Glory*, *Ramillies*, *Barfleur*, *Caesar*, *Bellerophon*, *Alfred*, *Invincible*, *Gibraltar* and *Circe* were affected as well as the *Valiant*, *Majestic* and *Southampton* – nearly half the fleet. The *Queen Charlotte* seems to have saved herself by enjoying her status as fleet flagship: Howe had immediately sent the sick prisoners on to the hospital ship *Charon*.

Trotter and the ships' surgeons then got to work. It was a bad blow for a victorious fleet but the response is deeply impressive and reminiscent of the sailors' own efforts to repair their ships in the heat of battle. The ships were fumigated every morning by those who believed in it; the walls, decks and bulkheads of all ships were whitewashed; 'constant attention' was paid to the cleanliness of the sailors' clothes and their bedding was aired every day; the sailors were ordered to pay close attention to their own cleanliness and to 'shift' more frequently; fires were kindled throughout the ship to combat humidity; great care was taken that air could circulate by setting up windsails and even studding sails to funnel air deep into the ship; the main hatchways were kept open at night when the ships' ports were lowered; vinegar was poured into an iron pot and then vaporised with a red-hot poker and more vinegar was sprinkled on the decks. Particular attention was paid to the dark and musty store rooms which were also emptied, whitewashed and ventilated 'so that not a particle of impure air could lodge anywhere'.

More importantly, the sick were immediately isolated from the healthy crew and sent ashore and the officers were sent on regular rounds with careful instructions to spot symptoms of impending sickness. They were ordered to look out for men appearing 'dejected or solitary' in their berths and the symptoms were listed as 'great debility with pain in the back, and redness of the eyes, with a wildness in their looks, and tremor of the tongue'. Sailors from the *Ramillies, Invincible* and *Bellerophon* displayed curious symptoms: sore throats and pain in the shin bones.

The cure involved a complex mixture of strange treatments. Trotter started with an emetic of ipecac (*ipecacuanha*, a native plant of Brazil but common in English medicine from the mid-1600s) to induce vomiting. He then prescribed diaphoretics (such as cayenne or yarrow) to induce sweating, combined with pectorals (herbs such as lobelia and blood root) used to strengthen the lungs. The patients were occasionally prescribed 'a scruple' or 'half a dram' of one of the neutral salts, with a few grains of rhubarb, to ease the constipation associated with the disease. The cure was then completed by 'tonics and opium' washed down with a little water and brandy.[30] This was all Trotter's personal preference. Leonard Gillespie, surgeon of the *Majestic* and the man who in eleven years' time would tend the dying Nelson at Trafalgar, preferred treating typhus with opiates and 'blisters'.[31]

From the return of the fleet to the end of the fever epidemic 800 sailors were incapacitated by sickness and sent to Haslar but, because of the precautions taken, only forty died. The only strange decision in this entire episode was made in the midst of the crisis when the Admiralty allowed the suffering Vice-Admiral Graves to bring the surgeon of the *Royal Sovereign* ashore with him, leaving that huge First Rate, with a crew of 850 men, in the hands of only two surgeon's mates.[32] No other information survives surrounding this decision and we simply do not know if it is indicative of a rash Admiralty pandering to the personal whim of a flag officer or evidence of the impressive capabilities of the

*Royal Sovereign*'s surgeon's mates. With the health of nearly a thousand men at stake the latter is the more likely.

Some logistical problems also affected the condition of the British fleet. Caulkers and shipwrights sent to Plymouth and Portsmouth from the eastern yards to repair the ships were 'mislaid'. By 24 June, the sailors of the *Defence* and *Marlborough*, whose hammocks had all gone overboard with the masts in the battle, had still not received any replacements: by now they had all been sleeping rough on deck for over three weeks.[33] Every captain complained about a lack of fresh fruit available to the injured. Of all the ships in the fleet only one ship, the *Royal Sovereign*, had been issued with sufficient wine to care for her wounded and even then they were only allowed between a quarter and a half a pint, which was wholly inadequate. Only if a man was fainting from weakness was he allowed a pint and only on that ship.[34]

It was the end of July before any of the infected ships were ready for sea and in mid-August the *Canada* was still unable to sail until she had received men back from the hospital. She had to wait a fortnight before enough of her crew had recovered sufficiently to take her to sea. Two months later, more than four months after the prisoners had first come on board the British ships, the *Gibraltar* was still suffering with forty-four cases of fever and on 25 June the *Diamond* was victualled for a four-month cruise but did not have enough men 'to work the ship as a man-of-war'.[35]

All this exacerbated the manning troubles and Howe was soon complaining about the quality of the 'men' he had been sent: 'some of those parties were not above the class of boys and several of the men too feeble of person and low in stature to befit, in my opinion, to have been received.' Howe was particularly worried about the state of those being returned from hospital to his fleet because, though cured, they remained very weak and unable to do their duty.[36]

With so many ships in need of repair and so many men struck down by illness – to add to the 1,098 killed or injured in the battle – the British Channel Fleet was incapacitated for some time. Between June and December it was at sea for less than a month and effectively useless in June or July. It was not until February that Howe attempted once more to lead the fleet out in force; to escort an outward-bound convoy. The ships made it out of Torbay before being driven back by a fierce storm and were then very nearly destroyed in Torbay as the wind turned easterly, a fatal quarter for that anchorage.

Nothing then happened until the following summer when Cornwallis and Hood both patrolled the Channel and fought Villaret. Jeanbon's claim that the prairal campaign '*étoit de metre l'arméee Anglaise hors d'état de tenir la mer*'[37] (left the English fleet unable to keep the sea) is not as far-fetched as one might suspect from this mouthpiece of Jacobin propaganda. The battle had no impact on the powerful frigate squadrons hunting out of Falmouth, and the Royal Navy was quite capable of finding ships to escort vulnerable convoys, but a significant number of those ships that had fought with Howe were forced to stay in port, tying up resources for a significant period of time. The Glorious First of June undoubtedly limited the potential of British naval power in the summer and autumn of 1794.

And what of the six captured French ships? Naval warfare is easy enough to measure in terms of numbers of enemy ships captured or sunk, but the First of June is a classic example of why such an approach can mislead as much as it can inform. Mary Howe's claim that the captured 80-gunners were 'ten feet longer than our First Rates'[38] is true. The *Juste* and *Sans Pareil* were very large with gun decks at least ten feet longer than the *Royal Sovereign*, the smallest British First Rate.[39] It is true to say, however that, rate for rate, the French ships tended to be larger than the British, but that in no way made them necessarily 'better'.

The magnificent and appropriately named 80-gun *Sans Pareil* certainly went on to enjoy a long service career in the Royal Navy. She had been built by the famed Jacques-Nöel Sané at Brest only five years previously. She was fitted out at Portsmouth and went on to lead an active life in the Royal Navy from March 1795 until September 1802, and seven years of service was a fine return for a captured ship. She then served as a prison hulk at Plymouth for three years, perhaps incarcerating some of the men who had once sailed her. The 80-gun *Juste* also enjoyed a career of seven years and the 74-gun *América* served for even longer, until 1812. The *Impétueux* was of the same class as the *América* and she should have enjoyed a lengthy career if she had not been burnt by accident at Portsmouth in the August of 1794. Only the *Northumberland* and *Achille* were not put into service and were broken up in the winter of 1795 and New Year of 1796. Thus only three of the six prizes went on to serve in the Royal Navy. The *América*, an elderly ship which had been recommissioned by the French from a terrible condition, was still in such bad shape that it cost £42,030 to get her into a fit state to serve as a British warship, about the same cost as a brand-new British Third Rate, and substantially more expensive than some other classes of ship that were built.

Only the *Juste* and *Sans Pareil* represented value for money, the *Juste* costing £20,331 to repair and fit out and the *Sans Pareil* £19,051, but combined, the money spent on these two would have paid for a new Third Rate.[40] The British may have captured six warships, therefore, but in real terms they only benefited by one. We know that, later in life, a bristling Villaret declared with some bravura, 'What did I care for half a-dozen rotten old hulks which you took'.[41] Indignant, perhaps, but there is more than a hint of truth here. Another French witness to the battle claimed that, with the exception of the *Sans Pareil*, the ships that were captured were 'no better than hulks … and only fit to make pontoons'. The same man, without giving specifics, said that some of the French fleet, as they lay at Brest before the battle, were so worm-eaten that they had gained the nickname 'the drowners' and could only be kept afloat by constant pumping. The contemporary historian Edward Brenton, and a serving sailor at the time, was also free with his admiration of the *Sans Pareil* but quite clear that it would have been far better, and much cheaper, to have burned the rest.[42]

Even in London there were signs that the Glorious First of June divided as much as it unified. We have seen how the battle was hijacked to make political, social and cultural attacks against the Government and Navy and in many respects it fuelled the fires of opposition to the war. In August 1794 London suffered the Crimp Riots, an anti-war or specifically anti-recruitment protest and one of the most serious public disruptions of the wartime period. It was only quelled when twenty-three people were arrested and four executed.[43] Pitt became increasingly associated with the pro-war stance and there was even an anti-recruitment riot outside his house in the summer of 1795. That October the King's personal carriage was attacked by protesters and in December Pitt himself was attacked in St James's Park.[44] The British may have hated the regicide of Louis XVI and feared the extremism of the Jacobins, but they hated and feared the idea of a standing army and enforced conscription even more.

Pitt fell to the nadir of his political fortunes. In the summer of 1795 a cartoon was published showing a mounted Pitt riding over a 'swinish multitude' and kicking those politicians who campaigned to end the war – Norfolk, Stanhope, Grafton, Wilberforce, Sheridan and Lansdowne – backwards into hell. It is one of the most hostile cartoons of the entire period and a powerful reminder of the tension in Britain after the Glorious First of June.[45] The entire episode is best summed up by Admiral Jervis, who commented ruefully: 'I am grieved to learn that the consequences were not so propitious as the resolution of the parties who were engaged most merited ...'[46]

There are, therefore, numerous ways in which the Glorious First of June was either counter-productive to British was aims or was not as helpful as might suspect and we know this was not missed by the contemporary public. With the advantage of more than two centuries of comment and scholarship, however, we can now advance a few reasons why the battle was also beneficial to the British war effort.

The captured ships had some influence on ship design. The Admiralty was now under the command of Lord Spencer and he was keen to learn lessons from French designers. Eight new 74-gunners were ordered that year, six based on French designs, and two, the *Renown* and *Impetueux* of the Northumberland Class, built to the lines of the captured *Impétueux*.[47] Both went on to enjoy lengthy and distinguished careers and received fine reports from their captains.

It was clear to British officers who took the time to examine their prisoners that the French sailors were 'in a very bad state both with Respect to Discipline and Knowledge of their profession'[49] and the First of June made their manning problems worse. The scenes in and around Brest when the French crews disembarked from their battered ships were shocking. Injured sailors were grouped together for treatment that for many never came; the roads to the hospitals at St Louis and Lesneven were lined with stretchers; the men's wounds rotted with gangrene. Jeanbon toured the hospitals to boost morale and at least one land-based French surgeon was sufficiently perky to reassure a boy injured in the face that he would 'still be a mirror for some whores', but the reality was that the French had lost 4,200 dead and 3,300 wounded, that is 10 per cent of all of the seamen in France incapacitated from a pool that was very difficult to fill. As one French sailor noted of his battered navy, '... finally, and this was the most serious, our most experienced sailors and gunners were missing, and half of those who remained were incapacitated by wounds'.[49] It was a blow from which the French navy would never truly recover.

The British treatment of French prisoners certainly did not help. In spite of numerous orders from the Admiralty, British prisons and prison ships were unprepared for the French prisoners: 'about 2,300', Howe had first warned the Admiralty in an uncharacteristically vague way.[50] But as early as 11 June they believed that 4,000–5,000 prisoners, far more, they realised, than could be held in Forton or Mill prison, would need accommodating and they ordered nine ships to be converted into temporary prison ships. They also began to investigate other options for holding men ashore. The King waded in to protect his house at Winchester from becoming a prison and suggested that Portchester Castle was a better idea.[51] Orders themselves are not enough, however, and there was a catastrophic breakdown in the middle management that was supposed to deal with the preparations which were, as a result, simply not made.

With nowhere ready to receive them, some prisoners were forced to endure as much as eight weeks[52] of incarceration in cramped conditions in the lowest decks of British warships before they were transferred to newly converted prison ships or the jails in Tavistock, Forton, Falmouth, Plymouth and Portchester.[53] This was still very early in the war and there was plenty of space: Ashburton, Tiverton, Callington, Bristol, Bodmin, Ilfracombe, Lynn and Norman Cross were yet to become holding camps for prisoners of war.[54] On one ship the prisoners were all crammed into the fore cockpit where they were 'totally deprived of fresh air and the common means of purifying it'.

The surgeons of the *Thunderer* and the *Queen Charlotte* were so horrified by the conditions in which some of the prisoners were held that they wrote a joint letter directly to Howe. As early as 17 June, still two months or so before any of the prisoners were moved ashore, the Admiralty received a letter from Caldwell of the *Impregnable* expressing his grave concerns about the health of the French prisoners and the conditions in which they were being kept.[55] The Admiralty immediately re-ordered the *Bienfaisant* and *Prudente*, both elderly French prizes, to be fitted as prison ships 'with all possible dispatch', having already cancelled their own original order to do this on 14 June.

Caldwell eventually got the firehearths and boilers of the *Bienfaisant* and *Prudente* up and running but only once labour could be spared from repairing Howe's fleet. There was still a great deal to be done before any prisoners could be let aboard. Caldwell was explicit that 'neither that ship [the *Prudente*] nor any other at this port is other ways in any state whatever for reception of prisoners.'[56] The Admiralty ordered Caldwell to put some of the sick prisoners on a ship in Ordinary and to send 250 to Falmouth. There was no ship available to take them by sea, however, and so the prisoners were forced to march to Falmouth from Plymouth overland, a long and exhausting march over barren moor.[57]

All of this was done at the instigation of an irate flag officer and far too late to prevent the infection of the British fleet and the death of many hundreds of French sailors. The man whom Caldwell held primarily responsible for this sorry state of affairs was Mr Thomas Reynolds, agent for the prisoners of war in Plymouth. Reynolds had told Caldwell that his prison was fit only for 700 men but, after a personal inspection, Caldwell felt that it could house 600–630 more than the agent's estimate. It then took several days and 'many carts' to empty the prison of the 'dirt and filth' that had accumulated there. Caldwell was furious. As a direct result of Reynolds' incompetence British sailors were put at great risk and the ships' repair was delayed because carpenters could not get into the holds where the prisoners were kept. Caldwell also cared greatly about the French: 'Scarce a day passed that from two to nine prisoners was not obliged to be landed with malignant fevers … and some had Died soon after they were sent on shore.'[58] The total number of French who died in British care is unrecorded but Trotter said that they suffered a 'vast mortality'. The only surviving evidence tells us that 338 died at Forton prison in Portsmouth in less than four months.[59] It is likely that hundreds more died on British warships before they were even transferred to prison. A certain Mr Blair from the Sick and Wounded Board stepped into the breach left by the incompetent Reynolds. Caldwell could not praise him highly enough and recommended him to the Admiralty as a man 'unacquainted with the word trouble'. Caldwell then demanded that Reynolds be the subject of an immediate enquiry 'who I have no hesitation in saying should be instantly dismissed from his employment' and the Admiralty were more than happy to agree to his request.[60]

These combined losses exacerbated existing weaknesses in French naval manpower, particularly among its officer corps.[61] A small balancing factor, however, was that, in the aftermath of the fall of Robespierre, some of those experienced French officers who had abandoned France during the Terror now returned. Moreover, the politically motivated trials of the eight officers arrested for their poor conduct in the battle were cancelled when Robespierre died. The men were swiftly released, albeit after a traditional court martial from which some of them escaped politically or physically unscathed only by the skin of their teeth.[62] Allary, Dumoutier, Gassin and Bompard may not have fought as Jeanbon expected but at least they were now more experienced in fleet warfare than they had been before the action. The same can be said of the other four captains who had been punished after the battle. If Robespierre's grip on power had endured, eight more French captains would have been lost to the service. They may have been adjudged incompetent at the First of June, but at least they had all been blooded in fleet battle.

Still, a lack of unity persisted in the French navy. It is clear that the French navy retained an impressive sense of cohesion during the battle itself but, as soon as the ships were alongside, the old cracks that Jeanbon had attempted to heal fractured again.[63] The logistical arm of the French navy was also in very poor shape after the battle. Jeanbon had left no stone unturned when equipping his fleet and when it returned the cupboards and storehouses were empty. There was little food for the men and very few materials to repair the damaged ships. The British had forced the French to sea to defend their convoy and in doing so they had driven them to over-extend their capability. The British may have suffered from logistical problems in sourcing material for repairs but their dockyards were in far better shape than the French.

All this meant that when the French fleet was forced to sea in December 1794 the cruise was a disaster. It was successful in capturing an impressive quantity of merchant ships but in all other respects it was ill-disciplined chaos from start to finish. Three ships of the line sank very soon after the fleet had left the safety of Brest Roads and three more were driven ashore. The rest were blown deep into the Atlantic. Only equipped with provisions for a fortnight's cruise, the main fleet then raided the holds of six of its number destined for the Mediterranean. With insufficient stores, those ships were then unable to reinforce the Toulon fleet that was to be sent to the relief of Corsica. The starving, battered fleet did not make it home until 2 February 1795.[64]

Villaret continued to rant about the inexperience and sheer incompetence of his officers and, in particular, his gunners and the captains of his three-deckers.[65] These deficiencies, which had done so much to cause his defeat on 1 June, continued to shackle the French navy. In 1796 an army officer, secure in the tradition of success now well established by the Republican armies, turned his gaze on the navy and found nothing but rot: 'Our hateful navy cannot and will not do anything ...What a bizarre mixture! The commissioned officers chaotic and divided, organized indiscipline in a fighting service ... arrogance, ignorance, vanity and folly.'[66]

With the exception of the odd, very rare, French triumph, it was British success that continued consistently in the following months and years, so often marked by the overwhelming scale of victory. From 1793 to 1800 the Royal Navy captured 250,000 tons of prizes and the French a mere 48,000.[67] Consider also the death rates of certain actions. Three frigate actions in the spring of 1796 make the point clearly. On 12 April when the British *Revolutionnaire* captured the French *Unité*, the British lost no sailors and the French twenty; on 20 April when the British *Indefatigable* fought the *Virginie*, the British lost no sailors and the French forty-two; and on 8 June when the *Unicorn* captured the *Tribune*, the British lost none and the French fifty-one. And the pattern continued. This disparity of casualties was even a significant feature of the French capture of the British *Alexander* in November 1794. The French won, but at the cost of more than ten times the casualties suffered by the British: there were 450 French casualties, forty British.[68] Even good ships with good guns primed with good gunpowder cannot be sailed and fought without an experienced and trained crew, and every time that the French fought, their ability to fight again was reduced – a self-defeating pattern that was jump-started at the First of June. This in turn affected the confidence of both sides, diminishing that of the French while stimulating the British self-belief in victory: they knew that if they fought for long enough the French would stop firing back.

A minor lesson that Howe took from the battle, but a significant one nonetheless for the benefit of the service, concerned surgeons' stores. These were dramatically improved to provide more bandage linen and flannel and more food and drink to help the wounded recover quickly. Howe insisted that greater quantities of tea, cocoa, sago, rice, ginger, barley and sugar were allocated to each surgeon together with a particular order that they were to be given one large saucepan to heat their remedies rather than two or three small ones, which was then the case. Perhaps equally crucial in operating the ship in action more effectively, Howe ordered greater quantities of small hatchets to be allocated to each ship to help cut away damaged rigging. Steps such as these helped to secure the foundations for British naval supremacy: fewer men would die for lack of medical care and fewer ships would be forced out of action for want of an axe to clear the decks. This is how battles and wars were won.[69]

Success at the First of June also reinforced the British willingness to believe in and trust the navy. There was certainly no good news coming from the army in the Caribbean, the only British field army active in the aftermath of the First of June. The army's early successes in the Caribbean had come to nothing and at a cost of 14,000 men dead, most from yellow fever, dysentery and malaria.[70] For some young men the news of naval victory inspired an immediate and powerful desire to join up. One of those men was James Goddard. When his father finally consented to James joining the Royal Navy he wrote to a connection of his who was in turn connected with Captain John Payne of the *Russell*. Payne received a letter recommending the young boy that read:

> If ever there was a lad found to play the Devil with the French at sea it is the bearer James Goddard ... [he] will not be persuaded to think of anything but the sea ... I don't know the regular way of getting him made a midshipman, but he is so impatient that tho' young has promised his brother shall provide for him, when he returns in the *Boyne*. He will not wait nor miss the sailing of the Fleet from Portsmouth ...[71]

For those less inclined to go and fight the French at sea, the victory was still a powerful fillip. The Duke of Portland wrote to Burke:

> It opens scenes to my mind, where I can contemplate with a sort of satisfaction which I think no other Event could have afforded me – I think I see an English fleet covering the coast of France and the white Plumes and Standards erected and advancing to restore Order Religion and law to that unhappy Country and tranquillity and security to the rest of the civilized world. Don't say that I dream and I shall indulge this vision with confidence and make every exertion in my power to realize it.[72]

The King shared his hope and commented: '... which in the same time that it adds lustre to the British arms, must in its consequences be of great consequence for the whole naval campaign'. Collingwood, too, shared that vision: 'I hope this battle will be attended with happy consequences, and tend to promote a peace', and another anonymous correspondent had hoped, rather optimistically, that the battle would 'settle the fate of Europe'.[73]

The reality was far more complex than any of these men believed it could be and, in spite of the widespread optimism of June 1794, those who looked to the future were facing twenty-one more years of war with France. The best that could be hoped for was summed up by Collingwood, a practical man at heart, who wrote to a close friend: 'I hope, however, their naval force is done for this summer: those that remain must be in a ruined and shattered state.' This, Collingwood believed, would provide some much-needed respite for British trade that the French had targeted with great success.[74] Another immediate effect was that the threat of invasion that had hung like a dull cloud over England for several months was lifted instantly and so too was the imminent danger of an anti-British armed neutrality of Sweden and Denmark, possibly with the additional weight of the United States, all of whom shared deep anger at British trade interference. The British victory was sufficient to counter the momentum of their anti-British alliance.[75]

It also carried sufficient weight to bolster Pitt and his supporters through the troubling times ahead when mobs rioted, Britain became isolated in Europe, and politicians bayed for the heads of those who supported the war. The First of June was proof enough that a maritime policy could work; that the French were weak at sea compared with the British; that a policy to destroy French maritime power and her colonial empire was valid. Defeats on the continent and the collapse of alliances could be endured because of the Royal Navy: it became a source of hope and reassurance; it became both a comfort blanket and a guiding star.

# Epilogue

*J'avais rêvé une république que tout le monde eût adorée.*

Camille Desmoulins to his wife from prison. 4 April, 1794.[1]

For many of the combatants, and for many historians since, the Glorious First of June was an opportunity to see the navies of France and Britain squaring up for the first time in the Revolutionary War. The British sailors got to see the French regicides, butchers and tyrants that they had heard about from the rumour mill; and the French first got to see the British 'leopards' that, according to both Jacobin propaganda and ancient maritime tradition, threatened their homes and their ideology. It was all too easy, therefore, to paint the battle in black and white. On one side were the French who, in the words of one contemporary historian, had been animated 'to a degree of phrenzy' by the Republicans. An early British historian even claimed that, in a state of 'savage ferocity', they drank brandy mixed with gunpowder as they fought.[2] On the other side were the British who, in obvious and direct contrast, retained their skill, organisation and discipline throughout. In the difference between the two sides, it was argued, lay the seeds of victory. We now know, however, that the result is not so easily explained.

That the French fought with extraordinary courage is overwhelmingly confirmed by the sources and is an important reminder that the Revolution inspired Frenchmen in many different ways and places. The sea is a location in its own right, just as Paris was different from Marseille, Toulon was different from Brest and the Vendée was different from Provence. For a few long hours on 28 and 29 May and 1 June the political and social wounds that had threatened to ruin the navy were ignored in the presence of their age-old enemy. The sailors were not Montagnards, Jacobins, *sans-culottes*, aristocrats, Girondins, Dantonists, Hébertistes or Indulgents: they were united as French. These men fought together in spite of, rather than because of, Jacobin interference in the navy. Their unity is testament to the power of the cultural brotherhood of fighting sailors. In moments of idleness they could be riven by faction but in the heat of action they could rise above their squabbles. It was proof that the Republic could exist without being crippled by introspection; that an outward-looking military-based unity could give the new Republic the focus it needed to take it further than anyone had dreamed possible.

The French fleet was manned with inexperienced sailors, but so too were many of the British ships and both sides were undermanned. Yet there was still a visible and distinctive gap in the professionalism and competence of both sets of crews. There was the odd example of British cowardice but the unmistakable pattern is of British gun crews silencing their opponents and then working through the exhaustion and pain to repair their ships and fight on. The British gun crews were, without doubt, more effective than the French. More Frenchmen died more quickly; fewer Frenchmen survived both to lead and then to fight a renewed engagement. The explanation for this does not lie solely in numbers or experience, but in a mixture of training and tactics and in the design, construction and manufacture of ships, guns and gunpowder.

Another clear factor is that the British officers were more experienced leaders in fleet warfare than the French because so many French officers had emigrated during the Terror. The French officers were not necessarily less experienced at fighting, because many had been promoted from the naval ranks, nor were they necessarily less experienced at seamanship, because many were skilled maritime hands, but when it came to leadership in battle, to understanding what needed to be done and then knowing how to get a team of men to do it, the British were far more experienced than the French. This had a telling impact at the lower levels of leadership, among small groups of men on dark gundecks with limited views of the action and a limited perception of the unfolding events. Naval historians may focus too much on grand tactics and strategy but to understand this battle we must look to the junior officers.

Jeanbon may have saved the navy in the short-term by galvanising it into action, but long-term it had been crippled by the Revolution. Too much infrastructure had been cut, too many ties of service and loyalty had been broken and too much experience jettisoned. That kind of damage could take generations to mend. The French army had access to the right number of people and the right sort of materiel but the navy simply did not. They could provide for a small navy but not a large one. Even if given enough notice, the problems were simply too acute. The Glorious First of June gave the French the opportunity for a healing process to begin by blooding so many of their new recruits and officers, nevertheless five thousand sailors were killed or taken prisoner. This could have been the foundation of a navy for the new Republic but it was not; Howe's victory ensured it was still-born.

The question of fleet seamanship is particularly interesting. The inexperience of the French captains clearly suggests that they were likely to be incompetent, and at times they were, not least in their inability to form a line of battle when the fleets first met on 28 May. Thereafter, however, the battles are coloured by impressive and sustained French competence and ability. In the aftermath of the final battle, Howe chose to discontinue the action and to call back the chase of some disabled Frenchmen because he feared that Villaret would bear down once again, in good formation, as he had twice before on 29 May. After the line was cut on 1 June, Howe's fleet was completely dislocated and Villaret stood off, in excellent formation. He had manoeuvred his fleet with great discipline under the ferocious guns of the British to such an extent that Howe was forced to back off. Even more impressively, Villaret achieved this with crews devastated by sickness, crippled by ill-advised transfers to crew prizes back to France and hampered by youngsters stuttering with inexperience. Remember that there were 150 men unable to fight for sickness aboard the *Sans Pareil* and aboard the *Trajan* 240 of her crew were, one way or another, absent, either through sickness, death, or having been put on prizes.[3] Figures such as these make the French achievement stand out even more.

And what of the perception of British competence at the levels of ships' captains and fleet admiral? The British captains' performance has been disparaged by a number of naval historians who have pointed out that so few of the British ships actually broke through the French line as Howe had intended. We now know, however, that Howe was sufficiently realistic that he neither expected all of his captains to break through, nor did he criticise those who could not. Howe has also been criticised for his inability to make himself understood and also for failing to form his captains into a Nelsonian-style 'band of brothers', but the evidence suggests that every captain understood Howe's intentions, even if they were unable to realise them, and that an atmosphere of great brotherliness existed throughout the fleet which manifested itself in sustained and repeated examples of mutual support. Time and again British ships drew fire from damaged or overwhelmed colleagues and sailed to the assistance of those in distress. Throughout this series of actions, the British captains both thought and fought as a unit without the constant urging and recrimination by senior officers that characterised so many other battles such as Benbow's last fight in 1702, the Battle of Toulon in 1744, the Battle of Ushant in 1778 or the Battle of the Chesapeake in 1782. By contrast, the Glorious First of June is an outstanding example of command success and fleet cohesion. That the British fleet lost no ships at all to the French in three significant actions fought over five days is testament to this sense of camaraderie and devotion.

It is useful to add here that such a victory could be regarded as impressive and fairly labelled 'glorious' even though there are numerous examples of British ships firing into each other, some examples of command confusion and several occasions when the cohesion of the British fleet completely fell apart, not least on 28 May when a squall destroyed the British line and 'Nothing but confusion was visible in our Fleet, whilst the enemy's line was in perfect order'.[4] The label 'glorious' carries with it certain assumptions about behaviour and performance which, in a battle such as this, do not apply. Such seamanship hiccups and friendly fire incidents were the norm in sailing warfare: they were both expected and acceptable. A glorious battle could boast examples of incompetence, cowardice and shame as easily as examples of skill, courage and pride. A glorious battle could be glorious for both sides, and it could be more or less glorious than it was. There were also so many people affected by the battle that inevitably it would be glorious for some and not for others. Collingwood, Montagu and Molloy are the clearest examples of British naval officers for whom it was not glorious, and from the French fleet Tardy, Langlois, Barrade, Benoît, Allary, Dumoutier, Gassin and Bompard were all forced to defend their conduct. From the art world we must not forget poor old Loutherbourg, who went to such great lengths to paint a magnificent work of art that was rejected and then neglected. Two of these men very nearly lost their lives, most were professionally ruined and a few deeply insulted and personally upset. The adjective 'glorious' is misleading, therefore, and when applied to naval warfare must always be qualified. It is a word that is so characteristic of our general perception of naval victory but at the same time so inadequate in its description.

The scale of the victory is deeply impressive. Naval warfare is so often, so easily and so erroneously measured by the number of ships captured and yes, in other battles in the age of sail the scale of victory might appear greater, but it is exactly the scale of this victory that makes the battle so important. The French were heavily beaten but they still only surrendered six ships, and they only did so when there was absolutely no hope of rescue. None of the ships surrendered during the battle itself but were boarded in the aftermath when the majority of the French fleet had sailed over the horizon. Never again would so many French ships in fleet battle sell themselves so dearly.

And yet, despite that dogged resistance, this was still the greatest British victory for 102 years; since the great Battle of Barfleur of 1692 in which the cream of Louis XIV's navy was destroyed, and, if things had worked out slightly differently between 28 May and 1 June the British might well have secured six more prizes: one on 28 May, two on 29 May and three more on 1 June, all of which had been silenced by British fire. All of those ships would have been made English prizes if not for the ebb and flow of battle shifting at that precise moment toward France.

The scale of the victory and the means by which it was achieved therefore combine to make this a very special battle indeed, a reputation the Glorious First of June was denied by the subsequent overwhelming scale of Nelson's victories. Nelson was also personally responsible for the suppression of this battle's reputation by making a disparaging remark about a 'Lord Howe's victory', perhaps with reference to the number of prizes secured on 1 June. But this should be taken as evidence of Nelson's competitive, vain character rather than as evidence of the inadequate performance of Howe's fleet on 1 June. Quite to the contrary, by fighting so well and securing such a victory against such a determined foe, Howe set a benchmark for British performance. That it was met and then surpassed actually enhances that achievement. Excellence does not exist without expectation. Nelson could not whip his captains to such a level of skill without the weight of expectation: Howe does not exist in the shadow of Nelson, but Nelson exists in the shadow of Howe. For too many years Nelson's influence has been wrongly allowed to go backward as well as forward in time. That must now change: Howe must assume his rightful position as the first fleet commander since Hawke in the late 1750s to generate a thorough sense of fleet cohesion and purpose.

His contemporaries certainly appreciated his ability. As Collingwood wrote: 'The proceedings of the 1st of June were like magic, and could only be effected by skill like his.'[5] The parents of the future famous naval captain Charles Fremantle were so impressed that they christened their son Charles Howe Fremantle because he was born on 1 June 1800.[6]

Where the British clearly failed, however, was in their ability to cope with such a scale of victory. When the fleet should have been united in celebration it was divided in misery because Howe had, and perhaps understandably, mismanaged the new medal system. Because of the nature of fleet warfare, particularly this battle which was fought over such an enormous passage of time in a vast area of sea and in foggy weather, Howe and his flag officers simply had no idea what many of their captains were doing at any given moment. And yet his political masters demanded names and answers immediately. It would be weeks, perhaps even months, before a fair perception of events could be achieved. Howe responded too quickly, too vaguely and many people were hurt.

The British were also wholly unprepared for the number of prisoners that they received, even if the Admiralty was aware that thousands of Frenchmen were rapidly descending on British shores in the cramped holds of British ships. The failure was not at the level of Admiralty Board but between the board and the dockyards and prisons where the men were supposed to be housed. The yards were warned, orders were given, but nothing was done and the direct result was that thousands of British sailors were infected with typhus. The British ships had been damaged, certainly, but it was nothing that the fleet could not handle given a week or so to repair. Everything was of timber, oak and iron, and the British had plentiful supplies, but they did not have an instant cure for typhus. The fleet, already disabled by French shot, was now disabled by French disease and it remained that way for the duration of the summer. In the aftermath of the First of June the British therefore learned the hard way that naval victory was a transient thing, its advantages as easily lost at home as gained at sea.

All of these complications were linked specifically to naval victory. The British had fought a 'glorious' action, but the Admiralty was now faced with an infected and already depleted pool of manpower, disabled ships, the worry and expense of housing thousands of French prisoners and an irate officer corps. In France, meanwhile, the grain convoy had arrived, the hungry were fed and the navy had demonstrated a measure of competence. But how much more pure and effective would capturing the grain convoy have been? The French would have been demoralised and starved; the navy labelled incompetent again and perhaps ignored politically and militarily; and the British would have secured thousands of tons of merchant shipping and grain to enrich and feed the British war machine. The British Channel Fleet would have been ready to fight, blockade or launch amphibious operations.

The British did, however, win a clear victory, and there was nothing, nothing at all, that could compare with naval victory in the hearts and minds of the general public. The politicians, Pitt, Chatham and Dundas, realised this and, by cooking up a scheme to parade none other than the King himself around the navy, *his* navy, they fed this public hunger for naval pride and naval victory. It is a display of political savvy that has not been awarded sufficient respect by historians. They strengthened a pre-existing bond between the general public, the Royal Navy and the King. The result was priceless to British security and British prospects in the coming war. By concentrating on the 'glory' of naval victory, rather than the missed opportunity of strategic advantage or the hideous and expensive reality of prisoners of war, the general public began to create a concept of British naval victory in its mind's eye that the navy was continually forced to live up to. And because the *people* believed in the navy, the navy retained its political support. With political support the navy retained its funding that enabled it to build fine ships and to feed, clothe and nurse its men. The navy was cared for by its country and in turn the navy cared for its country. The mystique of the navy was therefore created by the politicians, public and the press as much as it was by the men who fought the battles in the eighteenth century. Each was inadequate in its own way but together they produced something truly powerful that defeated Britain's enemies at sea and brought the sea and naval history into the heart of British national identity for well over a century. Naval battles rarely affected wars through military advancement and the Glorious First of June makes that point very clear. Rather, seapower affected politics, economics and popular culture in a profound way, which then went on to have an indirect effect on the outcome of wars.

In France, popular pride in the navy was boosted by its performance at the First of June, but it was never reciprocated by the politicians as it was in England. The navy was simply not cared for. The crews fought bravely, but the ships were dirty and with a handful of exceptions, rotten. The men were sick. Sick men on dirty, rotten ships could be beaten, however brave they were. The British knew this as surely as they knew that a strong gust of wind would split a thin sail and snap a weak line. After the First of June, the British did not just think that they were better; they knew that they were better, and that confidence ultimately won them the war at sea.

That war, however, would continue with only one very short break for the next twenty-one years and the two navies would stalk each other in a never-ending cycle of maritime violence fought worldwide. The Revolution had changed naval warfare and naval warfare had changed the Revolution. In many ways the battle was the final missing piece for the new Republic. Until the French had fought with sufficient loyalty and bravery on the Glorious First of June, no one had really known how the navy would react in battle. In the preceding year the Toulon fleet had surrendered to the British without a shot being fired and then the Brest fleet had mutinied. There was nothing to suggest that the navy could be relied upon to defend the Republic, and yet everyone knew that the navy was urgently required if the Republic was to survive.

Those questions were answered by the Glorious First of June, which was, in effect, trial by sea for the new Republic. It was the final proof that the Republic had the necessary ingredients to survive and even to expand. Priorities could now change. The Terror as it was first conceived, as a tool to unite through punishment and to inspire through fear, was no longer necessary. The armies were winning on land and now the navy had demonstrated itself to be reliable and loyal, if weak. The summer of 1794 and the death of Robespierre were, therefore, by no means the end of the Revolution but a rebirth, a re-energising and a conviction that it could succeed.

The navy then became an integral, though not prioritised, part of the new Republic. The British and French fleets would repeatedly meet, the British would repeatedly win, but the French would repeatedly rebuild their navy to keep it sufficiently strong to pose a threat. The perception that the British ever 'ruled the waves' is simply not true. Even at the very height of British dominance after Trafalgar, the French navy still existed in some numbers and powerful French squadrons targeted British trade in far-off locations, constantly irritating and weakening the British economy that was so reliant on foreign trade. Naval warfare was a constant grind throughout the eighteenth century, therefore, and no one realised this more than the sailors. They had won a battle but that did not mean that they could all go home.

As with any victorious fleet, squadron, army or battalion in the whole of history, a successful one is not disbanded but given another task. Naval service therefore stretched out far into the distance for the

British sailors who had fought at the Glorious First of June. They had survived battle once but they would have to do so again, and in the interim they would have to cope with the boredom of service life so neatly encapsulated when one sailor wrote to his sister immediately after the battle: 'pray write as often as possible, and, when you do write, write good long letters, about something or other.'[7] The ships had to be cleaned and painted; the decks scrubbed; the sails bent; the rope wormed, parcelled and served; the blocks oiled and tallowed; the iron chipped of rust; the cables whipped and coiled; the brass polished; the holds stowed; the guns cleaned and practised; the swords sharpened and oiled. Service life just continued as ever. For those who had fought, the change was invisible; it was internal; it was private. Some dreaded the next battle while others were impatient for it. And more battles came. In the immediate future loomed some of the greatest naval actions fought in the age of sail, the battles of Cape St Vincent (1797), Camperdown (1797), The Nile (1798), Copenhagen (1801), Trafalgar (1805), San Domingo (1806), and in between those great fleet actions were countless single-ship actions and fierce battles fought between smaller squadrons. Thousands of British and French sailors died in all of these battles, but none of them would be as hard fought as the Glorious First of June.

Nor would any of these battles be fought over such a significant cause as the Revolution. One French sailor who witnessed the battle later reflected on the strength of the combined fleets: 'I asked myself why, instead of this scene representing the prelude to a battle between the two greatest nations in Europe, it was not a crusade undertaken mutually to deliver other peoples from slavery.'[8] This is a fine example of the philosophy that made the Revolution truly revolutionary; the purest form of the ideology that had led the French people to conquer their oppressors. It is a sentence that could not have been uttered if it was not for the Revolution because it is indicative of a new perception of popular power.

Before the fall of the Bastille and the execution of Louis XVI, war was fought over dynastic insecurity or greed, but now it was being fought for the hopes and fears of the people. Politicians at the time grumbled that the Glorious First of June had little effect on the progress of the war and did nothing to stop the Revolution, and British historians ever since have criticised Howe for failing to make the victory what it could have been. It is time to be thankful that he did not. The Revolution survived the land and sea attacks of the First Coalition, it survived the Civil War and it survived the Terror, and in the long run its survival has benefited us all. It has left a legacy of boundless possibility – proof that a new and better world can always be both imagined and achieved.

# APPENDIX I

# The Chronology of Years I and II of the French Republic

An important part of the French Revolution was its adoption of an entirely new calendar. It is one of the most powerful examples of how the Revolutionaries were prepared to sweep aside accepted wisdom and the practice of centuries in an attempt to install order, regulation and fairness to their world. The bizarreness of the Gregorian calendar was an obvious, if ambitious, target.

The Republican calendar was officially adopted and used for twelve years from 1793 to 1805. The calendar began at the autumnal equinox and consisted of twelve months, each consisting of thirty days. The months were all renamed:

Vendémiaire (from Latin *vindemia* meaning grape harvest) lasted for thirty days from the autumnal equinox 22, 23 or 24 September
Brumaire (from French *brume* meaning fog) from 22, 23, or 24 October
Frimaire (from French *frimas* meaning frost) from 21, 22 or 23 November
Nivôse (from Latin *nivosus* meaning snowy) from 21, 22 or 23 December
Pluviôse (from Latin *pluvius* meaning rainy) from 20, 21 or 22 January
Ventôse (from Latin *ventosus* meaning windy) from 19, 20, 21 February
Germinal (from Latin *germen* meaning germination) from 20 or 21 March
Floréal (from Latin *flos* meaning flower) from 20 or 21 April
Prairial (from French *prairie* meaning pasture) from 20 or 21 May
Messidor (from Latin *messis* meaning harvest) from 19 or 20 June
Thermidor (from Greek *thermon* meaning summer heat) from 19 or 20 July
Fructidor (from Latin *fructus* meaning fruit) from 18 or 19 August

Each week then consisted of ten days, every single one of which was individually named for an animal, tool, plant or mineral. While the British date the battle as being fought on 1 June 1794, therefore, the French knew that date as Pois Prairial An II. And they didn't stop there. Each day was divided into ten hours, each hour into 100 minutes and each minute into 100 seconds. To make matters even more confusing, the Republican calendar, although it started on 22 September 1792, was not officially adopted until 5 October 1793.

# Year I

**1792**

*22 September (1 Vendémiaire).* Proclamation of the French Republic.

**1793**

*21 January (2 Pluviôse).* Execution of Louis XVI.

*1 February (13 Pluviôse).* France declares war on Britain and the Dutch Republic.

*14 February (26 Pluviôse).* British capture Tobago.

*24 February (6 Ventôse).* French decree for the raising of 300,000 men.

*7 March (17 Ventôse).* France declares war on Spain.

*March.* The Vendée breaks out in revolt.

*10 March (20 Ventôse).* Establishment of the Revolutionary Tribunal.

*22 March (2 Germinal).* France declares war on Austria.

The First Coalition (Spain, Holland, Britain and Austria) is complete.

April. British attack Martinique and Saint Domingue.

*6 April (19 Germinal).* Creation of the Committee of Public Safety.

First meeting of the Revolutionary Tribunal in Paris.

*2 June (14 Prairial).* Expulsion of the Girondin deputies from the National Convention, leaving the way clear for Jacobin dominance.

*27 July (9 Thermidor).* Robespierre voted on to the Committee of Public Safety.

*23 August (6 Fructidor).* Declaration of mass conscription in France.

*29 August (12 Fructidor).* Toulon is surrendered to Samuel Hood.

*5 September (19 Fructidor).* The National Convention declares: 'Terror is the order of the day.'

*6–8 September (20–22 Fructidor).* British and Dutch defeated at Hondschoote, outside Dunkirk.

*11 September (25 Fructidor).* Grain Maximum decreed – fixing maximum prices for grain and fodder.

*17 September (Jour de la Vertu).* The Law of Suspects is passed – widening the definition of 'suspect'.

# Year II

**1793**

*29 September (8 Vendémiaire).* Return of mutinous French fleet to Brest. Law of General Maximum is passed on all foodstuffs and commodities.

*5 October (14 Vendémiaire).* Adoption of Republican calendar.

*15–16 October (24–25 Vendémiaire).* Austrians defeated at Wattignies.

*20 October (29 Vendémiaire).* James Saumarez captures the French frigate *Réunion* but his frigate the *Crescent* is badly damaged by a resolute French defence.

*21–22 October (30 Vendémiaire – 1 Brumaire).* Nelson's frigate *Agamemnon* badly beaten by the French frigate *Melpomène*.

*24 October (3 Brumaire).* The British frigate *Thames* badly mauled by the French *Uranie*.

*4 December (14 Frimaire).* Law of 14 Frimaire – centralises power of the Committee of Public Safety. Bureaucratisation of the Terror.

*19 December (29 Frimaire).* Toulon retaken by the French.

*22 December (2 Nivôse).* Vendée rebellion crushed.

*29 December (9 Nivôse).* Fifty-eight 'representatives en mission' sent into the provinces to enforce the Law of 14 Frimaire.

*2 January (13 Nivôse).* Mutiny on board the *América* in Brest roads.

*13 January (24 Nivôse).* Four mutineers from the *América* guillotined in Brest roads.

*29 January (10 Pluviôse).* Creation of Central Surveillance Committee in Brest.

*5 February (17 Pluviôse).* Establishment of Revolutionary Tribunal in Brest.

*12 February (24 Pluviôse).* Vanstabel arrives in Chesapeake Bay.

*22 March (2 Germinal).* British capture Martinique.

*24 March (4 Germinal).* Hébertists executed.

*4 April (15 Germinal).* British capture St Lucia.

*5 April (16 Germinal).* Execution of the Dantonists.

*10 April (21 Germinal).* Vanstabel leaves America with a convoy 156-strong.

*16 April (27 Germinal).* Committee of Public Safety assumes policing powers.

*23 April (4 Floréal).* Sir John Warren's frigate squadron captures the *Babet*, *La Pomone* and *Engageante*.

*2 May (13 Floréal).* The British Channel Fleet leaves St Helens, Isle of Wight.
*6 May (17 Floréal).* Nielly leaves Rochefort.
*16 Mai (27 Floréal).* Villaret leaves Brest.
*23 May (4 Prairial).* Cécile Renault attempts to assassinate Robespierre.
*26 May (7 Prairial).* French decree forbidding taking of British or Hanoverian prisoners.
*28 May – 1 June (9–13 Prairial).* British and French fleets fight.
*4 June (16 Prairial).* Robespierre unanimously elected President of the Convention.
*8 June (20 Prairial).* Festival of the Supreme Being – Robespierre is master of ceremonies.
*10 June (22 Prairial).* Law of 22 Prairial passed – the Terror accelerates and reaches its peak over the next eight weeks.
*11 June (23 Prairial).* Howe's report of the action published in the *London Gazette Extraordinary*.
*12 June (24 Prairial).* Return of Vanstabel to Brest.
*20–30 June (2–12 Messidor).* House of Commons adjourns to 'enable' Royal visit to Portsmouth.
*23 June (5 Messidor).* Jeanbon orders the arrest of eight captains who failed to meet his expectations of Republican duty in battle.
*24 June (6 Messidor).* Jeanbon leaves Brest for Paris.
*26 June (8 Messidor).* French victory over the Allies at Fleurus (Belgium).
*8 July (20 Messidor).* French army enters Brussels.
*11 July (23 Messidor).* Portland Whigs join Pitt's government.
*26 July (8 Thermidor).* Robespierre's last speech to the National Convention. He is arrested the next day.
*28–30 July (10–12 Thermidor).* Robespierre and 105 of his followers are executed.
*1 August (14 Thermidor).* Repeal of the Law of 22 Prairial.
*5–10 August (18–23 Thermidor).* Mass release of suspects from Paris prisons.
*11 August (24 Thermidor).* Revolutionary Tribunal suspended.
*24 August (7 Fructidor).* Restructuring and decentralising of French government.

# APPENDIX II
# The Fleets

## THE BRITISH FLEET

**Launch place.** Warships of this period were built in Royal Dockyards and private shipyards. If a ship was built in a Royal Dockyard the location is given; if in a private yard the location and builder's name are given.

**Dimensions and tonnage**. The measurements are, in order, length of gun-deck (not length of keel, which is used to calculate tonnage) x breadth x depth in hold. In this period the tonnage was known as the 'Builders Measurement' hence the figures are given as 'bm'. The figure was achieved by a complex formula involving dividing the final figure into 94. Hence the tonnages are quoted in ninety-fourths.[1]

**Order.** The ships have been divided up into rate – this is not the order in which they went into battle.

### First Rates

***Queen Charlotte*** **(100)**

- Chatham. Launched 15.4.1790. 190ft 0in x 52ft 5½in x 22ft 4in
- 2,286 34/94bm
- Men: 787, 86 per cent (of full complement)
- Captain Roger Curtis; Admiral Earl Howe
- 14/29 (killed/wounded)
- One of her midshipmen was James Brisbane, who went on to become a naval officer of immense experience and skill, particularly in coastal bombardment and riverine warfare. Graham Hammond, future admiral of the fleet, was another midshipman. Edward Codrington, the future admiral, was her signal lieutenant. Serving as captain's aide-de-camp was Peter

Heywood, who had been a midshipman aboard the *Bounty* when mutineers took it by force from Captain William Bligh on 28 April 1789. In spite of being an officer, Heywood had remained aboard the *Bounty* but his reputation was saved at the subsequent court martial. Alexander Hood and Howe were influential patrons. Heywood went on to become a hydrographer of some significance. Serving as a volunteer was John Hunter, who went on to become governor of the convict colony in New South Wales, a post he fulfilled with little success. Another lieutenant was Henry Raper, who went on to become an admiral.

***Royal Sovereign*** **(100)**

- Plymouth. Launched 11.9.1786. 183ft 10½in x 52ft 1in x 22ft 2½in
- 2,175 29/94 bm
- Men: 762, 86 per cent (of full complement)
- Captain Henry Nicholls; Vice-Admiral Thomas Graves
- 14/44 (killed/wounded)
- Went on to lead the lee column at Trafalgar under the command of Collingwood

***Royal George*** **(100)**

- Chatham. Launched 16.9.1788. 190ft 0in x 52ft 5½in x 22ft 4in
- 2,286 34/94 bm
- Men: 710, 81 per cent (of full complement)
- Captain William Domett; Vice-Admiral Alexander Hood
- 20/72 (killed/wounded)
- An army officer commanding a company of Queen's Royals was Andrew Pilkington, who went on to enjoy a distinguished career in the army, reaching the rank of lieutenant-general.

## Second rates

***Impregnable*** **(98)**

- Deptford. Launched 15.4.1786. 177ft 7in x 49ft 3½in x 20ft 10½in
- 1,886 47/94 bm
- Men: 664, 87 per cent (of full complement)
- Captain George Westcott; Rear-Admiral Benjamin Caldwell
- 7/21 (killed/wounded)

• One of her midshipmen was Robert Otway, a future admiral of great courage and skill and a man held in the highest professional regard by his colleagues. Her flag captain was George Westcott, who became one of Nelson's 'Band of Brothers' but died at the Battle of the Nile (1798).

***Barfleur* (98)**

• Chatham. Launched 30.7.1768. 177ft 8in x 50ft 5in x 21ft 0in
• 1,947 47/94 bm
• Men: 640, 83 per cent (of full complement)
• Captain Cuthbert Collingwood; Rear-Admiral George Bowyer
• 9/25 (killed/wounded)
• One of her lieutenants was William Prowse, a man of humble origins, raised as a child on a trading vessel, who went on to become a rear-admiral through steady professional competence.

***Glory* (98)**

• Plymouth. Launched 5.7.1788. 177ft 5in x 50ft 1 5/8in x 21ft 2in
• 1,944 17/94 bm
• Men: 647, 100 per cent (of full complement)
• Captain John Elphinstone; Rear-Admiral George Keith Elphinstone
• 13/39 (killed/wounded)

***Queen* (90)**

• Woolwich. Launched 18.9.1769. 177ft 6in x 49ft 6in x 21ft 9in
• 1,876 74/94 bm
• Men: 650, 85 per cent (of full complement)
• Captain John Hutt; Rear-Admiral Alan Gardner
• 36/67 (killed/wounded)
• One of her lieutenants was Samuel Ballard, who went on to become a vice-admiral and distinguished officer in the Napoleonic Wars. Another lieutenant was Aiskew Hollis, who went on to fight throughout the Napoleonic Wars and became a rear-admiral.

## Third rates

***Caesar* (80)**

• Plymouth. Launched 16.11.1793. 181ft 0in x 50ft 5in x 22ft 11in

- 2,002 74/94 bm
- Men: 609, 83 per cent (of full complement)
- Captain Anthony James Pye Molloy
- 18/71 (killed/wounded)
- Captain Molloy was dismissed his ship following a court martial for failing to prosecute action to his best ability.

***Gibraltar* (80)**

- Havana. 178ft 10¾in x 53ft 3¾in x 22ft 4in
- 2,184 25/94 bm
- Men: 551, 85 per cent (of full complement)
- Captain Thomas Mackenzie
- 2/12 (killed/wounded)
- *Gibraltar* was an ex-Spanish prize captured in Rodney's action off Cape St Vincent in 1780.

***Bellerophon* (74)**

- Edward Greaves & Co, Frindsbury. Launched 17.10.1786. 168ft 0in x 46ft 10½in x 19ft 9in
- 1,612 78/94 bm
- Men: 572, 93 per cent (of full complement)
- Captain William Hope; Rear-Admiral Thomas Pasley
- 4/27 (killed/wounded)
- A nine-year-old boy aboard was John Hindmarsh, who though only fourteen, distinguished himself at the Battle of the Nile (1798) and went on to become a rear-admiral. One of her midshipmen was the twenty-year-old Matthew Flinders, who became one of the most successful cartographers of his age who, among many other achievements, circumnavigated Australia. His narrative of the battle is one of the most detailed, but least well-known, including magnificent battle-plans [see figs. ii–vii] *Bellerophon* herself continued to serve until the end of the wars and received Napoleon's surrender in 1815.

***Leviathan* (74)**

- Chatham. Launched 9.10.1790. 172ft 3in x 47ft 10in x 20ft 9in
- 1,707 85/94 bm
- Men: 553, 85 per cent (of full complement)

- Captain Lord Hugh Seymour
- 10/33 (killed/wounded)

***Russell*** **(74)**

- Thomas West, Deptford. Launched 10.11.1764. 168ft 6in x 47ft 5¾in x 19ft 9in
- 1,642 57/94 bm
- Men: 518, 86 per cent (of full complement)
- Captain John Payne
- 8/26 (killed/wounded)

***Marlborough*** **(74)**

- Deptford. Launched 25.10.1764. 168ft 8½in x 46ft 11in x 19ft 9in
- 1,642 12/94 bm
- Men: 529, 88 per cent (of full complement)
- Captain George Berkeley
- 29/90 (killed/wounded)
- One of her marines was James Lyon, who went on to become a significant and highly decorated army officer. He particularly distinguished himself against Napoleon in Egypt on 21 March 1801 and commanded the 6th Hanoverian Brigade at Waterloo. Berkeley also held the post of surveyor general of the ordnance.

***Defence*** **(74)**

- Plymouth. Launched 31.3.1763. 168ft 0in x 46ft 9in x 19ft 9in
- 1,603 8/94 bm
- Men: 505, 84 per cent (of full complement)
- Captain James Gambier
- 18/39 (killed/wounded)
- One of her midshipmen was William Dillon, a future admiral and a man of great influence on the development of the Royal Navy in the nineteenth century.

***Tremendous*** **(74)**

- William Barnard, Deptford Green. Launched 30.10.1784. 170ft 4in x 47ft 7½in x 20ft 4in
- 1,680 22/94 bm

- Men: 507, 85 per cent (of full complement)
- Captain James Pigott
- 3/8 (killed/wounded)

***Invincible*** **(74)**

- (John & William) Wells & Co, Deptford. Launched 9.3.1765. 168ft 6in x 47ft 3in x 19ft 9in
- 1,630 59/94 bm
- Men: 504, 84 per cent (of full complement)
- Captain Thomas Pakenham
- 14/31 (killed/wounded)
- Her first lieutenant was Henry Blackwood, who went on to become one of Nelson's 'Band of Brothers' and commanded the frigate squadron at the Battle of Trafalgar. John Hill, another midshipman, went on to reach flag rank and became a significant factor in maintaining dockyard efficiency. He became superintendent of Sheerness Dockyard and was the last-ever captain of HMS *Téméraire* before she was taken to Rotherhithe for demolition in that famous journey captured by Turner in his painting *The Fighting Téméraire*. Thomas Ussher, future rear-admiral, was one of her midshipmen. In April 1814 Ussher commanded the frigate *Undaunted* and took the recently abdicated Napoleon to exile on the island of Elba.

***Culloden*** **(74)**

- John Randall, Rotherhithe. Launched 16.6.1783. 170ft 0in x 47ft 8¾in x 20ft 3⅞in
- 1,683 29/94 bm
- Men: 489, 82 per cent (of full complement)
- Captain Isaac Schomberg
- 2/5 (killed/wounded)
- Schomberg went on to become a naval historian of note, and wrote his *Naval Chronology* that was first published in 1802 and reprinted with additions in 1815. One of her lieutenants was Edward Rotherham, who went on to fight alongside Collingwood at Trafalgar and thereafter command the *Bellerophon*, but he lacked both skill and judgement. William Owen, a future vice-admiral, was one of her midshipmen. As a hydrographer, Owen went on to survey the Great Lakes of Canada, the upper St Lawrence River, and delineated the border between Canada and America.

***Brunswick* (74)**

- Deptford. Launched 30.4.1790. 176ft 2½in x 48ft 9in x 19ft 6in
- 1,836 13/94 bm
- Men: 552, 85 per cent (of full complement)
- Captain John Harvey
- 41/114 (killed/wounded)
- Brother of Henry Harvey of the *Ramillies*. John Harvey also had his eleven-year-old son aboard, Edward Harvey, who went on to become an admiral. Her master's mate was John Pilfold (sometimes Pilford), who commanded the *Ajax* at Trafalgar as an inexperienced lieutenant. One of the powder monkeys was sixteen-year-old Mary Talbot. Her right ankle was shattered with grapeshot but she recovered and went on to serve again in the navy. She left a valuable memoir of a woman's life in a warship.

***Valiant* (74)**

- Chatham. Launched 10.8.1759. 171ft 2¾in x 49ft 4in x 21ft 2¾in
- 1,799 41/94 bm
- Men: 520, 80 per cent (of full complement)
- Captain Thomas Pringle
- 2/9 (killed/wounded)
- *Valiant* was a member of the *Triumph* class, which were the first 74-gun ships to carry a 24pdr armament on the upper deck.

***Orion* (74)**

- William Barnard, Deptford. Launched 1.6.1787. 170ft 5in x 46ft 10½in x 20ft 6½in
- 1,645 48/94 bm
- Men: 513, 86 per cent (of full complement)
- Captain John Duckworth
- 5/24 (killed/wounded)
- Duckworth went on to become an admiral and commanded the British fleet at the last fleet Battle of the Napoleonic Wars, the Battle of San Domingo (1806).

***Ramillies* (74)**

- Randall & Brent, Rotherhithe. Launched 12.7.1785. 170ft 4in x 47ft 6in x 19ft 11½in

- 1,677 17/94 bm
- Men: 502, 84 per cent (of full complement)
- Captain Henry Harvey
- 2/7 (killed/wounded)
- Brother of John Harvey, Captain of the *Brunswick*. Like his brother, John, Henry also had his son, Thomas, aboard, who was only seven. Thomas went on to become a rear-admiral.

***Alfred* (74)**

- Chatham. Launched 22.10. 1778. 169ft 0in x 47ft 2in x 20ft 0in
- 1,638 37/94 bm
- Men: 504, 84 per cent (of full complement)
- Captain John Bazely
- 0/8 (killed/wounded)

***Montagu* (74)**

- Chatham. Launched 28.8.1779. 169ft 0in x 47ft 1in x 19ft 11½in
- 1,631 16/94 bm
- Men: 508, 85 per cent (of full complement)
- Captain James Montagu
- 4/13 (killed/wounded)
- Montagu, having requested command because of the ship's name, was killed in the battle. One of her midshipmen was Frederick Irby, who went on to become an officer of note in the Napoleonic wars and eventually a rear-admiral.

***Majestic* (74)**

- William Barnard, Deptford. Launched 11.2.1785. 170ft 6in x 46ft 9½in x 20ft 6in
- 1,642 8/94 bm
- Men: 500, 83 per cent (of full complement)
- Captain Charles Cotton
- 3/18 (killed/wounded)
- Her doctor was Leonard Gillespie, who went on to be Nelson's doctor on HMS *Victory* at Trafalgar, the man who tended him as he died. *Majestic* herself was 'cut-down' to a frigate in 1813 as a reaction to the large American frigates and was part of squadron which captured the American frigate USS *President* in 1815.

***Thunderer*** **(74)**

- John & William Wells, Deptford. Launched 13.11.1782. 170ft 8in x 47ft 7in x 19ft 11in
- 1,679 1/94 bm
- Men: 487, 81 per cent (of full complement)
- Captain Albemarle Bertie
- 0/0 (killed/wounded)
- Bertie, whilst commander-in-chief at the Cape of Good Hope, participated in the capture of the Île de France (Mauritius) in 1810.

## Fifth rates

***Phaeton*** **(38)**

- John Smallshaw, Liverpool. Launched 12.6.1782. 141ft 0in x 39ft ½in x 13ft 10¼in
- 944 ?/94 bm
- Men: 253, 87 per cent (of full complement)
- Captain William Bentinck
- 3/4 (killed/wounded)
- Francis Beaufort, hydrographer and future inventor of the Beaufort Scale, was aboard as a twenty-year-old midshipman.

***Latona*** **(38)**

- Edward Greaves & Mr Purnell, Limehouse. Launched 13.3.1781. 141ft 3in x 38ft 11¾in x 13ft 6in
- 944 20/94bm
- Men: 256, 88 per cent (of full complement)
- Captain Edward Thornborough
- 0/0 (killed/wounded)

***Niger*** **(32)**

- Sheerness. Launched 25.9.1759. 125ft 0in x 35ft 2in x 12ft 0in
- 679 67/94 bm
- Men: 185, 84 per cent (of full complement)
- Captain Arthur Legge
- 0/0 (killed/wounded)
- One of her lieutenants was James Walker, future rear-admiral. He com-

manded the *Monmouth* at the Battle of Camperdown (1797) and the *Isis* at the Battle of Copenhagen (1801).

***Southampton* (32)**

- Robert Inwood, Rotherhithe. Launched 5.5.1757. 124ft 4in x 35ft 0in x 12ft 1in
- 671 64/94 bm
- Men: 184, 84 per cent (of full complement)
- Captain Robert Forbes
- 0/0 (killed/wounded)
- One of her midshipmen was Frederick Maitland, who was the naval captain of the *Bellerophon* who negotiated Bonaparte's surrender and took him from France to England in July 1815.

***Venus* (32)**

- John Okill, Liverpool. Launched 11.3.1758. 128ft 4½in x 35ft 9in x 12ft 4in
- 722 29/94 bm
- Men: 171, 78 per cent (of full complement)
- Captain William Brown
- 0/0 (killed/wounded)

***Aquilon* (32)**

- Young and Woolcombe, Rotherhithe. Launched 23.11.1786. 129ft 2in x 35ft 8in x 12ft 7½in
- 724 bm
- Men: 171, 78 per cent (of full complement)
- Captain Robert Stopford
- 0/0 (killed/wounded)
- One of her lieutenants was Sir James Hillyar, who went on to become a rear-admiral.

**<u>Sixth rates</u>**

***Pegasus* (28)**

- Deptford. Launched 1.6.1779. 120ft 6in x 33ft 6in x 11ft 0in
- 593 89/94 bm
- Men: 182, 91 per cent (of full complement)

- 0/0 (killed/wounded)
- Captain Robert Barlow
- The artist Nicholas Pocock was aboard

## BRITISH POWDER EXPENDITURE

This list[2] is not complete as it does not include figures for the *Marlborough*, *Tremendous*, *Montagu* or *Brunswick* because the list was compiled in Plymouth when those ships were either in Portsmouth or at sea.

These figures are important because they are exceptionally high for a contemporary naval action. The highest figures here, the *Royal George* with over 309 barrels, the *Queen* with 296 and the *Valiant* with 225 far exceed expectations. Nelson's *Victory* at Trafalgar, for example, used up only 160 barrels.[3] The *Bellerophon* at Trafalgar used up 61, an average figure for a 74-gunner at that battle, but at the Glorious First of June her return was 136. The amount of powder used per charge had certainly dropped by the time that Trafalgar was fought in 1805, but not enough to significantly alter these figures. The increased powder usage reflects the fact that the Glorious First of June was one of the longest actions of the century, with several ships heavily engaged on three separate days.

| Ships | Whole barrels | Half barrels | Pounds | Total |
|---|---|---|---|---|
| *Queen Charlotte* | 120 | | | |
| *Royal Sovereign* | 154 | | | |
| *Royal George* | 309 | 2 | | |
| *Barfleur* | 100 | 2 | 41 | |
| *Impregnable* | 80 | 1 | | |
| *Queen* | 296 | | | |
| *Bellerophon* | 136 | | | |
| *Caesar* | 134 | | | |
| *Leviathan* | 160 | | | |
| *Russell* | 154 | | | |
| *Audacious* | 32 | | | |
| *Defence* | | | | 3 tons 16 cwt 1 [illeg] |
| *Culloden* | 92 | | 85 | |

| Ships | Whole barrels | Half barrels | Pounds | Total |
|---|---|---|---|---|
| *Invincible* | 134 | | 73 | |
| *Gibraltar* | 74 | | | |
| *Valiant* | 225 | | | |
| *Orion* | 135 | | | |
| *Ramillies* | | | | 10,000lb |
| *Alfred* | 88 | | 24 | |
| *Majestic* | 122 | | 57 | |
| *Glory* | | | | 7,653lb |
| *Thunderer* | 83 | | | |
| *Phaeton* | | | | 2,220 lb |
| *Venus* | | | | 112 lb |
| *Pegasus* | | | | 8lb |

# THE FRENCH FLEET

**Obusiers.** Following the introduction of the carronade into the Royal Navy during the American War of Independence the French responded by fitting obusiers onto some of their warships. These were not carronades in the British style but howitzers and, unlike the British iron carronade, the French obusier was made of brass.

**Perriers.** A perrier was a small 1pdr cannon used as a swivel gun on French warships. These were also usually made of brass.

**Gun Weight.** A French pound was heavier than a British pound. A French 36pdr cannon would have been equivalent to approximately 39.3 pounds in British weight.

**Names.** Following the Revolution those French warships with names linked to the monarchy were renamed. The previous name of renamed ships is listed.

*Captured by the British during the battle
**Sank following the battle

The ships have been listed according to their size: this is not the order in which they went into battle.

The data for each ship is listed in the following order:

- **Place built**. Launch date. Dimensions
- **Previous name** (if any)
- **Tonnage** (not displacement)
- **Designer**
- **Full complement**: note that we do not have figures for the actual number of men each ship carried as we do for the British ships
- **Armament**

## Three-decked ships

***Montagne* (118)**

- Brest. Launched 8.11.1790. 196ft 6in x 51ft x 25ft
- *États de Bourgogne; Côte d'Or*
- 2,794 tons
- Jacques-Noël Sané
- 1,120 men
- 32 x 36pdr, 34 x 24pdr, 34 x 12pdr, 18 x 8pdr, 4 x 36pdr obusiers

***Terrible* (110)**

- Toulon. Launched 27.1.1780. 186ft 8in x 50ft x 35ft
- 2,500 tons
- Joseph-Marie-Blaise Coulomb
- 1,055–1,151 men
- 30 x 36pdr, 32 x 24pdr, 32 x 12pdr, 16 x 8pdr

***Républicaine* (110)**

- Brest. Launched 20.3.1780. 186ft x 50ft x 24ft 6in
- *Royal Louis*
- 2,500 tons
- Pierre-Alexandre Forfait (from the plans of Léon-Michel Guignace)
- 1,055–1,151 men
- 30 x 36pdr, 32 x 24pdr, 32 x 12pdr, 12 x 8pdr, 4 x 36pdr obusiers

## 80-gun ships

***Scipion***

- Brest. Launched 12.10.1795. 184ft 4in x 48ft 6in x 23ft 2in
- *Saint Esprit*
- 2,050 tons
- Joseph-Louis Ollivier
- 864–867 men
- 30 x 36pdr, 32 x 24pdr, 18 x 8pdr, 6 x perriers

***Jacobin***

- Brest. Launched 18.9.1778. 188ft x 48ft 6in x 23ft 2in

- *Auguste*
- 2,100 tons
- Joseph-Marie-Blaise Coulomb
- 851–856 men
- 30 x 36pdr, 32 x 24pdr, 18 x 10pdr, 6 x 36pdr obusiers

***Juste****

- Brest. Launched 13/17.9.1784. 184ft x 46ft 6in x 23ft
- *Deux Frères*
- 1,900 tons
- Pierre-Augustin La Mothe (from the plans of Antoine Groignard)
- 852–856 men
- 30 x 36pdr, 32 x 24pdr, 18 x 8pdr, 4 x 36pdr obusiers

***Sans Pareil****

- Brest. Launched 8.6.1793. 182ft 6in x 47ft x 23ft 6in
- 2,000 tons
- Jacques-Noël Sané
- 856 men
- 30 x 36pdr, 32 x 24pdr, 18 x 12pdr, 4 x 36pdr obusiers, 6 x perriers

**74-gun ships**

***Vengeur du Peuple*****

- Toulon. Launched 16.7.1766. 168ft x 43ft 6in x 21ft
- *Marseillais*
- 1,550 tons
- Joseph Chapelle
- 718–732 men
- 28 x 36pdr, 30 x 18pdr, 16 x 8pdr, 4 x 36pdr obusiers

***Neptune***

- Brest. Launched 20.8.1778. 168ft 6in x 44ft x 22ft
- 1,500 tons
- Pierre-Augustin La Mothe
- 662–751 men
- 28 x 36pdr, 30 x 18pdr, 20 x 8pdr, 4 x 36pdr obusiers, 6 x perriers

***Achille****
- Brest. Launched 5.10.1778. 168ft x 44ft x 21ft 6in
- *Annibal*
- 1,478 tons
- Jacques-Noël Sané
- 701–751 men
- 28 x 36pdr, 30 x 18pdr, 16 x 8pdr, 4 x 36pdr obusiers, 6 x perriers

***Northumberland****
- Brest. Launched 3.5.1780. 168ft x 44ft x 21ft 6in
- 1,478 tons
- Jacques-Noël Sané
- 701–751 men
- 28 x 36pdr, 30 x 18pdr, 16 x 8pdr, 4 x 36pdr obusiers, 6 x perriers

***Convention***
- Brest. Launched 9.9.1780. 166ft 6in x 44ft 3in x 21ft 6in
- *Sceptre*
- 1,585 tons
- Pierre-Augustin La Mothe
- 700–751 men
- 28 x 36pdr, 30 x 18pdr, 20 x 8pdr, 4 x 36pdr obusiers, 6 x perriers

***Pelletier***
- Toulon. Launched 5.7.1783. 173ft 3in x 43ft 8in x 22ft
- *Séduisant*
- 1,550 tons
- Joseph-Marie-Blaise Coulomb
- 707 men
- 28 x 36pdr, 30 x 18pdr, 16 x 8pdr

***Téméraire***
- Brest. Launched 17.12.1782. 172ft x 44ft 6in x 22ft
- 1,537 tons
- Jacques-Noël Sané
- 703–723 men
- 28 x 36pdr, 30 x 18pdr, 16 x 8pdr, 4 x 36pdr obusiers, 6 x perriers

***Patriote***

- Brest. Launched 3.10.1785. 172ft x 44ft 6in x 22ft
- 1,537 tons
- Jacques-Noël Sané
- 703–723 men
- 28 x 36pdr, 2 x 24pdr, 28 x 18pdr, 16 x 8pdr, 4 x 36pdr obusiers, 6 x perriers

***Mucius***

- Rochefort. Launched 18.4.1787. 172ft x 44ft 6in x 22ft
- *Orion; Mucius Scaevola*
- 1,537 tons
- Pierre Train and Joseph Niou (on the plans of Jacques-Noël Sané)
- 703–723 men
- 28 x 36pdr, 30 x 18pdr, 16 x 8pdr, 4 x 36pdr mortars

***Jemmapes***

- Rochefort. Launched 16.1.1794. 172ft x 44ft 6in x 22ft
- 1,537 tons
- Jacques-Denis Chevillard (on the plans of Jacques-Noël Sané)
- 707 men
- 28 x 36pdr, 30 x 18pdr, 16 x 8pdr

***Tyrannicide***

- Lorient. Launched 28.6.1793. 172ft x 44ft 6in x 22ft
- 1,537 tons
- Charles Segondat-Duvernet (on the plans of Jacques-Noël Sané)
- 720 men
- 28 x 36pdr, 30 x 18pdr, 16 x 8pdr, 4 x 36pdr obusiers

***Trente-et-un Mai***

- Rochefort. Launched 13.8.1791. 172ft x 44ft 6in x 22ft
- *Pyrrhus; Mont Blanc*
- 1,537 tons
- On the plans of Jacques-Noël Sané
- 703–723 men
- 28 x 36pdr, 30 x 18pdr, 16 x 8pdr

***Trajan***

- Lorient. Launched 24.1.1792. 172ft x 44ft 6in x 22ft
- 1,537 tons
- Charles Segondat-Duvernet (on the plans of Jacques-Noël Sané)
- 703–723 men
- 28 x 36pdr, 30 x 18pdr, 16 x 8pdr, 4 x 36pdr obusiers

***Éole***

- Lorient. Launched 15.11.1789. 172ft x 44ft 6in x 22ft
- 1,537 tons
- Charles Segondat-Duvernet (on the plans of Jacques-Noël Sané)
- 703–723 men
- 28 x 36pdr, 30 x 18pdr, 16 x 8pdr, 6 x perriers

***Entreprenant***

- Lorient. Launched 11.10.1787. 172ft x 44ft 6in x 22ft
- 1,537 tons
- Charles Segondat-Duvernet (on the plans of Jacques-Noël Sané)
- 703–723 men
- 28 x 36pdr, 30 x 18pdr, 16 x 8pdr, 4 x 36pdr obusiers, 6 x perriers

***Impétueux****

- Rochefort. Launched 25.10.1787. 172ft x 44ft 6in x 22ft
- 1,537 tons
- Henri Chevillard (on the plans of Jacques-Noël Sané)
- 703–723 men
- 28 x 36pdr, 30 x 18pdr, 16 x 8pdr, 4 x 36pdr obusiers

***Apollon***

- Rochefort. Launched 21.5.1788. 172ft x 44ft 6in x 22ft
- *Gasparin*
- 1,537 tons
- Joseph Niou (on the plans of Jacques-Noël Sané)
- 703–723 men
- 28 x 36pdr, 30 x 18pdr, 16 x 8pdr

***América****

- Brest. Launched 21.5.1794. 172ft x 44ft 6in x 22ft
- 1,537 tons
- Jacques-Noël Sané
- 703–723 men
- 28 x 36pdr, 30 x 18pdr, 16 x 8pdr, 4 x 36pdr obusiers, 6 x perriers

***Tourville***

- Lorient. Launched 16.12.1788. 172ft x 44ft 6in x 22ft
- 1,537½ tons
- Charles Segondat-Duvernet (on the plans of Jacques-Noël Sané)
- 703–723 men
- 28 x 36pdr, 30 x 18pdr, 16 x 8pdr, 4 x 36pdr obusiers

## APPENDIX III

# The Pocock Sketches

The experienced seaman Nicholas Pocock was the first specialist maritime artist to witness a naval battle since Willem Van der Velde the Elder, who was present at the Battle of Scheveningen on 31 July 1653. Van der Velde's subsequent depiction of that battle is a unique representation of seventeenth-century naval war (see fig. 9). A little under 141 years later Pocock was aboard the repeating frigate *Pegasus* at the Glorious First of June. He sketched frantically throughout the battle and several of his sketchbooks survive at the National Maritime Museum in Greenwich. They are crammed with sketches of some of the most significant events of the battle and offer a unique insight into naval warfare in the Age of Sail. This appendix showcases some of the most significant of Pocock's sketches.

## 26. Battle View 1: *The Engagement of 28 May*

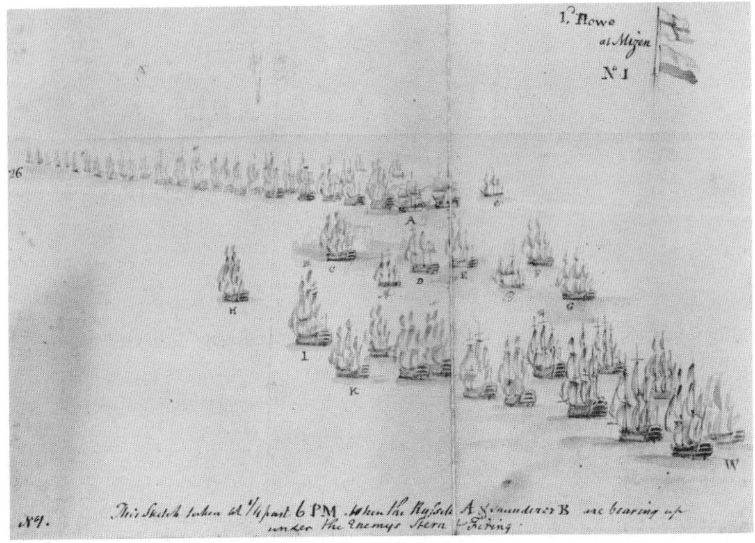


This bird's-eye view, soon a characteristic of Pocock's battle paintings, shows the two fleets on the evening of 28 May. The French fleet has formed into line and is now leading the British away from the arrival point of Vanstabel's convoy. The British chase with energy, the *Russell*, *Thunderer* and *Bellerophon* attacking the rearmost ship of the French fleet, the giant *Révolutionnaire*. The rest of the British fleet failed to catch up before nightfall and the French fleet continued its course, unwilling to come to the aid of the *Révolutionnaire* or perhaps even ignorant of her plight.

Pocock's notes say:

This sketch was taken at ¼ past 6 PM. When *Russell* A & *Thunderer* B are bearing up under the Enemy's Stern & Firing. A. *Russell* firing on the Enemy's rear ship; B. *Thunderer*, firing but farther astern; C. *Bellerophon*, firing on the Enemy's Quarter; D. *Marlborough* having fired and dropped into the Rear; E. *Leviathan* coming up under Crowded Sail; H. The *Caesar* gaining ahead of the *Queen Charlotte*; I. *Queen Charlotte*; K. The Remainder of our fleet in chase, and without any prescribed order; A. *Pegasus*; *B. Niger*; *C. Latona*; No 1. The Sternmost Ship of the Enemy's line a 3 deck; 26. Their van Ship.

## 27. Battle View 2: *The Engagement of 29 May*

The French fleet stretches out at the top of this image and the British tack at the far left to bring themselves upwind to attack the French van at the far right. Shortly after the moment depicted, Howe ordered his fleet several times to tack, and all of the signals were ignored. Howe then led the British attack by tacking the *Queen Charlotte* (K) and heading toward the French rear, followed by his seconds, the *Leviathan* (I) and the *Bellerophon* (L).

Pocock's notes say:

This sketch taken at ½ past 11 when Ld. Howe made the Signal to Tack in succession from the Van. A. *Caesar* not being able to comply with the Signal to Tack; B. *Queen*; C. *Russell*; D. *Valiant*; E. *Royal George*; F. *Invincible*; G. *Orion*; H. *Majestic*; I. *Leviathan*; K. *Queen Charlotte*; L. *Bellerophon*; M. *Marlborough*; N. *Royal Sovereign*; O. *Ramillies*; P. *Tremendous*; Q. *Montagu*; R. *Alfred*; S. *Brunswick*; T. *Culloden*; U. *Gibraltar*; V. *Barfleur*; W. *Glory*; X. *Impregnable*; Y. *Thunderer*; Z. *Defence*.

## 28. Battle View 3: *The Battle of 1 June*

The sketch is from the perspective of the British line, looking toward the French at the moment that Howe breaks through under the stern of the French flagship. The ships in the immediate foreground are the fleet's message carriers. One can just make out the stern of the *Brunswick* (M) just after she has collided with the *Vengeur* and is about to drive her out of the line. This sketch is slightly confusing because there are two groups of letters A–G and the leading ships of the British fleet are actually shown above the main action at top right.

Pocock's notes say:

This Sketch is at ½ past 10 when the *Queen Charlotte* (K) is hawling up under the *Montagne*'s Stern. Her foretopmast going over the Side. The *Marlbro* [*sic*] G foul of 2 F{rench} ships – A. *Caesar* Van Ship of Our fleet Engaging their Van; B. *Bellerophon*; C. *Leviathan*; D. *Royal Sovereign* driving & chasing a 3 decker out of the line; E. *Barfleur*, F. *Impregnable*; G. *Marlborough*; H. *Defence*; I. *Invincible*; J. *Tremendous* M. *Brunswick* Stays and Rigging cut to pieces; K. *Queen Charlotte* luffing up under *Montagne*'s Stern; L. *Gibraltar*, M. *Brunswick* on board a French ship (*Vengeur*); N. *Queen*; O. *Orion*; P. *Royal George*; Q. *Montagu*; R. *Glory*; S. *Thunderer*, A. *Latona*; B. *Niger*; C. *Comet*; D. *Southampton*; E. *Pegasus*; F. *Charon*; G. *Aquilon*.

## 29. Battle View 4: *The End of the Battle*

A sketch that powerfully suggests the scale of the battle-ground. There are as many shattered British ships as there are French. Some of Pocock's notes appear to be missing as there is no key to some of the numbers. Generally speaking, the British fleet are to the left of the picture and the French are to the right. Notice the *Brunswick* at top right, isolated from the rest of the British fleet. She is under full sail attempting to escape. Notice how the frigates (A, B, C) are now in the thick of things trying to extract certain disabled ships such as the *Queen* (W) and *Marlborough* (U).

Pocock's notes say:

A. *Bellerophon.* Fore & Main Topmast gone & much damaged; C. *Royal Sovereign.* No Masts or yards gone in this Action but not much shattered; D. *Russell.* Foretopmast and Gib boom gone; E. *Caesar*, not materially damaged to Outward View but Several shot through her sails; F. *Barfleur.* Masts Rigging & Sails Much Cut; G. *Impregnable.* Ditto; H. *Defence* – Totally dismasted; J. *Invincible*, not much damaged in this Action; K. *Orion* Main Topmast & Main Yard Gone; L. *Queen Charlotte* Fore & Main topmasts gone Yards much wounded hanging up and down. Signal to Wear; M.

*Thunderer* Sails and rigging Cut but not very Materially; N. *Gibraltar*. Ditto; O. *Alfred* – ditto. P. *Ramillies* ditto; Q. *Glory* – Foretopmast gone. Otherwise not much disabled; R. *Montagu.* Sails & Rigging much damaged; S. *Royal George* Foremast Main topmast gone, Much disabled; T. *Culloden* much disabled in Sails & Rigging; U. *Marlborough*, totally dismasted; V. *Brunswick* Mizen [*sic*] Mast gone & running before the Wind to get Clear of the French Fleet; W. *Queen* Main Mast Mizen topmast & fore yard gone Firing on Enemy in Passing; X. *Leviathan*, Foremast & Foreyard much wounded Sails & Rigging much damaged; A. *Pegasus* being ordered to take the *Queen* in Tow; B. *Niger*, C. *Aquilon*, taking the *Marlborough* in Tow.

# 30. Battle Plan 1 June

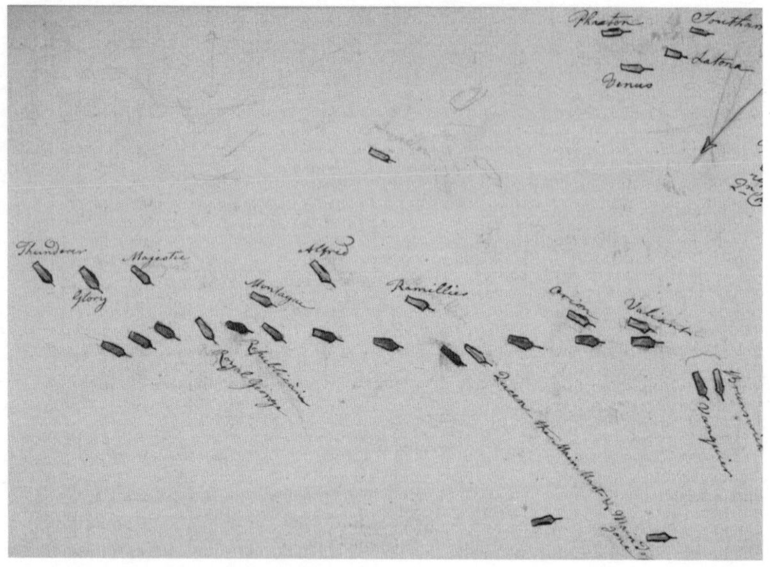


This plan shows the battle on 1 June shortly after Howe has broken the line when the two flagships, *Queen Charlotte* and *Montagne*, were locked in battle. The French *Jacobin* is also engaging the *Queen Charlotte* to leeward. They are all shown on the far right. Shortly after this, the massive *Montagne* broke free of the crippled *Queen Charlotte* and began to cause havoc in the British line ahead of Howe. The *Brunswick* and *Vengeur* are shown just to leeward of this group. At this stage they were locked together and their combined momentum now drove them clear of the main battle where they would continue their intense combat. Note the fine sketched 'bracket' to the stern of these two ships – this is the exact viewpoint Pocock assumed for both his sketch (see below) of the *Brunswick*/*Vengeur* action and the subsequent oil painting (see fig. 17). To the top right is a group of British frigates, Pocock's own *Pegasus* clearly visible. They are handily located to view and then repeat Howe's signals made on the *Queen Charlotte*.

## 31. HMS *Invincible* raking *La Juste*

This shows the British *Invincible* raking the bows of *La Juste*. The gunsmoke from the British ship sweeps toward the Frenchman and is then blown along and up by the powerful wind. The British ensign stands stiff in that breeze and the topsails shiver. It is a picture full of motion that depicts the power and impact of the elements as much as it depicts the power of the warships themselves. It is also a fine depiction of the dense fog of gunsmoke that enveloped the fleets; the smoke which made fleet warfare so disorientating and friendly fire such a distinct possibility. Hulls and masts of other ships, not distant but still anonymous, loom out of the fog. This image is particularly valuable because the log of the *Invincible* makes no reference to the combat, just that, at 4 p.m., she hove to and 'took possession of the *Juste*'.

## 32. HMS *Brunswick* and *Le Vengeur du Peuple*

Another sketch of a single-ship action in the midst of fleet battle. This shows Pocock's first impression of the *Brunswick*/*Vengeur* action that he later chose as the subject for one of his oils, a painting which became recognised as one of his finest achievements (see fig. 17). As with the image of the *Invincible* and *La Juste*, this sketch emphasises the poor visibility intrinsic to the battle and the stiff breeze that helped bring down so many damaged masts. The smoke is particularly bad at this stage because, according to the *Brunswick*'s log, she was on fire in four places. The *Brunswick*'s mizzen mast went by the board moments afterwards and the two ships drifted apart. Notice the convincing angle of the ships' hulls as they struggle in the rolling swell and the mass of wreckage encumbering the lee side of the *Vengeur*. If this was not cut away it would act as an anchor, slowing the ship down, and forcing her to heel toward the damage.

## 33. Frigate towing HMS *Defence*

The stern of James Gambier's *Defence* is shown here in a sketch that gives a markedly different impression of the battle. In this image the claustrophobic battle-ground is replaced by a barren sea-wilderness with the foreground occupied by the helpless, dismasted *Defence.* She is being towed by an unidentified frigate that appears to be steering out of the way of another, unidentified, ship which is descending on both the frigate and the *Defence.* The large three-decker with the damaged rig to the right is probably Howe's *Queen Charlotte.* The random disposition and direction of the ships is entirely convincing.

## 34. HMS *Queen* and HMS *Queen Charlotte*

Another sketch emphasising the wilderness of a battle-ground shortly after the fighting has stopped. What is important here is the vast size of the area that Pocock is depicting yet it is, still, only a fraction of the actual area of battle. The dismasted ship at the front right may well be another view of the *Defence*, with the *Queen Charlotte* just to the right and just above where Pocock has written her name. To the right again, and noted by Pocock, is the shattered *Queen*. Observe the floating wreckage in the very foreground. This powerful sketch gives a strong impression of the difficulty of regrouping and the dangers of collision after such an event.

## 35. *The French Admiral … No. 1*

One of two related sketches that concentrate on individual actions in the midst of the main battle. This shows the *Royal Sovereign* to the left engaging a French three-decker, either the *Terrible* or the *Républicain*. We know it is not Villaret's *Montagne* because the ship here is shown flying the early flag of the Republic – white with the tricolour in the top right-hand corner – when we know that the *Montagne* flew the Republic's new flag – the full tricolour. The sketch shows the exact moment that the Frenchman's main and mizzen masts went by the board. The mizzen mast has broken midway up the lower mast. It is unclear exactly how this relates to the next Pocock sketch but this has been marked by Pocock as No.1. Note the subtle but significant difference in size between these two great three-decked ships shown so close together. The hull of the French ship to leeward is significantly higher.

## 36. *French Ships to Windward … No. 2*

Sketch No. 2 is another focused on a specific engagement, this time as the *Marlborough* engaged two French ships. As Pocock notes, shortly after the *Marlborough*'s attack the main mast of the French ship (in the centre) fell on board her countryman to leeward; the mizzen mast of that leeward ship also seems to be falling toward the ship in the centre. The *Marlborough* has hauled up her foresail and backed her fore topmast to stay abreast of the Frenchmen. She is well positioned to rake both French ships across the bows. In fact her gunnery was so effective that she prevented the French ship (centre) from boarding her and then forced her to collide with the other Frenchman to leeward. The *Marlborough*'s luck ran out, however, and soon after this she was attacked by the British *Culloden* and *Gibraltar* and then raked by a huge French three-decker. She ended the battle with her captain severely injured along with 102 other members of her crew; twenty-seven of the *Marlborough*'s sailors died. Note the flags of the early Republic being flown by the French ships – white with the tricolour only in the top left-hand corner. The French ships are painted red, distinctly different from the *Marlborough*, which Pocock has painted in the dull-yellow that was typical of the *Royal Navy*.

## 37. The captured *América* and *La Juste*

These sketches are slightly confusing because they have been begun in pencil and then partially completed in ink. They were made on the fleet's return to Portsmouth and, as with so many of Pocock's sketches, were used as inspiration for a more detailed work that the artist would paint at a later date. The hull of the *América* is badly scarred, and that of *La Juste* is missing huge chunks of superstructure. Both ships went on to have lengthy careers in the Royal Navy but the *América*, apparently the least damaged of the two here, cost a fortune to repair – £42,030 – about the same price as a brand-new British-built Third Rate.

## 38. Lord Howe to windward …

Another picture by Pocock that was probably drawn when the fleet returned to Portsmouth. It has a much more finished look than the hastily sketched images made at the scene of the battle. Here, we see Lord Howe to windward of the French line and this is probably that period in the battle of 29 May when Howe successfully forced his way through the French line from to leeward. Note the quality of the French line. We know from other sources that it was particularly well formed on this day and, together, this must all be used as evidence of the surprising quality of French fleet seamanship. Shortly after the moment depicted here the leading French ships disappearing across the horizon tacked and then bore down in good order to force Howe and the ships that had followed him through the line to back off.

# APPENDIX IV

# The Biographies

I have included here some basic facts relating to the lives of the key naval and political players mentioned in this book.

## The British

**SIR BENJAMIN CALDWELL (1739–1820)**
Born in Liverpool on 31 January 1739 to Charles Caldwell and Elizabeth Heywood. He entered the navy on the *Isis* in 1756, and three years later he transferred to the *Namur*. Caldwell commanded several ships during the American War before transferring to the *Agamemnon* in 1781 as part of the Channel Fleet. Caldwell played a significant role in the Battle of the Saints and remained on the North America and West Indies station until the peace. He was MP for Knocktopher 1776–83 and Harristown 1783–90. Caldwell was promoted rear-admiral of the white in 1793 and of the red a year later. He served in Lord Howe's fleet, in the *Cumberland* and the *Impregnable*, where he experienced the Glorious First of June. Caldwell was among the officers not mentioned in Lord Howe's report and had his gold medal withheld. That year Caldwell was promoted vice-admiral of the blue and also married Charlotte Osborn, who bore his son, Charles. In 1795 Caldwell was sent to the Leeward Islands, where he was appointed commander-in-chief. Although entitled to the command, Caldwell was supplanted the following June, and believed it to be a continuation of the same slight that had cost him his medal. Caldwell returned to England, accepting no new appointments. He was omitted from the honours conferred after the war and his efforts only acknowledged following the death of George III. Caldwell died in November 1820.

## CUTHBERT COLLINGWOOD (1748–1810)

Born in September 1748 in Newcastle upon Tyne to an impoverished family. He joined the frigate *Shannon* in 1761 and, after a long apprenticeship, Collingwood was promoted lieutenant in June 1775. In 1780 he was made post captain and was sent to Nicaragua. In 1783 he sailed for the West Indies, where he spent two years policing illegal trade. Collingwood returned home in 1786 and in 1791 he married Sarah Blackett, with whom he had two daughters. He was overlooked for a medal for his conduct as captain of the *Barfleur* on 1 June 1794. Collingwood distinguished himself aboard the *Excellent* in his 1797 defeat of a much larger Spanish fleet off Cape St Vincent. He refused his gold medal in protest after he came away empty-handed from 1 June, but received both medals in due course. In 1799 he was promoted rear-admiral of the white, and of the red in 1801. In April 1804 Collingwood was advanced to vice-admiral of the blue and in October he moved his flag to the *Royal Sovereign,* in which he took the flagship *Santa Ana* at Trafalgar. With Nelson dead, Collingwood assumed command of the damaged yet victorious British fleet, humanely sending wounded Spanish prisoners ashore. In 1805 Collingwood was promoted vice-admiral of the red and was created Baron Collingwood of Caldburne and Hethpoole. As Napoleon's focus shifted east, Collingwood took command in the Mediterranean, where he originated many important naval policies. The ailing Collingwood finally turned over his command in March 1809 and died en route to England.

## HENRY DUNDAS, FIRST VISCOUNT MELVILLE (1742–1811)

Born on 28 April 1742 in Edinburghshire, to Lord Arniston and Ann Gordon. He took the degree of doctor of laws in 1789. In August 1765 Dundas married Elizabeth Rannie, with whom he had four children. He squandered her fortune on bad investments and they divorced in 1778. He remarried in 1793. In 1766 he became solicitor-general for Scotland, and soon set his sights on Parliament. In 1775 he became lord advocate, and in 1782 he was appointed treasurer of the navy. In 1790 he became MP for Edinburgh. Dundas' close friendship with Pitt the Younger proved key to his career. In 1791 he was appointed home secretary, remaining in the cabinet until 1801. Dundas took a keen interest in the colonies and, as president of the new Board of Control, transformed the chaotic Indian government into an imperial administration. In July 1794 Dundas became secretary of state for war. He strove to expel Napoleon's forces from Egypt, but despite victory in 1801, the government soon fell and Dundas gave up all his offices, except keeper of the great seal of Scotland. In 1801 he was raised to the peerage as Viscount Melville and Baron Dunira. Under Pitt again, Melville was made first lord of the Admiralty in 1804. Melville became the focus of an inquiry after failing to adhere to his own financial regulations and the Commons voted for his impeachment. He was acquitted of nearly all charges but the expensive trial was ruinous. Melville died on 27 May 1811.

## SIR WILLIAM HENRY DILLON (1780–1857)

Born 8 August 1780 in Birmingham, illegitimate son of John and Elizabeth Talbot Dillon. Dillon joined the navy in 1790 as a midshipman on the *Defence*. He was stunned by a splinter during the action of 1 June 1794, and served on the *Glenmore* during the 1798 rebellion at Wexford. Detained by the Dutch following the breach of a truce in 1803, the captive Dillon became a commander and on his release in 1807 took command of the *Childers*. In 1808, the worn-out *Childers* successfully drove off a Danish brig on the Norwegian coast. Dillon was gravely injured in the action which pitted his crew of sixty-five men and fourteen guns against one hundred and sixty Danes and twenty guns. His bravery was recognised with a sword presented by the Patriotic Fund at Lloyd's. He was later made naval equerry to the Duke of Sussex and, following his knighthood in 1835, obtained flag rank in 1846. He became vice-admiral of the blue in March 1853, and of the red four years later. Dillon was a skilled linguist and a Tory. He married three times, but fathered no children. Dillon died on 9 September 1857 in Monaco, leaving an account of his professional career, later published by the Navy Record Society.

## ALAN GARDNER (1742–1808/9)

Born 12 April 1742 in Staffordshire to Lieutenant-Colonel William and Elizabeth Gardner. He joined the *Medway* in 1755 and ascended swiftly through the ranks, commanding the flagship *Preston* on its 1766 voyage to Jamaica. There he married Susannah Hyde, fathering seven sons and one daughter. Gardner spent three years as commander-in-chief in Jamaica and on his return to England held a seat on the Admiralty board until 1795. Gardner became MP for Plymouth in 1790 and transferred to Westminster in 1796. In 1793 he achieved flag-rank and went to the West Indies on the *Queen,* where he achieved little, despite commanding a considerable squadron. The *Queen* suffered heavy losses in the Glorious First of June, after which Gardner was created a baronet, advancing to vice-admiral in July 1794 and admiral of the blue in 1799. During the 1797 Spithead mutiny Gardner was second-in-command of the Channel Fleet, but was then overlooked for command by Lord Spencer, who believed that Gardner did not want the role. Gardner was grievously offended but was pacified with an appointment to command the Irish station. Gardner was created Baron Gardner in the Irish peerage in 1800, and in 1806 he became Baron Gardner of Uttoxeter. In 1807 Gardner was eventually appointed commander of the Channel Fleet, but poor health forced his resignation and he died soon after.

### THOMAS GRAVES, FIRST BARON GRAVES (1725–1802)

Born on 23 October 1725 in Cornwall to Rear-Admiral Thomas Graves and Elizabeth Budgell. He joined the *Norfolk* in 1741 and advanced to lieutenant two years later and captain in 1755. He took temporary command of the *Oxford* in 1760 and in May 1761 became governor of Newfoundland. In 1771 he married Elizabeth Peere-Williams, with whom he had four children. He assumed command of the North American station in July 1781 towards the end of the War of American Independence, and with Samuel Hood he launched a largely unsuccessful campaign against the formidable French fleet in the Chesapeake. In October Graves led a relief expedition to reinforce Lord Cornwallis in Yorktown, but on arrival discovered that Cornwallis had already surrendered. Graves turned over his command in November and returned to England to rebut widespread criticism for failure in North America, exacerbated by Hood's condemnation of his conduct. Graves became an unlucky scapegoat, but in reality he had been the victim of poor decisions and poor preparation. Graves continued to further employment and in 1787 became vice-admiral of the blue. In 1793 he was appointed second in command of Lord Howe's Channel Fleet and in April 1794 he was promoted admiral of the blue. He was honoured with an Irish peerage for his performance on 1 June 1794, but the resulting injury ended his active career. He died on 9 February 1802.

## ALEXANDER HOOD, FIRST VISCOUNT BRIDPORT (1726–1814)

The younger brother of Samuel Hood (see below). He joined the Navy in 1741 and was made a lieutenant by 1746, following an identical career path to his brother. He also fought in numerous actions of distinction, notably the Battle of Quiberon Bay of 1759 during the Seven Years' War. Unlike his brother, Alexander fought in home and European waters during the American War, notably at the Battle of Ushant in 1778 and the 1782 relief of Gibraltar. He remained under Howe's command during the early years of the French Revolutionary war, serving as Howe's third in command aboard the HMS *Royal George* that fought with distinction at 1 June. He was created Baron Bridport for that heroism. When Howe was finally too ill to continue in command of the Channel Fleet, Hood took over and imposed a very tight blockade of Brest and had to deal with the Spithead mutiny of 1797. He sided firmly with the mutineers, ever a seaman who understood their grievances. His last few years of active service, however, did his reputation little good as he became notoriously strict and awkward.

## SAMUEL HOOD, FIRST VISCOUNT HOOD (1724–1816)

Born in Somerset the son of a vicar, Hood joined the Navy in 1741 and became a lieutenant in 1746. His first experience of naval warfare was during the War of the Austrian Succession. He went on to fight with distinction during the Seven Years' War. By 1767 he was Commander-in-Chief of the North American Station. During the American War he fought under Rodney, who he had served with as a youngster in the 1740s. He fought at the Battle of the Chesapeake in 1782 with Thomas Graves and was in some measure responsible for failing to engage the French properly: his rear division stayed well out of range even when Graves wished to attack. Some clever seamanship and skilled command followed in the subsequent months and Hood fought the French once more at the Saints in 1782 with great success. In the subsequent peace he successfully ran for Parliament and became MP for Westminster. He was promoted to vice-admiral in 1787. When the Revolutionary war broke out he was sent to the Mediterranean where he stumbled into a civil war that ultimately led to the surrender of Toulon. With inadequate resources, however, Hood was unable to keep Toulon, which was retaken by Jacobin forces. In 1796 he was made Viscount Hood of Whitley with a pension of £2000 per year for life.

From the date until his death he was Governor of the Royal Naval Hospital at Greenwich and was a chief mourner at Nelson's funeral.

## EARL RICHARD HOWE (1726–1799)

Born in London on 19 March 1726 to Emanuel and Mary Scrope Howe. He joined the navy in 1735, and went on to serve aboard the *Severn* in failed attacks on Spanish colonies in the Pacific. He was promoted lieutenant in August 1744. In 1745 Howe took part in operations off Scotland against the Jacobites. He was made flag-captain in October 1748 and began to attract attention after firing the first shots of the Seven Years' War. In 1756 he led a small squadron in the Channel Islands and then distinguished himself in Hawke's 1757 expedition against Rochefort.

He held a seat as MP for Dartmouth from 1762 for twenty-five years and went to the upper house in April 1782. He married Mary Hartopp in February 1758 and in July succeeded to the viscountcy following the death of his brother George. He was appointed to the Admiralty Board in April 1763, where he remained for two years. The Rockingham administration made Howe treasurer of the navy and after a short period of resignation, he continued in the position until January 1770. In November Howe was appointed commander-in-chief in the Mediterranean over the heads of many older admirals.

He was made vice-admiral in December 1775 and was given command of the North American station, instructed to pursue the war aggressively. This was the most controversial appointment of his career. His younger brother William commanded the army in the colonies and Howe often gave priority to supporting the army over sustaining his own coastal blockade. A parliamentary investigation into his conduct in America was inconclusive. The Rockingham administration gave Howe command of the Channel Fleet in April 1782 and made him a full admiral and a British peer in the same month. In October 1782 he oversaw the relief of Gibraltar. Howe became first lord of the Admiralty in January 1783, but his tenure was hindered by poor relations with his colleagues and a total lack of interest in any non-naval matters.

In June 1790 Howe returned to active service and was appointed commander-in-chief of the Channel Fleet. He became vice-admiral in May 1792. Howe was once again given command of the Channel Fleet in February 1793. For his service 28 May – 1 June 1794 Howe was honoured with a diamond-hilted sword and received the Order of the Garter, but found himself unpopular among fellow officers after omitting a number of honourable mentions. In March 1796 he was appointed admiral of the fleet and general of marines. During the Spithead mutiny, at the request of the king, Howe visited every ship, explaining the Admiralty's position, and agreed to the dismissal of fifty-nine unpopular officers. Howe's initiatives led to improvement in the command and control of fleets, and the sophisticated signalling system used in the Napoleonic wars was based on Howe's 1790 model. He died at home in London on 5 August 1799.

## SIR GEORGE MONTAGU (1750–1829)

Born on 12 December 1750 to Admiral John and Sophia Montagu. Joined the Navy in 1763 and in 1771 Montagu was promoted lieutenant and captain in 1773. He served on the North American station during the first years of the War of Independence. In 1783 Montagu married his cousin Charlotte, with whom he had five children. He became rear-admiral in April 1794 and joined Howe's Channel Fleet with his flag in the *Hector.* Montagu was sent to intercept the French grain convoy and made several captures. He ventured out again in June, and on discovering Villaret's fleet failed to prevent it reaching Brest. He was heavily criticised for his conduct, not least by the King, and never served afloat again. He was promoted vice-admiral in June 1795. In January 1801 Montagu was made admiral, and commander-in-chief at Portsmouth in 1802, a post which he held for five and a half years and was much esteemed by the captains of the ships fitted out during his command. He was nominated for a GCB in 1815 but had no service after the peace. Montagu died on 24 December 1829.

## SIR WILLIAM PARKER, FIRST BARONET (1781–1866)

Born on 1 December 1781 in Staffordshire, the third son of George Parker. Parker joined the navy in February 1793 and served as a captain's servant on the *Orion,* before joining Lord Howe's Channel Fleet and fighting on 1 June. He was confirmed in the rank of lieutenant some five years later and became captain in 1801. In November 1802 he was appointed to the *Amazon,* a frigate he would command for the next eleven years. Parker married Frances Biddulph in June 1810, and fathered eight children. The worn-out *Amazon* was eventually paid off in 1812 and Parker spent the next fifteen years living as a country gentleman. Parker was promoted rear-admiral in 1830. From September 1831 until 1834 Parker protected British interests in the Tagus during the Portuguese civil war. He was appointed lord of the Admiralty on his return to England and, after the change of ministry, was reappointed in April 1835. In 1841 Parker became commander-in-chief in China and was rewarded for his service with a GCB and a baronetcy. In 1845 he was appointed commander-in-chief in the Mediterranean and in 1846 was also given command of the Channel Fleet. Having dealt successfully with revolutionary turmoil and diplomatic crises, in September 1849 Parker began a unique second consecutive term in his Mediterranean appointment. He was promoted admiral in 1851. Between 1854 and 1857 Parker was commander-in-chief at Devonport and in 1862 was promoted rear-admiral. He was appointed admiral of the fleet in 1863 and died of bronchitis on 13 November 1866.

## SIR THOMAS PASLEY, FIRST BARONET (1734–1808)

Born in Dumfriesshire on 2 March 1734 to James and Magdalen Pasley. Pasley spent much of his early career serving under the Hon. Robert Digby, notably as lieutenant in the *Dunkirk,* after which he was given command of a fireship. In 1758 his cousin John Elliot appointed Pasley to the newly launched *Aeolus* and promoted him first lieutenant. Pasley advanced to commander on his return to England, and spent six years protecting coastal trade between Dublin and Plymouth. He was promoted to post-rank in 1771 and in 1774 married Mary Heywood, with whom he had two daughters. In 1776 Pasley successfully protected a convoy of West Indiamen and spent two years taking prizes on the Jamaica station. On the *Jupiter* off Havana in 1782, Pasley took five of thirteen enemy vessels and, despite considerable damage, escaped to Antigua. The *Jupiter* was decommissioned and Pasley saw no further action until 1788. In 1790 Pasley joined the Channel Fleet on the *Bellerophon* and in April 1794 was promoted rear-admiral of the blue. Pasley lost a leg during the action of 1 June and in July became rear-admiral of the red and a baronet. In 1795 Pasley advanced to vice-admiral of the white, in 1798 commander-in-chief at the Nore and at Plymouth in 1799. He was promoted admiral of the blue in 1801 and of the white four years later. Pasley died on 29 November 1808. A man of great humour and much-loved, Pasley's *Private Sea Journals*, published in 1931, offer a wonderful glimpse into life at sea in the eighteenth century.

## JOHN PITT, SECOND EARL OF CHATHAM (1756–1835)

Born on 9 October 1756 in Kent, the eldest son of William Pitt the Elder and his wife Hester. Pitt joined the army as an ensign in March 1774. His father opposed the American war and Pitt resigned his commission in 1776, returning as a lieutenant in June 1778. He was promoted captain in 1779 and served at the siege of Gibraltar. Pitt succeeded to the earldom in May 1778 and in July, at the invitation of his brother, William Pitt the Younger, Chatham became first lord of the Admiralty. In 1783 he married Mary Townshend, but fathered no children. He retired from the Admiralty in December 1794 but remained in the cabinet as lord privy seal, later president of the council. He became major-general in 1795 and was master-general of the ordnance from June 1801 to February 1806, and then again 1807–1810. In 1802 Chatham was made lieutenant-general, in March 1807 governor of Plymouth, and in September, of Jersey. Chatham owed many of his appointments to his friendship with George III. In June 1809 Chatham was given command of nearly 40,000 troops for the Walcheren expedition. After initial success against Flushing, the campaign failed, partly due to Chatham's mediocre talents and natural indolence. The resulting inquiry damaged his reputation and in March 1810 Chatham resigned his commission. He was nevertheless promoted general in 1812, and in 1820 became governor of Gibraltar, a post he held until his death. He died on 24 September 1835.

## WILLIAM PITT, PRIME MINISTER (1759–1806)

Born on 28 May 1759 in Hayes, Kent, the fourth child of the Earl of Chatham (William Pitt the Elder). Pitt studied law at Cambridge but soon changed his focus to politics and became an MP in 1781. Pitt was appointed Chancellor of the Exchequer under Shelburne in 1782, and in 1783 he took office as first lord of the treasury. Pitt became Prime Minister in 1784, and won great acclaim for his financial reforms. He stood firm in diplomatic crises and made tentative efforts to abolish slavery. By the end of the decade Pitt had won the support of the King and the Commons. However, he struggled to manage the war against France. Lacking in strategic understanding and initiative, Pitt was pulled in different directions by conflicting advisers, and was distracted by myriad domestic crises. The ministry fought to suppress political subversion and unrest, and Pitt suspended the habeas corpus act for the first time in 1794. In 1798 he established a single general tax, known as the triple assessment, but financial problems persisted, and in 1799 Pitt replaced the triple assessment with income tax. Following the 1798 Irish rebellion, Pitt proposed a legislative union to bring Ireland under Westminster's control. The bill was a personal triumph, but Pitt resigned in 1801, after George III refused to sanction his attempts for Catholic emancipation. He resumed office in 1804. Pitt suffered public embarrassment when an investigation into Melville's alleged misappropriation of naval funds scrutinised Pitt's own conduct. Pitt died a bachelor in London on 23 January 1806.

# The French

### JEAN-BAPTISTE ANDRÉ AMAR (1755–1816)

A prominent lawyer before his election to the Convention, Amar became known for his ferocious attacks on the King. He served on the Committee of General Security from June 1793, and in October contributed to the sentencing of the Girondins. He was suspicious of Robespierre and contributed to his overthrow. Amar was sentenced to life imprisonment for his involvement in the coup, but was amnestied in 1795. He was later arrested as a Babouvist.

### BERTRAND BARÈRE DE VIEUZAC (1755–1841)

Born 10 September 1755 in Tarbes to a middle-class family. Barère began a promising legal career as a magistrate in 1777, but on arriving in Paris, he became a member of the Jacobin club. He went on to serve on the Committee on Domains and edited a leading journal, the *Point du Jour*. Barère advocated the imprisonment and subsequent execution of Louis XVI. He was a supporter of Robespierre and was increasingly linked to the radical Montagnards. His 1793 Report to the French Nation espoused nationalism and war against royalist Europe to further the revolution. Barère was a founding member of the first Committee of Public Safety in April 1793, for which he worked tirelessly until mid-1794. As secretary, he formulated much of its propaganda. Barère was notorious for his pursuit of anyone suspected of royalist sympathies. He supported the 1794 Thermidor coup but his popularity suffered in the wake of Robespierre's execution and he fled to Bordeaux to escape arrest and deportation. Napoleon granted him amnesty in 1799 but Barère switched allegiance to the crown following the First Restoration of the Bourbon monarchy and was forced to escape to Belgium after the Second Restoration in 1815. Barère returned to Paris in 1830 and three years later was elected to the general council of the Hautes-Pyrénées. He died in Tarbes on 13 January 1841.

**FRANÇOIS LOUIS BOURDON 'DE L'OISE' (1758–1797)**

A former leader of the *basoche,* Bourdon had little success in his early revolutionary career, and was elected to the Convention by accident after a confusion over names. He aligned himself with the Montagnards and took part in the *journée* on 31 May 1793. Bourdon acquitted himself poorly whilst *en mission* in 1793 and was accused of corruption. He conspired against Robespierre at Thermidor. Deported following Fructidor

**GEORGES-JACQUES 'Show my head to the people' DANTON (1759–1794)**

Born 26 October 1759 in Arcis-sur-Arbe to Jacques Danton and Marie-Madeleine Camus. Danton trained as a lawyer and went to practise in Paris. In July 1789 he joined the civic guard of the Cordeliers district and was elected district president in October. In 1790 he founded the Cordeliers Club, where his speeches attracted much attention. Danton took refuge in London after the Cordeliers petitioned for the removal of Louis XVI; he returned to Paris and was elected second assistant to the procureur of the Paris Commune. As Minister for Justice, Danton made enemies of the Gironde, who accused him of complicity in the prison massacres of September 1792, which he had done nothing to prevent. Accounts demanded by the Girondins revealed enormous sums in secret expenditure, and they accused Danton of plotting with the Belgian General Dumouriez. Relations finally broke when Danton boldly accused the Girondins of the same crime. In 1793 Danton became the first president of the Committee of Public Safety. His policy of negotiation and compromise proved redundant and he was left out of the new July Committee. He adopted a more moderate political position and emerged as leader of the *Indulgents*. In the autumn of 1793 Danton withdrew from political life, and on his return in November, he attacked the anti-Christian movement. His increasing moderation and eventual opposition to Robespierre's Terror led to his arrest and Danton was guillotined on 5 April.

**JOSEPH FOUCHÉ (1763–1820)**
Principal of the College of Nantes, Fouché was elected to the Convention and won notoriety with his radical and de-Christianising policies while *en mission* in 1793. Returning to Paris in April 1794, Fouché plotted against Robespierre, who he saw as a threat. He became a protégé of Barras and was sent to the Cisalpine Republic as an ambassador. He continued his public life under Napoleon.

**ANTOINE QUENTIN FOUQUIER-TINVILLE (1747–1795)**
Fouquier-Tinville was carving out a legal career in Paris when the Revolution broke out. He was a keen participant in the early *journées* and was appointed to the newly created Revolutionary Tribunal in March 1793. He had a notorious appointment as public prosecutor. In the wake of the Thermidor coup, he claimed he had merely been acting on Robespierre's orders. Guillotined in May 1795.

**LOUIS LEGENDRE (1752–1797)**
A Parisian butcher and one of the founding members of the Cordeliers club, Legendre contributed to many of the revolutionary *journées* between 1789 and 1793. He had a brief appointment to the Committee of General Security. Legendre conspired against Robespierre at Thermidor, after which he became a reactionary and was elected an Ancien, member of the Coucil of Elders.

**JEAN-PAUL MARAT (1743–1793)**
Born on 24 May 1743 in Switzerland. Marat was a well-known doctor in 1770s London, where he authored a number of books on science and philosophy. His 1774 work *The Chains of Slavery* introduced the idea of an aristocratic conspiracy, a principal theme of his later articles. Returning to the Continent in 1777, Marat continued to experiment and write, but failed to be admitted to the Academy of Sciences, and joined those who opposed the established social and scientific order. From 1789 he edited *L'Ami du Peuple*, a newspaper which projected his radical and democratic ideas, and was forced into hiding on several occasions. The aristocracy were a particular target. In 1790 Marat began to direct his criticism towards moderate Revolutionary leaders and continued to warn against the émigrés, who were organizing a counter-revolution. By 1791 he was speaking out in favour of

the abolishment of the monarchy. In September 1792 Marat was elected to the Convention and became a prominent and popular member. Marat aligned himself closely with the radical Montagnards, and was targeted by the Girondins, who brought him before a Revolutionary tribunal, believing he had played a large part in the September massacres. His acquittal marked the beginning of the end for the Girondins. Marat became a martyr after his assassination on 13 July 1793 in Paris, stabbed to death in his bath by Charlotte Corday, a young Girondin conservative.

## AIMÈE CÉCILE RENAULT (1774–1794)

Born in 1774 in Paris, the daughter of a paper-worker. Renault tried to assassinate Robespierre in May 1794 but was discovered and arrested. She was guillotined a month later.

## MAXIMILIEN-FRANÇOIS-ISIDORE DE ROBESPIERRE (1758–1794)

Born on 6 May 1758 in Arras. He was raised by his maternal grandparents, and in 1769 was awarded a scholarship to the Parisian college of Louis-le-Grand where he shone in law and philosophy. Graduating in 1781, Robespierre became a lawyer in Arras, and was soon appointed as a judge at the Salle Episcopale. He became chancellor and then president of the Arras Academy. He was elected by Arras as a representative for the Estates-General in March 1789. Robespierre probably made his maiden speech on 18 May 1789 and attracted much attention for his pro-Jacobin, democratic opinions. In April 1790 he presided over the Jacobin Club and in June was elected secretary of the National Assembly. In October Robespierre was appointed as judge of the Versailles tribunal, where he fought for universal suffrage and the right to petition. He defended actors, black slaves and Jews, among others, his determination winning him enormous popular support.

He excluded himself from the new Legislative Assembly and resigned his lucrative appointment as public prosecutor of Paris, to which he had been elected in June 1791. He tried his hand at revolutionary journalism, founding the newspaper *Le Defenseur de la Constitution.* Robespierre was elected to the Commune Insurrectionnelle in August 1792, and was a member of the electoral assembly of Paris. He exonerated the mob responsible for the September massacres and was triumphantly elected to the Convention by the Parisian people.

By December 1792 Robespierre was an outspoken regicide. He soon made enemies of the Girondins, who made accusations of dictatorship from the very first sessions of the Convention. In May–June 1793 he supported the indictment of the Girondin leaders. He joined the Committee for Public Safety in July 1793 and strove to unite the divided revolutionaries. He promised to set up a Revolutionary militia to punish counter-revolutionaries and grain hoarders, and encouraged the Reign of Terror, but protested against senseless executions. He objected to factions calling for even more radical action, and de-Christianisation. In May 1794 he created the Cult of the Supreme Being, endeavouring to unite the revolutionaries around a civic religion. On 4 June he was elected president of the Convention.

Fears of a 'foreign plot' led Robespierre to support the purge of the Dantonists and Hébertists. He was closely associated with the unpopular Law of 10 June which reorganised the Revolutionary tribunal to produce more convictions. Battling ill-health and accusations of dictatorship, Robespierre began to distance himself from the Convention and then from the Committee of Public Safety. Continuing hardships in the wake of recent French victories lost him popular support. In July he returned to the Convention and the Committee. His apparent wish for further purges rallied his enemies for the successful Thermidor coup, and Robespierre was indicted with his brother. He was guillotined in front of an enthusiastic mob on 28 July 1794.

## JEANBON SAINT-ANDRÉ (1749–1813)

Born 25 February 1749 in Montauban, the son of a Huguenot businessman. He was employed as a captain in the French merchant navy until 1788, when he became a Protestant pastor. He welcomed the Revolution, hoping it would create a better life for French Protestants. He was elected to the National Convention and sat with the deputies from the Jacobin Club. When the Jacobins seized control in June 1793, the Convention elected Saint-André to the Committee of Public Safety, and although he was initially sent *en mission* with the army, Saint-André came to specialise in naval matters. In September 1793 he was sent to Brest to prepare the French fleet for war against Britain. Saint-André proved himself an able disciplinarian and instilled revolutionary spirit in the men. He worked hard to organise the construction of warships as well as the manufacture of essential supplies and then sailed with Villaret on the Prairial campaign. A staunch supporter of Robespierre, he was arrested after the Thermidor coup on grounds of terrorism but soon received amnesty. Saint-André was then sent by the Directory to Smyrna as a consul, but was imprisoned on arrival and only released under the Consulate. In 1798 he was appointed consul to Algiers, but was captured by the Turks in 1799 and held for three years. In 1802 Saint-André was made prefect of Mainz by Napoleon, in which post he yet again proved himself to be one of France's best administrators. He died of cholera in Mainz on 10 December 1813.

**LOUIS-ANTOINE-LÉON DE SAINT-JUST (1767–1794)**
Born 25 August 1767 in Decize, central France. An unruly youth, he fled to Paris in 1786 after the object of his affection married another man. He was sent to a reformatory and went on to take his law degree in April 1788. A year later the authorities seized his epic poem, *Organt*, a satirical work full of political allusion, and Saint-Just went into hiding. He was too young to play a major role in 1789 and soon realized that election to a significant post was the key to notoriety. Rather than joining a political club, Saint-Just established his reputation as the municipal corporation counsel of Blérancourt, becoming a spokesman for the voters and aligning himself with Robespierre. In September 1792, shortly after his twenty-fifth birthday, Saint-Just was elected to the National Convention by the Aisne. Skilled oratory and cold logic established Saint-Just among the most militant Montagnards. In May 1793 he was elected to the Committee of Public Safety and helped to draft the constitution. He was away *en mission* for much of the Terror, in Alsace and with the Army of the North. He was appointed president of the Convention on his return, and passed the radical Ventôse Decrees which gave confiscated lands to the needy. Ever more bloodthirsty, Saint-Just advocated execution of the Hébertists and Dantonists. He was arrested on 27 July and guillotined with Robespierre the next day.

**JEAN LAMBERT TALLIEN (1767–1820)**
A clerk and journalist for the radical *Ami du Citoyen*, Tallien joined the Commune Insurrectionnelle and was prominent in the September massacres. As a member of the Convention, he violently attacked the King and the Girondins and established repressive policies while *en mission* in

Bordeaux. Having been attacked by Robespierre in March 1794, Tallien helped to plot the Thermidor coup. He was elected to the Committee of Public Safety and was responsible for the closure of the Jacobin club and the suppression of the Revolutionary Tribunal. His position was largely sustained by his wife's salon, and Tallien lost much of his influence when they separated. In 1798 he began a new career in the diplomatic service.

## JACQUES ALEXIS THURIOT (1753–1829)

A lawyer and keen participant in the storming of the Bastille, Thuriot represented the Marne in the Legislative Assembly and sat with the Montagnards in the Convention. Between *missions*, he served in the Committee of Public Safety from July to September 1793 and again following Robespierre's execution. As acting president of the Convention, he had a significant role in the coup. He was arrested on suspicion of involvement in the Prairial rising but was freed in the 1795 amnesty.

## MARC GUILLLAUME ALEXIS VADIER (1736–1828)

A former army officer and magistrate, Vadier served on the Estates-General, the Convention and the Committee of General Security. He opposed Robespierre's religious policies, and helped to plot his overthrow. Attacked as a terrorist for his role in the coup, Vadier escaped deportation in 1795, but was subsequently imprisoned for his involvement in the Babeuf plot. He was released at the end of the 1790s.

# GLOSSARY

**abeam** In the direction at right angles to the ship's centreline.

**aboard** 1. On board a ship. 2. Alongside, touching another ship.

**Admiral of the Red, White, Blue** The officer nominally commanding ships of the Red, White or Blue squadron, ranking in seniority in that (descending) order; the rank of Admiral of the Red was created after the Battle of Trafalgar, the post having been occupied by Admiral of the Fleet. In practice, by the end of the eighteenth century the Admiralty created as many admirals of each rank as it required.

**assignat**, initially a government bond, but the French paper currency from 1790 – in principle 'assigned' (secured) on the nationalised property of the church.

**astern** Behind a ship, in the direction from which she is moving.

**athwart** Across.

**athwartships** Across, at right angles to the ship's centreline.

**Babouvist** Political supporter of François-Noël Babeuf, a Jacobin supporter and socialist, and a vocal critic of the Directory. Executed on 27 May 1797.

**Babeuf Plot** Failed *coup d'état* of May 1796 masterminded by François-Noël Babeuf known as the 'Conspiracy of Equals'. Babeuf planned to impose communal ownership, egalitarianism and the redistribution of property – what we know as communism.

**back** *vb* 1. To trim the sails so that they catch the wind on the wrong side and check the ship's way. 2. (Of the wind) to change in an anti-clockwise direction.

**ballast** Stones, gravel or other weight stowed low in a ship to improve her stability.

**Basoche** Body of clerks attached to the major high courts of appeal.

**battery** 1. The broadside guns mounted on one deck, or one side, of the ship. 2. A group of guns mounted ashore. 3. **floating** — a stationary raft or hulk mounting heavy guns.

**beam** 1. The width of the ship. 2. The direction at right angles to the centreline. 3. A timber running from side to side of a ship to support a deck.

**bend** *vb* To make a sail fast to its yard, mast or stay.

**bilge** 1. The angle of the ship's hull between side and bottom. 2. — **and bilge** close alongside, touching.

**Blérancourt** A commune in the department of Aisne in Picardy, Northern France.

**boatswain** A ship's officer responsible for sails, rigging and ground tackle. 2. —**'s call** a whistle used to convey orders.

**boom** 1. A light running spar, particularly one extending the foot of a sail. 2. A floating barrier protecting a harbour.

**bow** Either side of the foremost part of the ship's hull, as it widens from the stem. **on the —** said of a ship or object on a bearing somewhere between right ahead and abeam.

**bowline, bowling** Rope which holds the edge of a square sail tight against the wind.

**bowsprit** A spar projecting over the bows, spreading various items of rigging and one or more sails.

**broadside** 1. The side of the ship. 2. The number of guns mounted or bearing on one side. 3. the simultaneous fire of those guns. 4. The total weight of shot fired by all the guns of the ship. 5. — **on** of a ship showing her broadside at right angles to the observers line of sight, or to a named point of reference.

**bulkhead** A vertical partition within the ship.

**bulwark** A barrier around the side of a deck.

**butt** A cask holding two hogsheads – approximately 475–480 litres. Usually applied to ale or water.

**cable** 1. A large rope or hawser, particularly the anchor cable. 2. The standard length of an anchor cable, 120 fathoms.

**careen** *vb* To heel a ship over to expose one side of her underwater hull for cleaning or repairs.

**carronade** A type of short gun, of heavy calibre but small charge and short range.

**cartridge** A cloth or paper bag containing the propellant charge of a gun.

**caulk** *vb* To make seams watertight.

**chase** 1. The pursuit of one ship or squadron by another. 2. The ship pursued.

3. — **gun** a gun mounted to fire ahead or astern. 5. **general** — order to a squadron to pursue a beaten enemy without regard to order. 6. **stern** — pursuit in which the pursued lies dead ahead of the pursuer.

**close-hauled** *adv.* Steering as nearly towards the wind as possible.

**colours** Flags, especially the national ensign.

**commission** *vb* To establish a warship as an active unit for command, administrative and financial purposes.

**Committee of Public Safety (CPS)** Formed by the National Convention in April 1793 to act as the *de facto* Executive Government to protect the Republic from external attack and internal rebellion. Dissolved by the Directory in 1795.

**Commune Insurrectionelle** Name adopted by the renovated municipal government of Paris from 9–10 Aug 1792. Instrumental in the overthrow of Louis XVI.

**complement** The total ship's company authorised for her size or Rate.

**The Consulate** Government of France from the fall of the Directory 10 November 1799 until the Napoleonic Empire, 18 May 1804.

**Convention** See National Convention

**Cordeliers Club** An independent political club. Renowned for its denunciation of the misuse of power. Stong supporters of individual rights. Associated with the Indulgents.

**corvette** French term for a brig-sloop.

**Council of Elders** The upper house of the Directory, 22 August 1795–9 November 1799.

**course** 1. The direction of ship's movement. 2. The foresail or mainsail, the lowest square sails.

**court martial** A court held under naval or military law.

**crosstrees** Horizontal struts at the top of topmasts, used to anchor the topgallant stays.

**deck** A floor or platform within a ship. 2. — **head** the underside of the deck overhead. 3. **gun** — the deck carrying the main battery (seventeenth–nineteenth century). 4. **half** — the after end of the main deck, below the quarterdeck. 5. **lower** — a) the gun deck or (in a two- or three-decker) lowest gun deck; b) the ratings of the ship's company as a whole, those who berth on the lower deck. 6. **main** — the highest deck running the whole length of the ship. 7. **quarter** — a deck above the main deck over the after part of the ship. 8. **spar** — a light deck connecting quarter deck to forecastle. 9.

**upper** — a continuous weather deck incorporating quarterdeck and forecastle. 10. **weather** — a deck exposed to the sky.

**dead** Directly, straight.

**Directory** Body of five Directors that held executive power in France before the Consulate. The Directory was in power from 2 November 1795–10 November 1799.

**double, double on** *vb* To attack a ship or squadron from both sides.

**draught** 1. The depth of water required to float a ship. 2. A plan or chart. 3. The drawings showing the design of ship.

**Enragés** An early incarnation of the Hébertistes. Ultra left-wing popular radicals.

**ensign** A flag flown aft by warships and merchantmen to indicate nationality.

**Festival of the Supreme Being** 8 June 1794, the formal inauguration of the new sate religion, the Cult of the Supreme Being.

**fish** *vb* To strengthen a damaged spar or mast by lashing spars to it in the manner of splints.

**flag** 1. An admiral's distinguishing flag. 2. — **captain** the captain of a flagship. 3. — **rank**, admiral's rank. 4. — **ship** the admiral's ship.

**flotilla** 1. A group of small warships. 2. Coastal warships considered as a whole.

**forecastle** A deck built over the forward end of the main deck.

**foretopsail** The topsail on the foremast.

**freeboard** The minimum height of the ship's side above the waterline.

**frigate** 1. A small sailing warship of fine form and high speed (seventeenth century). 2. A cruising warship with an unarmed lower deck, mounting her battery on the main deck.

**furl** *vb* To bundle up a sail to its yard, mast or stay.

**gangway** 1. A light bridge connecting forecastle and quarterdeck. 2. **at the** — relating to that part of the quarterdeck where the gangways began, and where men were flogged

**get the wind** *vb* To gain the weather gage.

**Girondin** A political group expelled from the Jacobins and purged from the National Convention on 2 June 1793.

**grapeshot** Anti-personnel shot consisting of small shot that scatters on firing.

**gun** 1. A piece of artillery. 2. — **deck** see **deck**. 3. — **lock** a flintlock firing mechanism for a great gun. 4. — **port** a port cut to allow guns mounted below decks to fire out. 5. — **shot** the range of a gun. 6. — **tackle** tackle rigged to run out the gun after firing. 7. **chase** — see **chase**.

**gunlock** A flintlock mechanism that fired a cannon, operated by pulling a cord. A significant improvement on the traditional linstock, a length of burning match attached to a pole.

**heave-to** To stop by backing some of the sails.

**Hébertists** Political group associated with the journalists Jacques Hébert. Violent, anti-intellectual and populist. Strong supporters of the Reign of Terror.

**heel** *vb* (Of the ship) to incline or be inclined to one side or the other.

**hold** The lowest internal space of a ship, below all the decks.

**inboard** *adv.* In, into the ship.

**Indulgents** Supporters of George Danton. Defenders of individual rights, called for clemency and relaxation of the Terror.

**inshore** *adv.* Near, towards the shore.

**Jacobin** A member of the Jacobin Club, which dominated French politics in 1794. Initially moderate, the Jacobins became renowned for their implementation of the Reign of Terror.

**jack** A type of national flag flown forward, particularly by warships.

**jib** A triangular headsail hoisted on a stay set between the foretopmast and the bowsprit.

**jib boom** An extension to the bowsprit.

**keel** 1. The timber lying centrally along the length of the bottom of the ship, forming a spine upon which other parts of her frame are erected. 2. A type of square-rigged barge native to the River Tyne. 3. — **man** one of the crew of a keel. 4. **sliding** — a centre-board.

**landman/landsman** An unskilled member of the ship's company.

**landward** *adv.* Towards the land.

**langridge** Anti-personnel and dismasting shot made up of irregular pieces of iron, nails etc.

**larboard** Relating to the port or left-hand side of the ship.

**large** Relating to a course with the wind abaft the beam.

**lead** A weight on a marked line, used for sounding.

**leads** Inshore channels amongst the coastal islands of Norway, Sweden etc.

**league** Three miles.

**lee** 1. The direction towards which the wind is blowing. 2. The water sheltered from the wind by the land or by a ship. 3. — **shore** a coastline towards which the wind is blowing.

**leeward** Relating to the direction towards which the wind is blowing.

**leewardly** (Of a ship) tending to drift rapidly to leeward when trying to sail close-hauled.

**leeway** The extent to which the wind blows a ship to leeward of her apparent course.

**lieutenant** 1. A commissioned sea officer immediately junior to the captain. 2. — **commander/ — in command**, a lieutenant commanding a small warship. 3. **first (second, third** etc.) — lieutenant ranking first (second, third etc.) in seniority after the captain.

**line** 1. — **abreast** A formation in which the ships of a squadron sail on the same course abeam of one another. 2. — **ahead** a formation in which one or more ships follow a leader, imitating his movements. 3. — **of battle** a fighting formation in which the ships of a fleet form a straight line in a predetermined order. 4. — **of bearing** a formation in which a squadron of ships lie in a straight line diagonal to their course.

**longboat** The largest of the ship's boats, designed for carrying heavy weights.

**longitude** A position lying on a straight line drawn around the earth's surface from one pole to the other, hence fixed in an east-west direction.

**loose** *vb* To hoist or let drop sails, to make sail.

**lower deck,** On a two- or three-decker, the lowest deck carrying the ship's main battery.

**magazine** 1. A storehouse. 2. A storehouse for explosives. 3. A compartment in the ship for storing powder.

**mast** 1. A vertical spar or spars supporting sails, rigging and other spars. 2. **fore** —, the foremost mast. 3. **lower** — the lowest and principal element of fore, main or mizzen mast, on which the topmast is stepped. 4. **made** — a mast made up of more than one tree assembled together. 5. **main** —, the tallest (usually second) mast. 6. **mizzen** — see **mizzen**. 7. **topgallant** — **top** — see **topgallantmast topmast. 8.** — **dock** see **dock**. 9. — **head** the top of a lower, top or topgallantmast.

**maintopsail** The topsail on the mainmast.

**master** 1. On a warship, the warrant officer responsible for navigation. 2. The commanding officer of a merchant ship.

**master at arms** A petty officer responsible for ship's discipline.

**master's mate** A petty officer assisting the master.

**midshipman** 1. An inferior or petty officer. 2. A boy or young man hoping to become a commissioned officer.

**middle deck** On a three-decker, the deck between the lower deck and the upper deck.

**mizzen**, 1. The aftermost mast of a ship or ketch. 2. — **peak** the upper end of the mizzen yard or gaff. 3. **mizzentop** see **top**. 4. — **yard** the yard of the lateen mizzen sail (seventeenth to mid-eighteenth century).

**Montagnard or The Mountain** A left-wing political group known for their position in the National Convention, high up on the benches to one side. Fierce opponents of the Girondins. During the Reign of Terror synonymous with Jacobin. Dissolved after the death of Robespierre.

**moor** *vb* To secure a ship by two anchors, or by making fast to a buoy.

**The National Convention** The constitutional and legislative assembly from 20 September 1792 - 26 October 1795, though between 1793 and 1794 executive power was exercised by the Committee of Public Safety. The National Convention was succeeded from 2 November by the Directory.

**the Nore** An anchorage in the mouth of the Thames near the entrance to the River Medway, which led to Chatham naval dockyard.

**onshore** *adv.* Towards or on the shore.

**ordinance** 1. Heavy guns. 2. Relating to the Ordinance Board.

**outboard** *adv.* Relating to, towards, the outside of the ship.

**ordinary** Ships in reserve.

**orlop (deck)** The lowest deck.

**parallel** A meridian of latitude or longitude.

**pay** *vb* (of a ship in stays) to fall off on to one or other tack.

**pipe** A unit of wine and another word for a butt, holding two hogsheads – approximately 475–480 litres.

**pitch** *vb* To dip head and stern alternately into the waves.

**point** *vb* 1. (Of a ship) to head in a particular direction relative to the wind. 2. To lay a gun on some particular target. 3. — **high** (of a ship) to lie particularly close to the wind when close-hauled.

**poop** A short deck built over the after end of the quarterdeck.

**port** 1. An opening cut in a ship's side. 2. **gun** — a port out of which a gun is fired.

**Prairial Rising** Unsuccessful Parisian popular rising 20 - 23 May 1795.

**privateer** A privately owned warship licensed by letter of marque to capture enemy shipping for profit.

**pull** *vb* To row.

**purchase** An arrangement of rope led through pulleys in order to haul at a mechanical advantage.

**quarter** 1. The sides of the ship's stern. 2. (*pl*) Each man's post or station in action. 3. Mercy, safety on surrender. 4. — **deck** see **deck**. 5. **on the** — in a direction between abeam and right aft, diagonal to the ship's course. 6. — **gallery** A balcony projecting from the stern and quarter of large ships, accessed via the admiral's or captain's cabin.

**quoin** A wedge inserted between the breech of the gun and the bed of the gun-carriage, to adjust the elevation of the gun.

**rake** *vb* To fire down the length of an enemy ship from ahead or astern.

**razée** A ship modified by being 'cut down' by one deck.

**reach** *vb* To sail with the wind abeam.

**rear-admiral** 1. An admiral third in command of a fleet (seventeenth century). 2. The flag-officer commanding the rear division of a fleet (seventeenth century). 3. A rear-admiral's flagship (seventeenth century). 4. A flag-officer of the rank of Rear-Admiral of the Red, White or Blue (eighteenth century).

**reckoning** 1. A calculation of the ship's position. 2. **dead** —, an estimate of the ship's position without the benefit of observations, by calculating course, speed and drift from a known point of departure.

**reef** 1. A tuck taken in a sail to reduce its area. 2. A line of submerged rocks. 3. — **point** a short length of line secured through a sail in order to be made fast around the yard or boom to take in a reef.

**reef** *vb* To shorten sail by bundling part of the sail against yard or boom.

**red-hot shot** Shot which has been heated in a furnace before firing.

**road, roadstead** An open anchorage.

**roll** *vb* (Of a ship) to heed from one side to the other under the pressure of the waves.

**royal** A small square sail flown above the topgallant.

**sail** 1. A piece of cloth spread aloft by masts and rigging to catch the wind and propel a ship. 2. Some number of ships. 3. — **cloths** heavy canvas for sails. 4. — **plan** an arrangement of sails. 5. **easy** — a reduced sail plan, for slow speed. 6. **fore** — the fore course, the lowest square sail set on the foremast. 7. **head** — a sail set forward of the foremast. 8. **main** — the main course, the lowest square sail set on the mainmast. 9. **stay** — a triangular sail set on one of the stays supporting a mast from ahead. 10. **studding** —

a light sail temporarily spread outboard of a square sail in light airs. 11. **top** — a square sail hoisted on the topmast, above the course.

**sail** *vb* 1. (Of any sort of ship) to move, to proceed. 2. **make** — to hoist, spread sail. 3. **shorten** — to reduce, take in sail.

**sail loft** A large open space used by sailmakers to spread out sails.

**Sans-Culottes** Radical militants of the lower classes, was said to compromise individuals who wore workmen's trousers rather than knee-breeches (*culottes*).

**schooner** A small sailing vessel fore-and aft rigged on two masts.

**scuttle** A hole cut in the ship's deck or side, generally for ventilation.

**seaward** to **seaward** In the direction of the open sea.

**sextant** A navigational instrument capable of taking sights or angles up to 120°.

**sheet** A rope or tackle controlling the clew of a sail.

**shift** *vb* 1. To exchange, replace or move. 2. — **flag** (of an admiral) to change flagship.

**ship of the line** A warship large enough to lie in the line of battle.

**shot** 1. A bullet or (non-explosive) projectile fired from a great gun. 2. **canister** — see **canister**. 3. **chain** —, hollow shot formed in two halves containing and linked by a length of chain, designed to damage rigging. 4. **dismantling** — one of a number of types of shot designed to damage masts and spars. 5. **grape** — see **grape**. 6. **fire** — hollow shot filled with an incendiary compound.

**shroud** A stay supporting a mast from the side.

**slip (a cable)** To cast off; especially to sail without weighing anchor, in which case the anchor cable is let slip and buoyed for later retrieval.

**sloop** 1. A small cruising warship, having only one internal deck, and mounting her main battery on the upper deck.

**sound** *vb* To take a sounding, to measure the depth of water beneath a ship.

**spar** 1. A mast, pole or boom. 2. — **deck** see **deck**.

**Spithead** An area of the Solent, off Portsmouth.

**spring** A hawser led from the capstan, out of the ship aft and made fast some way along the anchor cable, hauling on which will cant an anchored ship to bring her broadside to bear as desired.

**spring** *vb* (Of a mast or spar) to split along the grain.

**spritsail** 1. A sail set on a yard below the bowsprit. 2. — **topsail** a sail set on a small mast stepped on the end of the bowsprit.

**squall** A sudden gust of wind that may last several minutes.
**starboard** Relating to the right-hand side of the ship.
**stay** *vb* 1. To tack. 2. **in stays** of a ship pointing into the wind while in the process of going about. 3. **miss stays** *vb* in tacking, to fail to turn into the wind and to fall back on to the original tack.
**step (a mast)** To place a ship's mast.
**stern** 1. The after end of the ship. 2. — **post** a straight timber erected on the after end of the keel, supporting both the rudder and the structure of the stern. 3. — **chaser** a chase gun pointing aft.
**strike (a mast)** To lower a mast.
**studdingsail** A light sail temporarily set outboard of a square sail in light airs.
**surge** Bodily movement of the ship ahead or astern.
**sway** Bodily movement of a ship from side to side.
**tack** 1. A rope or tackle serving to haul down the clew of a square sail. 2. The course held by a ship beating to windward. 3. **larboard —/port —** the tack on which the wind blows from the left-hand side of the ship. 4. **starboard —**, the tack on which the wind blows from the right-hand side of the ship.
**tack** *vb* 1. To shift tacks, to go about, to turn into the wind and so onto the opposite tack. 2. To beat to windward by successive tacks.
**Thermidor** The revolt of 27 July 1794 that led to the downfall of Robespierre and the end of the Reign of Terror.
**top** 1. A platform built at the head of the lower masts, serving to spread the shrouds of the topmast and provide a space for men working aloft. 2. — **gallant**, see **topgallant**. 3. — **hamper** ship's structure or equipment carried high up, tending to increase windage or reduce stability. 4. — **man** (likewise **foretopman** etc.) a seaman skilled in working aloft. 5. — **mast** a mast fitted to the top of the lower mast and extending it. 6. — **sail** see **sail**. 7. — **sides** the upper part of the ship's structure, clear of the water-line. 8. — **timber** a structural timber forming the uppermost section of a frame on each side. 9. — **weight** the weight of ship's structure or equipment carried high, hence tending to reduce stability. 10. **fore — main — mizzen —** a) the platform built at the head of the foremast, mainmast, mizzenmast; b) the fore, main or mizzen topmast head, the head of the topmast or topgallantmast.
**topgallant/topgallantsail** 1. A square sail set on the topgallantmast, above the topsail. 2. — **mast** a mast fitted to the top of the topmast and extending it. 3. — **yard** the yard set on the topgallantmast, spreading the topgallant.

**taffrail** Bulwark at the after end of the poop or quarterdeck.
**top (of a mast)** A platform built at the top of the lower mast.
**treenail, trenail** A wooden peg or pin used to fasten together the parts of the hull of a wooden ship.
**tumblehome** The inward slope of the ship's side above the waterline.
**unhandy** Unmanoeuvrable, clumsy.
**unmoor** *vb* To weigh anchor, to cast off a mooring.
**upperworks** The upper portion of the ship's structure.
**van division** The leading division of a fleet or squadron divided into van, centre and rear.
**vice-admiral** A flag officer ranking below admiral and above rear-admiral.
**wake** The track of the ship's passage through the water astern.
**way** 1. The movement of a ship through the water. 2. **in — of** in a line with, adjacent to. 3. **steerage** — movement at a speed sufficient to allow the ship to be controlled by the helm. 4. (*pl.*) Pairs of heavy timbers laid as rails on a launching slip down which the ship slides into the water. 5. **under** — moving through the water.
**wear** *vb* 1. To alter course from one tack to the other by turning before the wind. 2. To fly a particular flag or carry some distinguishing mark.
**weather** 1. Relating to the direction from which the wind is blowing. 2. — **gage** the windward position in relation to another ship or fleet.
**weather** *vb* To get to windward of something.
**weatherly** *adv.* (Of a ship) tending to ship seas easily.
**weigh** *vb* To raise something (most often an anchor) from the seabed.
**White Terror** A reactionary movement targeting real or suspected Jacobins after the fall of Robespierre. The name derives from the traditional use of white as a symbol of the Bourbon Monarchy – as opposed to the red of the Revolutionaries.
**wind** 1. The direction from which the wind blows. 2. The windward position, the weather gage. 3. **head** — a wind coming from ahead, one making progress on that course impossible. 4. **off the** — *adv.* sailing with the wind abaft the beam. 5. **on the** — *adv.* sailing close-hauled.
**yard** 1. A spar hung horizontally from a mast to spread the head or foot of a square sail. 2. An establishment to build, repair and supply warships.3. — **arm**, the extreme ends of a yard. 4. **main** — the yard spreading the mainsail.
**yaw** Deviations from side to side of the ship's course under pressure of wind and sea.

# NOTES

**Prologue**

[1] J. Gilchrist and W.J. Murray, eds, *The Press in the French Revolution*, 74.
[2] S. Dunn, *The Deaths of Louis XVI*, 10; M. Walzer, ed., *Regicide and Revolution*, 8; Gilchrist and Murray, eds, *The Press in the French Revolution*, 152.
[3] Walzer, ed., *Regicide and Revolution*, 1.
[4] J. Morrill, 'King-Killing in Perspective', 293–9.
[5] Quoted in M. Price, *The Fall of the French Monarchy*, 328.

**Introduction**

[1] NMM: MSS/82/150.0
[2] Anon, 'Description of the Monument', 363–4.
[3] This is explained in full in Appendix I.
[4] The French fought the British during the War of American Independence, a war fought by the Americans for ideological purposes, but by the French for dynastic aggrandisement.
[5] Since the Four Days' Battle of 1–4 June 1666.
[6] Since the Battle of Barfleur of 19–23 May 1692.
[7] Since the St James' Day Fight of 25 July 1666 witnessed by Willem Van de Velde the Elder.
[8] There are different views on the origins of the Terror. All are discussed here. H. Gough, *The Terror*, 2–6.
[9] R. Scurr, *Fatal Purity*, 296.
[10] E.A. Hughes, ed., *Private Correspondence*, 43.
[11] NMM: DUC/1/14.
[12] NMM JCD/12.
[13] NMM: BRK/14.
[14] NMM: FLI/8B.

**Chapter 1**

[1] R. Cobb and C. Jones, eds, *Voices of the French Revolution*, 206.
[2] N. Hampson, *Prelude to Terror*, x.
[3] *The Task* by William Cowper, 1785. For more on this see E. Royle, *Revolutionary Britannia*, 13ff.

[4] P. Griffith, *Art of War*, 29, 77; P.M. Jones, *French Revolution*, 58.
[5] Quoted in Scurr, *Fatal Purity*, 256.
[6] G. Best, *War and Society*, 97.
[7] There is a good description of French military panic in 1793 in Griffith, *Art of War*, 182–5.
[8] Quoted in T.C.W. Blanning, *French Revolutionary Wars*, 101.
[9] N. Aston, *French Revolution, 1789–1804*, 38.
[10] S. Schama, *Citizens*, 668.
[11] P. McPhee, *French Revolution*, 146.
[12] McPhee, *French Revolution*, 138.
[13] After the extraordinary French victory over a much larger Austrian army on 6 November 1792.
[14] I. Germani and R. Swales, eds, *Symbols, Myths and Images*, 14–15; J.A. Leith, *Space and Revolution*, 4.
[15] A. Forrest, *Soldiers of the French Revolution*, 109.
[16] W.S. Cormack, *Revolution*, 27.
[17] J.J. Keevil, *Medicine and the Navy 1200–1900*, 253.
[18] Cormack, *Revolution*, 86–7.
[19] Cormack, *Revolution*, 118.
[20] Guérin, *Histoire Maritime*, 17, 500 n. 2; N. Hampson, *La Marine*, 200.
[21] Griffith, *Art of War*, 131; Hampson, *La Marine*, 193.
[22] Quoted in Cormack, *Revolution*, 219.
[23] H.W. Hodges, ed., *Select Naval Documents*, 163.
[24] Cormack, *Revolution*, 220–222; Hampson, *La Marine*, 201.
[25] M. Acerra and J. Meyer, *Marines et Révolution*, 80–8.
[26] M. Duffy and R. Morriss, eds, *Glorious First of June*, 25; Dull, *Age of the Ship of the Line*, 130.
[27] Hampson, *La Marine*, 137.
[28] Acerra and Meyer, *Marines*, 32.

**Chapter 2**
[1] R.J.B Knight, *Pursuit of Victory*, 165.
[2] M. Bouloiseau, *Jacobin Republic*, 210.
[3] Quoted in Cormack, *Revolution*, 182.
[4] Quoted in M. Crook, *Toulon in War and Revolution*, 131.
[5] J. Holland Rose, *Lord Hood and the Defence of Toulon*, 12.
[6] Cormack, *Revolution*, 196–213.
[7] J. Mori, 'The British Government and the Bourbon Restoration', 706.
[8] C.J. Fox, *Napoleon Bonaparte and The Siege of Toulon*, 13.
[9] The idea that the fleet had received contradictory instructions to protect a convoy at the same time is unfounded. Hampson, *La Marine*, 74.
[10] Cormack, *Revolution*, 233.
[11] Holland Rose, *Defence of Toulon*, 8.
[12] Knight, *Pursuit*, 165; Holland Rose, *Defence of Toulon*, 8, 51, 77; Crook, *Toulon in War*, 150.

[13] Quoted in Crook, *Toulon in War*, 147.
[14] Quoted in Cormack, *Revolution*, 251, 255.
[15] Cormack, *Revolution*, 198–9.
[16] Bouloiseau, *Jacobin Republic*, 162.
[17] Quoted in Bouloiseau, *Jacobin Republic*, 171.
[18] R.R. Palmer, *Twelve who Ruled*, 183.
[19] Cormack, *Revolution*, 272.
[20] Cormack, *Revolution*, 235. For example, Pierre-Jean Vanstabel and François-Joseph Bouvet.
[21] Warner, *First of June*, 55; Lévy-Schneider, *Le Conventionnel*, 501; Griffith, *Art of War*, 121.
[22] E.H. Jenkins, *A History of the French Navy*, 210S.
[23] Cormack, *Revolution*, 253.
[24] *Gazette Nationale* 5 November 1793, 12 Jan 1794, 5 Feb 1794; Cormack, *Revolution*, 274.
[25] Palmer, *Twelve who Ruled*, 183, 228; Bouloiseau, *Jacobin Republic*, xv, 207.
[26] de Jonnès, *Adventures*, 54.
[27] Cormack, *Revolution*, 259.
[28] Acerra and Meyer, *Marines*, 168; Hampson, *La Marine*, 230; P. Henwood and E. Monange, *Brest: Un Port en Révolution*, 161–3, 217.
[29] Henwood and Monange, *Brest*, 188–91, 204–6.
[30] For a detailed breakdown of those executed, see Henwood and Monange, *Brest*.
[31] Blanning, *Revolutionary Wars*, 201.
[32] Hampson, *La Marine*, 241–4; W.J. James, *The Naval History of Great Britain*, 379–81.
[33] Palmer, *Twelve who Ruled*, 226.
[34] Best, *War and Society*, 95.
[35] Henwood and Monange, *Brest*, 217; C. Jones, *The Longman Companion to the French Revolution*, 32.
[36] J. Barrow, *The Life of Richard, Earl Howe*, 288.
[37] Biographical Memoir of Earl Howe, *Naval Chronicle* I (1799), 22.
[38] M.A. Lewis, ed., *Narrative*, 130; A. Phillimore, *The Life of Sir W. Parker*, 60.
[39] Hampson, *La Marine*, 213–4
[40] Quoted in Cormack, *Revolution*, 259.
[41] Hampson, *La Marine*, 193; C. Rouvier, *Histoire des Marins Français*, 139.
[42] Anonymous French writer, quoted in James, *Naval History* I, 123.
[43] This is contested by Hampson, *La Marine*, 140.
[44] Hampson, *La Marine*, 136.
[45] M. de Jonnès, *Adventures*, 53.
[46] Hampson, *La Marine*, 132–3, 216–17.
[47] Griffith, *Art of War*, 187.
[48] Acerra and Meyer, *Marines*, 171; Cormack, *Revolution*, 243.

## Chapter 3

[1] Nelson to Howe 8 Jan 1799, N.H. Nicholas, ed., *Dispatches*, III, 230.
[2] Barrow, *Life of Howe*, 421.
[3] *Felix Farley's Bristol Journal* 18 Oct 1783; *Whitehall Evening Post* 9–11 Oct, 11–14 Oct 1783; *Morning Chronicle and London Advertiser* 9 Oct 1783. Thanks to Mike Duffy for these references and for pointing out the difference between John Hervey, John Hervey and John Hervey. Roger Knight thought it was John Hervey, I thought it was John Hervey, but it turned out to be John Hervey. Who knew?
[4] Knight, 'Earl Howe', 279, 297.
[5] Knight, 'Earl Howe', 292.
[6] N.A.M. Rodger, *Command of the Ocean,* 355.
[7] Hodges, ed., *Naval Documents*, 186.
[8] D Syrett, 'Check List', 128.
[9] Hodges, ed., *Naval Documents*, 186.
[10] Knight, 'Earl Howe', 280.
[11] Hodges, ed., *Naval Documents*, 185.
[12] B. Lavery, ed., *Shipboard Life and Organisation*, 83.
[13] Lavery, ed., *Shipboard Life and Organisation*, 82–6.
[14] Anon, *Short Account of Naval Actions*, 126–7.
[15] Anon, *Short Account of Naval Actions*, 126–7.
[16] R Morriss, ed., *The Channel Fleet and the Blockade of Brest*, 36.
[17] Syrett, 'Check List', 128.
[18] C. Lloyd and J. Coulter, *Medicine and the Navy*, III, 159; Rodger, *Command of the Ocean*, 404; Lavery, ed., *Life and Organisation*, 497; Syrett, 'Check List', 128.
[19] Rodger, *Command of the Ocean*, 364.
[20] Webb, 'Nootka Sound', 141-5.
[21] Knight, 'Earl Howe', 285.
[22] Rodger, *Insatiable Earl*, 309.
[23] Knight, 'Earl Howe', 280-5.
[24] J.B. Bourchier, ed., *Memoir*, I, 12.
[25] O. Warner, *First of June*, 18.
[26] P.K. Ober, *Mark Twain and Medicine,* 137, 139, 142.
[27] Morriss, ed., *Channel Fleet*, 16.
[28] A. Aspinall, ed., *The Later Correspondence of George III*, 290.
[29] Bourchier, ed., *Memoir*, I, 29.
[30] Hughes, ed., *Collingwood Correspondence*, 36.
[31] Hughes, ed., *Collingwood Correspondence*, 36.
[32] All quoted in Webb, 'Nootka Sound', 151.
[33] S.J. Robertson, 'The Mobilization of the British Navy', 19–20.
[34] James, *Naval History* I, 178; Bourchier, ed., *Memoir*, I, 13; Robertson, 'Mobilization', 60.
[35] TNA: ADM 1/100 f. 72, 91.
[36] TNA: ADM 1/100 f.57, 86, 247, 266, 298.
[37] TNA: ADM 1/100 f. 264.

[38] TNA: ADM 1/100 f. 150.
[39] TNA: ADM 1/100 5 Jan 1794.
[40] Trotter, *Medicina Nautica*, I, 65–8.
[41] TNA: ADM 1/100 f. 137–9.
[42] TNA: ADM 1.100 f. 164.
[43] J.K. Laughton, ed., *Barham Papers*, II, 4; D Syrett, *Admiral Lord Howe*, 122.
[44] Bourchier, ed., *Memoir*, I, 19.
[45] For Collingwood's critical view of this campaign, see Hughes, ed., *Collingwood Correspondence*, 40–1.
[46] Hughes, ed., *Collingwood Correspondence*, 40.
[47] Bourchier, ed., *Memoir*, I, 18.
[48] TNA: ADM 1/100 f. 196, 205.

**Chapter 4**

[1] Quoted in H. Stoddart, *Rings of Desire*,86.
[2] P. Harrington, *British Artists and War*, 22.
[3] There is some suggestion that he painted the pictures from someone else's notes. See Dominic Serres (1722–93), *ODNB*. Also see A. Russett, *Dominic Serres R.A.*, 23, 34–5, 46.
[4] N.A.M. Rodger, 'Image and Reality in Eighteenth Century Naval Tactics'; Willis, *Fighting at Sea*.
[5] Quoted in N. Tracy, *Britannia's Palette*, 7.
[6] Thanks to Mark Barker of The Inshore Squadron for help with this.
[7] Quoted in N. Bentley, *The History of the Circus*, 11.
[8] Stoddart, *Rings of Desire*, 90.
[9] Stoddart, *Rings of Desire*, 85–86.
[10] Quoted in Stoddart, *Rings of Desire*, 86.
[11] H.P. Parker, 'Eminent Marine Artists', 41.
[12] C. Baugh, 'Philippe James de Loutherbourg', 116.
[13] S. Rosenfeld, *Georgian Scene Painters*, 31.
[14] J. Gage, 'Loutherbourg: Mystagogue of the Sublime', 333.
[15] Gage, 'Loutherbourg', 335.
[16] Gage, 'Loutherbourg', 334–5.
[17] Quoted in Tracy, *Britannia's Palette*, 44.
[18] *General Advertiser*, 1 Nov 1779.
[19] Baugh, 'Loutherbourg', 99; S. Rosenfeld, *A Short History of Scene Design*, 88; Tracy, *Britannia's Palette*, 44–5; E. Wind, 'The Revolution of History Painting', 118–19.
[20] Quoted in Tracy, *Britannia's Palette*, 44 and C. Baugh, *Garrick and Loutherbourg*, 80.
[21] Quoted in Baugh, *Garrick and Loutherbourg*, 80.
[22] Quoted in Gage, 'Loutherbourg', 332.
[23] Wind, 'Revolution', 118.
[24] L. Brandon, *Art and War*, 30–1; Wind, 'Revolution', 116.

[25] Harrington, *British Artists and War*, 69.
[26] J. Bonehill, 'Exhibiting War', 139-142; Harrington, *British Artists and War*, 51.
[27] Tracy, *Britannia's Palette*, 23-4.
[28] Harrington, *British Artists and War*, 69.
[29] Stoddart, *Rings of Desire*, 85.
[30] Quoted in D. Cordingly, *Pocock*, 40.
[31] Cordingly, *Pocock*, 40.
[32] Quoted in Cordingly, *Pocock*, 11.

**Chapter 5**

[1] Quoted in Warner, *First of June*, 56. It is unclear where Warner sourced the quote. See E.P. Brenton, *Naval History*, I, 245.
[2] Quoted in McPhee, *French Revolution*, 144.
[3] Scurr, *Fatal Purity*, 306.
[4] Scurr, *Fatal Purity*, 294–295.
[5] Quoted in Cormack, *Revolution*, 275.
[6] P. Crowhurst, *The French War on Trade*, 10; M.A.J. Palmer, 'Lord Nelson, Master of Command', 252–3.
[7] L. Evans, 'The Convoy', 122.
[8] P. Jarnoux, 'Autour des combats de Prairial', 174.
[9] Jarnoux, 'Convoi Vanstabel', 175 and n. 6.
[10] Jarnoux, 'Convoi Vanstabel', 170–1; L.S. Kramer, 'The French Revolution', 35.
[11] Kramer, 'French Revolution', 29–37.
[12] Black, *Crisis of Empire*, 176–7.
[13] Kramer, 'French Revolution', 41.
[14] Jarnoux, 'Convoi Vanstabel', 171; Kramer, 'French Revolution', 39.
[15] Jarnoux, 'Convoi Vanstabel', 171, 176–7.
[16] Quoted in M. Duffy, *Soldiers, Sugar, and Seapower*, 5.
[17] Blanning, *Revolutionary Wars*, 207.
[18] Duffy, *Soldiers, Sugar, and Seapower*, 44.
[19] D.P. Geggus, *Slavery, War, And Revolution*, 1.
[20] C. Ware, 'The Glorious First of June', 26.
[21] Geggus, *Slavery*, 108–14.
[22] Quoted in Duffy, *Soldiers, Sugar, and Seapower*, 95.
[23] TNA: FO 5/6 f.148, 192; Duffy, *Soldiers, Sugar, and Seapower*, 108.
[24] TNA FO 5/6 f. 161.
[25] TNA: FO 5/6 f. 175.
[26] TNA: FO 5/6 f. 176.
[27] Knowles to Stevens 11 June 1794, TNA: ADM 1/2016.
[28] TNA: FO 5/6 f. 161.
[29] TNA: FO 5/6 f. 179.
[30] Henwood and Monange, *Brest*, 211.
[31] Jarnoux, 'Convoi Vanstabel', 179.
[32] There is some uncertainty about the size of the convoy but 156 is the figure

given by Consul Hamilton, who saw it leave. M. Duffy, 'Man who Missed the Grain', 117 n. 11; Palmer, *Twelve who Ruled*, 343.

[33] TNA: FO 5/6; Cormack, *Revolution*, 275.

[34] Jarnoux, 'Convoi Vanstabel', 180.

[35] Duffy, 'Man who Missed the Grain Convoy', 117 n. 11; Jarnoux, 'Convoi Vanstabel', 178–9.

[36] TNA: FO 5/6 f. 162.

[37] TNA: FO 5/6 f. 187.

[38] Knowles to Stevens 4 April 1794, TNA: ADM 1/2016.

[39] Duffy, 'Man who Missed the Grain Convoy', 103.

[40] A. Jeanbon Saint-André, *Journal Sommaire*, 2.

[41] BL: Add. 35194 f. 297.

[42] Lewis, ed., *Dillon's Narrative*, I, 120.

[43] NMM: STT/3.

[44] These figures all come from the ships' musters in the National Archives. For each ship's figures, see Appendix II.

[45] BL: Add. 23207 f.10v, 98; TNA: ADM 1/100 f.290, 301; TNA: ADM 36/11700; www.queensroyalsurreys.org.uk/1661to1966/gloriousfirst/gloriousfirst.html

[46] TNA: ADM 1/2128.

[47] Lewis, ed., *Dillon's Narrative*, I, 121.

[48] Bourchier, ed., *Memoir*, I, 14.

[49] TNA: ADM 1/100 f. 56, 254.

[50] *Bellerophon* ADM 51/1162; *Royal Sovereign* ADM: 52/3361; *Impregnable* ADM 51/1142; *Queen Charlotte* ADM 51/4490; *Barfleur* ADM 51/90; *Queen* ADM 51/753; *Royal George* ADM: 51/774

[51] Howe's orders to these frigates, including some rare signalling orders for transmitting their intelligence, are here: BL: Add. 35194 f. 297.

[52] William Parker to his Father 17 June 1794, Duffy and Morriss, eds, *First of June*, 84.

[53] Lewis, ed., *Dillon's Narrative*, I, 121.

[54] Quoted in Warner, *First of June*, 56.

[55] A. Delaporte, 'The Prairial Battles: The French Viewpoint', 13; Jarnoux, 'Convoi Vanstabel', 181.

[56] Cormack, *Revolution*, 274.

[57] Prieur quoted in Cormack, *Revolution*, 242.

[58] Palmer, *Twelve who Ruled*, 344; Rouvier, *Histoire*, 145.

[59] O. Havard, *Histoire de la Révolution*, 366–7; Henwood and Monange, *Brest*, 226; L. Lévy-Schneider, *Le Conventionnel Jeanbon Saint André*, 793–4.

[60] Knowles to Stevens 4 April 1794, TNA: ADM 1/2016.

[61] Syrett, *Howe*, 131.

[62] James, *Naval History*, I, 129.

[63] James, *Naval History*, I, 128.

[64] Lewis, ed., *Dillon's Narrative*, I, 120.

[65] William Burgh of the *Queen Charlotte* to his sister, 2 June 1794. Private Collection.

[66] William Burgh of the *Queen Charlotte* to his sister, 2 June 1794. Private Collection.
[67] G.L. Newnham Collingwood, *Collingwood Correspondence*, 20.
[68] Duffy and Morriss, eds, *First of June*, 81.
[69] Lewis, ed., *Dillon's Narrative*, I, 120.
[70] R. Gardiner, ed., *Fleet Battle and Blockade*, 27.
[71] TNA: ADM 36/11660; ADM 36/12139; ADM 36/11406; ADM 36/11761.

**Chapter 6**

[1] Quoted in Cormack, *Revolution*, 277.
[2] Palmer, *Twelve who Ruled*, 344.
[3] Hampson, *La Marine*, 217; Rouvier, *Histoire*, I, 163.
[4] Cormack, *Revolution*, 277 n. 148.
[5] Warner, *First of June*, 74.
[6] Cormack, *Revolution*, 277 n. 150.
[7] Palmer, *Twelve who Ruled*, 344.
[8] See Chapter 3.
[9] J.S. Corbett, *Signals and Instructions*, 317.
[10] Quoted in Knight, *Pursuit*, 160–2.
[11] James, *Naval History* I, 62; L. Lévy-Schneider, *Le Conventionnel Jeanbon Saint André*, I, 567, 623–4.
[12] Syrett, *Howe*, 128; James, *Naval History*, I, 129.
[13] Knight, *Pursuit*, 162.
[14] James, *Naval History*, I, 105.
[15] Laird Clowes, *Royal Navy*, IV, 481–5.
[16] For more on the question of French carronades, see Hampson, *La Marine*, 30.
[17] M. Duffy, 'The Gunnery at Trafalgar', 7.
[18] Quoted in Delaporte, 'Prairial Battles', 14.
[19] Warner, *First of June*, 63.
[20] Lavery, *The Ship of the Line*, 122.
[21] E. Chevalier, *Histoire de la Marine Française*, II, 49; Laird Clowes, *Royal Navy*, IV, 543.
[22] Bourchier, ed., *Memoir*, I, 17–18.
[23] The ships Howe chose for the flying squadron were all 74-gunners, the fastest in the fleet, and there were four of them: *Bellerophon*, *Russell*, *Marlborough* and *Thunderer*.
[24] Bourchier, ed., *Memoir*, I, 19.
[25] Duffy and Morriss, eds., *First of June*, 15; T. Sturges Jackson, ed., *Logs*, I, 141.
[26] Palmer, *Twelve who Ruled*, 209.
[27] Log of the *Phaeton* 28 May, Jackson, ed., *Logs*, I, 148–50.
[28] NMM: FLI/8/B.
[29] BL. Add. 23207 f. 21; O. Troude, *Batailles Navales*, II, 351; Nicholas Pocock's Notebook in Duffy and Morriss, eds, *First of June*, 73; James, *Naval History*, I, 131.
[30] Jackson, ed., *Logs* I, 35.

[31] Lewis, ed., *Dillon's Narrative*, I, 123.
[32] Log of the *Thunderer* 28 May, Jackson, ed., *Logs*, I, 131.
[33] Warner, *First of June*, 73.
[34] Log of the *Culloden* 28 May, Jackson, ed., *Logs*, I, 141.
[35] de Jonnès, *Adventures*, 56.
[36] Lewis, ed., *Dillon's Narrative*, I, 122.

**Chapter 7**

[1] James, *Naval History*, I, 131.
[2] NMM: FLI/8/B; William Parker to his father 17 June 1794, Duffy and Morriss, eds., *First of June*, 85.
[3] Journal of Capt Wm Hope 28 May 1794, Jackson, ed., *Logs*, I, 72.
[4] Duffy and Morriss, eds, *First of June*, 85.
[5] BL Add: 23207 f. 5.
[6] In her log, however, the fact that she hauled down her colours as she fell across the *Audacious* is noted. Jackson, ed., *Logs*, I, 99.
[7] Log of the *Queen Charlotte* and *Latona* 28 May, Jackson, ed., *Logs*, I, 24, 162.
[8] Jackson, ed., *Logs*, I, 136.
[9] BL Add: 23207 f. 5–8; BL Add: 23207 f. 5–8; William Parker to his Father 17 June, Duffy and Morriss, eds., *First of June*, 85.
[10] Rouvier, *Histoire*, 140.
[11] Jackson, ed., *Logs*, I, 175.
[12] BL Add: 23207 f. 72; Jackson, ed., *Logs*, I, 36, 89, 108.
[13] BL Add: 23207 f. 9, 55 v; Jackson, ed., *Logs*, I, 99, 85.
[14] Jackson, ed., *Logs*, I, 37.
[15] BL Add. 23207 f. 9.
[16] Jackson, ed., *Logs*, I, 99; James, *Naval History*, I, 133; BL Add. 23207 f. 9.
[17] BL Add/ 23207 f. 6–10.
[18] James, *Naval History*, I, 133.
[19] Cormack, *Revolution*, 278 n. 152.
[20] Troude, *Batailles Navales*, 352.
[21] Jackson, ed., *Logs*, I, 56.
[22] Jackson, ed., *Logs*, I, 155.
[23] This could be a clerical error as the signal was made shortly after noon and all other leading ships picked it up.
[24] Jackson, ed., *Logs*, I, 39.
[25] Lewis, ed., *Dillon's Narrative*, I, 124.
[26] Bourchier, ed., *Memoir*, I, 21.
[27] Bourchier, ed., *Memoir*, I, 18–22.
[28] NMM: BRK/14; NMM: PAR/50; Duffy and Morriss, eds, *First of June*, 86.
[29] Duffy and Morriss, eds, *First of June*, 86.
[30] R. Bevan and W.G. Kemble, 'Narrative of the Engagement', 159.
[31] BL: Add 23207 f. 773; Jackson, ed., *Logs*, I, 68.
[32] Jackson, ed., *Logs*, I, 40.

[33] Lewis, ed., *Dillon's Narrative*, I, 125.
[34] BL Add. 23207 f. 73; Lewis, ed., *Dillon's Narrative*, I, 12–46.
[35] Jackson, ed., *Logs*, I, 73, 81, 120, 143.
[36] Duffy and Morriss, eds, *First of June*, 75; Hughes, ed., *Collingwood Correspondence*, 47.
[37] de Jonnès, *Adventures*, 58–9.
[38] James, *Naval History*, I, 139.
[39] BL Add. 23207 f. 74, 111.
[40] Taken in tow by *La Seine*. Met up with Vanstabel with whom he returned to Brest. Cormack, *Revolution*, 278.
[41] A.C. de Poggi, ed., *A Narrative*, 12, 37–9.
[42] James, *Naval History*, I, 143.
[43] BL Add: 23207 f. 83.
[44] Jackson, ed., *Logs*, I, 85, 103, 108, 109, 137; BL Add: 23207 f. 99.
[45] A contemporary suggestion of Howe's displeasure is Lewis, ed., *Dillon's Narrative*, I, 123.
[46] BL Ad: 23207 f. 125v.
[47] Duffy and Morriss, eds, *First of June*, 85–6.
[48] Jackson, ed., *Logs*, I, 86.
[49] R. Morriss, 'The Glorious First of June', 90 n. 5.
[50] Jackson, ed., *Logs*, I, 52, 82; James, *Naval History*, I, 140.
[51] Jackson, ed., *Logs*, I, 74.
[52] See for example Jackson, ed., *Logs*, I, 57.
[53] Jackson, ed., *Logs*, I, 151, 191.
[54] Jackson, ed., *Logs*, I, 69; BL Add. 23207 f. 57–60v.
[55] C. Ekins, *Naval* Battles, 190.
[56] Duffy and Morriss, eds, *First of June*, 57, 76; James, *Naval History*, I, 144.
[57] Two ships had become separated from his original squadron of five.
[58] Jackson, ed., *Logs*, I, 87, 118, 121.
[59] For more on the difficulty of keeping a ship dark, see NMM: TUN/130 p. 38.
[60] Jackson, ed., *Logs*, I, 69, 94.
[61] Jackson, ed., *Logs*, I, 138.
[62] Jackson, ed., *Logs*, I, 110.
[63] Jackson, ed., *Logs*, I, 52.
[64] Jackson, ed., *Logs*, I, 166.
[65] Jackson, ed., *Logs*, I, 116.
[66] Jackson, ed., *Logs*, I, 26.
[67] Jackson, ed., *Logs*, I, 110, 144; NMM: BRK/14.
[68] Jackson, ed., *Logs*, I, 43, 110.
[69] Jackson, ed., *Logs*, I, 28.
[70] Jackson, ed., *Logs*, I, 77, 87.
[71] James, *Naval History*, I, 146.
[72] Duffy and Morriss, eds, *First of June*, 87.
[73] Jackson, ed., *Logs*, I, 56.

[74] Jackson, ed., *Logs*, I, 44.
[75] BL: Add. 23207 f. 107.
[76] de Poggi, ed., *Narrative*, 13-14; Duffy and Morriss, eds, *First of June*, 76.
[77] Newnham Collingwood, *Collingwood Correspondence*, 21.
[78] de Jonnès, *Adventures*, 59.
[79] Lewis, ed., *Dillon's Narrative*, I, 127.

**Chapter 8**

[1] Barrow, *Life of Howe*, 278.
[2] Nelson, 'Plan of attack' 1803, J.S. Corbett, *Fighting Instructions*, 315; Memo. of a conversation between Nelson and Sir Richard Keats, N.H. Nicholas, ed., *The Dispatches and Letters of Lord Nelson*, VII, 241 n. 9; M. Czisnik, 'Admiral Nelson's Tactics', 557–8.
[3] James, *Naval History*, I, 149.
[4] See for example NMM: MSS/77/133.0; NMM: BRK/14.
[5] N. Pearce, *The Life and Adventures of Nathaniel Pearce*, 9. The *Orion* had a black streak down her side: Duffy and Morriss, eds, *First of June*, 87.
[6] de Jonnès, *Adventures*, 59.
[7] Duffy and Morriss, eds, *First of June*, 87.
[8] Lewis, ed., *Dillon's Narrative*, I, 128. Also see Hughes, ed., *Collingwood Correspondence*, 45.
[9] Bourchier, ed., *Memoir*, I, 31.
[10] It is interesting that the British swapped their ships around and not the French, as it was in the interests of both fleets to do so, but if both fleets reordered their lines it would never have worked. Perhaps Howe was simply the first to make the move and Villaret, concerned over the seamanship of his captains, was content to let him do so.
[11] Bourchier, ed., *Memoir*, I, 31.
[12] Anon, 'Proceedings of His Majesty's Ship the *Orion*' 298; BL: Add. 23207 f 112.
[13] Barrow, *Life of Howe*, 278.
[14] Pearce, *The Life and Adventures of Nathaniel Pearce*, 9.
[15] Lewis, ed., *Dillon's Narrative*, I, 128.
[16] de Jonnès, *Adventures*, 57–60.
[17] J. Greig, ed., *The Farington Diary*, VIII. 129.
[18] Pearce, *The Life and Adventures of Nathaniel Pearce*, 9–10.
[19] Lewis, ed., *Dillon's Narrative*, I, 128.
[20] Newnham Collingwood, *Collingwood Correspondence*, 21.
[21] Jackson, ed., *Logs*, I, 112.
[22] Lewis, ed., *Dillon's Narrative*, I, 128–9.
[23] Hughes, ed., *Collingwood Correspondence*, 45.
[24] Biographical Memoir of Earl Howe, *Naval Chronicle*, I (1799), 22.
[25] Bourchier, ed., *Memoir*, I, 21–23; Lewis, ed., *Dillon's Narrative*, I, 131.
[26] Duffy and Morriss, eds., *First of June*, 87; NMM: BRK/14; Hughes, ed., *Collingwood Correspondence*, 47.

[27] BL: Add 23207 f. 127.
[28] Many thanks to Dr Phil Weir for this.
[29] de Jonnès, *Adventures*, 60.
[30] Bourchier, ed., *Memoir*, I, 25.
[31] Ekins, *Naval Battles*, 189. Codrington agrees: he says the foretopmast of the *Queen Charlotte* fell as soon as she hauled her wind. Bourchier, ed., *Memoir*, I, 24; Duffy and Morriss, eds, *First of June*, 61.
[32] Bourchier, ed., *Memoir*, I, 160.
[33] James, *Naval History*, I, 152.
[34] BL: ADD 23207 f. 112; Bevan and Kemble, 'Narrative,' 160; Lewis, ed., *Dillon's Narrative*, I, 1.
[35] James, *Naval History*, I, 161 fn.*.
[36] M.A. Talbot, *The Life and Surprising Adventures of Mary Anne Talbot*, 155–8.
[37] Duffy and Morriss, eds, *First of June*, 95.
[38] Bevan and Kemble, 'Narrative' 165.
[39] Ekins, *Naval Battles*, 194.
[40] Bevan and Kemble, 'Narrative', 165; NMM: STT/3; NMM: FLI/8/B.
[41] Bevan and Kemble, 'Narrative', 166.
[42] Bevan and Kemble, 'Narrative', 168. For another ref. to the dead being thrown overboard, see Lewis, ed., *Dillon's Narrative*, I, 130. The British practice of doing so is well-known but it is curious that the French are also doing this: it is understood that at Trafalgar in 1805 the French did not throw their dead overboard but piled them up in the centre of the gun decks. See Duffy, 'Gunnery'.
[43] NMM: STT/3; Bevan and Kemble, 'Narrative', 164; James, *Naval History*, I, 162 fn.*.
[44] Bevan and Kemble, 'Narrative', 163; Jackson, ed., *Logs*, I 102; NMM: STT/3; Duffy and Morriss, eds, *First of June*, 94–5.
[45] BL: ADD 23207 f. 114.
[46] Duffy and Morriss, eds, *First of June*, 88. A French source for this action is Troude, *Batailles Navales*, 350ff.
[47] Cormack, *Revolution*, 279.
[48] Duffy and Morriss, eds, *First of June*, 98; Jackson, ed., *Logs*, I, 130.
[49] Jackson, ed., *Logs*, I, 70.
[50] Bourchier, ed., *Memoir* I, 28.
[51] Duffy and Morriss, eds, *First of June*, 81.
[52] Duffy and Morriss, eds, *First of June*, 77–88.
[53] Jackson, ed., *Logs*, I, 70.
[54] Barrow, *Life of Howe*, 289.
[55] BL: Add 23207 f. 13.
[56] Jackson, ed., *Logs*, I, 134.
[57] Three without masts standing *Scipion*, *Mucius* and *Jemappes*. Also the *Terrible* and *Républicain*.
[58] de Poggi, ed., *Narrative*, 23.
[59] NMM: STT/3.

[60] Biographical Memoir of Earl Howe, *Naval Chronicle*, I, (1799), 22 fn.†.
[61] Duffy and Morriss, eds, *First of June*, 89; Bevan and Kemble, 'Narrative', 169.
[62] Troude, *Batailles Navales*, II, 355.
[63] James, *Naval History*, I, 165.
[64] Duffy and Morriss, eds, *First of June*, 89.
[65] Duffy and Morriss, eds, *First of June*, 89; Hughes, ed., *Collingwood Correspondence*, 48.
[66] Duffy and Morriss, eds, *First of June*, 88.
[67] Jackson, ed., *Logs*, I, 113.
[68] Newnham Collingwood, *Collingwood Correspondence*, 23.
[69] de Jonnès, *Adventures*, 65.
[70] Bourchier, ed., *Memoir*, I, 26, 27; Jackson, ed., *Logs*, I, 113, 130; BL: Add 23207 f. 43, 107v.
[71] Jackson, ed., *Logs*, I, 113, 114, 130.
[72] Loir, M., 'L'adoption du pavillon Tricolore', 600–19; Henwood and Monange, *Brest*, 226; de Jonnès, *Adventures*, 60.
[73] de Jonnès, *Adventures*, 61–62.
[74] Lewis, ed., *Dillon's Narrative*, I, 131; Duffy and Morriss, eds, *First of June*, 80, 86; Newnham Collingwood, *Collingwood Correspondence*, 22.
[75] J. Greig, ed., *The Farington Diary*, I, 216–17; Cormack, *Revolution*, 286.
[76] Jackson, ed., *Logs*, I, 57.
[77] Jackson, ed., *Logs*, I, 58, 152–3.
[78] There is one entirely uncorroborated claim from a French historian writing in the mid-nineteenth century that the British also used red-hot shot. Rouvier, *Histoire*, I, 161; Newnham Collingwood, *Collingwood Correspondence*, 23.
[79] James, *Naval History*, I, 168.
[80] Duffy and Morriss, eds, *First of June*, 88.
[81] Bevan and Kemble, 'Narrative', 163; Also see NMM: STT/3.
[82] Lewis, ed., *Dillon's Narrative*, 131.
[83] Bevan and Kemble, 'Narrative', 164.
[84] Barrow, *Life of Howe*, 275–6; Laird Clowes, *Royal Navy*, IV, 230 n. 1. A similar story of a brave cockerel survives from the Battle of San Domingo, 1806. See NC, XV (1806), 451.
[85] Jeanbon Saint-André, *Journal Sommaire*, 26–7; James, *Naval History*, I, 174.
[86] NMM: BRK/14; G. Cole, 'The Office of Ordnance', 159, 163–5, 177.
[87] Jackson, ed., *Logs*, I, 148.
[88] Cormack, *Revolution*, 280 n. 163; James, *Naval History*, I, 160; Rouvier, *Histoire*, I, 165.
[89] Lewis, ed., *Dillon's Narrative*, I, 133.
[90] Jackson, ed., *Logs*, I, 112.
[91] A.B. Caruana, *The History of English Sea Ordnance*, II, 396; W. Falconer, ed., *Universal Dictionary of the Marine*, 64–5.
[92] Acerra and Meyer, *Marines*, 177; Lewis, ed., *Dillon's Narrative*, I, 130 n. 1, 133.
[93] TNA: ADM 1/1509 f. 111. I have not been able to find out if the invention was

widely adopted. A research project for somebody please!

[94] Caruana, *English Sea Ordnance*, II, 389–95.

[95] Bevan and Kemble, 'Narrative', 163; Lewis, ed., *Dillon's Narrative*, I, 130.

[96] Cormack, *Revolution*, 286; Chevalier, *Histoire de la Marine*, 141.

[97] Bevan and Kemble, 'Narrative', 162.

[98] BL: Add. 23207 f. 81v.

[99] Bevan and Kemble, 'Narrative' 161.

[100] For a detailed breakdown, see James, *Naval History*, I, 387; Lloyd and Coulter, *Medicine*, III, 181.

[101] NMM: FLI/8/B.

[102] Hughes, ed., *Collingwood Correspondence*, 45.

[103] Griffith, *Art of War*, 266 estimates a high-end figure of 4,270 dead and 3,254 taken prisoner. Also see Cormack, *Revolution*, 284.

[104] The most recent criticism is Syrett, *Howe*, 135; also see Barrow, *Life of Howe*, 253–5 and Lewis, ed., *Dillon's Narrative*, I, 126 for contemporary criticism.

[105] Bourchier, ed., *Memoir*, I, 27.

[106] Duffy and Morriss, eds, *First of June*, 81.

[107] Newnham Collingwood, *Collingwood Correspondence*, 19.

[108] Jackson, ed., *Logs*, I, 57, 118, 120, 165; NMM: HSR/B/9.

[109] Taken from the musters in the National Archives in ADM 36.

[110] Jackson, ed., *Logs*, I, 160.

[111] The term actually used is 'shook'. Jackson, ed., *Logs*, I, 97; Phillimore, *The Life of Sir W. Parker*, 44; NMM: PAR/50.

[112] TNA: ADM 36/13767.

[113] Pearce, *The Life and Adventures of Nathaniel Pearce*, 10.

[114] BL: ADD 23207 f. 80–1.

[115] Jackson, ed., *Logs*, I, 174.

[116] Lewis, ed., *Dillon's Narrative*, I, 134.

[117] Jackson, ed., *Logs*, I, 153.

[118] BL: Add. 23207 f. 61.

[119] BL: Add 23207 f. 53–4;

[120] NMM: PAR/50; J.J. Fresselicque, *A Sermon of Praise and Thanksgiving*, 22–5.

[121] Lewis, ed., *Dillon's Narrative*, I, 130.

[122] Jackson, ed., *Logs*, I, 139; TNA: ADM 1/100 f. 294.

[123] He had a cot, not a hammock because his captain, John Duckworth, believed that hammocks were bad for growing boys. Phillimore, *The Life of W. Parker*, 56.

[124] Phillimore, *The Life of W. Parker*, 46; TNA: ADM 1.100 f. 451.

[125] Jackson, ed., *Logs*, I, 88, 125; Lewis, ed., *Dillon's Narrative*, I, 132.

[126] de Jonnès, *Adventures*, 66.

[127] de Jonnès, *Adventures*, 65–8.

[128] Lewis, ed., *Dillon's Narrative*, I, 133.

[129] Duffy and Morriss, eds, *First of June*, 81.

[130] NMM: PAR/50; Duffy and Morriss, eds, *First of June*, 82 n. 6.

[131] Bourchier, ed., *Memoir*, I, 24.

[132] Lewis, ed., *Dillon's Narrative*, I, 131.
[133] de Jonnès, *Adventures*, 63.
[134] Barrow, *Life of Howe*, 287.
[135] NMM: ADL/M/8: TNA: ADM 36/11700.
[136] M Crumplin, 'Surgery', 72; Lloyd and Coulter, *Medicine III*, 160–1.
[137] de Jonnès, *Adventures*, 66.
[138] Duffy and Morriss, eds, *First of June*, 108.
[139] Duffy and Morriss, eds, *First of June*, 111.
[140] Troude, *Batailles Navales*, II, 362; Chevalier, *Histoire de la Marine Française*, 144.
[141] Chevalier, *Histoire de la marine Française*, 144.
[142] Duffy and Morriss, eds, *First of June*, 111. Jarnoux claims fifteen: Jarnoux, 'Convoi Vanstabel', 180–2.

**Chapter 9**

[1] Quoted in Cordingly, *Pocock*, 105.
[2] *Royal Sovereign*, *Impregnable*, *Marlborough*, *Tremendous*, *Gibraltar*, *Culloden*, *Orion*, *Alfred*, *Montagu*.
[3] NMM: POR/F/21; FLI/8/B.
[4] Biographical Memoir of Earl Howe, *Naval Chronicle*, I, (1799), 22–3.
[5] Thomas Hardy (1769–1839), *ODNB*.
[6] Greig, ed., *Farington Diary*, I, 53.
[7] TNA: ADM 2.605 f. 379–80; de Poggi, ed., *Narrative*, 23; Aspinall, ed., *Later Correspondence of George III*, II, 217. Prince Ernest later became King of Hanover.
[8] A.E. Aspinall, *The Correspondence of George, Prince of Wales*, 433; de Poggi, ed., *Narrative*, 23; Jackson, ed., *Logs*, I, 100; BL Add. 23207 f. 3.
[9] P. Van der Merwe, 'A battle of art and theatre', 137.
[10] P Jupp, ed., *The Letter-Journal of George Canning 1793–5*, 121.
[11] Quoted in Duffy and Morriss, eds, *First of June*, 1–2.
[12] P.J. Marshall and J.A. Woods, eds, *The Correspondence of Edmund Burke*, VII, 549.
[13] Jenks, *Engagements*, 44–5.
[14] J. Black and P. Woodfine, eds, *The British Navy*, 3; Jenks, *Engagements*, 3.
[15] Quoted in Jenks, *Engagements*, 27.
[16] Aspinall, *Correspondence of Prince of Wales*, 437.
[17] Barrow, *Life of Howe*, 290.
[18] The letter to Howe from the Speaker of the Commons is here NMM: AGC/13/6 and Howe's answer to the House of Lords is here: BL: Add. 35194 f. 297. Biographical Memoir of Earl Howe, *Naval Chronicle* I (1799), 22; Barrow, *Life of Howe*, 288.
[19] K. Douglas-Morris, *The Naval General Service Medal Roll*, 3–14; B. Tomlinson, 'The Battle Sanctified', 166.
[20] The first known examples of these gold anchors appear to have been distributed to officers in Rodney's fleet at the Battle of the Saints (1782). Within Lord Howe's fleet at the Glorious First of June there were a number of officers who had also

served with Rodney twelve years previously, so the practice may have been continued from those days. Whether the anchors were intended to be worn by the officers or were presents by the officers to their wives and sweethearts is open to question. Many thanks to Sim Comfort for help with this.

[21] TNA: ADM 7/706; Brenton, *Naval* History, I, 154; Barrow, *Life of Howe*, 269; Warner, *First of June*, 157 fn.*.

[22] Farington claimed it was £10,000 Tracy, *Britannia's Palette*, 71.

[23] See S.B.A. Willis, *The Admiral Benbow*, 91.

[24] TNA: ADM 1/1001 f. 116; Warner, *First of June*, 162–3.

[25] Barrow, *Life of Howe*, 269.

[26] Brenton, *Naval History*, I, 155; BL: Add. 35194 f. 297; Barrow, *Life of Howe*, 288.

[27] Trotter thought the figure was 1,800l. T. Trotter, *Medicina Nautica*, I, 78; O. Warner, 'Howe at the Glorious First of June', 153.

[28] Duffy and Morriss, eds., *First of June*, 90.

[29] Trotter, *Medicina Nautica*, I, 78.

[30] M. Lincoln, *Representing the Royal Navy*, 85.

[31] Crumplin, 'Surgery in the Royal Navy', 71.

[32] Barrow, *Life of Howe*, 288; Laird Clowes, *Royal Navy*, IV, 161; Warner, *First of June*, 163; BL: Add 35195; Brenton, *Naval History*, I, 155; Phillimore, *The Life of Sir W. Parker*, 58; I. Schomberg, *The Naval Chronology*, I, 271–4.

[33] Trotter, *Medicina Nautica*, I, 78, 87.

[34] NMM: XDUC/27/49.

[35] Aspinall, ed., *Later Correspondence of George III*, II, 216–20; Aspinall, *Correspondence of Prince of Wales*, 435.

[36] Jenks, *Engagements*, 51. Anon., *An historical account*, 3–6; Barrow, *Life of Howe*, 260, 282–9.

[37] Barrow, *Life of Howe*, 280–290;. Hughes, ed., *Collingwood Correspondence*, 49–50; Anon., *An historical account*, 3–6.

[38] The King had asked that it contain 'some remark on a nation attached to religion, good government and obedience to law, in opposition to those hurried on by anarchy, irreligion and every horrid excess Aspinall, ed., *Later Correspondence of George III*, II, 220.

[39] Barrow, *Life of Howe*, 260.

[40] Anon, *An historical* account, 3–6; Barrow, *Life of Howe*, 260; NMM: FLI/8/B.

[41] Barrow, *Life of Howe*, 282.

[42] Black and Woodfine, eds, *British Navy*, 16.

[43] Anon, 'Description of the Monument', 363.

[44] Tomlinson, 'The Battle Sanctified', 165.

[45] TNA: ADM 1/100 f.290; BL: Add. 23207 f. 10, 98.

[46] Schomberg, *The Naval Chronology*, I, 271.

[47] Barrow, *Life of Howe*, 269.

[48] Duffy and Morriss, eds, *First of June*, 90.

[49] Duffy and Morriss, eds, *First of June*, 20.

[50] Henwood and Monange, *Brest*, 268.

[51] Jeanbon Saint-André, *Journal Sommaire*, 4–9.
[52] Henwood and Monange, *Brest*, 229.
[53] Acerra and Meyer, *Marines*, 174–5.
[54] Best, *War and Society*, 97; Chevalier, *Histoire de la Marine*, II, 161.
[55] Best, *War and Society*, 97.
[56] Cormack, *Revolution*, 281.
[57] Biographical Memoir of Earl Howe, *Naval Chronicle*, I (1799), 22; Greig, ed., *Farington Diary*, I, 236.
[58] Rouvier, *Histoire*, I, 176.
[59] H. Schneider, 'Le Mythe du Vaisseau Le Vengeur', 71–5.
[60] TNA: FO 5/6 f. 243–4.
[61] A. Forrest, *The Legacy of the French Revolutionary Wars*, 32.
[62] Van der Merwe, 'Art and Theatre', 133.
[63] Van der Merwe, 'Art and Theatre', 137.
[64] NMM: BHC 0469.
[65] de Poggi, ed., *Narrative*, 100ff.
[66] Tracy, *Britannia's Palette*, 68.
[67] Quoted in D. Evans, *Mather* Brown, 128.
[68] Warner, 'Howe at the Glorious First of June', 2.
[69] Quoted in Harrington, *British Artists and War*, 71.
[70] Tracy, *Britannia's Palette*, 58–59.
[71] Tracy, *Britannia's Palette*, 59, 74; Warner, 'Howe at the Glorious First of June', 147.
[72] *The Naval Chronicle* I (1799), 24 and see 154; also see 300 for a depiction of Lord Hood's action off Lorient (1795) with an accompanying detailed description.
[73] Tracy, *Britannia's Palette*, 88.
[74] A copy is here TNA: ADM 7/884.
[75] Quoted in Warner, 'Howe at the Glorious First of June', 152.
[76] H. Owen, 'An Eyewitness Account', 336.

**Chapter 10**

[1] G. Montagu, *Statement of a Correspondence*, XXII.
[2] NMM: HOW/4; Barrow, *Life of Howe*, 285; Jupp, ed., *Letter-Journal of George Canning*, 126.
[3] Aspinall, *Correspondence of Prince of Wales*, 436.
[4] Jupp, ed., *Letter-Journal of George Canning 1793–5*, 122.
[5] NMM: XDUC 27/47–52.
[6] Phillimore, *Life of Sir W. Parker*, 45–47.
[7] NMM: AGC/8/33.
[8] See for example NMM: MSS/77/133.0; NMM: MSS/82/150.0; BL: ADD. 35194 f. 297; Hughes, ed., *Collingwood Correspondence*, 48.
[9] NMM: PAR/50; TNA: ADM 52/2812.
[10] J. Ehrman, *The Younger Pitt*, 349.
[11] See for example BL: Add. 23207 f. 40, 60v.

[12] J.B. Hattendorf et al., eds, *British Naval Documents*, 543.
[13] NMM: STT/3.
[14] Aspinall, *Correspondence of Prince of Wales*, 437.
[15] Aspinall, ed., *Later Correspondence of George III*, II, 221.
[16] Warner, *First of June*, 157.
[17] Barrow, *Life of Howe*, 240.
[18] Though he was mentioned in the first letter as one of the wounded officers.
[19] Hughes, ed., *Collingwood Correspondence*, 49.
[20] BL: Add. 23207 f. 40.
[21] Hughes, ed., *Collingwood Correspondence*, 49–52.
[22] Hughes, ed., *Collingwood Correspondence*, 49–52.
[23] de Poggi, ed., *Narrative*, 20–1.
[24] Morriss, 'British View', 68.
[25] BL: Add 23207 f. 57.
[26] See for example Acerra and Meyer, *Marines*, 177; M. Duffy and R. Mackay, *Hawke, Nelson and British Naval Leadership*, 150–1 and n. 81; Duffy and Morriss, eds, *First of June*, 68; Knight, 'Earl Howe', 296. For contemporary perception see Greig, ed., *The Farington Diary*, VIII, 129.
[27] BL: Add. 23207 f. 127.
[28] Duffy and Mackay, *Hawke*, 150–1 and n. 81; Rodger, *Command of the Ocean*, 430.
[29] Bourchier, ed., *Memoir*, I, 27.
[30] Barrow, *Life of Howe*, 240.
[31] Corbett, *Fighting Instructions*, 255.
[32] BL: Add. 23207 f. 61.
[33] The pick of the letters is in BL: Add 23207.
[34] BL: Add.23207 f. 62.v.
[35] BL: Add 23207 f. 62v, 63.
[36] Hughes, ed., *Collingwood Correspondence*, 51.
[37] See for example NMM: MSS/82/150.0.
[38] TNA: ADM 1/5332 f. 384.
[39] TNA: ADM 1/5332 f. 388.
[40] Cole, 'The Office of Ordnance', 211.
[41] Phillimore, *Life of Admiral Sir W. Parker*, 45.
[42] TNA: ADM 1/5332 f. 566.
[43] TNA: ADM 1/5332 f. 574–5. There is lots more in the same vein in his letters to the Admiralty in TNA: ADM 1/2128.
[44] Barrow, *Life of Howe*, 270; Bourchier, ed., *Memoir*, I, 29; Greig, ed., *The Farington Diary*, VIII, 129.
[45] TNA: ADM 1/5332 f. 527.
[46] Bourchier, ed., Memoir, I, 32–4. The jurors are listed at TNA: ADM 1/5332 f. 383.
[47] Aspinall, ed., *Later Correspondence of George III*, II, 221 n.1.
[48] Aspinall, ed., *Later Correspondence of George III*, II, 221.
[49] Hughes, ed., *Collingwood Correspondence*, 49.

[50] BL: Add. 23207 f. 78.
[51] Knight 'Earl Howe', 296.
[52] See for example Knight, 'Earl Howe', 285.
[53] Hughes, ed., *Collingwood Correspondence*, 50.
[54] Quoted in Tracy, *Britannia's Palette*, 53.
[55] Hughes, ed., *Collingwood Correspondence*, 42.
[56] Hattendorf et al., eds, *British Naval Documents*, 543.
[57] Ehrman, *The Younger Pitt*, 409.
[58] Aspinall, ed., *Later Correspondence of George III*, II, 224 n.1–2.
[59] D. Hill, *Mr. Gillray the Caricaturist*, 53–4.
[60] Jupp, ed., *The Letter-Journal of George Canning 1793–5*, 121.
[61] Hill, *Mr. Gillray the Caricaturist*, 54; Lincoln, *Representing the Royal Navy*, 60.
[62] Tracy, *Britannia's Palette*, 53.
[63] Ben's song, by Lord Mulgrave, C. Price, ed., *The Dramatic Works of Richard Brinsley Sheridan*, 772–3.
[64] G. Russell, *The Theatres of War*, 60–1.
[65] Jenks, *Engagements*, 37ff.; Russell, *The Theatres of War*, 61–3. For the background of the anti-war movement, see E.V. Macleod, *A War of Ideas*.
[66] Duffy, 'Man who Missed the Grain Convoy', 108.
[67] Montagu, *Statement*, xiv, xv n.
[68] Aspinall, ed., *Later Correspondence of George III*, II, 215–17.
[69] He was also shaken by the death of his brother, James Montagu, who died at the battle.
[70] Montagu, *Statement*, x in.
[71] BL: Add. MSS 31158, 161 f.98-100. Thanks to Mike Duffy for this reference.
[72] Edward Brenton (1774–1839), *ODNB*.
[73] Brenton, *Naval History*, I, 298; Montagu, *Statement*, xviii.
[74] Montagu, *Statement*, xi.
[75] Montagu, *Statement*, vi.
[76] G. Montagu, *Refutation*, 1–2.
[77] Montagu, *Refutation*, 18.
[78] Montagu, *Statement*, 13.
[79] Montagu, *Statement*, xxii.
[80] Brenton, *Naval History*, I, 151.
[81] Montagu, *Statement*, xiv fn.*.
[82] Barrow, *Life of Howe*, 247.
[83] Pearce, *The Life and Adventures of Nathaniel Pearce*, 10.
[84] Jeanbon Saint-André, *Journal Sommaire*, 866–8.
[85] Jeanbon Saint-André, *Journal Sommaire*, 10, 15.
[86] Cormack, *Revolution*, 286.
[87] Chevalier, *Histoire de la Marine Française*, II, 163; Ekins, *Naval Battles*, 191.
[88] Ekins, *Naval Battles*, 191; Jeanbon Saint-André, *Journal Sommaire*, 807.
[89] Cormack, *Revolution*, 291–302.
[90] Cormack, *Revolution*, 289.

[91] Cormack, *Revolution*, 287.
[92] Quoted in Duffy and Morriss, eds, *First of June*, 18.
[93] Chevalier, *Histoire de la Marine Française*, II, 145.
[94] Quoted in James, *Naval History*, I, 175.
[95] Guérin, *Histoire*, 45; James, *Naval History*, I, 160,74; Rouvier, *Histoire*, 165; Warner, *First of June*, 70; Jeanbon Saint-André, *Journal Sommaire*, 856.
[96] Quoted in Warner, *First of June*, 70.
[97] Rouvier, *Histoire*, 165.

**Chapter 11**

[1] Quoted in Scurr, *Fatal Purity*, 323.
[2] M. Lyons, 'The 9 Thermidor: Motives and Effects', 399; Bouloiseau, *Jacobin Republic*, 206.
[3] Gough, *The Terror*, 68.
[4] Jarnoux, 'Convoi Vanstabel', 182.
[5] Duffy and Morriss, eds, *First of June*, 6, 120ff.
[6] W. Doyle, *The Oxford History of the French Revolution*, 281; Gough, *The Terror*, 67; McPhee, *French Revolution*, 151.
[7] Doyle, *Oxford History*, 277; Gough, *The Terror*, 55.
[8] McPhee, *French Revolution*, 150–1.
[9] Gough, *The Terror*, 55; Jones, *French Revolution*, 67.
[10] Gough, *The Terror*, 54.
[11] Bouloiseau, *Jacobin Republic*, 211; Gough, *The Terror*, 58; Scurr, *Fatal Purity*, 307.
[12] Doyle, *Oxford History*, 281–92; Gough, *The Terror*, 70.
[13] Aston, *French Revolution*, 44; Doyle, *Oxford History*, 282.
[14] Crowhurst, *French War on Trade*, 11; Gough, *The Terror*, 72; Jones, *French Revolution*, 67.
[15] M. Duffy, 'British Diplomacy and the French Wars', 132.
[16] Blanning, *Revolutionary Wars*, 137.
[17] M. Crook, *Napoleon Takes Power*, 17; McPhee, *French Revolution*, 155.
[18] Crook, *Napoleon*, 39; Jones, *French Revolution*, 65.
[19] TNA: ADM 174/400.
[20] TNA: ADM 1/1001 f. 64; Havard, *Histoire de la Révolution*, 365; Acerra, *Marines et Révolution*, 186.
[21] Rodger, *Command of the Ocean*, 432; Acerra and Meyer, *Marines*, 182; Henwood and Monange, *Brest*, 258–9.
[22] Dull, 'Why did the French Revolutionary Navy Fail?', 130; Jarnoux, 'Convoi Vanstabel', 183.
[23] Acerra and Meyer, *Marines*, 211; Henwood and Monange, *Brest*, 259–60. Crowhurst puts French successes in the context of the entire British shipping industry. Crowhurst, *French War on Trade*, 31.
[24] R.V. Hamilton and J.K. Laughton, eds, *The Recollections of James Anthony Gardner, 1755–1814*, 158–9.
[25] J. Glete, *Navies and Nations*, II, 382–4.

[26] Dull, 'Why did the French Revolutionary Navy Fail?', 131.
[27] BL: Add 35195.
[28] Nine hundred bottles, each bottle containing between one and a half and eight and half gallons each, and the two hundred ten-gallon casks.
[29] TNA: ADM 1/100 f. 268; BL: Add. 23207 f. 118.
[30] Trotter, *Medicina Nautica*, I, 65–7, 77–89.
[31] Lloyd and Coulter, *Medicine*, III, 160; Trotter, *Medicina Nautica*, I, 65–7, 77–89.
[32] TNA: ADM 1/100 f. 188.
[33] TNA: ADM 2/605 f. 346, 357, 392; TNA: ADM 1/100 f. 451.
[34] TNA: ADM 1/100 f. 455 ff.
[35] BL: Add. 23207 f. 128; Trotter, *Medicina Nautica*, I, 84; TNA: ADM 1/1001 f. 126, 454.
[36] TNA: ADM 1.1001 f. 28, 37, 66.
[37] Jeanbon Saint-André, *Journal Sommaire*, 5.
[38] Barrow, *Life of Howe*, 286.
[39] Hampson, *La Marine*, 130.
[40] Figures from R. Winfield, *British Warships in the Age of Sail.*
[41] Quoted in Warner, *First of June*, 57.
[42] de Jonnès, *Adventures*, 53, 70–2; Brenton, *Naval History*, I, 152.
[43] Jenks, *Engagements*, 28, 47; J. Stevenson, 'The London "Crimp" Riots,' 40–58.
[44] M. Duffy, *The Younger Pitt*, 156.
[45] Hill, *Mr. Gillray the Caricaturist*, 55.
[46] Quoted in Warner, *First of June*, 72.
[47] Lavery, *The Ship of the Line*, 123, 125.
[48] NMM: FLI/8/B.
[49] de Jonnès, *Adventures*, 72.
[50] BL: Add 23207 f. 118.
[51] TNA: ADM 2/605 f. 346–7, 385; NMM: ADM/A/2857.
[52] TNA: ADM 103/319. Some at least were landed on 23 June. TNA: ADM 1/100 f. 445.
[53] TNA: ADM 103/128; 103/133; 103/275; 103/320; 103/319.
[54] TNA: ADM 103/601; ADM 103/411.
[55] TNA: ADM 1/100 f. 126, 420–1.
[56] TNA: ADM 1/100 f. 430.
[57] TNA: ADM 1/100 f. 428, 430.
[58] TNA: ADM 1/100 f. 445.
[59] Trotter, *Medicina Nautica*, 84; Lloyd and Coulter, *Medicine*, III, 160.
[60] TNA: ADM 2/605 f. 473; ADM 1/100 f. 445.
[61] de Jonnès, *Adventures*, 72; Jeanbon Saint-André, *Journal Sommaire*, 9; Acerra and Meyer, *Marines*, 178.
[62] Dumoutier, for example was found guilty but excusable by four votes to seven. Rouvier, *Histoire*, I, 163.
[63] Cormack, *Revolution*, 287–8, 291ff.
[64] Jenkins, *A History of the French Navy*, 217ff.

[65] Chevalier, *Histoire de la Marine Française*, II, 141; Jenkins, *A History of the French Navy*, 219–220.
[66] Quoted in Rodger, *Command of the Ocean*, 437.
[67] Glete, *Navies and Nations*, II, 382–4.
[68] Laird Clowes, *Royal Navy*, IV, 242, 520. Jenkins claims the casualty discrepancy after the capture of the *Alexander* was less. Jenkins, *A History of the French Navy*, 216.
[69] NMM: POR/G/1.
[70] Rodger, *Command of the Ocean*, 436.
[71] Aspinall, *Correspondence of Prince of Wales*, 440.
[72] Marshall and Woods, eds, *The Correspondence of Edmund Burke*, VII, 549.
[73] NMM: MSS/82/150.0; Aspinall, ed., *Later Correspondence of George III*, II, 215
[74] Hughes, ed., *Collingwood Correspondence*, 45.
[75] Duffy and Morriss, eds, *First of June*, 2, 28.

**Epilogue**
[1] Quoted in A. Alison, *History of Europe from the Commencement of the Revolution*, 202.
[2] Biographical Memoir of Earl Howe, *NC* I (1799), 22.
[3] Hampson, *La Marine*, 217.
[4] Lewis, ed., *Dillon's Narrative*, I, 124.
[5] Hughes, ed., *Collingwood Correspondence*, 46.
[6] Charles Fremantle (1800–1869), *ODNB.*
[7] Phillimore, *Life of Sir W. Parker*, 58.
[8] de Jonnès, *Adventures*, 57.

**Appendix II**
[1] The figures come from Winfield, *British Warships in the Age of Sail: 1793–1817: Design, Construction and Fates.*
[2] TNA: ADM 1/101
[3] Cole, 'The Office of Ordnance and the Arming of the Fleet in the French Revolutionary Wars, 1793-1815', 170.

# BIBLIOGRAPHY

Abbreviations:
BL – British Library
*MM* – Mariner's Mirror
*NC* – Naval Chronicle
NMM – The National Maritime Museum, Greenwich
NRS – Navy Records Society
*ODNB* – Oxford Dictionary of National Biography
TNA – The National Archives


Acerra, M., and J. Meyer. *Marines et Révolution* (Rennes, 1988).

Alison, A. *History of Europe from the Commencement of the Revolution to the Restoration of the Bourbons* (London, 1844–8, 10 vols).

Anon. 'Description of the Monument erected in Westminster Abbey, to the Memory of the Late Captains Harvey and Hutt'. *Naval Chronicle* 11 (1804), 363–4.

———. 'Proceedings of His Majesty's Ship the *Orion* …' *Naval Chronicle* 1 (1799), 293–300.

———. *A Short Account of the Naval Actions of the Last War … with observations on the discipline and hints for the improvement of the British Navy* (London, 1788).

Anon. *An historical account of the review of Lord Howe's fleet at Portsmouth honoured by the presence of the King, Queen and Royal Family* (1794).

Aspinall, A., ed. *The Later Correspondence of George III* (Cambridge, 1963, 5 vols).

Aspinall, A. E. *The Correspondence of George, Prince of Wales 1770–1812* (London, 1964, 8 vols).

Aston, N. *The French Revolution, 1789–1804* (Basingstoke, 2004).

Barrow, J. *The Life of Richard, Earl Howe* (London, 1838).

Baugh, C. *Garrick and Loutherbourg* (Cambridge, 1990).

———. 'Philippe James de Loutherbourg and the early pictorial theatre: some aspects of its cultural context'. In *The Theatrical Space*, edited by J. Redmond (Cambridge, 1987), 99–128.

Bentley, N. *The History of the Circus* (London, 1977).

Best, G. *War and Society in Revolutionary Europe, 1770–1870* (Bungay, 1982).

Bevan, R., and W. G. Kemble. 'Narrative of the Engagement between the *Brunswick* and the *Vengeur*, 1 June 1794'. In *The Naval Miscellany* III, edited by W. G. Perrin (London, NRS Vol. 63, 1927), 157–72.

Black, J. *Crisis of Empire: Britain and America in the Eighteenth Century* (London, 2008).

Black, J., and P. Woodfine, eds. *The British Navy and the Use of Naval Power in the Eighteenth Century* (Leicester, 1988).

Blanning, T. C. W. *The French Revolutionary Wars 1787–1802* (London, 1996).

Bonehill, J. 'Exhibiting War: John Singleton Copley's *The Siege of Gibraltar* and the staging of history'. In *Conflicting Visions: War and Visual Culture in Britain and France c.1700–1830*, edited by J. Bonehill and G. Quilley (Aldershot, 2005), 139–68.

Bouloiseau, M. *The Jacobin Republic 1792–4*. Translated by J. Mandelbaum (Cambridge, 1972).

Bourchier, J. B., ed. *Memoir of the Life of Admiral Sir Edward Codrington*. 2 vols. Vol. 1 (London, 1873).

Brandon, L. *Art and War* (London, 2007).

Brenton, E. P. *The Naval History of Great Britain from the year 1783 to 1836*. 3rd ed. (London, 1837, 8 vols).

Caruana, A. B. *The History of English Sea Ordnance 1523–1875* (Rotherfield, 1994–7, 2 vols).

Chevalier, E. *Histoire de la Marine Française sous la première République* (Paris, 1886, 8 vols).

Cobb, R., and C. Jones, eds. *Voices of the French Revolution* (Topsfield, Mass., 1988).

Cole, G. 'The Office of Ordnance and the Arming of the Fleet in the French Revolutionary Wars, 1793–1815'. PhD (University of Exeter, 2008).

Corbett, J. S. *Fighting Instructions 1530–1816* (London, NRS Vol. 29, 1905).

———. *Signals and Instructions 1776–1794* (London, 1971).

Cordingly, D. *Nicholas Pocock 1740–1821* (London, 1986).

Cormack, W. S. *Revolution and Political Conflict in the French Navy* (Cambridge, 1995).

Crook, M. *Napoleon takes power: dictatorship and democracy in France at the turn of the nineteenth century* (Cardiff, 1997).

———. *Toulon in war and Revolution* (Manchester, 1991).

Crowhurst, P. *The French War on Trade: Privateering 1793–1815* (Aldershot, 1989).

Crumplin, M. 'Surgery in the Royal Navy during the Republican and Napoleonic Wars'. In *Health and Medicine at Sea, 1700–1900*, edited by D. Boyd Haycock and S. Archer (Woodbridge, 2009), 63–89.

Czisnik, M. 'Admiral Nelson's Tactics at the Battle of Trafalgar'. *Journal of the Historical Association* 139, no. 296 (2004), 549–59.

de Jonnès, M. *Adventures in the Revolution* (London, 1969).

de Poggi, A. C., ed. *A Narrative of the Proceedings of His Majesty's Fleet, Under the Command of Earl Howe from the Second of May to the Second of June* (London, 1796).

Delaporte, A. 'The Prairial Battles: The French Viewpoint'. In *The Glorious First of June: A Naval Battle and its Aftermath*, edited by M. Duffy and R Morriss (Exeter, 2001), 12–24.

Demerliac, A. *La Marine de La Révolution: Nomenclature des Navires Français de 1792 à 1799* (Nice, 1999).

Douglas-Morris, K. *The Naval General Service Medal Roll, 1793–1840* (London, 1982).

Doyle, W. *The Oxford History of the French Revolution*. 2nd ed. (Oxford, 2002).

Duffy, M. 'British Diplomacy and the French Wars'. In *Britain and the French Revolution, 1789–1815*, edited by H. T. Dickinson (London, 1989), 127–46.

———. 'The Man who Missed the Grain Convoy: Rear Admiral George Montagu and the Arrival of Vanstabel's Convoy from America in 1794'. In *The Glorious First of June: A Naval Battle and its Aftermath*, edited by M. Duffy and R. Morriss (Exeter, 2001), 101–19.

———. *Soldiers, Sugar, and Seapower* (Oxford, 1987).

———. 'The Gunnery at Trafalgar: Training, Tactics or Temperament?' *Journal for Maritime Research* (2004).

———. *The Younger Pitt* (Harlow, 2000).

Duffy, M., and R. Mackay. *Hawke, Nelson and British Naval Leadership*

*1747–1805*. (Woodbridge, 2009).

Duffy, M., and R. Morriss, eds. *The Glorious First of June 1794: A Naval Battle and Its Aftermath* (Exeter, 2001).

Dull, J. R. 'Why did the French Revolutionary Navy Fail?' *Consortium on Revolutionary Europe, 1750–1850* 18, no. 2 (1989), 121–37.

———. *The Age of the Ship of the Line: The British & French Navies, 1650–1815* (London, 2009).

Dunn, S. *The Deaths of Louis XVI: Regicide and the French Political Imagination* (Princeton, 1994).

Ehrman, J. *The Younger Pitt: The Reluctant Transition* (London, 1983).

Ekins, C. *Naval Battles from 1744 to the Peace in 1814, Critically Reviewed and Illustrated* (London, 1824).

Evans, D. *Mather Brown: Early American Artist in England* (Middletown, 1982).

Evans, L. 'The Convoy, the Grain and their Influence on the French Revolution'. In *The Glorious First of June: A Naval Battle and its Aftermath*, edited by M. Duffy and R. Morriss (Exeter, 2001), 120–31.

Falconer, W., ed. *Universal Dictionary of the Marine* (London, 1771).

Forrest, A. *The Legacy of the French Revolutionary Wars: The Nation-in-Arms in French Republican Memory* (Cambridge, 2009).

———. *The Soldiers of the French Revolution* (London, 1990).

Fox, C. J. *Napoleon Bonaparte and The Siege of Toulon* (Washington, 1902).

Fresselicque, J. J. *A sermon of praise and thanksgiving … for the late victory obtained over the French fleet …* (London, 1794).

Furet, F. *The French Revolution 1770–1814* (Oxford, 1996).

Gage, J. 'Loutherbourg: Mystagogue of the Sublime'. *History Today* 13 (1963), 332–9.

Gardiner, R., ed. *Fleet Battle and Blockade: The French Revolutionary War 1793–1797* (London, 1996).

Geggus, D. P. *Slavery, War, And Revolution: The British Occupation of Saint Domingue 1793–1798* (Oxford, 1982).

Germani, I., and R. Swales, eds. *Symbols, myths and images of the French Revolution: essays in honour of James A. Leith* (Regina, 1998).

Gilchrist, J., and W. J. Murray, eds. *The Press in the French Revolution* (London, 1971).

Glete, J. *Navies and Nations: Warships, Navies and State Building in Europe and America 1500–1860* (Stockholm, 1993, 2 vols).

Gough, H. *The Terror in the French Revolution* (Basingstoke, 1998).

Greig, J., ed. *The Farington Diary* (London, 1922, 8 vols).

Griffith, P. *The Art of War of Revolutionary France 1789–1802* (London, 1998).

Guérin, L. *Histoire Maritime de France, depuis la fondation de Marseille jusqu'à la prax de Nimègue* (Paris, 1863).

Hamilton, R. V., and J. K. Laughton, eds. *The Recollections of James Anthony Gardner, 1755–1814* (London: NRS Vol. 31, 1906).

Hampson, N. *La Marine de l'An II: Mobilisation de la flotte d'océan 1793–4* (Paris, 1959).

———. *Prelude to Terror: The Constituent Assembly and the Failure of Consensus 1789–1791* (Oxford, 1988).

Harrington, P. *British Artists and War: The Face of Battle in Paintings and Prints, 1700–1914* (London, 1993).

Hattendorf, J. B., R. J. B. Knight, A. W. H. Pearsall, N. A. M. Rodger and G. Till, eds. *British Naval Documents 1204–1960* (Aldershot: NRS Vol. 131, 1993).

Havard, O. *Histoire de la Révolution dans les Ports de Guerre* (Paris, 1912, 2 vols).

Henwood, P., and E. Monange. *Brest: Un Port en Révolution* (Rennes, 1989).

Hill, D. *Mr. Gillray the Caricaturist* (London, 1965).

Hodges, H. W., ed. *Select Naval Documents* (Cambridge, 1922).

Holland Rose, J. *Lord Hood and the Defence of Toulon* (Cambridge, 1922).

Hughes, E. A., ed. *The Private Correspondence of Admiral Lord Collingwood* (London: NRS Vol. 98, 1957).

Hutchinson, W. *A Treatise on Practical Seamanship*. 2nd ed. (Liverpool, 1787).

Jackson, T. Sturges, ed. *Logs of the Great Sea Fights, 1794–1805*. Vol. 1 (London: NRS Vol. 16, 1981).

James, W. J. *The Naval History of Great Britain* (London, 1837, 6 vols).

Jarnoux, P. 'Autour des combats de Prairial: le convoi van Stabel et les approvisionnements américains en 1793–1794'. In *Les Marines Française et Britannique Face aux Etats-Unis (1776–1865)* (Vincennes, 1999), 169–86.

Jeanbon Saint-André, A. *Journal sommaire de la croisière de la flotte de la république, commandée par le contre-amiral Villaret; tenu jour par jour par le représentant du peuple Jeanbon Saint-André, embarqué sur le vaisseau la Montagne* (Paris, AN II).

Jenkins, E. H. *A History of the French Navy* (London, 1973).

Jenks, T. *Naval Engagements: Patriotism, Cultural Politics, and the Royal Navy 1793–1815* (Oxford, 2006).

Jones, C. *The Longman Companion to the French Revolution* (Harlow, 1988).

Jones, P. M. *The French Revolution: 1787–1804* (Harlow, 2003).

Jupp, P., ed. *The Letter-Journal of George Canning 1793–5* (London, 1991).

Keevil, J. J. *Medicine and the Navy 1200–1900*. Vol. 2: 1649–1714 (Edinburgh and London, 1958).

Knight, R. J. B. *The Pursuit of Victory: The Life and Achievement of Horatio Nelson* (London, 2005).

———. 'Richard, Earl Howe, 1726–99'. In *Precursors of Nelson: British Admirals of the Eighteenth Century*, edited by P. Le Fevre and R. Harding (London, 2000), 279–99.

Kramer, L. S. 'The French Revolution and the Creation of American Political Culture'. In *The Global Ramifications of the French Revolution*, edited by J. Klaits and M. H. Haltzel (Cambridge, 1994), 26–54.

Laird Clowes, W. *The Royal Navy. A History from the Earliest Times to 1900*. Vol. 4 (London, 1997).

Laughton, J. K., ed. *The Letters and Papers of Charles, Lord Barham*. Vol. 2 (London: NRS Vol. 38, 1910).

Lavery, B. *The Ship of the Line* (London, 1983, 2 vols).

———, ed. *Shipboard Life and Organisation 1731–1815* (Aldershot: NRS Vol. 138, 1998).

Leith, J. A. *Space and Revolution: Projects for Monuments, Squares, and Public Buildings in France 1789–99* (Montreal, 1991).

Lévy-Schneider, L. *Le Conventionnel Jeanbon Saint André*. 2 vols (Paris, 1901).

Lewis, M. A., ed. *A narrative of my professional adventures by Sir William Dillon*. Vol. 1 (London: NRS Vol. 93, 1953).

Lincoln, M. *Representing the Royal Navy: British Sea power, 1750–1815* (Aldershot, 2002).

Lloyd, C., and J. Coulter. *Medicine and the Navy 1200–1900*. Vol. 3 (London, 1961).

Loir, M. 'L'adoption du Pavillon Tricolore'. *Revue Maritime et Coloniale* 122 (1874), 600–19.

Lyon, D. *The Sailing Navy List* (London, 1993).

Lyons, M. 'The 9 Thermidor: Motives and Effects'. In *The French*

*Revolution In Social and Political Perspective*, edited by P. Jones (London, 1989), 395–413.

Macleod, E. V. *A War of Ideas: British Attitudes to the Wars Against Revolutionary France 1792–1802* (Aldershot, 1998).

Marshall, P. J., and J. A. Woods, eds. *The Correspondence of Edmund Burke*. Vol. 7 (Cambridge, 1968).

McPhee, P. *The French Revolution* (Oxford, 2002).

Montagu, G. *A Refutation of the Incorrect Statements and Unjust Insinuations Contained in Captain Brenton's Naval History of Great Britain* (London, 1823).

———. *Statement of a Correspondence Which Has Taken Place Between Admiral Sir George Montagu G. C. B. and Capt. Edward Pelham Brenton* ... (London, 1823).

Mori, J. 'The British Government and the Bourbon Restoration: The Occupation of Toulon'. *The Historical Journal* 40, no. 3 (1997), 699–719.

Morrill, J. 'King-Killing in Perspective'. In *Murder and Monarchy: Regicide in European history, 1300–1800*, edited by R. Von Friedeburg (Basingstoke, 2004), 293-299.

Morriss, R., ed. *The Channel Fleet and the Blockade of Brest 1793–1801* (Aldershot: NRS Vol. 141, 2001).

Morriss, R. 'The Glorious First of June. The British View of the Actions of 28, 29 May and 1 June 1794'. In *The Glorious First of June 1794: A Naval Battle and Its Aftermath*, edited by M. Duffy and R. Morriss (Exeter, 2001), 46–100.

Newnham Collingwood, G. L. *A Selection from the Public and Private Correspondence of Vice-Admiral Lord Collingwood* (London, 1828).

Nicholas, N. H., ed. *The Dispatches and Letters of Lord Nelson,* 7 vols (London, 1844–5).

Ober, P.K. *Mark Twain and Medicine: 'Any Mummery will Cure'* (Colombia, Mo., 2003).

Owen, H. 'An Eyewitness Account of the Glorious First of June, 1794'. *Mariner's Mirror* 80, no. 3 (1994), 335–8.

Palmer, M. A. J. 'Lord Nelson, Master of Command'. *Naval War College Review* 41 (1988), 105–16.

Palmer, R. R. *Twelve who Ruled: The Year of the Terror in the French Revolution* (Princeton, 1969).

Parker, H. P. 'Eminent Marine Artists: No. 12 Philippe James de

Loutherbourg'. *Mariner's Mirror* 3 (1913), 40–2.

Pearce, N. *The Life and Adventures of Nathaniel Pearce* (London, 1831).

Phillimore, A. *The Life of Admiral of the Fleet Sir W. Parker*. Vol. 1 (London, 1876).

Price, C., ed. *The Dramatic Works of Richard Brinsley Sheridan*. Vol. 2 (Oxford, 1973).

Price, M. *The Fall of the French Monarchy: Louis XVI, Marie Antoinette and the Baron de Breteuil* (London, 2003).

Robertson, S. J. 'The Mobilization of the British Navy at the Start of the French Revolutionary War 1793–4'. MA (Exeter, 2000).

Rodger, N. A. M. *The Command of the Ocean: A Naval History of Britain 1649–1815* (London, 2004).

———. 'Image and Reality in Eighteenth Century Naval Tactics'. *Mariner's Mirror* 89, no. 3 (2003), 280–296.

———. *The Insatiable Earl: A Life of John Montagu, 4th Earl of Sandwich 1718–92* (London, 1993).

Rosenfeld, S. *Georgian Scene Painters and Scene Painting* (Cambridge, 1981).

———. *A Short History of Scene Design in Great Britain* (Oxford, 1973).

Rouvier, C. *Histoire des Marins Français sous la République*. Vol. 1 (Paris, 1868).

Royle, E. *Revolutionary Britannia? Reflections on the threat of revolution in Britain 1789–1848* (Manchester, 2000).

Russell, G. *The Theatres of War: Performance, Politics, and Society 1793–1815* (Oxford, 1995).

Russett, A. *Dominic Serres R. A., 1719–1793: War Artist to the Navy* (Woodbridge, 1999).

Schama, S. *Citizens: A Chronicle of the French Revolution* (London, 1989).

Schneider, H. 'Le Mythe du Vaisseau Le Vengeur de 1794 à 1951 Textes – Images – Musique'. *Acta Musicologica* 77, no. 1 (2005), 71–121.

Schomberg, A. *A Sea Manual, Recommended to the Young Officers of the Royal Navy as a Companion to the Signal Book* (London, 1789).

Schomberg, I. *The Naval Chronology*. Vol. 1 (London, 1815).

Scurr, R. *Fatal Purity: Robespierre and the French Revolution* (London, 2007).

Stevenson, J. 'The London "Crimp" Riots'. *International Review of Social History* 16 (1971), 40–58.

Stoddart, H. *Rings of Desire: Circus History and Representation* (Manchester, 2000).

Sutherland, D. M. G. *The French Revolution and Empire. The Quest for a Civic Order* (Oxford, 2003).

Syrett, D. *Admiral Lord Howe* (Stroud, 2006).

———. 'A Check List of Admiral Lord Howe Manuscripts in United States Archives and Libraries'. *Mariner's Mirror* 67, no. 3 (1981), 273–84.

Talbot, M. A. *The Life and Surprising Adventures of Mary Anne Talbot …* (London, 1809).

Tomlinson, B. 'The Battle Sanctified: Some Memorials and Relics'. In *The Glorious First of June: A Naval Battle and its Aftermath*, edited by M. Duffy and R. Morriss (Exeter, 2001), 159–68.

Tracy, N. *Britannia's Palette: The Arts of Naval Victory* (London, 2007).

Trotter, T. *Medicina Nautica: An Essay on the Diseases of Seamen*. Vol. 1 (London, 1797).

Troude, O. *Batailles Navales de la France*. Vol. 2 (Paris, 1867).

Van der Merwe, P. 'The Glorious First of June. A battle of art and theatre'. In *The Glorious First of June 1794: A Naval Battle and Its Aftermath* edited by M. Duffy and R. Morriss (Exeter, University of Exeter Press, 2001), 132–58.

Walzer, M., ed. *Regicide and Revolution: Speeches at the Trial of Louis XVI* (Cambridge, 1974).

Ware, C. 'The Glorious First of June: The British Strategic Perspective'. In *The Glorious First of June: A Naval Battle and its Aftermath*, edited by M. Duffy and R. Morriss (Exeter, 2001), 25–42.

Warner, O. *The Glorious First of June* (London, 1961).

———. 'Howe at the Glorious First of June'. *Mariner's Mirror* 56 (1970), 2.

Webb, P. L. C. 'The Naval Aspects of the Nootka Sound Crisis'. *Mariner's Mirror* 61, no. 2 (1975), 133–54.

Willis, S. B. A. *The Admiral Benbow* (London, 2010).

———. *Fighting at Sea in the Eighteenth Century: The Art of Sailing Warfare* (Woodbridge, 2008).

Wind, E. 'The Revolution of History Painting'. *Journal of the Warburg Institute* 2, no. 2 (1938), 116–27.

Winfield, R. *British Warships in the Age of Sail: 1793–1817: Design, Construction and Fates* (London, 2005).

# INDEX


*Achille* 307, 348
Adams, John 102
*Agamemnon*, HMS 132–4
*Alexander*, HMS 299, 313
*Alfred*, HMS 169, 201–2, 247, 340
Alfred, Richard 174
Amar, Jean-Baptiste 287, 376
*América* 168, 307, 349–50
American Independence, War of xl, 15–16, 100–1, 141
amputations 220
Anson, George 45
Antoinette, Marie 23
*Apollon* 349
*Aquilon*, HMS 117, 187, 199, 203, 239, 343
*Arrogant*, HMS 58
artistic depictions of naval warfare 72–3, 75, 85–6
  and Copley 82–3
  and Glorious First of June 245–54
  and historical in/accuracy 73, 75, 81–2, 246, 248–9
  and Loutherbourg 77–81, 84
  and Pocock 86–9
  and Van de Velde 74–5
Astley, Philip 69, 75–7, 274
*Atalante* 135
*L'Audacieux* 159
*Audacious*, HMS 59, 118, 153–5, 156, 157–8, 159, 231
Austria 6, 299

*Babet* 137
Baker, Ned 260
Baker, William 260
Ballard, Samuel 335
Barère, Bertrand de 112, 243–4, 376–7
Barfleur, Battle of (1692) 234, 321
*Barfleur*, HMS 119, 169, 192, 204, 268, 335
Barker, Robert 254
Barlow, Captain Robert 344
Bath, and Howe's home in 43
Bazeley, Captain John 263, 340
Beaufort, Francis 341
*Bellerophon*, HMS 58, 117, 131, 147–8, 151, 153–4, 163, 164, 166, 203, 216–17, 336
Benbow, John 66, 72, 235
Bentinck, Captain William 341
Berkeley, Captain George 155, 199, 209–10, 262, 337
Bertie, Captain Albemarle 154–5, 341
Betjeman, John 227
Bevan, Rowland 196, 197
Bible, Abraham 219–20
*Bienfaisant* 310
*Black Joke*, HMS 60
Blackwood, Henry 338
Bligh, Captain William 334
Bonaparte, Napoleon xl, 26, 27, 245, 298–9, 301
Bourdon, François 287, 377
Bouvet, Rear-Admiral François Joseph 141
Bowen, James 60, 163–4, 193, 235, 242, 254
Bowyer, Rear-Admiral George 58, 212, 235, 262, 335
Brenton, Edward 91, 257, 277–80, 307
Brest fleet
  and 29 May engagement 159–70, 172, 173–4
  and 30-31 May, fog 177
  and achievement in fleet seamanship 319–20
  and cancellation of trials of officers 311
  and captured merchant ships 124
  and crew shortages 130
  and criticism of conduct 282
  and discipline 35, 171
  and disposition for Vanstabel's convoy 116
  and divisions within 282, 312
  and inexperience of officers 141–2
  and leaves port 121, 122–3
  and mutiny 26
  and optimism of 39
  and poor seamanship 130–1
  and post-1 June operations 299–300, 312
  and preparations for invasion of England 35, 36
  and purge of the disloyal 34–5
  and quality of ships 142–3
  and resolution and aggression of 132, 317
  and sails into Brest 224–5
  and shortcomings of 39
  and sickness in 39–40, 130
  and sighted by Montagu 224
  and sights British fleet 146–7
  and unity of 318
  and Villaret de Joyeuse appointed C-in-C 32

and witch-hunt for 'traitors' 281–2
*see also* Glorious First of June, Battle of
Brisbane, James 333
Bristol 86
British Army 118, 232–3, 239
Brown, Mather 210–11, 246, 248–9
Brown, Captain William 343
*Brunswick*, HMS xxxix, 117–18, 164, 194–8, 202, 207, 211–12, 268, 339
*Brutus* 173, 282
Burgh, William xlii

*Caesar*, HMS 58, 118, 142, 162, 166, 167, 170–1, 176, 194, 268–9, 335–6
Caird, Sir James 247
Caldwell, Rear-Admiral Benjamin 119, 120, 263–4, 310–11, 334, 367
calendar reform, and French Revolution xxxiv, 10–11, 329–30
Camperdown, Battle of (1797) 234, 326
*Canada*, HMS 305
Cancale 116
Canning, George 231, 238, 259, 273
Cape St Vincent, Battle of (1797) 277, 326
caricatures, and attacks on Howe 273–4
carronade 135
cartoons, and attacks on Howe 273–4
*Castor*, HMS 123
casualties
British 171, 199, 208, 212
and discrepancy in Anglo-French naval engagements 133–5, 207–8, 313
French 207–9, 212–13, 309
Catherine the Great xxix
Channel Fleet
and 29 May engagement 159–75
and 30-31 May 175–80
and attacks French rear 149–50
and chases after Villaret's Brest fleet 124–5
and competence of crews 318
and composition of 117
and crew shortages 57–8, 117–18
and discipline problems 58–9, 174, 261
and escorting trade convoys 59–61, 116–17
and exercised by Howe 57
and experienced officers 140–1, 318–19
and French prisoners on board 124–5, 310–11, 323
and gunnery 118–19, 209–11
and hostility towards Howe 54
and Howe appointed commander of 45, 55
and illness among crews 58
and political divisions in 54
and post-1 June incapacitation of 302–6
and prize ships burned 124
and quality of ships 142
and reception in Spithead 230
and repair of ships 305
and sails for home 222
and sails to intercept Vanstabel's convoy 111, 112–13
and shortcomings of 56–7
and sights French fleet 146–7
and signalling practice 120
and soldiers in crew 118
and typhus outbreak 302–5, 323
and unity in 271
*see also* Glorious First of June, Battle of
charity, and relief of wounded and dependants 235–6
Charlotte, Queen 238, 240, 254
Chatham, 2nd Earl of (John Pitt) 231, 240, 262, 277, 323–4, 375
Chatham Chest 236
Chesapeake, Battle of the (1781) xl, 72
Christianity, and Revolutionary hostility towards 9
circus 75–7
clearing for action 148–9
*Cléopâtre* 6
Cleveley, Robert 73, 246, 247–8, 253–4
Codrington, Edward 54–5, 56, 120, 145, 146, 163–4, 179, 191–2, 235, 267, 333
Collingwood, Captain Cuthbert xxxviii, 56–7, 180, 189, 191, 239, 263, 264–7, 268, 269, 270–1, 315, 335, 368
*Commerce de Marseille* 142–3
Committee of Public Safety (CPS) 4, 7, 8, 9, 29, 30–1, 93–5, 98–9, 137–8, 291, 293
*Concorde*, HMS 135
*Convention* 348
convoys
and area covered by 115
and interception of 113–16
*see also* Vanstabel's grain convoy
Copenhagen, Battle of (1801) 326
Copley, John Singleton 81–3, 248
Corday, Charlotte xxvi, 96
Cornic, Rear-Admiral Pierre-François 116
Cornwallis, Admiral William 300
Cotton, Captain Charles 340
Couthon, Georges 295
cowardice, in British fleet 206–7
*Crescent*, HMS 134
Crimp Riots 307–8
*Culloden*, HMS 146, 156, 164, 167, 169, 174, 201–2, 203, 204, 208, 214, 338
Curtis, Sir Roger 120, 199, 201, 231, 235, 241, 265, 273–4
Cuyler, Maj-Gen Cornelius 104–5
*Cybèle* 299

*Daedalus*, HMS 109–10, 123
Danton, Georges 94, 95, 377
Darby, George 55
decimalisation 10
*Defence*, HMS 118, 120, 142, 149–50, 166, 189, 190–1, 203, 206–7, 216, 337

Desmoulins, Camille 317
*Diamond*, HMS 305
Dillon, William 119–20, 121, 124, 149–50, 208, 217, 220, 337, 369
divisional system 52–3
Dodd, Robert 246–7
Domett, Captain William 263, 334
Douglas, Andrew Snape 60, 241
Drake, Francis 26
Duckworth, Captain John xli, 261, 262, 339
duels 44–5
*Duguay Trouin* 135
Dundas, Henry 104, 240, 263, 323–4, 368–9

East Indies 6–7
Edgeworth, Henry xxvi
Elphinstone, Rear-Admiral George Keith 335
Elphinstone, Captain John 117, 262, 335
*Engageante* 137
engravings 73
*Entreprenant* 349
*Éole* 163, 349
Erskine, Thomas 233, 263

Falconer, William 253
Farrington, John 230
Fauchet, Jean-Antoine 112
Fisher, Ebenezer 259
flags 204
fleet command and tactics 63–4
  and broadside to broadside battles 65
  and convoy interception 113–16
  and defensive actions 66–7, 138–9
  and difficulties in attacking from leeward position 169
  and difficulties in bringing fleets to action 62, 63–4
  and difficulties in implementing plans 68
  and doubling an enemy line 65
  and factors affecting battle strategy 62–3
  and French deficiencies 16
  and Howe's new form of attack 64, 66
  and Howe's skill in 48–50
  and manoeuvrability in battle 176
  and mathematical depictions of 73–4
  and myth of 'line of battle' 74
  and response to line-breaking manoeuvre 139–40
  and signal flags 49–51
  and time element in fleet battle 139, 140
  and Villaret's achievement 319–20
Fleurus, Battle of (1794) 289
Flinders, Matthew xli, 148, 336
Forbes, Captain Robert 343
Fouché, Joseph 287, 378
Fouquier-Tinville, Antoine Quentin 287, 378
France
  and American War of Independence 100–1
  and arrival of grain convoy 288
  and civil unrest 100
  and civil war 5
  and conscription (*grande levée*) 7–8
  and convoys from America 300
  and execution of Louis XVI xxvi, xxvii, xxviii–xxix
  and external threats to 6–7
  and food shortages 6, 98–100
  and importance of West Indian colonies 104
  and inflation 297
  and military and naval defeats (1793) 6–7
  and military successes 289, 297–8
  and power vacuum 7
  and regional separatism 29–30
  and stability of monarchy xxvi–xxvii
  and state control of economic resources 38
  *see also* Committee of Public Safety (CPS); French Revolution; Glorious First of June, aftermath in France; Terror
Franklin, Benjamin 101
Fremantle, Charles Howe 322
French army 7–8, 40, 93, 99, 289, 297–8
French navy xxxviii
  in American War of Independence xl, 15–16, 101
  and association with aristocracy and monarchy 11
  and *classes* manning system 12, 18
  and conflict with Revolutionaries 12–13, 15
  and confused lines of authority 15
  and continued threat of 302, 325
  and criticism of 312
  and damage done by Revolution 319
  and decline in proficiency of 15, 16–17
  and discipline 35
  and divisions within 15, 282, 312
  and dockyards 13
  and economic impact of 99
  and expansion of 301–2
  and failure in ship and fleet seamanship 16
  and financial problems 17
  and gunnery shortcomings 14, 16–17, 38
  and high casualty rates 133–5
  and influence on outcome of war 302
  and lack of political support for 324
  and lack of practice 15–17
  and living conditions 11–12
  and logistical problems 312
  and loss of officers 13–14
  and manpower shortages 18, 311
  and political unrest in 13
  and politicisation of 37
  and poor construction of ships 135
  and post-Robespierre return of officers 311
  and punishment in 12
  and quality of ships 142–3
  and recruitment 36–7
  and reform of 37
  and renaming of ships 37–8

and Republican distrust of 11, 12, 22
and reputation of 12
and resolution and aggression of 132–3
and Revolutionary reforms 12
and shipbuilding 17–18
and sickness in 39–40
and strengthening of anti-Jacobins 282–3, 284
and success of 1st June 289
and survival of the Republic 325
*see also* Brest fleet

French Revolution
and attempted abolition of Christianity 9
and backlash against Jacobins 296
and British praise for 4
and calendar reform xxxiv, 10–11, 329–30
and casualties of 4
and censorship 10
and change in 5
and Cult of the Supreme Being 290–1
and differential regional impact of 21
and factional divisions 93–5
and idealism of 9–10
and ideals of 3
and legacy of 327
and military successes 289, 297–8
and paranoia amongst Jacobin leaders 287
and politicisation of society 11
and potential for military dictatorship 298–9
and reinvigoration of 297
and revolt against 5
and Revolutionary names 10
and second anniversary celebrated 297
and social and economic reforms 10
and suppression of revolt 9
and White Terror 296
*see also* Committee of Public Safety (CPS); Terror

friendly fire 166–7, 203–4, 207

Fuseli, Johann 230

Galissonière, Marquis de la 67

Galles, Morard de 15, 34

Gambier, Captain James 166, 189, 190–1, 203, 235, 262, 337

Gardner, Rear-Admiral Alan 199, 235, 262, 271, 335, 369–70

Genêt, Edmond 103

George III xxv, xxviii, 54, 231, 276, 314–15
and visits fleet at Portsmouth 237–40

George IV 251

George Tavern 247

*Gibraltar*, HMS 118, 142, 203, 204, 305, 336

Gillespie, Leonard 304, 340

Girondins 5

Glorious First of June, Battle of
and battle between *Brunswick and Vengeur* 195–8, 211–12, 268
and becomes unstructured mêlée 198
and British attack French line 189–98
and British casualties 199, 208, 212
and British memorials to xxxi–xxxiii
and competence of British 318, 320
and conditions below deck 217
and courage of French 317
and cowardice, British 206–7
and crew reactions to battle 218–20
and crippled ships rescued by Villaret 201
and criticism of Howe 213, 221–2, 320
and damage to British ships 203
and damage to French ships 207
and discrepancy in casualties 207–8
and distinguishing features of xxxv–xxxvi
and duration of xxxviii–xxxix
and effect on young crew 218–19
and end of 202–3
and experience of British officers 318–19
and fleets sight each other 186–7
and food and water damage 217–18
and French attack HMS *Queen* 199–200
and French casualties 207–9, 212–13, 309
and French fighting abilities 205
and French memorials to xxxiv–xxxv
and French prisoners 214–15, 323
and French use of red-hot shot 206
and friendly fire 203–4, 207
and gunnery 209–11
as hardest-fought battle of Age of Sail 201
and Howe orders ships to break through French line 187–8
and Howe's expectations of French 185
as ideological battle xxxviii
and impact of xxxix–xl
and inappropriateness of 'glorious' label 320–1
and lack of mutual support by French 211, 212
and mutual support by British ships 211–12, 320
and Nelson's disparagement of 322
and political context of xxxvi–xxxvii
and refusal of French ships to strike 200–1, 203
and repair work, British 213–14, 215–16
and scale of victory 233–4, 321–2
and sharpshooters 196–7
and significance of 193
and sinking of *Vengeur* 201–2
and smoke of battle 204–5
and unfairness of French fighting 205–6
and unity of French 318
and victory claimed by both sides xxxix, 225
and Villaret engages British ships 198–9
and Villaret's achievement in 222–3, 319–20
and Villaret's uncertainty over British tactics 185–6

Glorious First of June, aftermath in Britain
and artistic commemoration of 245–54
and awards granted to Howe 234
and belief in Royal Navy 314
and beneficial effects on war effort 308–15

and British celebrations 230–2
and captured French ships 306–7
and connotations of name 229
and counter-productive effects on war effort 296–308, 323
and criticism of Howe 221–2, 267–8, 271–2, 273–4
and criticism of Montagu 275–6, 277–9
and discipline problems 261
and French prisoners 309–11, 323
and George III visits fleet at Portsmouth 237–40
and Howe's commendation of officers 262–3, 322–3
and Howe's report on battle 261–2
and Howe threatens resignation 271
and impact on naval manpower 302
and incapacitation of Channel Fleet 302–6
and invasion threat lifted 315
and learning fate of loved ones 259–60
and marquisate refused by Howe 272
and memorials 241
and military honours awarded 234–5
and Molloy's court martial 269–71
and naval self-confidence 324
and news reaches London 230–2
and offence caused by Howe's commendations 263–6, 322–3
and optimism generated by 314–15
as political and strategic failure 276–7
and political exploitation of 237–8, 323–4
and praise for officers and men 241–2
and prize money 237
and promotions 235
and reassurance of relatives of crew 260–1
and reception of Howe in Spithead 230
and relief of wounded and dependants 235–6
and surgeons' stores 313
and theatrical commemoration of 254–5, 274–5
and typhus outbreak on ships 302–5, 323
Glorious First of June, aftermath in France 242–4
and absence of artistic representation 245
and boost to morale 288, 289
and celebration of battle 243
and criticism of fleet 282
and denunciations of Saint-André 283–4
and dismissal of captains 281
and impact on naval manning levels 309
and myth of the *Vengeur* 243–4
and positive spin on 243–4, 283
and reaction against politicisation of navy 282–3
and strengthening of anti-Jacobins 282–3, 284
and witch-hunt for 'traitors' 281–2
*Glory, HMS* 117, 167–8, 335
Goddard, James 314
*Gorgon*, HMS 301
gout 55
Graham, George 236
Graves, Vice-Admiral Thomas 72, 142, 235, 262, 304, 334
Great Britain
and Anglo-American relationship 103
and Anglo-American tensions 109–11
and campaign against French West Indian colonies 103–7
and collapse of First Coalition against France 299
and economic sanctions against France 100
and opposition to war 273, 307–8
and Pitt seeks coalition government 272, 273
and plundering of West Indies 108–9
and praise for French Revolution 4
and seizure of American ships 108–9
and significance of naval victories 232–3
*see also* Glorious First of June, aftermath in Britain
Grey, Lt-Gen Sir Charles 104, 108
Guadeloupe 107, 300
guillotine xxvi, xxxvii
gunnery
and British innovations 209–11
and British tactics 211
and French shortcomings 16–17, 38, 211
and gunlocks 210–11
and hot guns 192
and myths of British and French approaches to 170
and naval fighting 16–17
and practice in Channel Fleet 118–19
and withholding fire 192, 221

Hamilton, Alexander 102
Hammond, Graham 333
Hanriot, François 295
Hardy, Thomas 230
Harvey, Edward 339
Harvey, Captain Henry 211, 235, 262, 340
Harvey, Captain John xxxii-xxxiii, 164, 195–8, 212, 236, 240–1, 262, 339
Harvey, Thomas 340
Haslar naval hospital 237, 303
Hawke, Edward 46, 47
Hawksmoor, Nicholas xxxi
d'Herbois, Collot 95–6
Hervey, Captain John Augustus 45
Heywood, Peter 333–4
Hill, John 338
Hillyar, Sir James 343
Hindmarsh, John 336
Holland 299
Hollis, Aiskew 335
Hood, Vice-Admiral Alexander 89, 212, 235, 262, 334, 371
Hood, Vice-Admiral Lord Samuel xxxviii, 22–3, 24, 56, 72, 371–2
Hope, Captain William 262, 263, 336

Howe, Mary 237, 238, 239, 240, 259, 306
Howe, Admiral Richard, Earl xxxix, 372–3
and 29 May engagement 159–75
and 30-31 May 175–80
and abilities as fleet commander 48–50, 51
and achievement of 322
and 'Additional Instructions' addressing fleet blunders 131–2
and appointed commander of Channel Fleet 45, 55
and attacked in cartoons 273–4
and attacks French line 191–2
and attacks French rear 149–50
and awards granted to 234
and bravery of 51
and breaks French line 192–4
and burns prize ships 124
and care for his men 51–2
and challenges Hervey to duel 44–5
and character 54–5
and chases after Villaret's Brest fleet 124–5
and collapses at end of battle 213
and commendation of officers 262–3, 322–3, 370
and concern over captains' behaviour 68
and criticism of conduct of battle 213, 221–2, 267–8, 320
and denied Garter 272
and destruction of family papers 43–4
and devotion of men to 238, 271
and discovers French have left Brest 123–4
and divisional system 52–3
and ensign of xlii
and exercises Channel Fleet 57
and expectations of the French 185
and experienced officers 140–1
and faith in his ships 142
on French fighting abilities 205
and gout 55
and health of seamen 53
and homes of 43
and hostility towards 54
and hygiene on ships 53
and inability to express himself 51, 67, 267
and influence over seamen 51
and lack of rest 213
and naval career 45–7
and new form of attack 64, 66
and offence caused by commendations of 263–6, 322–3
and orders breaking of French line 187–8, 189
and orders ships to carry a light 156–7
and paintings of 248–9
and political career 47, 53–4, 272–3
and popularity of 50
and praises officers and men 242
and press attacks on 271–2
and reception in Spithead 230
and refuses marquisate 272
and reluctance to return to active service 55
and report on battle 261–2
and riskiness of innovative tactics 140
and sails for home 222
as 'seaman's friend' 53
and secretiveness of 43
and sends *Bellerophon* to reconnoitre French fleet 147–8
and ship's order book 51–2
and signal flags 49–51
and surgeons' stores 313
and threatens resignation 271
and unity in fleet 271
Hughes, Charles 77
Hughes, Edward 55–6
Hunter, John 334
Hutt, Captain John xxxii-xxxiii, 212, 240–1, 263, 335

*Impétueux* 307, 308, 349
*Impetueux*, HMS 308
*Impregnable*, HMS 119, 120, 124, 216, 310, 313, 334–5
*Inconstant* 134
*Indomptable* 165, 167, 168, 173
injured sailors 220–1
*Invincible*, HMS 57–8, 124, 175–6, 194, 204, 215, 338
Irby, Frederick 340
Ireland 300
Isle d'Aix 46–7

*Jacobin* 192–3, 194, 199, 346–7
Jacobins xxxvi-xxxvii, 5, 10, 13, 21, 29, 287, 292–3, 296
Jefferson, Thomas 102
*Jemappes* 181, 186–7, 188–9, 203, 218, 220, 348
Jervis, Rear-Admiral John 54, 57, 104, 107, 108, 133, 308
*Juste* 194, 214, 306, 307, 347

Kean, Alexander 118
Kempenfelt, Richard 16, 50–1, 55
Keppel, Augustus 67, 72
Knowles, Sir Charles 46, 109–10, 112, 123

*La Bataille Prairial, see* Glorious First of June
Lafitte, Louis 245
Laforey, Sir John 104–5
Lángara, Admiral Juan de 142
Larcom, Thomas 235
*Latona*, HMS 155, 203, 214, 341
Lebrun, Pierre-Henri 10
Leeward Islands 107
Legendre, Louis 287, 378
Legge, Captain Arthur 341
Legge, Captain Edward 45
*Léopard* 13
Leveson-Gower, Edward 54

*Leviathan*, HMS 58, 154, 163, 164–5, 166, 336–7
Livesay, Richard 249, 254
Lloyd's 235–6
lookouts 145–6
Louis XVI xxv, xxvi–xxvii, xxviii–xxix
Louis XVII 23, 297
Louis XVIII 297
Loutherbourg, Philippe de xli, 77–81, 84, 246, 249–51
Louverture, Toussaint 106
Lucadou, Jean-Jacques 130–1
Lyon, James 337

Mackenzie, Captain Thomas 235, 241–2, 336
Madison, James 102
*Magnanime*, HMS 46, 47, 52
*Maire Guitton* 123
Maitland, Frederick 343
*Majestic*, HMS 118, 214, 302–3, 340
Malcolm, James 221
Malone, Dan 174
Marat, Jean-Paul xxvi, 96, 378–9
*Marlborough*, HMS 119, 153–4, 155, 199, 203, 204, 207, 209–10, 337
Marriot, Sir James 237
Marseillaise 33–4
Marseilles 23
Martinique 105, 106, 107
Maxwell, James 260–1
medals 234–5
medical emergencies 220–1
*Melpomène* 132–4
Minorca, Battle of (1756) 66, 72
Molloy, Captain Anthony James Pye 268–71, 336
Monroe, James 102
*Montagnard* 168
*Montagne* 32, 37, 186, 191, 192–3, 194, 198–9, 208, 243, 346
*Montagu*, HMS 57, 58, 119, 340
Montagu, Rear-Admiral George 223–4, 373
  and criticism of 275–6, 277
  and disliked by George III 276
  and dispute with Brenton 277–80
  and fails to gain another sea-going command 277
  and gains intelligence on Vanstabel's convoy 123
  and returns to Plymouth 144, 223, 224
  and sails to intercept Vanstabel's convoy 112–13, 223
  and sights Villaret's fleet 224
Montagu, Captain James xxxi-xxxii, 212, 241, 340
Moonlight Battle (1780) 55, 67–8, 142
*Mucius* 348
Mulgrave, Lord 238
mutiny
  in French navy 13, 26, 34–5
  in Royal Navy 58–9, 174, 261

National Convention xxv, 5, 6, 29, 35–6, 293, 294
National Gallery 73
National Maritime Museum 245–6, 247, 252, 254
naval battles, and complexity of 229
naval fighting, *see* fleet command and tactics
naval history, and nature of xliv
Neal, Sir Harry 88–9
Nelson, Horatio 19, 28, 41, 45, 54, 132–4, 322
*Neptune* 347
Nichols, Captain Henry 262, 263, 334
Nielly, Rear-Admiral Joseph-Marie 116, 123, 173, 299
*Niger*, HMS 155, 187, 215, 341–2
Nile, Battle of (1798) 234, 326
*Northumberland* 307, 348
*Nymphe*, HMS 6

Ochakov crisis (1791) 57
*Orion*, HMS 164, 167, 169–70, 171, 188, 192, 202, 203, 214, 261, 339
d'Orléans, Duc 83–4
*Orpheus*, HMS 135
Otway, Robert 335
Owen, William 338
Ozanne, Nicholas 245, 247

Pakenham, Captain Thomas 194, 200–1, 203, 212, 262, 338
Palliser, Sir Hugh 67, 72
Panoramic Theatre 254–5
Panthéon xxxiii–xxxiv, xxxiv
*Papillon* 121–2
Paris, and naval memorials xxxiv–xxxv
Paris, Treaty of (1783) 101
Parker, Captain William 59, 154, 156, 235, 242, 262, 373–4
Parker, Midshipman William 169–70, 171, 202, 217, 236, 242, 260, 261
Pasley, Rear-Admiral Thomas 117, 147–8, 153–4, 166–7, 212, 235, 262, 268–9, 271, 336, 374
*Patriote* 130–1, 195, 348
Payne, Captain John 153, 262, 263, 314, 337
Pearce, Nathaniel 186, 215, 281
*Pegasus*, HMS 89, 119, 120, 187, 200, 343–4
*Pelletier* 348
Pellew, Captain Sir Edward 6, 300
*Penelope*, HMS 134
*Phaeton*, HMS 60, 117, 146, 203, 206, 341
Pigott, Captain James 235, 268, 271, 338
Pilfold, John 339
Pilkington, Andrew 334
Pindar, Peter 80–1
Pitt, William, the Elder 82
Pitt, William, the Younger xxix, 240, 272, 284, 308, 315, 323–4, 375–6
Place de la République, and naval memorial xxxiv–xxxv
Pocock, Nicholas xli, 86, 88, 89, 162, 187, 195, 200, 253, 344

and becomes professional artist 87
and depictions of Glorious First of June 246, 251–3
and detail in naval paintings 88–9
and logbook images 86–7
and Reynold's advice to 87
and sketches of 352–66
and smoke of battle 204
Poggi, A C de 253
Polloy, John 220
*Pomone* 134, 137
Portland, Duke of 272, 284, 314
Portsmouth, and George III visits fleet at 237–40
Prieur, Pierre Louis 122
*Prince of Wales*, HMS 239
Pringle, Captain Thomas 194, 235, 262, 339
prisoners of war 124–5, 214–15, 309–11, 323
prize money 237
prizes, and difference in British and French attitudes 124
Prowse, William 335
*Prudence* 299
*Prudente* 310
Prussia 6, 299
psychological shock, and effects of battle 218–20

*Queen*, HMS 162, 165, 166, 168, 170, 172–3, 188, 199, 216, 335
*Queen Charlotte*, HMS 55, 57, 60, 117, 118, 119, 242, 333–4
and 29 May engagement 163, 166
and 1 June 189, 191–4, 204, 214, 310
Quiberon Bay, Battle of (1759) 47

*Ramilles*, HMS 119, 211–12, 339–40
Raper, Henry 334
*Rattler*, HMS 247
red ensign 204
red-hot shot, and French use of 206
regicide, in Europe xxvii–xxviii
relief funds for sailors 235–6
Renaudin, Jean François 202, 244
Renault, Cécile 96, 379
*Renown*, HMS 308
repair work
and Brest fleet 172, 173
and Channel Fleet 172–3, 213–14, 215–16
*Républicaine* 194, 346
*Résolue* 134, 137
*Réunion* 134
*Révolutionnaire* 150, 153–6, 158–9
*Revolutionnaire*, HMS 313
Reynolds, Sir Joshua 87
Reynolds, Thomas 310–11
Rioms, Albert de 13
Robespierre, Maximilien xl, xliv, xxxvii, 379–80
and appearance 3
and assassination attempts 95–6
and attacks enemies of the Revolution 294
and centralisation and intensification of Terror 291–2
and character 3
and Cult of the Supreme Being 290–1
and Danton's execution 95
on ending civil war 4–5
and *enragés/indulgents* divisions 94–5
and execution of 294–5
and imposition of Law of 22 Prairial 291
and increasing violence of 95, 284
and need for military victories 98
and opposition to 95, 287–8, 290, 292–3
and Vanstabel's grain convoy 111–12
and violent rhetoric of 97
and withdraws from Committee of Public Safety 293
Rodney, Admiral George xl, 53, 55, 67
Rogers, Josias 108
Ross, Lieutenant Francis 241
Rotherham, Edward 338
Rowland, Hamilton 296
Rowlandson, Thomas 246
*Royal George*, HMS 117, 118, 162, 166, 170, 171, 215, 334
Royal Navy
and abandonment of Mediterranean 301
and belief in 314, 315
and crew shortages 57–8, 117–18
and divisional system 52–3
and failures of 68
and French influence on ship design 308
and gunnery practice 118–19
and health of seamen 53
and hygiene on ships 53
and low casualty rates 133–5
and monarchy 240, 324
and mystique of 324
and political and public support of 240, 324
and political divisions in 53–4
and relief of wounded and dependants 236
and reputation of 232, 233
and routines of service life 326
and ship's order book 51–2
and shortcomings of 56–7
and signal flags 49–51
and successes of 313
and typhus outbreak 302–5
and uneven record of 67–8
*see also* Channel Fleet
*Royal Sovereign*, HMS 117, 118, 142, 199, 203, 214, 304–5, 334
*Russell*, HMS 118, 153–4, 162, 170, 337

sails
and setting and trimming 129–30
and use in signalling 145–6
Saint-André, Jeanbon xxxviii, 29, 31, 293, 380–1
and appointment of new C-in-C for Brest

fleet 32
and asserts control in Brest 34–5
and claims political victory after battle 283
and complains of poor seamanship 130, 173
and criticism of 283–4
and imprisonment of 296
and influence of 38
and inspects Brest fleet 32–3
and introduces disciplinary code 35
and naval recruitment 36–7
and naval reform 37
and politicisation of navy 37
and purge of the disloyal 34–5
and report on battle 243
and sails with Brest fleet 122
and Vanstabel's grain convoy 113
and witch-hunt for 'traitors' 281–2
Saint Domingue 104, 105–7
Sainte-Maranthe family 96–7
Saint-Julien de Chambon, Rear-Admiral 24, 36
Saint-Just, Louis Antoine de 31, 94–5, 294, 295, 381
Saints, Battle of the (1782) xl, 67
San Domingo, Battle of (1806) 326
Sané, Jacques-Nöel 306
*sans-culottes* 9, 93, 290
Sanson, Charles xxvii
*Sans Pareil* 130, 188, 303, 306–7, 347
Sardinia 6
Sargent, John Singer 71
Schomberg, Captain Isaac 134, 146, 176–7, 201, 263, 338
*Scipion* 206, 346
scurvy 53
seamanship
and poor quality of French 130–1
and setting and trimming sails 129–30
*see also* fleet command and tactics
*Seine* 282
Serres, Dominic 73, 79, 83, 249
Seven Years' War (1756-63) 46, 141
Seymour, Captain Lord Hugh 166, 235, 262, 337
sharpshooters 196–7
Sheridan, Richard 235–6, 274, 275
ship design, and French influence on British 308
signalling 49–51, 120, 145–6
slave revolts 106
Smith, Easley 259
smoke of battle 204–5
Snodgrass, Gabriel 143
Society for the Encouragement of Arts, Manufacture and Commerce 73
*Southampton*, HMS 215, 303, 343
Spain 27, 28, 142, 299
squadron command and tactics 136–7
station-keeping 48, 115, 156–7, 177
St Lucia 107
Stopford, Captain Robert 343
Sullivan, Pat 174
surgeons
and improvements in surgeons' stores 313
and treating injured 220–1
and typhus outbreak 302–5
*Swiftsure*, HMS 135

tacking 62, 139
Talbot, Mary Anne 195–6, 339
Tallien, Jean 287, 381–2
*Téméraire* 348
*Terrible* 166, 199, 346
Terror xxxvi-xxxvii, 8–9
and centralisation and intensification of 291–2
and dismantling of machinery of 296–7
and *enragés*/*indulgents* divisions over 93–5
and inauguration of 29
and lack of justification for continuation of 292
and Law of 22 Prairial 291
as weapon of social war 292
*Thames*, HMS 133
theatre 77
and character of contemporary 85
and commemoration of Glorious First of June 254–5, 274–5
and Loutherbourg's scenic effects 77–81
as mouthpiece of political propaganda 275
Thornborough, Captain Edward 341
*Thunderer*, HMS 119, 153, 154, 201, 310, 341
Thuriot, Jacques 287, 382
time, and fleet battle 139, 140
Tobago 6, 104–5
Toulon
and French recapture of 27
and impact of siege of 28–9
and Jacobin extremism 21
and military geography of 26–7
and partial destruction of French fleet 28
and rebels accept British help 23
and reprisals against rebels 27–8
and revolt against Jacobins 21–2
and Revolutionary army sent to quell revolt 22
and surrender of French fleet 24–5, 31
Toulon, Battle of (1744) 66, 72
*Tourville* 15, 350
Trafalgar, Battle of (1805) 234, 326
*Trajan* 130, 186, 188, 189, 208, 349
*Tremendous*, HMS 124–5, 149, 169, 174, 204, 268, 269, 271, 337–8
*Trente-et-un Mai* 348
*Tribune* 313
Trinity House 236
Trogoff de Kerlessy, Jean-Honoré de 22, 24
Trotter, Thomas 236, 237, 302, 303, 304, 311
Troubridge, Captain Thomas 183, 188, 303
Turner, J M W 251
Turreau, General Louis 1
typhus, and Channel Fleet 302–5, 323
*Tyrannicide* 165, 167, 168, 348

*Unicorn*, HMS 313
*Unité* 313
United States 102
and Anglo-American relationship 103, 109–11
and British seizure of American ships 108–9
and convoys to France 300
and divisions over French Revolution 102–3
and Proclamation of Neutrality (1793) 103
and reaction to battle 245
and support for French Revolution xxxix, 101–2, 109–10
*Uranie* 133
Ure, Andre 220
Ushant, Battle of (1778) xl, 67, 72
Ussher, Thomas 338

Vadier, Marc 287, 293, 382
*Valiant*, HMS 58, 117, 124, 142, 157, 162, 188, 194, 303, 339
Van de Velde, Willem, the Elder 74–5
Van de Velde, Willem, the Younger 74
Vanstabel, Rear-Admiral Pierre-Jean 111, 133, 224–5
Vanstabel's grain convoy
and Anglo-French naval dispositions 116
and British intelligence on 112, 113, 123
and capture of a British priority 112
and Channel Fleet sets out to intercept 112–13
and difficulties with interception of 113–16
and distribution of grain 288
and gathers in the Chesapeake 111
and protection of the French priority 137–8
and sails into Brest 224–5, 281
and size of 115
and uncertainty over destination of 114–15
and value of 112
Vendée, and revolt in 5, 9
*Vengeur du Peuple* xxxix, xxxvii, 134, 191, 202, 347
and artistic depictions of sinking of 245, 247
and battle with HMS *Brunswick* 195–8, 211–12
and British rescue some crew 201–2
and myth of 243–4
and sinking of 202
*Venus*, HMS 58, 119, 123, 156, 187, 343
Victoria, Queen 234
Victoria and Albert Museum 255
Villaret de Joyeuse, Louis Thomas xxxix, 14, 91, 116, 121, 198
and 29 May engagement 159–69
and 30-31 May, leads British away from convoy 180
and achievement in fleet seamanship 168–9, 319–20
and appointed C-in-C of Brest fleet 32
and attacks HMS *Queen* 199–200
and career of 32
and failure of ships to offer mutual support 212
and fleet sighted by Montagu 224
and inexperience of officers 141–2, 312
and instructions from Committee of Public Safety 137–8, 143
and isolated by anti-Jacobins 283
and lack of fleet command experience 49
and optimism of 39
and political scrutiny of 121, 122
and post-1 June operations 299–300
and promoted Governor of Martinique 243
and reprimands ships 131
and rescues crippled ships 201
and sails into Brest 224–5, 281
and sails out of Brest 121, 122–3
and strategic success of 222–3
and tactical challenges facing 138–40
and uncertainty over British tactics 185–6
*Virginie* 313

Wainwright, Sam 220
Wales, and French troops landed in 300
Walker, James 341–2
Walpole, Horace 54, 271
war artists, *see* artistic depictions of naval warfare
War of the Austrian Succession (1739-58) 141
Warren, Sir John 134, 135–7, 300
Washington, George 102, 103
Webber, John 80
West, Benjamin 82, 248
Westcott, Captain George 334, 335
West Indies 6, 104, 107–8
and British campaign against French colonies 103–7
and British plundering of 108–9
Westminster Abbey, and naval memorials xxxi–xxxiii, 241
Wilkinson, Jonathan 200, 213, 219
wind, and impact of 144–5
Windward Islands 104–7
Wolfe, James 82

Yowell, William 221